W9-DBE-734

ADULTS WITH LEARNING DISABILITIES

ADULTS WITH LEARNING DISABILITIES

Theoretical and Practical Perspectives

Edited by

NOEL GREGG
CHERI HOY
ALICE F. GAY

THE GUILFORD PRESS
New York   London

© 1996 The Guilford Press
A Division of Guilford Publications, Inc.
72 Spring Street, New York, NY 10012

Printed in the United States of America

This book is printed on acid-free paper.

Last digit is print number: 9 8 7 6 5 4 3 2 1

Library of Congress Cataloging-in-Publication Data

Adults with learning disabilities : theoretical and practical
 perspectives / [edited by] Noel Gregg, Cheri Hoy, and Alice F.
 Gay
    p.   cm
  Includes bibliographical references and index.
  ISBN 1-57230-037-X
  1. Mentally handicapped—Services for. 2. Learning disabled—
Services for. I. Gregg, Noel. II. Hoy, Cheri
III. Gay, Alice F.
HV3004.A455   1996
362.3′8—dc20   95-33485
                                                            CIP

*In memory of Dian Ridenour—
a visionary and dedicated advocate
for adults with learning disabilities*

Contributors

Susan Sigalas Bonham, Ed.S., Private Practice, Statesboro, Georgia

Jim Brackett, Ed.D., Department of Education, The University of South Carolina-Spartanburg, Spartanburg, South Carolina

Cindy A. Darden, Ph.D., Learning Disabilities Center, The University of Georgia, Athens, Georgia

Beth Ferri, M.Ed., Department of Special Education, The University of Georgia, Athens, Georgia

Anna H. Gajar, Ph.D., Department of Educational and School Psychology and Special Education, Pennsylvania State University, University Park, Pennsylvania

Alice F. Gay, M.Ed., Learning Disabilities Research and Training Center, The University of Georgia, Athens, Georgia

Noel Gregg, Ph.D., Learning Disabilities Center, The University of Georgia, Athens, Georgia

Robin Hawks, M.S., Center for Learning Potential, Mount Sidney, Virginia

Stephen R. Hooper, Ph.D., Clinical Center for the Study of Development and Learning, University of North Carolina-Chapel Hill, Chapel Hill, North Carolina

Cheri Hoy, Ph.D., Department of Special Education, The University of Georgia, Athens, Georgia

George W. Hynd, Ed.D., Center for Clinical and Developmental Neuropsychology, The University of Georgia, Athens, Georgia

Yvonne Johnson, M.Ed., Division of Rehabilitation Services, Georgia Department of Human Resources, Atlanta, Georgia

Michael King, Ph.D., Roosevelt Warm Springs Institute for Rehabilitation, Warm Springs, Georgia

Elaine Manglitz, M.Ed., Department of Special Education, The University of Georgia, Athens, Georgia

Carolyn McKinley, M.Ed., Roosevelt Warm Springs Institute for Rehabilitation, Warm Springs, Georgia

Anne McPherson, Ph.D., Department of Special Education, The University of South Carolina-Spartanburg, Spartanburg, South Carolina

Esther H. Minskof, Ph.D., Department of Special Education, James Madison University, Harrisonburg, Virginia

Carolyn Moreland, M.Ed., Roosevelt Warm Springs Institute for Rehabilitation, Warm Springs, Georgia

Anna W. Morgan, M.Ed., Learning Disabilities Center, The University of Georgia, Athens, Georgia

J. Gregory Olley, Ph.D., Clinical Center for the Study of Development and Learning, University of North Carolina-Chapel Hill, Chapel Hill, North Carolina

Carolyn Phillips, B.A., First Presbyterian Church, Marietta, Georgia

Cynthia A. Riccio, Ph.D., Department of Educational and School Psychology, University of Alabama, Tuscaloosa, Alabama

Jovita M. Ross-Gordon, Ed.D., Center for Adult Learning Services, St. Edward's University, Austin, Texas

Judith Osgood Smith, Ph.D., Department of Education, Purdue University Calumet, Hammond, Indiana

Neil A. Sturomski, M.Ed., National Adult Literacy and Learning Disabilities Center, Washington, DC

Elisabeth H. Wiig, Ph.D., Private Practice, Arlington, Texas

Joseph Wisenbaker, Ph.D., Department of Educational Psychology, The University of Georgia, Athens, Georgia

Contents

1

Adults with Learning Disabilities: Empowering Networks of Inclusion, Collaboration, and Self-Acceptance

NOEL GREGG
CAROLYN PHILLIPS

The term "consumer empowerment" is used by both adults with learning disabilities and professionals in discussing a wide variety of concepts. Armchair critics are quick to focus on the ambiguity surrounding the term and suggest replacing the word "consumer" or documenting select examples whereby the term did not help lead to change. Rather than continuing the debate for or against the term, it is the purpose of this chapter to concentrate on consumer empowerment specific to adults with learning disabilities, examining past and future directions necessary to examine whether the term is to move past ideals to political action. As bell hooks (1994) notes, "the possession of a term does not bring a process or practice into being" (p. 61). Whether one is a consumer or a professional, the practice of using the term "consumer empowerment" does not necessarily mean an individual has examined the meaning of the term in relation to self or others.

The term "consumer empowerment" is certainly not new to the vocabularies of either the public or the private sector. During the 1960s, rehabilitation and special education specialists began recognizing and talking about the need for greater consumer input into policy decisions. Following the Vietnam War, the United States witnessed an upsurge of consumer involvement in such issues as housing, employment, and training related to issues of disabilities (Childers & Rice, 1993). As Holmes and Saleeby (1993) discuss, although consumers became vocal during this time, unfortunately sharing power with professionals often was and continues to be undermined by the sociopolitical realities of the system. As the public sector began eliciting consumer input, the private sector, separate from issues of disabilities, quickly recognized the importance of listening to U.S. consumers' perception of items marketed by companies (Peters & Austin, 1986). Naisbitt and Aburdene (1985) warn that if industry does not accept the input of consumers, consumers will become more militant in the next decade. Certainly, on the political scene, one of the best examples of this move toward militancy is the philosophical revolution that occurred in the 1994 elections.

One of the clear lessons for the administration in the 1994 elections was the strength of an empowered system. For change to occur, all the factors of the group must work together toward a common mind-set. Emener (1991) encourages a model that examines empowerment across key factors and areas of locus of control. Within the term "key factors," he includes (1) systems, (2) professionals, (3) families, and (4) clients. In addition, he suggests examining all these factors across external and internal areas of locus of control. For instance, a consumer needs certain system laws to negotiate on critical issues (external factor). Yet a particular system's philosophy, policies, and procedures (internal factor) might work counter to providing the consumer empowerment to make those changes. Or, a system philosophy (internal factor) can encourage and provide equal empowerment, but the consumer's own self-concept (internal factor) might have a negative impact on decision making.

The success of consumer empowerment requires all key factors (i.e., systems, professionals, families, friends, and consumers) to examine themselves, as well as to be examined by others both externally and internally. Both consumers and professionals across disciplines (private and public) must reevaluate. One such assumption is that client empowerment somehow robs professionals of their own power. As Swift and Levin (1987) note, "empowerment of some is possible without reducing the power of others" (Holmes & Saleeby, 1993, p. 62). Consumers must also be ready to reexamine past and future practices in dealing with systems, professionals, families, and, most important, themselves. For all factors involved, the key to empowerment for adults with learning disabilities appears to rest with a willingness for self-reflection and proactive change (Emener, 1991; Emener, Luck, & Smits, 1981; Emener & Stephens, 1982; Hahn, 1986).

CHANGING PARADIGM?

Searching for the means to nurture an empowered network for all factors might require a new paradigm by which to better understand sociopolitical change. Gregg and Ferri (Chapter 2, this volume) explore past and current paradigms and theories that have influenced the field of adults with learning disabilities. Although they focus on the concepts of control, knowledge, and power, this chapter enters the debate as it centers on the issue of individualism. The concept of individualism is central to any discussion of consumerism, be that a focus on the person, system, or policy related to such matters. According to Sampson (1988), individualism is defined in the literature by two distinct theories governed by contrasting paradigms that have very different interpretations of the role of the personal, interpersonal, and societal functioning. Sampson's (1988) research is based on cross-cultural, historical, and intracultural evidence applied only to individualism in the United States.

The two universal concepts discussed by Sampson (1988) that have direct application to adults with learning disabilities relate to (1) the self–nonself boundary and (2) the location of power and control. Chapter 2 of this volume discusses power and control in great depth and the issue of the self–nonself boundary is the primary focus of this chapter. According to Sampson (1988), the two indigenous psychologies of individualism prevalent in our society are Type 1, which he calls self-contained individualism, and Type 2, or ensembled individualism. The self-contained psychology of the individual identifies a sharp boundary that "stops at one's skin and clearly demarks self from nonself" (Spence, 1985, p. 1288). In addition, such a psychology advocates control as mediated solely within the person. One's conception of self or person is exclusionary. Opposite to this form of individualism is the ensembled person whose self–other boundary is fluid and whose power and control go beyond the person. The ensembled psychology of self identifies others within the region defined as self (Sampson, 1988). Such a psychology, according to Lyke (1985, p. 373), describes the "self as an ensemble of social relations," supporting the sociohistorical perspective of self. Cultures whose dominant view of individualism is ensembled would be African American, Native American, Japanese, and Islamic.

Sampson's (1988) Type 1 or self-contained individual psychology is prevalent in the core values dominant in the United States today. The values of freedom, responsibility, and achievement are often presented as possible only through a society stressing the self-contained individual. This is a message advocated by many professionals and families involved in the lives of adults with learning disabilities. Certainly, researchers exploring issues of locus of control, so popular in the early 1980s, support such a perspective. Yet Sampson (1988) presents intracultural evidence from feminist and social class analyses that indicates possibilities of freedom, responsibility, and achievement to be obtained by the ensembled individual. In addition, Deutsch (1949, 1973) explores issues of cooperation and competition, providing evidence of the achievements of cooperative groups—where each person's act helps move the entire group toward its product goals more effectively and efficiently than does the act of an individual working in isolation.

> When persons' sense of self is defined through relationships and connection, achievements will occur, not from separate actors seeking somehow to mesh their behavior together, but rather from thoroughly interdependent actors whose very design for being includes working on behalf of larger interests. (Sampson, 1988, p. 21)

Readers are encouraged to review Chapter 2 (Gregg & Ferri, this volume) for a more in-depth exploration of current paradigms influencing the decision making that has an impact on adults with learning disabilities.

This chapter does not explore new paradigms in depth but rather raises the question whether the paradigm so prevalent in our society, one that advocates the self-contained individual, is an obstacle to adults with learning disabilities. Staples (1990) stresses that a key to empowerment is the collective strength among individuals. Thus, systems that advocate self-contained individualism work in opposition to those systems supporting the collective community. According to Holmes and Saleeby (1993), the way to consumer empowerment is through inclusiveness and collaboration, stressing the need for professionals to become part of the consumer's community. The reverse is equally true in that consumers must be willing to take the risk of becoming part of the world of professionals, exploring from within the environment in which professionals operate on a daily basis. The issue of community and coempowerment is explored further in this chapter because it requires all parties to be receptive to such a process—both consumers and professionals.

HISTORICAL OVERVIEW
OF THE SELF-HELP MOVEMENT

To explore new directions that encourage an inclusive and collaborative empowered network across all factors we must first understand the impact of the self-help movement on the adult population with learning disabilities. This chapter focuses solely on the self-help movement. It does not represent an inclusive history of all the variables, including individuals and situations, that have an impact on the adult movement. It must be kept in mind that the self-help movement occurred within the context of a much larger awareness of disability. Readers are encouraged to explore other resources for a more thorough background of the social and disability movements leading to consumer involvement (Childers & Rice, 1993).

The public agencies serving children with learning disabilities in the late 1960s did not focus at all on the future of such children as they reached adolescence and adulthood. It became apparent to the adults with learning disabilities who were attempting to gain access into rehabilitation, employment, and postsecondary academic settings during the early 1970s that the system was in great need of transformation. In order to empower themselves, these pioneer adults with learning disabilities recognized that they could not allow themselves to transfer responsibility solely to society; they would need to initiate a dialogue with the different systems to which they sought access rather than a polemic argument of past wrongs. "During this time, also, consumer advocacy groups began to spring up in communities across the country with a focus on self-help, community care alternatives and improvement on the quality of life of children and adults" (Childers & Rice, 1993, p. 24).

Within this societal atmosphere, groups of adults with learning disabilities across the country took the first step toward open dialogue, a step that carved future paths. It would be impossible to mention every individual and group responsible for the progress made by these first adult self-help organizations. Thus, only key figures and groups are discussed in an attempt to summarize the philosophy behind the movement. The problems were and continue to be sociopolitical in nature; the task from the start has been to heighten awareness of the needs of adults with learning disabilities. In the early 1970s, adults with learning disabilities, with varying perspectives on the issue of needs, began to work together in an attempt to seek solutions that, as of now, are still unformulated. "Participation is not a convenient pedagogical tool, it is the heart of the pedagogical process" (Smith, 1976, p. 4).

The parents of adolescents and adults with learning disabilities provided one of the first forums for these adults to express their concerns to the public. In February 1977, at the national conference of what was then called the Association of Children with Learning Disabilities (ACLD), now the Learning Disabilities Association (LDA), four young adults with learning disabilities were invited to share their experiences of "growing up" with a learning disability. This panel of young adults included Rob Coursin, Ross Glider, Ed Sickles, and Kathy Rice. The conference room was packed for the entire presentation, a first of its kind at the LDA. Those present reported that the audience demonstrated a sensitivity to and respect for these adults who were willing to share their narratives. A field whose focus had only been on young children was beginning to recognize the problems faced by these young adults. What to do remained the question at large for professionals, families, and consumers. At the end of the presentation of this panel at the ACLD, the four presenting adults decided to form a committee within the organization for adults with learning disabilities.

The critical needs of adolescents and adults with learning disabilities were beginning to be conceptualized in the minds of professionals and families working with this population. By May 1977, another panel of young adults was asked to present at the Illinois ACLD state conference. Members of this panel included Dian Ridenour, Mary Grigar, Charles Rumble, Loraine Lorick, and Marge Wilson. This panel decided to form an organization separate from the ACLD designed for and by adults with learning disabilities. Such a split represented a healthy sign of autonomy from the ACLD, the parent advocacy group. By June 1977, this group of adults with learning disabilities incorporated and called themselves Time Out to Enjoy. Time Out to Enjoy became one of the early models for many other organizations developed for and by adults with learning disabilities. In fact, Project Building, funded by the U.S. Department of Justice in 1981, used the Time Out to Enjoy model of self-help as a means of reaching adolescents living in high-crime areas and helping them become more positive about their future. Mentorship and modeling is nothing new to the adult movement. Dian Ridenour, the national coordinator of Time Out to Enjoy at its inception, remained a source of inspiration for many adults with learning disabilities throughout her life.

By the late 1970s, the number of self-help organizations developed by and for adults with learning disabilities began to increase across the United States. Puzzle People, under the leadership of Jo Ann Hazeltine, was formed in California during 1977. This adult self-help group has been one of the few groups to remain active to this day. The Association of Learning Disabled Adults (ALDA) began in the Washington, DC, area through the efforts of Dale Brown, a longtime advocate for the adult movement. Breaking from Time Out to Enjoy, the ALDA incorporated in 1978. Leadership, Action, Unity, Nurturing, Citizenship, Harmony (LAUNCH) also incorporated during 1978 under the leadership of John Moss. The voices of adults with learning disabilities began to get louder and attract greater attention than ever before in the United States.

At the national ACLD (LDA) conference in Kansas in 1978, a few of these self-help organizations sent representatives to the ACLD Youth and Adult Committee to discuss the best direction for the adult movement. A controversy over leadership split the movement. Time Out to Enjoy felt that it could not work with the ACLD Youth and Adult Committee if the committee continued to be directed by a parent rather than an adult with learning disabilities. The first major intrastrife bubbled within the adult movement. The complexity between ideas and actions became an issue that would require resolution. Emotional rhetoric divided the movement; standard prescriptions for cohesion failed to work.

In an attempt to mend the division stirring among the groups, Time Out to Enjoy invited all the officers of the different adult organizations representing adults with learning disabilities to a special meeting at the Pathways to Employment conference in 1979. At this meeting, sponsored by the President's Committee on the Employment of the Handicapped, Dale Brown proposed the idea of a centrally controlled network which could facilitate communication between the adult groups. The time was too soon, however, for advocating centralization. The officers from the separate self-help organizations voted down Brown's visionary idea. Dissension continued between the groups.

At this time, Roa Lynn (1979), an adult with learning disabilities, published one of the first books describing what it was like to grow up with a learning disability. The professional press was not yet ready just to let her tell her story; the book had to be a professional explanation of learning disabilities as well as her narrative. The underlying theme in her book was one being expressed all over the country by adults with learning disabilities attending self-help organizations. Lynn (1979) reported that many adults with learning disabilities had been forced to feel like con artists because of the double burden of having to do their work while maintaining the image that they were working in the same way as everyone else. It is interesting to note that in 1991 this same message was expressed by Lee and Jackson in a book called *Faking It*. However, this time the professional press was willing to let the sole focus of the book be on growing up with a learning disability.

By February 1980, at the national ACLD conference, several breakthroughs for the adult movement occurred. The ACLD decided that the Youth and Adult Committee should and would be led by a consumer. Susan Hastings, chairperson of the Virginia Division of Adults and Youth, was elected chairperson of the national Youth and Adult Committee. By September of that year, the adults obtained separate status under the Youth and Adult Committee. Hastings worked closely with Time Out to Enjoy to encourage the adult self-help organizations throughout the country to begin working closely together to strengthen the impact of adults with learning disabilities. The ACLD Adult Section under Hastings worked to change the system within the ACLD structure. Dian Ridenour urged Time Out to Enjoy to work externally from the ACLD in encouraging other systems to be more sensitive to the needs of adults with learning disabilities. Through the cooperation and understanding between Hastings and Ridenour, the movement became less fragmented.

The idea of a national network, seeded at the Pathways to Employment Conference in 1979, became a reality at the President's Conference on the Employment of the Handicapped in 1980. Dale Brown was elected chairperson the first year. She continues to take a proactive role at the national level to the present. The Network was designed to be the umbrella structure over all adult groups focusing on learning disabilities. One of the primary focuses of the Network was to provide greater communication between the groups and their officers. Time Out to Enjoy and the ACLD Adult Section, while cooperating with the Network, refused to become official chapters. They believed that intercooperation could be achieved without the establishment of a superstructure with satellites. The Network soon fell under the incorporation of LAUNCH.

Independently, each of the adult groups continued to make monumental strides in educating the public and providing support for individual adults with learning disabilities. A major breakthrough in morale for the adult movement occurred in 1981, when Hastings was asked to be the keynote speaker at the national ACLD (LDA) conference in Atlanta, Georgia. Her speech, full of emotion, described the struggle of growing up with a learning disability, reinforcing the fact that a learning disability affects other areas of one's life outside academics.

Another benchmark in the history of the adult movement was recorded again at an ACLD (LDA) national conference in Atlanta, Georgia in 1981. Dian Ridenour conceived the idea for a discussion session with both consumers and professionals. Encouraged by other self-help group leaders, the ACLD Youth and Adult Committee provided meeting space for Ridenour. She then invited major self-help groups to submit issues of concern. Those issues numbered 14. All lists were distributed to heads of consumer self-help groups asking that they have their group members prioritize them. The chairperson of the caucus, Eleanor Westhead, Ph.D., University of Virginia, chose four major issues to be addressed. Above all, this session illustrated that adults with learning disabilities and professionals could productively work together, learn from each other, and support the efforts of the other.

At this same conference in Atlanta, Susan Hastings was elected to the ACLD National Governing Board, the ACLD Governmental Affairs Committee, the ACLD Advocacy Committee, and the ACLD Early Childhood Committee. Such appointments indicated that the parent organization realized the necessity of input from adults with learning disabilities and was willing to give the adults direct input into the policy decision making of this powerful advocacy organization. This foresight in recognizing and including adults with learning disabilities within the decision-making process of the LDA was the result of many different professional pioneers in the field of learning disabilities who had long been concerned with the service, training, and research activities on adults with learning disabilities. Dialogue would now be ongoing; it would be heard at the time of a crisis rather than post facto. After Hastings's appointment, other adults with learning disabilities followed in her footsteps to sit on the LDA Governing Board, as well as various other subcommittees within the LDA organization.

During the 1980s and 1990s, numerous individuals with learning disabilities convinced private, nonprofit organizations to foster greater public awareness of the political and social needs of the adult population. Some of these individuals worked in cooperation with professionals and parent organizations, whereas others operated independently. The impact of such individuals on the adult movement should not be underestimated. What has not happened, however, is a nurturing of grassroots self-help groups. As the sociological trend in the United States supports self-contained individualism, the collective community of the adult movement at local levels is, in large part, unattended or underrated. The result is that fewer local and state self-help groups are available for adults with learning disabilities *across the severity range*, and there is little communication between existing groups.

SELF-HELP GROUPS: PURPOSE AND NEED

Paulo Freire (1973), through his work in the slums of Brazil, labels the process of consciousness raising as *conscientizacano*; it is the degree to which individuals are able to see the social system critically. The early adult movement clearly illustrates how a few individuals, consumers, and professionals laid the groundwork for the needs of adults with learning disabilities to become visible. The self-help groups that led to the early organizations for adults with learning disabilities represent a conceptual balance between individual and group needs. Four major goals of this early self-help movement for adults with learning disabilities include (1) self-help, (2) resource dissemination, (3) interagency cooperation, and (4) self-advocacy. Some of these early adult groups stressed one goal more than another as they advocated for the needs of the adult population with learning disabilities. The movement as a whole, however, incorporated the development of all these goals.

Self-help groups are successful on the local level. Such groups provide a community network for adults to seek friendship and understanding. At meetings the adults express their frustrations with the daily work world or the educational institutions with which they are directly involved at the moment. Input from others, as well as being part of a community, is integral to self-help organizations.

A major goal of the adult movement is to educate different systems, professionals, family members, and friends to the specific problems faced by adults with learning disabilities. Therefore, resource dissemination is a function of all adult organizations. Some groups focus on public speaking, whereas others direct more energies to the publishing of newsletters, articles, training packets, and other printed material. Dale Brown's early attempts to elicit a systemized, cooperative network between the self-help groups for adults with learning disabilities should be reevaluated by the adult movement. The joint effort across advocacy groups provides a louder voice in the political arena, where policy and social change are constructed.

Self-help organizations, by encouraging self-advocacy, also provide an avenue for meeting some of the emotional and social needs of adults with learning disabilities. Adults with learning disabilities must inform themselves of the legislation and litigation affecting their lives. By providing material and resources, adult self-help groups encourage adults to become more their own self-advocates.

The importance of self-help groups at both a local and a national level cannot be underestimated. Their past and future success lies in the questions they raise in the field as well as the answers they provide to social and political issues. The 1980s and 1990s have seen more of a focus on stories of individuals with learning disabilities rather than the nurturing of self-help groups or collective experiences leading toward a network of empowerment. Although individual stories remain an important means of better understanding problems, more change occurs through a collective agenda. The adult movement continues to be an instrument of education for the adults as well as for the various factors (i.e., systems, professionals, families, and friends) involved in change in the academic and employment arenas. Self-help organizations that remain strong today, such as Puzzle People, Rebus, or state groups like the LD Adults of Georgia, stress the nurturing of internal self needs to confront an external world. Yet none of these adult organizations can meet all four goals of the movement with maximum strength. Rather, it takes all these separate self-help groups working in cooperation with professionals across disciplines to help society better understand the strengths of adults with learning disabilities. This openness to working with professionals implies a reciprocal obligation from professionals working in various different systems, as well as from family members and friends of the adults. Such an opportunity provides everyone with a creative obligation to listen and learn from others, not to exclude any party's ideas and experiences. The future direction of the adult movement will allow for practical solutions as well as more dialectic problem solving. The time has come to push aside hollow rhetoric and begin creative problem solving for the good of the movement, not only for the individual members of any group or system.

MOVING TOWARD SYSTEM CHANGE

One of the federal agencies that has encouraged collaboration and inclusion of all the factors to better identify solutions and future direction is the National Institute on Disability and Rehabilitation Research (NIDRR). The research and training activities that the NIDRR supports require systematic and frequent input from consumers to help determine their direction so that all activities are relevant and maintain social responsiveness. The underlying framework of this practice is participatory action research and training. Participatory action research and training has three central components: (1) maximum involvement of ultimate and intermediate beneficiaries, (2) systematic action resulting from the project to achieve change or applications, and (3) the dynamic interaction of consumers and constituents in all phases of projects. The NIDRR developed the following working definition of participatory action research (PAR):

> Participatory Action Research (PAR) recognizes the need for persons being studied to participate in the design and conduct of all phases (e.g., design, execution, and dissemination) of the research that affects them. PAR is an approach or a strategy for research, not a methodology. (K. D. Seelman, personal communication, November 15, 1994)

The PAR approach requires that adults with learning disabilities of all degrees of severity and types would be represented across all research and training activities. The data generated from this PAR must be summarized and disseminated quickly and efficiently. Training activities, therefore, must meet the following criteria: (1) be socially relevant and responsive to consumers and intermediate beneficiaries, (2) provide training to all key factors, and (3) rapidly disseminate research and training results using the latest technology.

The NIDRR enacted a policy in 1994, Constituency-Oriented Research and Dissemination (CORD), that governs all PAR activities. The CORD policy requires that any activity undertaken and funded by the NIDRR must be governed by a committee that consists of all the key factors representing that constituency. Therefore, a CORD committee must be established that includes consumers, professionals across disciplines, family members, and system representatives. These CORD committees must be active in establishing, carrying out, and disseminating information related to any training and research activity. For instance, in the Learning Disabilities Research and Training Center (LDRTC) at the University of Georgia and Roosevelt Warm Springs Institute for Rehabilitation, seven CORD committees with a total of 92 individuals direct the research and training activities of this center. In addition to these CORD committees, the LDRTC has 39 members on a separate advisory council from the CORD committees that oversee the operation of the entire center.

The NIDRR has led the way in establishing a system's creative response to inclusiveness and collaboration. The LDRTC is currently demonstrating the impact of this for adults with learning disabilities, as well as for the professionals and family or friends who are part of this system. Other agencies such as the Department of Education and the National Institutes for Health should be encouraged to enact such a policy. In addition, state and local governmental agencies and institutes of higher education might explore such options within their systems. It is time to stop talking about consumer input—the time has come for action. Examples such as the NIDRR's CORD and PAR are available to all consumers and professionals as future social and political issues come up for review in this new political climate.

MOVING TOWARD INDIVIDUAL CHANGE

Two major areas important for consumers to explore pertain to issues of essentialism and narcissism (not that these are problems only for consumers; certainly professionals across disciplines provide ample evidence of how these characteristics work against professional goals). Essentialism and narcissism can easily become blocks to the successful outcome of taking a leadership role in the adult movement. The products of essentialism or narcissism are often inflexibility and rigidity. As Tuchman (1984) illustrates, these two characteristics have led governments to establish policies contrary to their own interests.

Essentialism

One of the key barriers facing many adults with learning disabilities rests as much with self as with systems. bell hooks (1994), in discussing her growth as an African American female, states the problem eloquently: "And when I was not desperately seeking to belong to this family community that never seemed to accept or want me, I was desperately trying to discover the place of my belonging" (p. 60). One of the means by which bell hooks was able to find this "place of my belonging" was her search for theory and knowledge. Knowledge became a means of healing. As she cautions, however, knowledge "is not inherently healing, liberatory, or revolutionary" (p. 61). It becomes a means to heal if directed and nurtured by what hooks (1994) calls collective sources. hooks is not the first to discuss the liberation of knowledge for marginalized, oppressed groups; many other advocates and theorists have written extensively on this topic (Freire, 1973; Smith, 1976). Freire (1973) and hooks (1994) state often that oppressed people do not see the connection between current theory and practice. Rather than searching for alternative theories and practices, they reject knowledge, usually addressed as theory, as having any relevance to their everyday life. hooks (1994), rather than rejecting knowledge as a means to gain power, suggests that marginalized groups need to seek "new theories rooted in an attempt to understand both the nature of our contemporary predicament and the means by which we might collectively engage in resistance that would transform our current reality" (p. 67). In addition, professionals often work under the assumption that consumers are incapable of understanding or creating knowledge or theories that lead to solutions for current problems. Such stereotypes of consumers on the part of professionals block the development of a source for creative solutions to the complex issues facing adults with learning disabilities.

Belief by either consumers or professionals that there is a split between theory and practice, or that one group is more in control of one domain, leads to what Freire (1973) or hooks (1994) would refer to as collective exploitation and repression. For instance, if consumers do not provide professionals time to tell their professional stories or life narratives, a significant body of knowledge is purposely being omitted. It is time to put knowledge and theory into what hooks (1994) calls "a holistic framework of liberatory activism" (p. 69). But she goes on to warn consumers, "It is not easy to name our pain, to theorize from that location" (p. 74).

One of the important points that hooks (1994) makes in her call for collaboration is that oppressed groups use the power of experience as the only means of authenticity. For instance, consumers often respond that a professional who does not demonstrate a learning disability really cannot help resolve problems or understand future directions for the movement. Such a politics of essentialist exclusion can be more dangerous than many of the barriers placed in front of adults with learning disabilities. Just because individuals demonstrate a learning disability, they are not empowered with the knowledge of all solutions. Such an insider-versus-outsider mentality inhibits everyone. Although it is an important piece of the decision making, the consumer's experience is only part of a collection of knowledge. It is no better or worse than the experience of any of the players who construct the whole. hooks (1994) discusses the importance of personal experience in relation to African American females:

> Then there are times when personal experience keeps us from reaching the mountaintop and so we let it go because the weight of it is too heavy. And sometimes the mountaintop is difficult to reach with all our resources, factual and confessional, so we are just there collectively grasping, feeling the limitations of knowledge, longing together, yearning for a way to reach that highest point. Even this yearning is a way to know. (p. 92)

The future requires consumers and professionals to work toward taking each other's perspective, using the knowledge and experiences of the collective whole as future directions for the adult movement are reviewed and planned. Respect, not fear of what all parties can contribute, will lead to creative and innovative practices.

Narcissism

The term "narcissism," particularly the definition used by the *Diagnostic and Statistical Manual of Mental Disorders,* fourth edition (American Psychiatric Association, 1994), has at times been used to hurt adults with learning disabilities because professionals have been unwilling to look beyond superficial behavior to the source of narcissistic behavior. Unfortunately, narcissism has a mainly negative connotation in our society—a trait to deny or reject in self as well as in others. Narcissism is a far more complex trait, which we all demonstrate positively and negatively at times. Narcissistic behavior as a psychological construct affecting adults with learning disabilities needs further exploration by professionals willing to keep an open mind. For consumers, understanding narcissism and its strengths and weaknesses is vital for becoming empowered.

Moore (1992) uses the ancient myth of Narcissus, as told in the *Metamorphoses* of the Roman writer Ovid, to illustrate the concept of narcissism. Narcissistic personalities, according to Moore (1992), are always searching for love and no matter how much they get, it is never enough. Accordingly, the problem that narcissistic personalities face is that they fall in love with the surface images of themselves, forgetting that their other images are just as lovable. The solution to narcissistic personalities then becomes allowing themselves to be open to new images of self. Moore (1992) advocates a focus on object relations psychology, where the individual moves to love self by seeing self as an object to love.

Narcissistic behavior among consumers can be illustrated by two common profiles. Profile A s always down themselves; they are never any good. Moore (1992) calls this "narcissism in reverse" (p. 72), for denial of oneself requires a significant amount of time focusing negatively on the ego rather than on the pleasures of every day, others, and self. Profile B is the individual who always takes credit for anything that has occurred in his or her environment—the constant bragger or manipulator. A consumer with this type of profile often has a "habit of repeating many ideas he had heard from several sources as though they were his own—one of the telltale signs of narcissism" (Moore, 1992, p. 68). Although any dichotomy or subgroup of personality must be viewed with caution, these profiles can be used to explore narcissism and adults with learning disabilities. According to Moore (1992), the reaction of others to a narcissistic personality is usually one of countertransference.

The solution to understanding the narcissistic personality, whether in ourselves or in others is not by using countertransference (i.e., grow up; get real; what a bore). Rather, according to Moore

(1992), "The secret in healing narcissism is not to heal it at all, but to listen to it" (p. 73). What pieces of the self does the consumer consider not acceptable to his or her identity? Does the consumer focus only on talking about his or her story? Do consumers reject knowledge and learning of others, really a clear message of fear of what they have constructed as their fatal flaw—their learning disability? It may not be their identity as individuals with a learning disability but, rather, their identity, such as a woman or part of a minority population, they are struggling to accept. Consumers working with other consumers help the most by being willing to listen and better understand the multiple identities of each person. Professionals might begin to better explore the concept of narcissism from an object relations and developmental perspective as to the impact on consumers representing multiple identities. Working with consumers as they construct honest and loving perceptions of themselves requires a listener, not a director. As Moore (1992) states: "By being the curator of our images, we care for our souls" (p. 65). Both consumers and professionals might benefit from nurturing the soul as much as the mental and physical body.

Kristeva (1991) talks about a problem faced by many nations and individuals—dealing with the foreigner within us. The word "foreigner" represents differences. Many adults with learning disabilities are not comfortable with their multiple identities or the foreigners within their person. This can lead to a conception that there is a right and wrong way of being an individual—a right and wrong way of learning and feeling. As Kristeva (1991) states: "The foreigner comes in when the consciousness of my difference arises, and he disappears when we all acknowledge ourselves as foreigners, unamenable to bonds and communities" (p. 1). Applying this concept of foreigner to adults with learning disabilities, many adults with learning disabilities become foreigners in the academic and work world because they are already foreigners from within. Kristeva (1991) would encourage consumers and professionals working with the adult population demonstrating learning disabilities to learn to "accept new modalities of otherness" (p. 2). Otherness must be constructed from a sociopolitical perspective—not just from the hegemonies of a given society.

FUTURE DIRECTIONS

The future direction for adults with learning disabilities rests within the creative talents of this population. Recent directions advocated by new alternative paradigms (see Gregg & Ferri, Chapter 2, this volume) stress the need in society for connections and relationships rather than a focus on boundaries and separateness. Adults with learning disabilities and those professionals committed to empowering this population might review these paradigms as a foundation for future models. For as Lykes (1985) states, the self might be best viewed as "an ensemble of social relations" (p. 356). Whatever the paradigm and theory chosen, a major focus of the movement will require a call for inclusiveness and collaboration among and between consumers and professionals across disciplines (Holmes & Saleeby, 1993).

Part of the call for collaboration might be for adults with learning disabilities to review whence they came—the self-help movement. Greater emphasis on creating a community for adults with learning disabilities at the grass roots should be explored. Then a network of communication among existing organizations or self-help groups will need to be operationalized. With the use of assistive technology, this goal will be easier than it was for the pioneers of the adult movement.

Professionals across disciplines and agencies would be well advised to review the NIDRR's current PAR and CORD policies to develop similar policy within their institutions. Professional and consumer input at all levels and stages of policy, research, and training are no longer luxuries but necessities if socially responsible institutions are to remain answerable to the people. Such policy leads to constructive self-reflection.

Concern about adults with learning disabilities is certainly still not a major focus of the field of learning disabilities, which is a child-oriented discipline in mission. Reviewing four journals, the *Journal of Learning Disabilities*, the *Learning Disabilities Quarterly*, the *Journal of Special Education*, and the *Rehabilitation Counseling Bulletin* from 1980 through 1994, only 147 articles were identified as dealing with the adult population demonstrating learning disabilities. Sixty-seven of the 147 articles pertain to assessment issues, focusing on cognitive, achievement, and social–emotional issues of this population. Certainly this documents the prevailing concern of finding the source of the problem within the adult with learning disabilities rather than within a network of factors. Such a philosophy does not encourage openness to consumer viewpoints, particularly those from culturally different communities. In addition, the majority of articles pertaining to the adult population with learning disabilities focus on the college or high-achieving population. Few articles explore the adult population with severe disabilities or the importance of cultural differences in the adult population with learning disabilities. As Holmes and Saleeby (1993) observe, "The question is, to what degree do clinical beliefs about clients rest more upon stereotypes of clienthood than upon the validity of evidence and the factuality of the world" (p. 64). More research focusing on the complex issues surrounding the adult population with learning disabilities is crucial to future social and political decision making.

Consumers will also have to involve themselves in self-reflection, particularly related to issues of essentialism and narcissism. Rogers (1965) notes that in therapy, "clients move generally from examinations of symptoms to examination of self" (Holmes & Saleeby, 1993, p. 64). The foreigner within us, Kristeva (1991) notes, "is the hidden face of our identity, the space that wrecks our abode, the time in which understanding and affinity founder" (p. 1). Acceptance of all the identities that each individual finds within will do nothing but enhance a better understanding of the adult population with learning disabilities. While the field will benefit from such introspection, all adults with learning disabilities owe this to themselves.

Finally, and most important, all key factors (i.e., consumers, systems, professionals, families, and friends) will need to, as bell hooks (1994) labels it, "authentically help" each other. She defines this term in the following manner:

> Authentic help means that all who are involved help each other mutually growing together in the common effort to understand the reality which they seek to transform. Only through such praxi—in which those who help and those who are being helped help each other simultaneously—can the act of helping become free from the distortion in which the helper dominates the helped. (p. 54)

Real change will require a mind-set among the entire community involved in working for the adult movement (whether that be consumer, professional, system, family, or friends). The beginning of change, however, will start in our own introspections of the foreigner within each of us—only by this means can we eliminate the fears that grip our perceptions of reality and begin to work for a positive change in relation to adults with learning disabilities.

REFERENCES

American Psychiatric Association. (1994). *Diagnostic and statistical manual of mental disorders* (4th ed.). Washington: Author.
Childers, D., & Rice, D. (1993). *Consumer involvement in rehabilitation re-*

search and practice: Nineteenth institute on rehabilitation issues [Monograph]. Arkansas: Arkansas Research and Training Center in Vocational Rehabilitation.

Deutsch, M. (1949). An experimental study of the effects of cooperation and competition upon group processes. *Human Relations, 2,* 199–232.

Deutsch, M. (1973). *The resolution of conflict: Constructive and destructive processes.* New Haven, CT: Yale University Press.

Emener, W. G. (1991). Empowerment in rehabilitation: An empowerment philosophy for rehabilitation in the 20th century. *Journal of Rehabilitation, 5,* 7–12.

Emener, W. G., Luck, R. S., & Smits, S. J. (Eds.). (1981). *Rehabilitation administration and supervision.* Baltimore: University Park Press.

Emener, W. G., & Stephens, J. (1982). Improving quality of working life in a changing rehabilitation environment. *Journal of Rehabilitation Administration, 6,* 114–124.

Freire, P. (1973). *Education for critical consciousness.* New York: Seabury Press.

Hahn, H. (1986). Public support for rehabilitation programs: The analysis of U.S. disability policy. *Disability, Handicap and Society, 1,* 121–137.

Holmes, G. E., & Saleeby, D. (1993). Empowerment, the medical model, and the politics of clienthood. *Journal of Progressive Human Services, 4,* 61–78.

hooks, b. (1994). *Teaching to transgress: Education as the practice of freedom.* New York: Routledge.

Kristeva, J. (1991). *Strangers to ourselves.* New York: Columbia University Press.

Lee, C., & Jackson, R. (1992). *Faking it: A look into the mind of a creative learner.* Portsmouth, NH: Boynton/Cook.

Lynn, R. (1979). *Learning disabilities: An overview of theories, approaches, and politics.* New York: Free Press.

Lykes, M. B. (1985). Gender and individualistic vs. collectivist bases for notions about the self. *Journal of Personality, 53,* 356–383.

Moore, T. (1992). *Care of the soul: A guide for cultivating depth and sacredness in everyday life.* New York: HarperCollins.

Naisbitt, J., & Aburdene, P. (1985). *Re-inventing the corporation.* New York: Warner Books.

Peters, T., & Austin, N. (1986). *A passion for excellence.* New York: Warner Books.

Rogers, C. (1965). *Client-centered therapy: Its current practice, implications and theory.* Boston: Houghton Mifflin.

Sampson, E. E. (1988). The debate on individualism: Indigenous psychologies of the individual and their role in personal and societal functioning. *American Psychologist, 43,* 15–22.

Smith, W. A. (1976). *The meaning of conscientizacao: The goal of Paulo Freire's pedagogy* [Monograph]. Amherst, MA: University of Massachusetts, Center for International Education.

Spence, J. T. (1985). Achievement American style: The rewards and costs of individualism. *American Psychologist, 40,* 1285–1295.

Staples, L. H. (1990). Powerful ideas about empowerment. *Administration in Social Work, 14,* 24–42.

Swift, C. & Levin, G. (1987). Empowerment: An emerging mental health technology. *Journal of Primary Prevention, 8*(112), 71–94.

Tuchman, B. W. (1984). *The march of folly from Troy to Vietnam.* New York: Knopf.

2

Paradigms: A Need for Radical Reform

NOEL GREGG
BETH FERRI

> The Enlightenment is dead, Marxism is dead, the
> working class movement is dead . . . and the
> author does not feel very well either.
> —SMITH (cited in Harvey, 1989, p. 325)

In the midst of a paradigm shift, knowledge claims previously taken as universal become the site of questioning and debate. The tensions between paradigms appear across disciplines and have a direct impact on research, methods, and theory (Kavale & Forness, 1994). For example, supporters of the positivist paradigm currently suggest the possibility of an objective and measurable external and independent truth or reality. Reductionism and the linear, sequential links drawn between cause and effect are characteristic of the positivist paradigm (Gergen, 1994; Heshusius, 1991; Poplin & Stone, 1992). Critics of the positivist paradigm call into question such issues as objectivity, causality, independence, and an accessible and representational truth (Fine, 1992; Heshusius, 1991; Lather, 1991).

The questioning of positivist assumptions is either liberating or threatening to the field of learning disabilities, depending on how one is situated; however, the basis for any paradigm shift is the persistent failure to solve "crisis-provoking" problems within existing paradigms (Kuhn, 1993). Problems can lead to reform. In education, a succession of reforms led to predictable pendulum swings and reversals rather than real change or progress (Kauffman, 1993). It may be that hegemony is at work such that the prevailing paradigm so constrains thinking and imagination that it becomes difficult to envision real change. The current positivist paradigm constrains the ability for many to envision alternatives (Heshusius, 1991). Some theorists suggest that it may be possible to envision existing theories with a new angle, so disregarding past knowledge and progress is shortsighted (Schrag, 1992).

This chapter evolved from the contention that the field of learning disabilities has only begun to see a glimmer of an alternative paradigm. Most of what is presented as new paradigms are really simply differences in theory within the prevailing positivist paradigm rather than paradigmatic changes. The difference between a paradigm and a theory is important to note. As Heshusius (1991) suggests, paradigms represent ways of seeing and not seeing the "beliefs, values, and assumptions about what counts as real and how we are allowed to claim knowledge" (p. 407). Paradigms are overarching frameworks that determine our view of reality and what we can ultimately see or hear. It is therefore impossible to combine theories and call it a paradigm, just as we cannot approach paradigms eclectically—paradigms determine what counts as evidence and theories proceed within the parameters determined by the prevailing paradigm (Kuhn, 1993). Theories represent models of inquiry, capable of delineating specific phenomena within the angle of vision afforded by the paradigm (Heshusius, 1989). Much of the debate within the field of learning disabilities is really a debate at the theory or method level, leaving unexamined the larger, underlying principles or paradigm at work (Kavale & Forness, 1994).

The field of learning disabilities is embedded within larger historical, social, and political contexts that influence reform efforts. As Kavale and Forness (1994) note, "Although logical positivism as a philosophy might be considered dead, its influence remains and is seen most clearly in the research process. The scientific method promulgated by logical positivism is viewed as the model for LD [learning disabilities]" (p. 42). The field of learning disabilities, however, cannot ignore the rumblings in every field of inquiry that suggests a paradigm shift or what amounts to a crisis of reason. Whether we call it modern versus postmodern, mechanistic versus holistic, or reductionist versus constructivist, it is clear that current ways of seeing and knowing are being challenged. It is perhaps in times of questioning that marginalized voices and alternative visions become clearer, and existing theories can be seen with new perspectives.

In this chapter several theories are described as they have evolved and contributed to our understandings and knowledge base in the field of learning disabilities. Skinner's radical behaviorism, cognitive, and constructive models, as well as alternative theories, are briefly described.

These and all theories, however, are seen as embedded within historical and social contexts, informed and constrained by the ways of thinking of the prevailing positivist paradigm. Without careful acknowledgment of prior thinking any talk of reform is left uninformed and destined to forever re-create itself. It seems important at this juncture to examine both existing theories and emerging voices as they inform our understanding of individuals with learning disabilities.

Many existing theories are important to the adult population with learning disabilities, but it is impossible to discuss all of them in this chapter. Thus, we decided to structure this chapter around several evolving key issues as they relate to adults with learning disabilities. The issues of cause, sources of control, and processes of knowledge are used to delineate the contributions of various theories and the similarities and differences in how they frame both the problems and the solutions for adults with learning disabilities.

The final section of the chapter focuses on factors evolving from oppositional discourses of both feminist scholars and scholars writing from a disability rights perspective. These scholars critique the politics of difference and call for reform. The issue of identity evolved from the work of Fine and Asch (1990), who describe disability as a social construct rather than a deficit located within an individual. They purport that disability, like identity, is shifting, multiple, and partial. They also recognize the diverse impact of ethnicity, class, and gender on how individuals experience disability. Educational reform scholarship recognizes that future reform efforts must be collective and sensitive to diversity of context, community, and culture (Honig, 1994) as well as to political and social contexts (Schrag, 1992).

Attention to knowing and power is rooted in the writings of Foucault (cited in Rabinow, 1984). The connections (Gergen, 1994; Lather, 1991) between knowledge and power are referred to as a politics of knowing, which encourages the changing roles and responsibilities in claims to authority and access to knowledge (Schrag, 1992). The Constituency-Oriented Research and Development (CORD) policy (see Gregg & Phillips, Chapter 1, this volume) attempts to put into practice different ways of authorizing knowledge and a commitment to hearing the voices of individuals with disabilities in the production of knowledge claims.

The factors of identity, power, knowing, and voices seem to be critical and interconnected issues in what must be seen as a paradigm shift in how both the constructs of learning disabilities and individuals with learning disabilities are viewed. Alterations in how these issues are constructed reflect a changing world view—a paradigm shift that will drive future reform efforts and theory production. We therefore hope to open further dialogue about existing and emerging paradigms and how they inform these issues.

RADICAL BEHAVIORISM

Radical behaviorism is one of the numerous theories that come under the heading of behaviorism (e.g., Skinner, 1969; Tolman, 1959; Watson, 1924). In fact, Chiesa (1992) notes that much of contemporary U.S. psychology belongs to a behavioral tradition. The theoretical model identified as radical behaviorism—Skinner's behaviorism—is distinct, however, from other models of behaviorism both in the constructs governing the theory and in the methodology. Radical behaviorism focuses on the relationships between behaving persons, the settings, the conditions of the behavior being observed, and the consequences of the behavior in context. Skinner (1969), drawing on the work of Mach (1893/1960), identifies the functional relationship between the change in the independent and dependent variables as the crucial interaction of behavior rather than a cause-and-effect reaction.

Causation

Newtonian models are based on the concept of "force" and "agency" as the nucleus of causation (Russell, 1946). Metaphors of behavioral responses, such as "causal chains" or "links in the chain," are examples of Newtonian models utilizing a serial power of force and agency. Many popular models that come under the heading of behaviorism, particularly social learning theory (e.g., Bandura, 1977, 1989), are built on the premises of force and agency.

An important aspect of radical behaviorism is the nonsequential and noncontiguous explanation of causation. Radical behaviorists view causation over time (life history, experience), as well as consider variation of a species or individual over time (Chiesa, 1992). Selection, therefore, is not only the result of temporal or spatial factors but the result of behavioral history. Experience (personal history) becomes a vital link in explaining current behavior.

Sources of Control

Skinner advocates that the source of control of an individual is in the environment rather than in the mental functions and processes of that person's mind. Skinner (1953, 1969, 1974) criticizes the adherence of psychological models that contribute significant power to "mental functions." The term "mental" to Skinner (1974) includes "the non-physical, the 'other stuff' of dualism, the fictional" (Baum & Heath, 1992, p. 1312). However, thoughts, feelings, images, and memories are termed "physical" by Skinner (1974). According to Skinner (1974), private events, which he labels "physical," are observable even if only by one person, unlike mental data, which he feels are abstract concepts (intelligence, intention, belief, knowledge, etc.) unable to be validated.

Control in Skinner's radical behaviorism rests in operant behavior. In the area of verbal behavior, Skinner recognizes a need to expand operant behavior into two categories: contingency shaped and rule governed. Radical behaviorists define rule-governed behavior as occurring when "the individual is behaving in accordance with explicit rules, advice, instructions, modeling performances, plans, maxims, and the like. Rules are contingency-specifying stimuli" (Delprato & Midgley, 1992, p. 1507). Skinner (1957) proposes that all processes referred to as thinking are operant behavior. As he states, "Man Thinking is simply Man Behaving" (p. 452) and cognitive processes are "behavioral processes: they are things people do" (Skinner, 1989, p. 23). Higher cognitive functioning, particularly Skinner's verbal behavior, is where the division between radical behaviorism and other theories of cognitive psychology is not clear.

A basic tenet of radical behaviorism is that the primary purpose of science or a theory is prediction and control. As Skinner (1953) notes: "We undertake to predict and control the behavior of the individual organism" (p. 35). Therefore, Skinner feels comfortable in determining an individual's needs, collecting functionally related facts about that person, and finally inductively explaining the problem. The entire foundation of radical behaviorism is the observer determining the knowledge the individual lacks and then acting on the individual or training the individual in how to act in order to change behavior. Skinner clearly describes the importance of prediction and control in the theory of radical behaviorism when he states, "The ultimate criterion for the goodness of a concept is not whether two people are brought into agreement but whether the scientist who uses the concept can operate successfully upon his material—all by himself if need be" (1945, p. 293). While Skinner (1971), in *Beyond Freedom and Dignity*, stresses the need for individuals to recognize controlling factors in their environment, the emphasis is not on constructing reality but on the awareness of the restrictions of reality.

Process of Knowledge

Guerin (1992), in a critique of behavior analysis and the social construction of knowledge, applies the work of Ryle (1949) to distinguish between two distinct types of knowledge, "knowing how" and "knowing that." According to Ryle (1949), knowing how means behavior shaped directly by the environment, and knowing that refers to behaving with the appropriate verbal behavior. Theorists from a radical behaviorist perspective emphasize the knowledge how or the knowledge that is generated from the interaction of individuals with the nonsocial environment. As Guerin (1992) noted, however, radical behaviorists do not fully account for social control in verbal communities, and socially constructed knowledge is missing from their explanation of the processes of knowledge. In return, the field of social psychology might benefit from radical behaviorists exploring the "role of social consequences in maintaining the contingencies of behavior" (Guerin, 1991, p. 1428), particularly social representations.

Application to Adults with Learning Disabilities

One of the most important aspects of radical behaviorism theory for adults with learning disabilities is the opposition to hypothetical or abstract constructs (i.e., memory, perception, and intelligence) being the entire predictor of future potential, becoming self-sustaining entities. According to Neisser (1982), such hypothetical constructs have diverted the attention of professionals from examining variables such as context, type of material, and past learning and knowledge. Even more of a threat to many adults with learning disabilities is how labels (e.g., learning disabilities, social skills deficits, dyslexia, and attention-deficit disorder), with varying definitions, are used to deny access to services or employment. In addition, many adults with learning disabilities describe horrifying events in which professionals have mistakenly used test scores to predict potential without the use of other qualitative data collected over time (Lee & Jackson, 1991). A few standardized test scores are not the total measure or predictor of success of a person. As Rose (1989) states:

What we define as intelligence, what we set out to measure and identify with a number, is both in us and out of us. We have been socialized to think of intelligence as internal, fixed, genetically coded. There is, of course, a neurophysiology to intelligence, but there's a feeling to it as well, and a culture. (p. 241)

Radical behaviorism provides a methodology to help adults with learning disabilities to gain the skills, either academic or social, to improve their current status through instruction. If behavior is seen as changeable, not all inherent in the individual, change is a realistic goal. Recognizing that locus of control is both internally and externally manifested allows individuals to change long-standing behaviors that might be having a negative impact on their daily lives.

COGNITIVE MODELS

Different theorists of cognitive development propose models to help professionals grasp the concept of learning ability (Case, 1985; Fodor, 1983; Gardner, 1983; Sternberg, 1985). Placing theorists into categories runs the high risk of oversimplifying theories to fit labels. In the area of cognitive development, this is certainly true as all contemporary theories must address the affective and cognitive processes that affect learning. The day of ignoring the functional integration of environmental, cognitive, and affective factors is certainly past. The source and degree of power given each of these processing functions, however, differ across models. As Roschelle and Clancey (1992) note in calling for a dialogue between social and neural theories, "Representation and meaning are not prior to social and physical interaction but are constructed in activity" (p. 444). A weakness with many older models of cognition was an oversimplification of the processes of learning, as well as a significant degree of power given to isolated, abstract cognitive functions. Often the cognitive processes presented in such models were defined with little empirical validity to support their existence. As an example, Wilensky (1983) discusses the weaknesses of Rumelhart's (1975) story grammar approach, which focuses on abstract structural features of stories at the expense of the social and motivational functions behind these stories.

The best-fit cognitive model may in the future result from cross-disciplinary cooperation between theorists exploring issues of learning from varying perspectives. Gergen (1985) discusses the current discontinuity between psychological processes and social construction processes. He suggests that rather than "looking towards the natural sciences and experimental psychology for kinship, an affinity is rapidly sensed with a range of what may be termed *interpretive disciplines*, that is, disciplines chiefly concerned with rendering accounts of human meaning systems" (p. 270; see also Gergen, 1988).

Causation

The philosophical theory of Fodor (1983), from his treatise entitled *Modularity of Mind*, has been chosen as one model to examine the issue of cognitive processing. "Modularity" is a term that appears to adequately describe the current research generated by professionals exploring the complexity of cognitive development from various disciplines (e.g., neurology, neurolinguistics, and sociolinguistics). Ceci (1990) defines modularity as the view that "mental life is best seen as a concatenation of many isolable cognitive processes, possessing various organizations" (p. 214). According to Foder's (1983) model of thinking, two sets of faculties exist, one that is "encapsulated within" specific knowledge domains and one that spreads across information obtained from many sources, which he calls unencapsulated sources. Some researchers propose that language, perception, and motor are examples of encapsulated sources and broad problem-solving ability is an example of unencapsulated (Ceci, 1990). According to this theory, encapsulated processes and unencapsulated processes are not always available to each other. Drawing heavily from Fodor's (1983) model, Ceci (1990) proposes what he calls the bioecological model of intelligence. The emphasis of causation in this model is on both the environment and the neurological makeup of an individual. Context and an individual's cognitive profile influence performance. Context used in this manner refers to the learning material and environmental constraints rather than cultural factors.

Pioneering researchers first exploring the correlation between cognitive processes and learning ability depended on the then popular serial hierarchical processing model that viewed cognitive functions as contained in fixed neuroanatomical pathways (Johnson & Myklebust, 1967; Orton, 1925; Roach & Kephart, 1966). According to these early cognitive theories, damage to a structure within this serial pathway results in functional deterioration. Rather than serial pathways, current research from the fields of neurology and neuropsychology is providing evidence to support the concept of interacting neural networks. In neural network theories, functional demand structures the networks of neuroanatomic configurations; thus, a single neuroanatomic network could affect various functions or task demands differently (Deuel, 1992; Deuel & Collins, 1984; Grimm,

1983). Several published studies apply this theory to understanding laterally directed spatial attention and motor behavior (Deeke, Kornhuber, Lang, Lang, & Schreiber, 1985; Getting, 1989; Wise & Desimone, 1988). Neural network theory proposes that a breakdown in learning can occur during a specific stage of execution or under unique task demands but not at other times (Deuel, 1992).

Connectionist models are a relatively new means of understanding cognitive processing. They are based on the neural network premise that learning takes place through the interaction of large numbers of cognitive processing units (Barden & Pollock, 1991; Schneider & Graham, 1992). Utilizing algorithms, such models implement parallel distribution connection-based processing descriptions of cognitive behavior. One of the conclusions, however, from such research is that learning is dynamic, requiring transient structures that are continually reproduced and re-formed as the need arises (Bickhard & Richie, 1983). "At the level of neural architecture the formation of new categories looks more like chaotic settling into a new activation state, rather than incremental modification of existing structures" (Roschelle & Clancey, 1992, p. 436).

Sources of Control

Contemporary cognitive psychologists utilize the term "intentional learning" to refer to cognitive processes that put learning as a goal rather than an incidental outcome (Bereiter & Scardamalia, 1989). Therefore, according to many cognitive researchers, learning develops across time and experience rather than being something we are simply born with the competence to perform. This does not discount the neurological network theory; it simply allows a better understanding of types of learning (e.g., intentional and automatic) and the context in which learning takes place. Iran-Nejad, Hidi, and Wittrock (1992) stress the multiplicity of sources that affect an individual's ability to learn. Phylogenetic, ontogenic, and social factors influence the biological organism from the perspective of today's cognitive psychologists. "The emergence of new categories is a matter of reusing transient organizations of neural maps; structured cues from the physical and social world gradually can stabilize new relations of features and the world" (Roschelle & Clancey, 1992, p. 449).

Process of Knowledge

Three aspects of knowledge on which cognitive psychologists have focused include an individual's understanding of (1) schema-based knowledge (i.e., scripts), (2) the structure of knowledge, and (3) the transformative nature of knowledge (Bereiter & Scardamalia, 1989). The emphasis of much of this discussion of knowledge has been on learning skills and strategies in both academic and social settings (Brown, Bransford, Ferrara, & Campione, 1983; Pressley, Forrest-Pressley, Elliott-Faust, & Miller, 1985). According to Pressley, Borkowski, and O'Sullivan (1985) and Borkowski, Milstead, and Hale (1988), more time has been given to the investigation of specific strategy knowledge rather than executive process and general strategy knowledge. Executive functions are the "self-regulatory mechanisms that give metacognitive knowledge its transituational applicability" (Groteluschen, Borkowski, & Hale, 1990, p. 92).

Knowledge in cognitive processing models is seen as an agreed-on set of information that is presented by others for the individual to assimilate. The type, structure, and presentation of information all influence the motivation of the individual to learn. Cognitive models rest on the ability of an individual to take in information to be acted on by cognitive networks that will allow for the storage of this information. While social and cultural experiences, along with the intention of the learner, influence the product according to such models, it is also believed that a set body of knowledge exists to be absorbed by the learner. The learner has a cognitive processing profile that makes it easier to learn some types of information and by some types of instruction than by other types and means of instruction. Less emphasis is placed on the impact of the environment and more credit is allocated to the cognitive architecture of the thinking organism. According to Watkins (1990), "Mechanistic theories are neither compelled nor constrained by the data" (p. 334).

Application to Adults with Learning Disabilities

It will be particularly important for future researchers to explore the cognitive and social processes adults with learning disabilities utilize across a multitude of task demands. Unfortunately, far too often, as Vygotsky (1981) observed, "Experimental procedures become surrogates for psychological processes" (p. 67). These experimental procedures can be in different forms (single-subject, case study, statistical), but the end will defeat the purpose. Any experimental procedure or model has its own narrowness. Future cognitive processing models, it is hoped, will integrate many different perspectives obtained by the use of a variety of experimental procedures.

Cognitive models have given way to a better understanding of the processes involved in the learning of tasks, be they cognitive or social. Cognitive models, such as Baddeley and Hitch's (1974) "working memory" model, have provided a heuristic to begin to understand the complexity of memory and semantic organization. Although behaviorists would rather emphasize the functional or environmental relationships in Baddeley and Hitch's (1974) model of memory, terms such as Baddeley and Hitch's (1974) "central executive," "visuospatial scratchpad," and "articulatory loop" focus on the process and not just on the objects or products involved in learning. Such models have been informative in the development of appropriate accommodations, modifications, and instruction matched to an individual's learning profile. The problem occurs when theorists relegate more power to hypothetical components than to the behaving person.

CONSTRUCTIVIST MODELS

The various interpretations of constructivist thought are described by Ernest (1995) as "the one and the many," capturing the very essence of the different forms of constructivist models. Constructivist models share several common assumptions (Neimeyer & Neimeyer, 1993). One assumption is that individuals are active in the process of constructing meaning pertaining to their lives. Access to reality is seen as partial and mediated by interests and perceptions. It is through the gaze of the observer that difference is created and made distinctive from the rest of reality; therefore, no clear boundary is visible between internal and external reality. This perception of a partial reality allows for alternative constructions as opposed to a reality that is seen as fixed or stable. Constructivist models contrast sharply from behaviorist models that assume the possibility of objective observation. These commonalities represent what Ernest (1995) describes as "the one" of constructivist thought. The remainder of this section describes several different interpretations of constructivist thought (i.e., radical constructivism, social–cultural constructivism, and alternative theories).

Radical Constructivism

The theoretical contributions of Piaget inform much of radical constructivist thought (Heshusius, 1991). Piaget, according to Ernest (1995), emphasizes internal cognitive processes of the individual as being the necessary means for the construction of knowledge. These constructions do not follow a linear path from experience to acquisition but are subject to self-regulation, reflection, and abstraction and are constrained by an individual's general level of development and existing cognitive system (Case, 1993; von Glasersfeld, 1995). Radical constructivists propose an evolutionary model of learning. Individuals are viewed as "acquiring new systems of cognitive operations that radically alter the form for learning of which they are then capable" (Case, 1993, p. 219). The emphasis, according to von Glasersfeld (1995), is on the construction of experiential realities that are biologically constrained by an individual's mental structures.

Causation

According to a radical constructivist view, individuals are biologically constricted by their mental processes (von Glasersfeld, 1995). Viability and adaptation to a specific context are the exerting influences on the individual. The cause of a learning disability might then be attributed to a biological difference in cognitive structures, but the adaptation of an individual's constructions would be evaluated in terms of practical adaptation to an individual's own context rather than external norms for performance. The drawback of an evolutionary or developmental view of the mind is that it fails to challenge false universals regarding developmental stages, hierarchical conceptions of cognitive ability, and the "biology is destiny" myth of human potential.

Sources of Control

The radical constructivist frame allows for considerable individual agency and control. Von Glasersfeld (1995) stresses the importance of individual learners being able to solve problems that are personally meaningful and chosen. In addition, he discusses the role of self-regulation, reflection, and abstraction in an individual's construction of knowledge. Because all knowledge is seen as temporary, failures are not seen as negative but actually necessary for individuals to reconstruct knowledge in light of additional or contradictory information (von Glasersfeld, 1995). The purpose of knowledge is driven by an essential need for individuals to gain predictability and control over their experience, so that learners are characterized as active, self-regulative, and innately driven to construct meaning (Confrey, 1995). Radical constructivism appears to place the learner at the center and in control of learning, constricted by biology alone.

Process of Knowledge

One of the strengths of radical constructivism is its detailed account of how individuals come to know (Ernest, 1995). The construction of knowledge occurs over time and in relation to an individual's cognitive stage of development. Learning is seen as an "essentially inner, intellectual process" (Shotter, 1995, p. 41) and knowledge is the ordering or organizing of the world through the individual's experiences. Thus, knowledge is not something independent of the individual to be discussed in the external world but something an individual does in his or her world representing successful adaptation with the physical world (von Glasersfeld, 1995). Radical constructivists have been criticized for emphasizing internal cognitive processes at the expense of social interaction, for their "tendency towards isolated individualism" (Ernest, 1995, p. 477) and for privileging cognitive over other factors (Heshusius, 1991). Recent presentations of the radical constructivist frame do address the role of social and cultural forces on how individuals construct knowledge (Ernest, 1995; von Glasersfeld, 1995).

Application to Adults with Learning Disabilities

All theories of learning are political in that they are value-laden, particularly in the ways in which the learner is positioned in the construction of knowledge (Ernest, 1995). The radical constructivist frame is politically and educationally useful for adults with learning disabilities in some ways and incomplete in others. The role of the learner as active, self-regulating, and capable of agency is certainly empowering to adults with learning disabilities. The fact that the cause of a learning disability according to a radical constructivist perspective might be attributed to biological cognitive structures justifies the claim for accommodations or modifications in the learning and work environment by adults with learning disabilities. The drawback to this definition of cause is that it leaves unchallenged the myth of "normal" cognitive structures and ignores other factors that may impede an individual's adaptation to a particular context such as cultural, economic, and personal factors. Finally, with an insistence on the individual's inner construction of knowledge, radical constructivist thought leaves the role of social interaction and other politically charged factors that place limits on an individual's ability to act as an independent agent and gain access to certain types of knowledge largely unexamined.

Social–Cultural Constructivism

In keeping with all constructivist frames, social–cultural constructivists recognize connections between individuals and their environment.

Whereas radical constructivism focuses on the physical reality in which individuals interact, sociocultural approaches focus on the individual's social and cultural interactions. In this frame, knowledge is constructed as a result of individuals interacting in communities rather than in their nonsocial environment (Guerin, 1992). Sociocultural approaches recognize mental functioning as inherently situated in cultural, historical, and institutional contexts (Wertsch & Toma, 1995).

Causation

Vygotsky (1934/1962) writes that all forms of higher mental functions are the result of internalized social interactions; an emphasis, therefore, is on social knowing. Accordingly, Vygotsky (1934/1962) states that interpsychological processes are internalized to intrapsychological processes by egocentric speech, leading to inner language. One of the functions then of egocentric speech and later inner language is to help plan and regulate human action. Wertsch (1985b) illustrates, through mother–child dialogues, the transformation of interpsychological processes involved in children's ability to solve problems. Language according to Vygotsky (1934/1962) plays a significant role in the knowing process.

Theorists (Ivanov, 1974; Wertsch, 1985a) support the thesis that inner language is inherently dialogical, constructed through the knowing process. Wertsch (1985b) supports Vygotsky's (1934/1962) claim that "egocentric speech . . . grows out of its social foundation by means of transferring social, collaborative forms of behavior to the sphere of the individual's psychological functioning" (p. 40). The regulative speech acts initially develop on the interpsychological (social) level according to Vygotsky (1934/1962) but become mirrored on the intrapsychological plane. The source of difficulty processing social rules for many adults with learning disabilities leads to difficulty in regulating their own behavior. The problem is a breakdown in the development of inner language.

Sources of Control

The issue of control and agency is less clear in a sociocultural framework. The individual is seen as clearly imbued within a social context. Sociocultural approaches recognize other social and structural controls on individuals' ability to act as autonomous agents. Further, as Guerin (1992) notes, social norms with historical, political, and economic consequences exert influences on an individual. The influence of Marxist thought in Vygotsky's (1934/1962) theory, while downplaying biological control, advocates cultural and political access to power. In fact, according to Wertsch and Toma (1995), Vygotsky's view of agency, although it did not fully consider cultural and historical factors, recognizes that agency is afforded not to individuals but to groups of individuals that share mediational means. Still left unexamined in sociocultural models is a critical analysis of power and its impact on an individual's ability to actively construct reality within a social context.

Process of Knowledge

Rather than viewing knowledge as a noun, social constructivists propose that the unit of activity, rather than individual, static, psychological processes (e.g., skills, concepts, and information processing units), be the focus of study. According to Wertsch (1985b), the Russian concern for the action or verb form of knowledge finds its roots in Vygotsky's favorite philosopher Spinoza. Spinoza (1675/1979) stated: "Thinking is not the product of an action but the action itself, considered at the moment of its performance, just as walking for example, is the mode of action of the legs, the 'product' of which it transpires is the space walked" (p. 35). Action theory, as social constructivists describe, places motives and concepts as dialectically related beginning with the unit of activity (Leontiev, 1978). According to Vygotsky (1934/1962), inner language is structured around abbreviated syntax, or "predicativity." Again, the verb form of knowing is the critical component rather than the noun form of knowledge. One of the most important characteristics of an activity, according to Wertsch (1985b), rests with the fact that it is "a sociocultural interpretation or creation that is imposed on the context by the participants" (p. 203). Unlike Newtonian or mechanistic paradigms, the self in such a theory is integrally involved in the process of knowing. Therefore, to study this process of knowing, Vygotsky places the focus of attention on the activity surrounding a "microcosm of consciousness" rather than on a static unit behavior (Wertsch, 1985b).

Application to Adults with Learning Disabilities

Future research is needed to better explore the regulative speech acts that Vygotsky (1934/1962) describes as initially developing on the interpsycholgical (social) level and later mirrored on the intrapsychological plane. In particular, research investigating the regulative speech acts, both cognitive and social, of adults with learning disabilities has direct implications for intervention.

The designing of effective assessment (dynamic) and intervention (proleptic instruction) will be a result of more research utilizing a sociocultural perspective. The focus of such assessment and intervention will be on the dialogical and action processes involved in knowing. Sociocultural approaches demand that learning go beyond gaining knowledge or information and actually provide the means to become involved in the discourse or actual doing of that knowledge. This requires access to the tools and signs necessary to engage in the process, as well as the understanding of the ways that knowledge is produced within that context (Carey & Smith, 1993). The role of technology as providing access to consumers to information and modes of discourse in an educational or work setting would be seen as a means of access to the context. Providing services to adults with learning disabilities would involve assisting individuals with the means to access the desired context so that they could, through their own efforts, assume full control of their own learning or training (Moll, 1990). Again, this frame seems useful in support of acquiring accommodation and modifications for adults with learning disabilities. A strength of a sociocultural model is that access is dictated by the context, not by a deficit or a biological impairment.

Alternative Theorists

Theorists proposing alternative models appear to present reinterpretations of previous theories to incorporate issues of diversity, culture, and power informed by a postmodern perspective that recognizes partiality in all knowledge claims. In these models there is a sense that knowledge is constructed through socially, personally, and politically charged ways.

A postmodern perspective is informed by both social activism and "high" theory, creating a cultural politics of difference that remains always paradoxical, openly contradictory, and self-undermining (Natoli & Hutcheon, 1993). Lather (1991) characterizes postmodern theory as capable of grasping the complexities of people and the cultures they create, although she recognizes that postmodern theory offers more questions than answers. The need to hear a plurality of voices, while acknowledging that no one voice is universal and that every voice is partial, is critical to recognizing the value and importance of difference and representation. In a postmodern analysis there is no essence, no absolute truth, no privileged discourse or center, but a recognition of the local and the particular as opposed to the universal and the eternal (Natoli & Hutcheon, 1993).

Heshusius (1991) defines a holistic frame as "not a new theory, but a new way of seeing" (p. 431) in which theory and basic assumptions are *transformed*. In a holistic frame, the "whole is both *more than* and *different from* the sum of its parts" (Heshusius, 1991, p. 442). In a holistic paradigm, learning is both personally and socially constructed and emotions, feelings, and desires are intricately welded to thinking. Knowledge and the learner are seen as inextricably connected so that the learner creates what is known (Poplin & Stone, 1992). Alternative models suggest possibilities for connections and departures from previous constructivist frames. It is the points of departure from previous frames that will be analyzed in the following paragraphs.

Causation

Postmodern, as well as alternative, theorists view competence or ability as evolving, subject to social, cultural, and historical factors (Lather, 1991; Lyotard, 1993). The focus is on difference and process rather than origin or cause (Hassan, 1993). Heshusius (1991) is perhaps most explicit in suggesting that searching for isolated causes of learning disabilities is a futile task. She believes that intellect, emotion, desire, and will are inextricably connected. Therefore, trying to separate any part from the whole creates only artificial abstractions. She disallows objective independent observation. In her view, it is impossible to observe external phenomena independent of thought and bias. Poplin and Stone (1992) speak of the integrity of the mind and different intelligences, recognizing that individuals are forever learning. They do recognize, however, the possibility of an individual not learning in terms of developmental unreadiness. Yet, Poplin and Stone (1992) propose that the problems that learners demonstrate might also be attributed to interests, cultural factors, inexperience, and inactive teaching techniques.

Sources of Control

Alternative theorists speak directly to power and control in the context of learning, suggesting that learning contexts segregated from an individual's reality are disempowering. Heshusius (1991) notes that when an individual has control over a learning task "his/her needs, experiences, and interests are intimately involved" (p. 457). Alternative theorists recognize the significant role of diversity, power relations, and multiple identities influenced by culture (Confrey, 1995). Such theorists take a self-conscious and critical stance regarding the relationship among the learner, knowledge and power, and assumptions of universality.

Some feminists have been wary of postmodern perspectives and theory. As bell hooks (1990) notes, the postmodern focus on difference and "otherness" occurs mainly on a theoretical plane without the benefit of the perspectives and the concrete, lived experiences of marginalized groups. Other feminists, according to Flax (1993), voice concern with the loss of identity, even an essentialist one, as a loss of political grounding. This is certainly important to consider for adults with learning disabilities who look to a shared identity from a minority group standpoint for political strategies. A postmodern frame, however, might "open new possibilities for the construction of self and the assertions of agency" (hooks, 1990, p. 28) for marginalized, essentialized groups. Certainly, the postmodern deconstruction of the "master narrative" provides opportunity to hear and learn from other voices.

Process of Knowledge

The concept of knowledge from the perspective of alternative and postmodern theorists is characterized as competence determined by historical, cultural, and social criteria specific to the context (Lyotard, 1993). Knowledge is viewed as being constructed by the learner who is socially, culturally, and personally invested, attending always to his or her most passionate interest (Poplin & Stone, 1992). Social and radical constructionist theories are criticized by alternative theorists for stressing cognitive ways of knowing—ignoring feelings, intuition, and noncognitive ways of problem solving (Poplin & Stone, 1992) and for failing to fully address cultural factors (Confrey, 1995). Alternative models recognize that learners are self-preserving, as well as self-regulating, so that withdrawing from a task could be seen as an act of resistance from a learning situation perceived by the learner as too difficult, too inconsistent with previous knowledge, or simply uninteresting (Poplin & Stone, 1992). The suggestion that a learner must have ownership and control of learning requires that the individual's needs, experiences, and interest be considered (Heshusius, 1991). In situations in which there are inherent power imbalances, the ownership and control of the learning are undermined (Heshusius, 1991). The importance of learning not from just a more experienced other, in a Vygotkian sense, but with a trusted other is an important axiom of alternative theorists (Poplin & Stone, 1992).

Application to Adults with Learning Disabilities

The alternative theories are presented as tentative perspectives. This does not necessarily reflect the potential for such frames to illuminate important issues for adults with learning disabilities. For example, when Confrey (1995) speaks of knowledge as being relative both temporally and communally, she allows that knowledge gained through observation or assessment is, at least to a degree, relative to the evaluator, the culture, and the context. Therefore, an evaluator's personal definition of a learning disability influences the perceptions and assessment of the construct and filters observed facts. The postmodern linkage of knowledge to power and cultural context recognizes hegemony in any claims to standards or norms on which to judge competence.

The recognition of multiple and shifting identities is useful for recognizing the many ways that individuals with learning disabilities are situated within diverse experiences and contexts. This viewpoint suggests that individuals with learning disabilities are a diverse, multiply situated group, questioning the salience of the very category. More important, "normal" is presented as a politically charged myth. Feminist strategies may prove useful in the debate between the efficacy of a shared identity as a place from which to act politically and the possibility of a decentered, multiply situated, constructed subject (Lather, 1991).

The recognition of resistance and dissent in the self-preservation of learners allows us to question which knowledge and ways of knowing are privileged and powered in a particular culture or context and which are disempowered. The added interrogation of the politics of knowing is potentially emancipatory as it questions both what counts as knowledge and what ways of knowing are privilege in a particular context. Again, feminist theory is useful to this discussion as it represents a challenge to hegemony as an outsider discourse with emancipatory goals.

EMERGING ISSUES FOR FUTURE PARADIGMS

It could be argued that a truly alternative paradigm has yet to be born. In the midst of a paradigm shift it is difficult to envision beyond current ways of seeing and knowing. However, it may be possible to gain new insights on existing theories by listening to emergent voices and reconstructing meanings based on current understandings, values, and purposes. Rather than advocating a particular lens or theory as "the" paradigm that will be useful for adults with learning disabilities, several themes or issues that appear to be critical to any new angle of vision are presented in the following sections.

Power, Control, Agency

The issue of power, control, and agency is central to efforts to redefine the relationship between professionals and consumers or the very definition of learning disabilities. A relatively new way of thinking about individuals with learning disabilities (as well as other disabilities) is from a minority group perspective (Fine & Asch, 1988, 1990; Funk, 1987; Hahn, 1987; Scotch, 1988; Shapiro, 1993). In redefining learning disabilities in terms of civil rights and a minority model, the definition of disability is seen as less an issue of biology inherent within the individual and more a label for a group of people who are unfairly excluded from or denied access to mainstream social institutions (Scotch, 1988). Dworkin and Dworkin (cited in Fine & Asch, 1990) report that the criteria for minority group status is an identifiable group subjected to differential and pejorative treatment by others. The group must have less power than the dominant group and must share some group awareness. It is not surprising then that individuals with learning disabilities are considered a minority group.

The focus of a minority model is ensuring that all individuals have the right to access social, educational, and vocational contexts regardless of any impairment. This movement places the consumer at the center of inquiry and reform efforts, acting on his or her own behalf. It recognizes that inequities, restrictions, and barriers are products of political decisions (Hahn, 1987). The CORD policy statement is testimony to this effort to create a space for consumers to have active and meaningful input into all phases of the research process. The move to more collaborative research designs recognizes the impact of power relations, subjugated knowledges, and the importance of the "silenced coming to voice" (Lather, 1991, p. 51).

The difficulties for adults with learning disabilities to develop a minority group consciousness and a political standpoint include insufficient financial resources, disincentives of self-identification, and the lack of a shared identity or community (Scotch, 1988). A missing shared political consciousness for individuals with hidden disabilities, like learning disabilities, must be understood in light of the fact that a disability rights movement requires individuals to identify and organize around a label or an aspect of identity that is most stigmatized by society (Hahn, 1987). The fact that organizations and services are organized around specific diagnostic categories reduces the likelihood of coalitions or alliances across a range of disabilities and creates a barrier to collective political action (Hahn, 1987). Social and historical attitudes behind the welfare or charity model are problematic as services to individuals with disabilities are granted "special rights" rather than unconditionally guaranteed civil rights. It is telling that racial and sex discrimination are seen as social injustices yet disabilities are stilled framed as biological and personal injustices (Fine & Asch, 1988).

The issue of control or "power to" rather than "power over" requires that learners must be agents in the construction of knowledge rather than recipients of that knowledge (Lather, 1991). In keeping with this view of power, the term "producer" might be more fitting than "consumer." According to Lather (1991), teachers and service providers must actively work to restructure power relations, value alternative ways of knowing, and act as facilitators creating spaces in which individuals can act and speak on their own behalf rather than position themselves as "masters of truth and justice" (p. xi). Power and control in this context would also be facilitated by the acquisition of skills that empower individuals to have command of their culture (Lather, 1991).

Lather (1991) draws from Foucault's "regimes of truth" (cited in Rabinow, 1984) and suggests that power and authority, which are informed by race, class, gender, and disability, influence which knowledge is legitimized and whose voices are heard in any culture. It is power over or domination over others that positions certain aspects or characteristics as the norm by which others deviate (Lather, 1991). Lather (1991) recognizes that efforts to include diversity must go beyond a multicultural perspective and actually challenge hegemony; therefore, efforts toward reform must go beyond including the voices and perspectives of individuals with learning disabilities and actually challenge the "myth" of normal. Questions Lather (1991) might ask are: Who decides what is the norm? For whom? Who benefits from these decisions?

Ellsworth notes that adding voices without recognizing that all voices do not carry the same "legitimacy, safety, and power" (cited in Lather, 1991, p. 43) will not effectively interrupt power imbalances. According to Lather (1991), to do this requires a constant questioning of the ways that we contribute to patterns of domination, despite our emancipatory aims as service providers. Scotch (1988) also presents the possibilities that dependency and stigma can be reinforced by the very persons and structures designed to help by presenting the individual using services as in need of professional, medical, and rehabilitative assistance. The political and historical importance of this more self-critical shift is the positioning of the consumer from a marginal and passive recipient to a place of empowerment. This truly represents a change of vision from deficit-driven medical models which locate the source of the disability within the consumer and the solution to the "problem" with the professional.

With a sociopolitical or minority group model, the solution does not lie in remediating or rehabilitating the individual but in the eradication of bias, segregation, and discrimination. The focus shifts from service delivery to public policy. Challenging cultural values and attitudes become the major issues confronting individuals (Hahn, 1987). The deficit shifts from being considered within the individual to within the environment or attitudes of society. The rehabilitation and educational efforts change from helping the individual with a learning disability to fit into an unchanging environment to looking toward creative ways for restructuring the environment, encompassing the individual's strengths and abilities. The "disabled environment" then becomes the object of remediation, according to Stubbins (cited in Finkelstein, 1980). Gartner and Joe (1987) note that it is political decisions rather than individual impairments that prevent the creation of structures and environments that meet the needs of people with a wide range of functional capabilities. As Fine and Asch (1988) note, it is time for us to stop thinking about the social and attitudinal environment as a given.

Identity

Redefining disability is both an issue of control and one of identity. The issue of self-definition for individuals with disabilities challenges us to view identity as multiple and shifting. In much of the research on individuals with learning and other disabilities, the disability is uncritically accepted as the independent variable—the variable that predicts the outcome (Fine & Asch, 1988). Fine and Asch (1990) suggest that a "disability may be more salient to the researcher studying it than to the people being studied" (p. 67). Research on individuals with learning disabilities typically ignores and treats as irrelevant issues of race, class, gender, and culture, thereby defining the person only by his or her learning disability. The label of a learning disability fails to acknowledge ways that individuals are multiply situated and the varying impact of culture and context. Lather (1991) notes that categories are never stable or pure but rather are contingent and partial, interacting within a specific context. What Lather (1991) is suggesting is that there is no "one essence" that describes an individual and that our efforts to recognize diversity must consider the ways that individuals within any group are more different than similar. Other researchers suggest a "disability continuum" (Zola, 1993) to replace a functional limitation model to focus on the external forces and social barriers and their impact on individuals.

Issues of identity for individuals with learning disabilities might call into question the ways that disability is constructed by society. Feminist theory examines gender construction, which is parallel to the ways that disability is constructed. Irigaray's idea of the phallic feminine, or "woman as man sees her," suggests ways that gender difference in a patriarchy must be exaggerated to reinforce the stereotypical images of woman as other (cited in Tong, 1989). This image of a reverse mirror illuminates the ways that differences in physical size and power between males and females is exaggerated. In similar ways, the nondisabled perpetuate myths about people with disabilities as being overly dependent and tragic victims. What purpose do these exaggerations serve—as Lather (1991) would ask: Who benefits? It may be that these exaggerated stereotypes serve to make the nondisabled feel less vulnerable, and more abled, just as exaggerations between women and men serve to make men feel more powerful. Whether one considers learning disabilities as a social construction or a biological fact, it is possible to question the significance of the attitudes, assumptions, and social meanings that are attached to the label and the implications behind such meanings.

One reasonable response to negative representations of learning disabilities is "passing." Actually, it is encouraged in our society by rehabilitation and other professionals working with individuals with disabilities to "pass" for as normal as possible. The limited images presented in literature and film champion the people who overcome their disability or succeed "against the odds." The issue of "passing" is particularly relevant to individuals with such hidden disabilities as learning disabilities, who may face additional pressure to "pass." The damaging result of "passing" is that it leaves intact the implicit assumption that to be nondisabled is normal, rather than calling into question the unsteady and mythical construction of normal. Finkelstein (1980) notes that redefining disability will require turning "normal" upside down and reminds us that if society were structured for people in wheelchairs, for example, abled-bodied people would be disabled by structures and environments systematically designed not to meet their needs.

The political implications of identity or Anspach's "identity politics" (cited in Scotch, 1988) suggests the link between identity and power. The impact of diagnostic categories that presume biological inferiority, the same assumption that has been used to oppress other minorities, creates and reinforces subordination that then appears "natural" (Hahn, 1987). The issues of identity and representation are critical to the ability of individuals with learning disabilities to create meaningful self-presentations that reflect their multiple positions in society. In this way self-knowledge, self-presentation, and self-advocacy are intimately linked to the self-construction of identity and empowerment.

Knowledge/Knowing

Knowledge in Newtonian or mechanistic paradigms is treated as a construct quite separate from the knower, and as an entity to be objectively studied and controlled by the knower. Knowledge is viewed as a noun and the knower as self. The knower becomes separate from the objective knowledge, giving the self power over the knowledge. Feminist theorists complain that the positivist paradigm positions knowledge as something to be mastered in the way that women have been mastered through the centuries (Ruthven, 1984). Currently, paradigms or theories focusing on the verb form of knowledge appear to provide a critical perspective necessary in addressing many of the issues related to the adult population with learning disabilities.

The design of effective assessment and intervention programs for adults with learning disabilities has in the past often neglected the dialogical and action processes involved in knowing. Traditionally, most diagnostic procedures have been static, leading only to diagnostic labels and eligibility decisions for services. Recently, the concept of process or dynamic assessment has led professionals to reevaluate traditional diagnostic models. Dynamic assessment is based on the following principles (Meyers, 1987): (1) there must be a link between assessment and intervention; (2) assessment must be tied to the environment; (3) assessment must focus on the process as well as the product of behavior; and (4) assessment must involve a means of generating and testing hypothesis. The work of Feurenstein (1979), Brown and Campione (1987), and Vygotsky (1934/1962, 1935/1978) provide a theoretical and empirical base for restructuring the purpose and means of assessment.

Dynamic models of learning advocate that greater attention be given the process of knowing than the end product "knowledge." Stone and Wertsch (1984) use the term "proleptic instruction" to describe the importance of students constructing an understanding of a concept rather than simply viewing an adult demonstrate or explain a task. It is the dialogical interaction between the adult and learner that helps the learner grasp the concept and later transfer it to another context.

Dynamic assessment and intervention models primarily use the work of Feurenstein's (1979) mediation principles or Brown and Campione's (1987) graduated prompting model. The research results of Vye, Burns, Deldos, and Bransford (1987) illustrate that a mediational model may be better suited than graduated prompting models as a diagnostic–prescriptive device because it has a greater emphasis on contingency in instruction and use of metacognitive skills. Graduated prompting models, however, seem more effective for the prediction of behavior.

Specific research is needed that focuses on the use of dynamic assessment and instruction for the adult population with learning disabilities. Attention to the dialogical dynamics involved in the development of knowing, as well as sensitivity to the role of the learner characteristics as mediators to problem solving, will help in creating more sensitive and effective accommodation and modifications, as well as instructional programs for the adult population with learning disabilities. A focus on knowing rather than knowledge appears to be a critical factor in the construction of future paradigms or theories.

VALUING THE VOICES OF ADULTS
WITH LEARNING DISABILITIES

Valuing the voices of consumers, thereby allotting power to such voices, is a key factor to incorporate into future paradigms or theories. Feminist theories from varying perspectives state that the different voices of women are often discounted or ignored, particularly in academic writing. Wertsch (1991) terms this abstract, third person voice of academics the "disengaged image of the self" (p. 69). He purports that the power given to the disengaged image of the self is the result of "western scholars who hold to the underlying assumptions of approaches such as behaviorism, in spite of what he sees as overwhelming evidence that these assumptions lead to untenable claims" (p. 69). Brown and Gilligan (1992), in an analysis of the oral text of young women, come to the conclusion that developmental progress leads to a loss of the female voice. Hegemony, it appears, is given the power to set the standards for normality and acceptance despite overwhelming evidence that diversity is often not equally represented. The problems women relate to not having their voices recognized have certainly been an issue for individuals with learning disabilities in our society.

The current recognition that many voices are interested participants in helping to solve the problems facing individuals with disabilities led to the development of the National Institute on Disability and Rehabilitation Research's CORD policy (see Chapter 1, this volume, for a detailed discussion). Consumers (adults with learning disabilities), researchers, and practitioners are beginning to better recognize the need to collaborate in the development of research and service projects. The critical focus on listening to the voices of all constituencies involved in seeking solutions for adults with learning disabilities will, it is hoped, provide more access to educational and employment opportunities for the adult population with learning disabilities. Recent social shifts that view persons with learning disabilities as contributors to the solutions rather than passive recipients of services are constructing positive changes in both research and practice.

The word "voices" is a key variable in future paradigms and theories. The CORD policy recognizes that there are many voices (e.g., consumer, practitioners, and researchers) involved in working on solutions to problems facing the adult population with learning disabilities. A critical point is that the consumer voice is not a homogeneous group but rather a heterogeneous group of adults representing various social and cognitive profiles, as well as different genders, classes, and cultures. Casden (1994), in a critique of the sociolinguistic theories of Bakhtin, Hymes, and Vygotsky, discusses the impact of social experiences on voice: "We acquire words through hearing or reading the utterances of others, and they are thereby marked with the voices of these prior context" (pp. 45–62). Wertsch (1991) elaborates on Vygotsky's (1934/1962) and Bakhtin's (1986) theories related to the voice or dialogue of discourse by stressing that there are *voices* rather than *a voice* involved in our creation of discourse. Adults with learning disabilities, therefore, must be sensitive to the multiplicity of voices influencing them (e.g., self, other, and culture). Voice is a heuristic for interpreting meaning and exists explicitly in dialogical interaction (Gregg, Sigalis, Hoy, Wisenbaker, & McKinley, in press). Claude Bernard (1978) eloquently discusses the concept of our *milieu intérieur* or our "in-vironment." He wrote about the in-vironment as the inner relationships that impact on our thinking and feeling and "en-vironment" as the everyday external relationships that change our thinking. One hears and reacts to many voices in both the "in" and "en" vironments. Discrepancies in messages from the "in" and "en" vironments or voices can lead to confusion and ambiguity.

Valuing the voices of adults with learning disabilities is a critical aspect of a policy such as CORD. The definition for valuing will need to be examined carefully and selected to fit the paradigm of choice. The verb form "value" defined as "to determine or estimate the worth" of an individual (*American Heritage Dictionary*, 1975, p. 1414), stresses the *worth of a voice*. The use of this definition or perception is illustrated in the research on resilience (Spekman, Goldberg, &

Herman, 1992) and successful adults with learning disabilities (Ginsberg, Gerbera, & Reiff, 1994). Other instances of this use of the word "valuing" are apparent when adult superstars with learning disabilities from science (e.g., Einstein), sports (e.g., Greg Louganis), or the movies (e.g., Cher and Tom Cruise) are held up as examples of potential success for adults with learning disabilities. Although it is helpful for young persons to use superstars as models, such examples can also be seen as the only level of success valued in our society.

"Valuing" defined as "regarding highly: prize; esteem" (*American Heritage Dictionary*, 1975) focuses on the multiplicity of all voices. Rukeyser (1974) once stated that the reality of art is imagination. If applied to life choices, imagination is a plan or scheme to deal creatively with reality. For many adults with learning disabilities, fear of accepting and valuing their own voices can be an indication that they are cast off from their own reality. Helping such adults value and not discount their own voices leads to personal success. Quality of life consists of much more than material or social success. Future research is critical to help consumers, researchers, and practitioners better understand quality-of-life issues for the adult population with learning disabilities. Hoy and Manglitz (Chapter 10, this volume) provide an excellent discussion of the research issues pertaining to quality of life and the adult population with learning disabilities.

Valuing all adults with learning disabilities, not just those identified by some measure as successful, is more in line with CORD policy. This is not to discount the need for research on investigating resiliency and the success factors of adults with learning disabilities. It is simply a call to focus not on "determining or estimating the worth" of individuals but rather on "regarding all adults with learning disabilities highly" for who they are, not just for their contributions to the world.

FUTURE DIRECTIONS

The fields of learning disabilities and rehabilitation are in the midst of significant changes. Some of the changes being seen represent a shift in paradigms—a change in how we view individuals with learning disabilities and disability as a social and political construct. Collaborative research between activists, action researchers, and consumers will disrupt and transform the relationships, boundaries, and claims of expertise between researchers and the researched. Thinking about individuals with learning disabilities as a minority group while recognizing the multiple and diverse contexts of culture presents a challenge to build coalitions across differences as well as to understand differences in new ways. Finally, challenging stereotypes, oppression, and the institutions or practices that perpetuate and reinforce them is further evidence of a changing perspective—a changing paradigm.

Kavale and Forness (1994) speak of some of these changes as "paradigm wars" and many discussions frame paradigms as opposing dichotomies. It might be that a new paradigm will not win over the other but rather will transform the other—rendering it unrecognizable in its previous form. As Heshusius (1989) suggests, "Paradigms, when made self-conscious and articulated, make explicit how we think about the phenomena of interest . . . [they] describe who we are in our epistemological make up" and who we are as knowers (p. 403). A paradigm shift results in changes at the very core of our thinking. The struggle to demonstrate the changes seen in the field of learning disabilities may not be fully articulated, and we may not ever be in a position to disregard previous victories and knowledges, but we are perhaps at an important juncture. This juncture of shifting paradigms may be just the place where possibilities and promises of change and real reform begin to take focus within a changing lens.

REFERENCES

American Heritage dictionary of the English language. (1975). New York: Houghton Mifflin.

Baddeley, A. D., & Hitch, G. J. (1974). Working memory. In G. H. Bower (Ed.), *Recent advances in learning and motivation* (pp. 47–89). San Diego, CA: Academic Press.

Bakhtin, M. M. (1986). *Speech genres and other late essays* (C. Emerson & Michael Holquist, Eds.; V. W. McGee, Trans.). Austin: University of Texas Press.

Bandura, A. (1977). Self-efficacy: Toward a unifying theory of behavioral change. *Psychological Review, 84*, 191–215.

Bandura, A. (1989). Human agency in social cognitive theory. *American Psychologist, 44*, 1175–1184.

Barden, J. A., & Pollock, J. B. (Eds.). (1991). *Advances in connectionist and neural computation theory* (Vol. 1). Norwood, NJ: Ablex.

Baum, W. M., & Heath, J. L. (1992). Behavioral explanations and intentional explanations in psychology. *American Psychologist, 44*, 1312–1318.

Bereiter, C., & Scardamalia, M. (1989). Intentional learning as a goal of instruction. In L. B. Resnick (Ed.), *Knowing, learning and instruction: Essays in honor of Robert Glaser* (pp. 261–292). Hillsdale, NJ: Erlbaum.

Bernard, C. (1978). *Lettres parisiennes: 1869–1878/Claude Bernard.* Lyon, France: Fondation Marcel Merient.

Bickhard, M. H., & Richie, D. M. (1983). *On the nature of representation: A case study of James Gibson's theory of perception.* New York: Praeger.

Borkowski, J. G., Milstead, M., & Hale, C. (1988). Components of children's metamemory: Implications for strategy generalization. In F. E. Weinert & M. Perlmutter (Eds.), *Memory development: Universal changes and individual differences* (pp. 73–100). Hillsdale, NJ: Erlbaum.

Brown, A. L., Bransford, J. D., Ferrara, R. A., & Campione, J. C. (1983). Learning, remembering, and understanding. In J. H. Flavell & E. M. Markman (Eds.), *Handbook of child psychology: Vol. 3. Cognitive development* (4th ed., pp. 77–166). New York: Wiley.

Brown, A., & Campione, J. C. (1987). Psychological theory and the study of learning disabilities. *American Psychologist, 41,* 1059–1068.

Brown, L., & Gilligan, C. (1992). *Meeting at the crossroads: Women's psychology and girls' development.* Cambridge, MA: Harvard University Press.

Carey, S., & Smith, C. (1993). On understanding the nature of scientific knowledge. *Educational Psychologist, 28*(3), 235–251.

Casden, C. (1994). Vygotsky, Hymes, and Bakhtin: From word to utterance and voice. In L. Steffe (Ed.), *A constructivist approach to teaching* (pp. 45–62). Hillsdale, NJ: Erlbaum.

Case, R. (1985). *Intellectual development: Birth to adulthood.* Orlando, FL: Academic Press.

Case, R. (1993). Theories of learning and theories of development. *Educational Psychologist, 28*(3), 219–233.

Ceci, S. J. (1990). *On intelligence . . . more or less: A bio-ecological treatise on intellectual development.* Englewood Cliffs, NJ: Prentice Hall.

Chiesa, M. (1992). Radical behaviorism and scientific frameworks: From mechanistic to relational accounts. *American Psychologist, 47,* 1287–1299.

Confrey, J. (1995). How compatible are radical constructivism, social–cultural approaches, and social constructivism? In L. Steffe (Ed.), *Constructivism in education* (pp. 185–226). Hillsdale, NJ: Erlbaum.

Deeke, L., Kornhuber, H., Lang, W., Lang, M., & Schreiber, H. (1985). Timing function of the frontal cortex in sequential motor and learning tasks. *Human Neurobiology, 4,* 143–154.

Delprato, D. J., & Midgley, B. D. (1992). Some fundamentals of B. F. Skinner's behaviorism. *American Psychologist, 47,* 1507–1520.

Deul, R. (1992). Motor skill disorders. In S. Hooper, G. Hynd, & R. Mattison (Eds.), *Developmental disorders: Diagnostic criteria and clinical assessment* (pp. 239–281). Hillsdale, NJ: Erlbaum.

Deul, R., & Collins, R. C. (1984). The functional anatomy of frontal lobe neglect in the monkey: Behavioral and quantitative 2-deoxyglucose studies. *Annals of Neurology, 15,* 521–529.

Dworkin, A., & Dworkin, R. (Eds.). (1976). *The minority report.* New York: Praeger.

Ernest, P. (1995). The one and the many. In L. Steffe (Ed.), *Constructivism in education* (pp. 459–486). Hillsdale, NJ: Erlbaum.

Feurenstein, R. (1979). *The dynamic assessment of retarded performers: The learning potential assessment device, theory, instruments and techniques.* Baltimore: University Park Press.

Fine, M. (1992). *Disruptive voices: The possibilities of feminist research.* Ann Arbor: University of Michigan Press.

Fine, M., & Asch, A. (1988). *Women with disabilities: Essays in psychology, culture, and politics.* Philadelphia: Temple University Press.

Fine, M., & Asch, A. (1990). Disability beyond stigma: Social interaction, discrimination, and activism. In M. Nagler (Ed.), *Perspectives on disability* (pp. 61–74). Palo Alto, CA: Health Markets Research.

Finkelstein, B. A. (1980). *Attitudes and disabled people: Issues for discussion* [Monograph No. 5]. New York: World Rehabilitation Fund.

Flax, J. (1993). Thinking Fragments (excerpts). In J. Natoli & L. Hutcheon (Eds.), *A postmodern reader* (pp. 419–425). Albany: State University of New York Press.

Fodor, J. A. (1983). *The modularity of mind.* Cambridge, MA: MIT Press.

Funk, R. (1987). Disability rights: From caste to class in the context of civil rights. In A. Gartner & T. Joe (Eds.), *Images of the disabled, disabling images* (pp. 7–30). New York: Praeger.

Gardner, H. (1983). *Frames of mind: The theory of multiple intelligences.* New York: Basic Books.

Gartner, A., & Joe, T. (Eds.). (1987). *Images of the disabled, disabling images.* New York: Praeger.

Gergen, K. J. (1985). The social constructionist movement in modern psychology. *American Psychologist, 40,* 266–275

Gergen, K. J. (1988). If persons are texts. In S. B. Messer, L. A. Sass, & R. L. Woolfolk (Eds.), *Hermeneutics and psychological theory* (pp. 28–51). New Brunswick, NJ: Rutgers University Press.

Gergen, K. J. (1994). Exploring the postmodern. *American Psychologist, 49*(5), 412–416.

Getting, P. (1989). Emerging principles governing the operations of neural networks. *Annual Review of Neuroscience, 12,* 185–204.

Ginsberg, R., Gerber, P., & Reiff, H. B. (1994). Employment success for adults with learning disabilities. In P. J. Gerber & H. Reiff (Eds.), *Learning disabilities in adulthood: Persisting problems and evolving issues* (pp. 204–213). Boston, MA: Andover Medical.

Gregg, N., Sigalis, S., Hoy, C., Wisenbaker, J., & McKinley, C. (in press). Sense of audience and the adult writer: A study across competence levels. *Reading and Writing.*

Grimm, R. (1983). Program disorders of movement. In J. Desmedt (Ed.), *Motor control mechanisms of health and diseases* (pp. 1–12). New York: Raven Press.

Groteluschen, A. K., Borkowski, J. G., & Hale, C. (1990). Strategy instruction is often insufficient: Addressing the interdependency of executive and attributional processes. In T. E. Scruggs & B. Y. L. Wong (Eds.), *Intervention research in learning disabilities* (pp. 81–101). New York: Springer-Verlag.

Guerin, B. (1991). Anticipating the consequences of social behavior. *Current Psychology: Research and Reviews, 10,* 131–162.

Guerin, B. (1992). Behavior analysis and the social construction of knowledge. *American Psychologist, 47*(11), 1423–1432.

Hahn, H. (1987). Civil rights for disabled Americans: The foundation of a political agenda. In A. Gartner & T. Joe (Eds.), *Images of the disabled, disabling images* (pp. 181–203). New York: Praeger.

Harvey, D. (1989). *The condition of postmodernity.* Oxford: Basil Blackwell.

Hassan, I. (1993). Toward a concept of postmodernism. In J. Natoli & L. Hutcheon (Eds.), *A postmodern reader* (pp. 273–286). Albany: State University of New York Press.

Heshusius, L. (1989). The Newtonian mechanistic paradigm, special education, and contours of alternatives: An overview. *Journal of Learning Disabilities, 22*(7), 403–415.

Heshusius, L. (1991). Future perspectives. In D. K. Reid, W. P. Hresko, & H. L. Swanson (Eds.), *A cognitive approach to learning disabilities* (pp. 431–467). Austin, TX: Pro-Ed.

Honig, B. (1994). How can Horace best be helped? *Phi Delta Kappan,* 75(10), 790–796.

hooks, b. (1990). Postmodern blackness. In *Yearnings* (pp. 23–31). Boston: South End Press.

Iran-Nejad, A., Hidi, S., & Wittrock, M. C. (1992). Reconceptualizing relevance in education from a biological perspective. *Educational Psychologist, 27,* 407–414.

Ivanov, V. V. (1974). The significance of M. M. Bakhtin's ideas on sign, utterance, and dialogue for modern semiotics. In H. Baran (Ed.), *Semiotics and structuralism: Readings from the Soviet Union* (pp. 27–45). White Plains, NY: International Arts and Science Press.

Johnson, D., & Mykelbust, H. (1967). *Learning disabilities: Educational principles and practices.* New York: Grune & Stratton.

Kauffman, J. M. (1993). How we might achieve the radical reform of special education. *Exceptional Children, 60*(1), 6–16.

Kavale, K. A., & Forness, S. R. (1994). Models and theories: Their influence on research in learning disabilities. In S. Vaughn & C. Bos (Eds.), *Research issues in learning disabilities: Theory, methodology, assessment, and ethics* (pp. 38–65). New York: Springer-Verlag.

Kuhn, T. (1993). The resolution of revolutions. In J. Natoli & L. Hutcheon (Eds.), *A postmodern reader* (pp. 376–389). Albany: State University of New York Press.

Lather, P. (1991). *Getting smart: Feminist research and pedagogy with/in the postmodern.* New York: Routledge.

Lee, C., & Jackson, R. (1991). *Faking it: A look into the mind of a creative learner.* Portsmouth, NH: Boynton/Cook.

Leontiev, A. N. (1978). *Activity, consciousness, and personality.* Englewood Cliffs, NJ: Prentice Hall.

Lyotard, J. F. (1993). The postmodern condition: A report on knowledge (excerpts). In J. Natoli & L. Hutcheon (Eds.), *A postmodern reader* (pp. 71–90). Albany: State University of New York Press.

Mach, E. (1960). *The science of mechanics: A critical and historical account of its development.* Peru, IL: Open Court. (Original work published 1893)

Meyers, J. (1987). The training of dynamic assessors. In C. S. Lidz (Ed.), *Dynamic assessment: An interactional approach to evaluating learning potential* (pp. 403–425). New York: Guilford Press.

Moll, L. C. (Ed.). (1990). *Vygotsky and education: Instructional implications and applications of sociohistorical psychology.* New York: Cambridge University Press.

Natoli, J., & Hutcheon, L. (Eds.). (1993). *A postmodern reader.* Albany: State University of New York Press.

Neimeyer, G. J., & Neimeyer, R. A. (1993). Defining the boundaries of constructivist assessment. In G. J. Neimeyer (Ed.), *Constructivist assessment: A casebook* (pp. 1–30). Newbury Park, CA: Sage.

Neisser, U. (1982). *Memory observed: Remembering in natural context.* San Francisco: Freeman.

Orton, S. (1925). "Word-blindness" in school children. *Archives of Neurology, 14,* 582–615.

Poplin, M. S., & Stone, S. (1992). Paradigm shifts in instructional strategies: From reductionism to holistic/constructivism. In W. Stainback & S. Stainback (Eds.), *Controversial issues confronting special education: Divergent perspectives* (pp. 153–180). Boston: Allyn & Bacon.

Pressley, M., Borkowksi, J. G., & O'Sullivan, J. (1985). Children's metamemory and the teaching of memory strategies. In D. L. Forrest-Pressley, D. MacKinnon, & T. G. Wallter (Eds.), *Metacognition, cognition, and human performance* (pp. 111–153). San Diego, CA: Academic Press.

Pressley, M., Forrest-Pressley, D. L., Elliott-Faust, D., & Miller, G. (1985). Children's use of cognitive strategies, how to teach strategies, and what to do if they can't be taught. In M. Pressley & C. J. Brainerd (Eds.), *Cognitive learning and memory in children* (pp. 1–47). New York: Springer-Verlag.

Rabinow, P. (Ed.). (1984). *The Foucault reader.* New York: Pantheon.

Roach, E., & Kephart, N. (1966). *The Purdue Perceptual Motor Survey.* Columbus, OH: Merrill.

Roschelle, J., & Clancey, W. J. (1992). Learning as social and neural. *Educational Psychologist, 27,* 435–453.

Rose, M. (1989). *Lives on the boundary: The struggles and achievement of America's underprepared.* New York: Free Press.

Rukeyser, M. (1974). *The life of poetry.* New York: Morrow.

Rumelhart, D. E. (1975). Notes on a schema for stories. In D. G. Bobrow & A. Collins (Eds.), *Representation and understanding* (pp. 211–236). New York: Academic Press.

Russell, B. (1946). *A history of Western philosophy.* London: Allen & Unwin.

Ruthven, K. K. (1984). *Feminist literary studies.* New York: Cambridge University Press.

Ryle, G. (1949). *The concept of mind*. London: Hutchinson.

Schneider, W., & Graham, D. J. (1992). Introduction to connectionist modeling in education. *Educational Psychologist, 27*, 513–530.

Schrag, J. (1992, March). Educational reform: The future is a continuation of times past. In *Education reform: A step forward or a step backward for students with learning disabilities* (pp. 5–14). Atlanta: Learning Disabilities Association of America.

Scotch, R. K. (1988). Disability as the basis for a social movement: Advocacy and the politics of definition. *Journal of Social Issues, 44*(1), 159–172.

Shapiro, J. P. (1993). *No pity: People with disabilities forging a new civil rights movement*. New York: Times Books.

Shotter, J. (1995). In dialogue: Social constructionism and radical constructivism. In L. Steffe (Ed.), *Constructivism in Education* (pp. 64–83). Hillsdale, NJ: Erlbaum.

Skinner, B. F. (1945). The operational analysis of psychological terms. *Psychological Review, 52*, 270–277, 291–294.

Skinner, B. F. (1953). *Science and human behavior*. New York: Macmillan.

Skinner, B. F. (1957). *Verbal behavior*. Englewood Cliffs, NJ: Prentice Hall.

Skinner, B. F. (1969). *Contingencies of reinforcement: A theoretical analysis*. Englewood Cliffs, NJ: Prentice Hall.

Skinner, B. F. (1971). *Beyond freedom and destiny*. New York: Knopf.

Skinner, B. F. (1974). *About behaviorism*. New York: Knopf.

Skinner, B. F. (1989). *Recent issues in the analysis of behavior*. Columbus, OH: Merrill.

Spekman, N., Goldberg, R. J., & Herman, K. L. (1992). Learning disabled children grow up: A search for factors related to success in the young adult years. *Learning Disabilities Research and Practice, 7*, 161–170.

Spinoza, B. de (1979). *Etica [Ethics]*. Madrid: Editora Nacional. (Original work published 1675)

Sternberg, R. J. (1985). *Beyond IQ: A triarchic framework for intelligence*. New York: Cambridge University Press.

Stone, A., & Wertsch, J. V. (1984). A social interaction analysis of learning disabilities remediation. *Journal of Learning Disabilities, 17*, 194–199.

Tolman, E. C. (1959). Principles of purposive behavior. In S. Koch (Ed.), *Psychology: A study of science* (Vol. 2, pp. 92–157). New York: McGraw-Hill.

Tong, R. (1989). *Feminist thought: A comprehensive introduction*. Boulder: CO: Westview Press.

von Glasersfeld, E. (1995). A constructivist approach to teaching. In L. Steffe (Ed.), *Constructivism in education* (pp. 3–16). Hillsdale, NJ: Erlbaum.

Vye, N. J., Burns, S., Deldos, V. R., & Bransford, J. D. (1987). A comprehensive approach to assessing intellectually handicapped children. In C. S. Lidz (Ed.), *Dynamic assessment: An interactional approach to evaluating learning potential*. New York: Guilford Press.

Vygotsky, L. S. (1962). *Thought and language* (E. Hanfmann & G. Vakar, Trans.). Cambridge, MA: MIT Press. (Original work published 1934)

Vygotsky, L. S. (1978). Interaction between learning and development. In

Mind in society: The development of higher psychological processes (M. Cole, V. Jon-Steiner, S. Scribner, & E. Souberman, Eds. & Trans.; pp. 79–91). Cambridge, MA: Harvard University Press. (Original work published 1935)

Vygotsky, L. S. (1981). The instrumental method in psychology. In J. V. Wertsch (Ed.), *The concept of activity in Soviet psychology*, (pp. 134–143). Armonk, NY: M. E. Sharpe.

Watkins, M. J. (1990). Mediationism and the obfuscation of memory. *American Psychologist, 45*, 328–335.

Watson, J. (1924). *Psychology from the standpoint of a behaviorist* (2nd ed.). Philadelphia: Lippincott.

Wertsch, J. V. (Ed.). (1985a). *Culture, communication and cognition: Vygotskian perspectives*. New York: Cambridge University Press.

Wertsch, J. V. (1985b). *Vygotsky and the social formation of mind*. Cambridge, MA: Harvard University Press.

Wertsch, J. V. (1991). *Voices of the mind: A sociocultural approach to mediated action*. Cambridge, MA: Harvard University Press.

Wertsch, J. V., & Toma, C. (1995). Discourse and learning in the classroom: A sociocultural approach. In L. Steffe (Ed.), *Constructivism in education* (pp. 159–174). Hillsdale, NJ: Erlbaum.

Wilensky, R. (1983). Story grammars versus story points. *Behavioral and Brain Sciences, 6*, 579–623.

Wise, S., & Desimone, R. (1988). Behavioral neurophysiology: Insights into seeing and grasping. *Science, 242*, 736–741.

Zola, I. K. (1993). Disability statistics, what we count and what it tells us: A personal and political analysis. *Journal of Disability and Policy Studies, 4*(2), 9–40.

3

Clinical Model versus Discrepancy Model in Determining Eligibility for Learning Disabilities Services at a Rehabilitation Setting

CHERI HOY
NOEL GREGG
JOSEPH WISENBAKER
SUSAN SIGALAS BONHAM
MICHAEL KING
CAROLYN MORELAND

Rehabilitation counselors currently face serving an increasing number of individuals identified as demonstrating a specific learning disability. The National Institute on Disability and Rehabilitation Research (NIDRR, 1992) reports that in state rehabilitation programs, the percentage of clients demonstrating specific learning disabilities rose from 1.3% in 1983 to an estimated 5% in 1990. In addition, the percentage of persons with specific learning disabilities as a secondary disability rose from 0.2% to 5%, making individuals with specific learning disabilities the fastest-growing disability population served by state and federal vocational rehabilitation programs (NIDRR, 1992). Currently, there are no national standards for diagnostic and eligibility criteria for the adult population requesting services from vocational rehabilitation. The identification of learning disabilities by the public school is not a binding determination of services at postsecondary institutions (Rothstein, 1986). However, institutions such as rehabilitation agencies must have a policy by which the definition of learning disabilities is clearly stated and the eligibility criteria operationalized. As Gregg (1994) states, without articulated objective criteria, institutions of rehabilitation will be faced with serving a large number of individuals with questionable documentation of learning disabilities. The result will be fewer available services and poorer-quality services for those individuals who really do demonstrate specific learning disabilities. Learning disabilities by definition encompass a heterogeneous group of individuals. Heterogeneity, however, should not preclude clear operational criteria for defining service eligibility.

There are three broad methods for determining eligibility for learning disabilities services: underachievement cutoff scores, discrepancy formulas, and what has been labeled "the clinical model" (Gregg, 1994). An extreme example of an underachievement eligibility model is one proposed by Seigel (1990). She suggests the abandonment of the IQ test in the identification of learning disabilities with total reliance only on achievement measures. In the area of reading, she proposes using only a word identification measure (i.e., Wide Range Achievement Test—Revised [WRAT-R]; Jastak & Wilkinson, 1984) and declaring anyone scoring below the twenty-fifth percentile as having a learning disability with respect to reading. The four assumptions that underlie Seigel's arguments against the use of IQ tests in the identification of learning disabilities have been debated in the literature. Her first assumption, that IQ tests do not measure intelligence, has been argued to represent too narrow a view of the use of intelligence tests (Graham & Harris, 1989), as well as indicative of a confusion between intelligence and predicted achievement (Meyen, 1989). Seigel's second assumption, that a reading disability can affect IQ test performance and thus mask a discrepancy, demonstrates a perceived lack of need to differentiate the reading disabled from other poor readers. Arguing against Seigel's third assumption, that IQ scores do not predict achievement, Stanovich, Nathan, and Vala Rossi (1986) provide research indicating correlations between reading achievement and IQ between .3 and .5 in younger children and increasing to .6 and .7 by adulthood. As Graham and Harris (1989) point out, no one has tried to argue that IQ is a perfect predictor of reading. Seigel's fourth assumption is that her reading-disabled subjects did not differ on cognitive tasks across IQ, therefore eliminating the need for the administration of cognitive tasks. Graham and Harris (1989) identified significant methodological errors with the Seigel (1988a) studies, undermining any conclusions drawn from these data. Seigel's (1990) proposal to identify learning disabilities solely through the use of an achievement test has not been evaluated by empirical research. Seigel's proposal, however, raises some important issues regarding the identification of individuals who have specific learning disabilities, particularly pertaining to the efficacy and effectiveness of using an IQ measure.

Individuals with learning disabilities typically present an uneven performance profile: demonstrating difficulty with some tasks and success with others relative to their overall cognitive ability. Discrepancy between broad cognitive ability and achievement has become the hallmark in the identification of individuals as having specific learning disabilities. Unfortunately, underachievement has come to be seen as equivalent to having a learning disability. Kavale (1987) warns professionals that "discrepancy alone cannot diagnose learning disabilities; it can only indicate that a primary symptom is present. Discrepancy may be a necessary condition for LD but it is hardly sufficient" (p. 19). The theoretical (Scruggs, 1987), statistical (Wilson, 1987), developmental (Parrill, 1987), and educational (Hessler, 1987; Mellard, 1987) problems with using only an ability–achievement discrepancy model have been thoroughly reviewed in the literature. However, the ease of using simple discrepancy models has contributed to their popularity among professionals involved with the diagnosis of individuals as having specific learning disabilities.

The methods most often employed to identify a severe performance discrepancy can be grouped into four categories (Chalfant, 1989; Cone & Wilson, 1981; Frankenberger & Harper, 1987; Gregg, 1994; McNutt, 1986). The four categories of methods, all of them controversial, used to determine a significant discrepancy include (1) ability–achievement, (2) regression, (3) intracognitive, and (4) intraachievement. Concerned that these models do not reliably identify adults with learning disabilities, some researchers are suggesting a clinical model as an alternative (Brackett & McPherson, in Chapter 4, this volume; Gregg, 1994). The clinical model is suggested as a more ecologically sound model for identifying adults with learning disabilities because it provides a context for using information beyond norm-referenced standard scores in decision making. Professionals in the field of rehabilitation, while considering eligibility criteria, will need a clear understanding of the possible models currently being debated across disciplines. The ability–achievement discrepancy model identifies the amount of disparity between a student's assessed level of intellectual functioning and assessed academic achievement (Woodcock, 1984). A regression equation discrepancy model is an ability–achievement model with a mathematical correction to take explicit account of measurement error (Reynolds, 1984–1985). Scores that are considerably high or considerably low are unreliable because they tend to regress toward the mean when performance is assessed a second time (Cone & Wilson, 1981). An intra-achievement discrepancy model evaluates divergent achievement performance within and between academic achievement areas (Seigel, 1988b; Woodcock, 1984). For example, a student may perform within the average range in reading but have math performance one and one-half or more standard deviations below the mean. An intracognitive model examines discrepancies in performance tests and subtests designed to assess cognitive abilities needed in acquiring, storing, integrating, retrieving, and expressing information (Woodcock, 1984).

The clinical model has recently been receiving more attention, as professionals are calling for the use of more functionally and ecologically sound assessment tools in addition to norm-referenced tests (Best, Howard, Kanter, Mellard, & Pearson, 1986; Gregg & Hoy, 1990; Vogel, 1989). The clinical model integrates (1) quantitative data, (2) qualitative data, (3) self-reported background information, and (4) the clinical judgment of a multidisciplinary team to determine learning disabilities eligibility for special services. According to such a model, learning disabilities should not be diagnosed by test scores alone or solely by the presence of a severe performance discrepancy based on two norm-referenced measures (e.g., regression model). In the clinical model, the impact of gender, severity of disability, ethnicity, age, motivation, experience, correlation between intelligence measures and achievement, and the reliability and validity of psychometric instruments can be incorporated into the decision-making process. As Gregg (1994) noted, with the growing number of individuals demonstrating specific learning disabilities who seek special services from state and federal rehabilitation agencies, there is an urgent need to develop an appropriate diagnostic model that (1) determines whether an individual is eligible for learning disabilities services and (2) provides information to counselors and learning disabilities specialists charged with program planning.

Brackett and McPherson (in Chapter 4, this volume) report a research project in which they applied the five eligibility models just described to the assessment profile of 169 college students identified as demonstrating a specific learning disability by a clinical model.

They found very low correlations between all models with respect to those individuals identified as demonstrating a specific learning disability. In addition, they found that the regression and the ability–achievement models identified as learning disabled more individuals with intelligence scores higher than 100 and fewer with intelligence scores lower than 100. The overidentification of individuals with higher intelligence scores has also been documented when such models are applied to younger children (Branden, 1989; Cone & Wilson, 1981). Such a finding has significant implications for language-impaired, multicultural, and dually diagnosed individuals being considered for learning disabilities services. Therefore, individuals with moderate to severe learning disabilities might be at risk for being misidentified.

Research investigating the discrepancy models alone (e.g., ability–achievement, regression, intracognitive, and intra-achievement) supports the regression equation model as most accurate in determining discrepancy (Branden, 1989; Cone & Wilson, 1981). However, the regression equation model, which is totally dependent on norm-referenced measures, cannot control for problems such as the gradual increase in the heterogeneity of obtained achievement scores as individuals progress in age, the high correlation between cognitive and achievement measures, the high amount of measurement error of psychometric tools, the lack of norm groups appropriate for adults, and the dynamic information obtained from behavioral observations and informal functional assessment tools. The purpose of this study was to compare the decisions made using the regression equation model to those from the clinical model.

METHOD

Subjects

Subjects (n = 80) selected for this study were all clients at Roosevelt Warm Springs Institute for Rehabilitation, Warm Springs, Georgia, currently being served under a diagnosis of learning disabilities. Their diagnoses were derived from public and private evaluations. Many of the clients were identified by public schools and served by special education during their secondary schooling. For the purposes of this study, each subject underwent a 2-day psychological assessment to determine whether they met the criteria under the clinical model as described next. Information gathered and reported for each client in the study is consistent with the marker variable system that Keogh (1983) suggests researchers in the area of learning disabilities use to describe study populations.

Study-Specific Assessments and Classification Procedures

Each subject was diagnosed using clinical criteria and three different regression-based criteria. Subjects who fit all the following criteria were classified as having learning disabilities according to the clinical model: (1) evidence of academic underachievement as defined by results from one or more areas of achievement (measured by tests such as the Woodcock–Johnson Psychoeducational Tests of Achievement— Revised, Standard Battery; Woodcock & Johnson, 1989) being at least one and one-third standard deviations below the individual's Wechsler Adult Intelligence Scale—Revised (WAIS-R; Wechsler, 1981) Full Scale standard score; (2) evidence of cognitive processing deficits as defined by results from one or more areas of cognitive processing (measured by standardized cognitive instruments designed to assess cognitive processing areas of perception, reasoning, symbolic representation, and memory such as the Woodcock–Johnson Tests of Cognitive Ability—Revised) being at least one and one-third standard deviations below one of the individual's WAIS-R scale scores (Verbal IQ [VIQ], Performance IQ [PIQ], Full Scale IQ [FSIQ]); (3) no evidence of sensory impairment or mild intellectual deficits as defined by detailed background information (i.e., visual and audiological reports, school transcripts, birth and educational histories, and prior psychological and educational evaluations; and (4) no evidence of primary psychiatric disorder as evaluated by the psychiatric interview used for the *Diagnostic and Statistical Manual of Mental Disorder*, third edition, revised (American Psychiatric Association, 1987), diagnosis that was administered individually. There were 54 adults classified as having learning disabilities according to the clinical model, 41 males and 13 females.

Next, Severe Discrepancy Analysis II (Reynolds, Stowe, & Stanton, 1987), an IBM personal computer program based on a regression model, was used to determine whether the 80 clients would be considered to have mild learning disabilities, severe learning disabilities, or no learning disabilities according to their criteria. Variables used in the regression equation decision included the WAIS-R Full Scale score and, individually, the reading, math, and spelling scores from the WRAT-R. Means and standard deviations on these variables for the groups identified by clinical and regression models appear in Table 3.1. The degree of agreement between the resulting classification based on the regression and clinical models was determined by cross-tabulating the four resulting diagnoses. Finally, whether the classification based on the clinical model differed significantly from those provided by the regression models was examined.

TABLE 3.1. Means and Standard Deviations for Critical Variables

| | WAIS-R | | | | | | | | WRAT-R | | | | | |
| | Age | | Full Scale | | Verbal | | Performance | | Reading | | Math | | Spelling | |
	X̄	SD	X̄	SD	X̄	SD	X̄	SD	X̄	SD	X̄	SD	X̄	SD
Clinic model														
LD	22.57	3.52	84.61	7.20	85.48	9.32	85.96	10.57	73.46	14.61	74.39	12.46	71.72	14.95
Not LD	23.15	4.66	76.81	8.03	78.27	8.34	77.46	12.13	60.04	13.28	68.69	11.23	71.50	13.99
Regression—reading														
LD	22.38	2.63	83.38	7.21	82.68	8.24	86.70	10.63	61.05	8.45	72.86	14.13	62.24	10.89
Not LD	23.09	4.74	80.95	9.04	85.53	10.68	80.19	11.90	81.47	11.14	72.26	10.58	79.74	12.32
Regression—math														
LD	22.30	2.83	85.45	8.13	86.91	10.46	85.82	11.90	69.73	16.22	66.67	12.20	69.88	16.49
Not LD	23.09	4.51	79.70	7.62	80.49	8.01	81.36	11.37	73.64	12.64	76.66	10.63	72.89	13.07
Regression—spelling														
LD	22.35	2.29	85.91	8.75	83.27	8.11	90.00	13.80	70.44	13.37	71.40	13.12	69.14	8.57
Not LD	22.68	3.95	80.30	8.94	83.19	10.42	79.78	11.74	77.46	14.21	75.59	10.10	79.86	14.03

RESULTS

Each of the three regression-based diagnoses was cross-tabulated with the diagnoses provided under the clinical model. Figures 3.1, 3.2, and 3.3 show the results of those cross-tabulations. A chi-square test for proportions using related samples (Glass & Hopkins, 1984) was then used to determine whether the clinical method differed significantly

Regression—Reading

	LD	Not LD	Totals
LD	27	27	54
Clinic Not LD	10	16	26
Totals	37	43	

FIGURE 3.1. Cross-tabulation of clinic diagnosis with regression using *reading* scores.

Regression—Math

	LD	Not LD	Totals
LD	24	30	54
Clinic Not LD	9	17	26
Totals	33	47	

FIGURE 3.2. Cross-tabulation of clinic diagnosis with regression using *math* scores.

Regression—Spelling

	LD	Not LD	Totals
LD	16	21	37
Clinic Not LD	5	16	21
Totals	21	37	

FIGURE 3.3. Cross-tabulation of clinic diagnosis with regression using *spelling* scores.

from each regression model in the proportion identified with learning disabilities. Using a critical value of 3.84 with one degree of freedom, significant differences were found between the clinic method and the regression using reading data ($\chi^2 = 7.81$), using math data ($\chi^2 = 11.31$), and using spelling data ($\chi^2 = 3.90$). In each instance, the regression-based diagnoses identified a smaller proportion of subjects as learning disabled than did the diagnoses afforded by the clinical model.

DISCUSSION

Professionals responsible for providing services to adults with learning disabilities, whether at a university or in a rehabilitation setting, need to be cognizant that the kind of model used in determining eligibility affects the numbers and types of individuals identified (Best et al., 1986; Chalfant, 1984; Reynolds, 1984–1985; Torgesen, 1987). The weak degree of diagnostic agreement between currently used discrepancy models, coupled with their inability to differentiate individuals demonstrating learning disabilities from individuals with other cognitive and emotional disorders based on standardized tests, supports the need to use a clinical model in the identification of learning disabilities, particularly at the adolescent and adult levels (Brackett & McPherson, Chapter 4, this volume; Sengupts, 1991). A simple ability–achievement discrepancy model fails to integrate the multiple factors (i.e., cognitive, oral language, achievement, social, and emotional) involved in a reliable diagnostic decision.

The three methods most commonly used by professionals in determining eligibility for learning disabilities services include (1) looking simply at cutoff scores (Seigel, 1990), (2) applying a discrepancy equation (regression), or (3) using a differential diagnostic (clinical) model (Gregg, 1994). The purpose of this study was to examine the impact of a clinical model and a discrepancy formula model on the identification of 80 consumers with documented past histories of learning disabilities served by vocational rehabilitation. It was clear from the results that neither the clinical nor the regression model identified the numbers of adults as demonstrating a learning disability, as did simply taking past documentation. If one applies Seigel's (1990) cutoff score method for determining eligibility, approximately 89% of the population examined would have qualified as reading disabled, 86% as math disabled, and 90% as spelling disabled. It is obvious from these results that rehabilitation services are being provided based on data that are documenting underachievement as the primary means of eligibility. Approximately 30% of the subjects currently provided services for their learning disability by rehabilitation would not be eligible for services under a clinical or regression model. This is a significant number when one considers the dollars spent per client.

Also investigated in this research was the correlation between those subjects identified as demonstrating a learning disability with the clinical model applied to their psychological data and those with the regression model. The results indicated significant differences between the clinical method and the regression model using reading, spelling, and math data in the specific individuals identified as demonstrating a learning disability. Therefore, the results of this research support the hypothesis that the type of eligibility model used determines the number and type of individuals served for learning disabilities. Using a cutoff score method or a regression equation model stresses the underachievement component of learning disability and ignores the other criteria that determine learning disabilities. Such an overuse of underachievement as the only critical factor in diagnosing learning disabilities has significant implications for intervention and program planning.

Looking only at underachievement in program planning suggests that strategies that are effective for underachievers classified as schizophrenic or mentally retarded should work for persons with learning disabilities. Swanson (1991) has clearly documented with empirical research, however, that strategies and methods that are effective with individuals who do not demonstrate a learning disability are not always effective with the population with learning disabilities. He stresses that (1) strategies serve different purposes, (2) processing competencies must be considered when investigating strategy development, (3) strategies must be considered in relation to an individual's knowledge base, and (4) expert strategy use is not always the result of strategy intervention. Therefore, one might question the usefulness of eligibility models that can do nothing more than identify underachievement.

The discrepancy model (regression formula) utilized in this study also emphasizes underachievement as measured solely by two standardized assessment instruments. Although norm-referenced tests are powerful tools, indispensable for psychological assessment, their results should be interpreted cautiously, particularly when isolated from other documentation (e.g., background information, social–emotional, or oral language). The limitations of using norm-referenced measures such as the gradual increase in range of heterogeneity of obtained achievement scores as individuals progress in age, the high correlation between cognitive and achievement measures, the regression to the mean, the amount of high measurement error of many tests, and norm groups appropriate for the adult population must all be kept in mind when making decisions based on psychometric measuring. Socioeconomic level must also be considered when specific instruments are chosen to be incorporated into discrepancy formulas.

The clinical model provides for the integration of norm-referenced tools as well as dynamic assessment methods. Vygotsky (1934/1962) was one of the first to introduce the concept that assessment should stress the process rather than the product (i.e., scores); therefore, evaluation should be dynamic in nature. Dynamic assessment, as it is currently called, advocates the principles first discussed by Vygotsky (1934/1962). According to Meyers (1987), dynamic assessments should (1) provide a link between assessment and intervention and (2) involve a means of generating or testing hypothesis. Clinical models of eligibility are the only models that allow for the dynamic nature of learning to be factored into the decision-making process. Such a model of assessment is more ecologically sound and provides the functional information requested by consumers and service providers.

The growing number of individuals demonstrating learning disabilities who seek special services from rehabilitation and federal agencies presents an urgent need to develop reliable and valid means to determine service eligibility. The purpose of evaluations should also be to provide consumers and counselors with ecologically valid and functional information pertaining to learning strengths and weaknesses and to how they impact on job success. Future eligibility models must be robust enough to identify those individuals with diagnosis of a primary learning disability, as well as the ever-increasing number of adults who are dually diagnosed (having hearing impairments and learning disabilities, visual impairments and learning disabilities, etc.), for whom rehabilitation means providing services (NIDRR, 1992). Empirical research is needed to help formulate clearly stated and understood criteria for the diagnosis of individuals with learning disabilities that will assist in the development of appropriate accommodations and interventions.

REFERENCES

American Psychiatric Association. (1987). *Diagnostic and statistical manual of mental disorders* (3rd ed., rev.). Washington, DC: Author.

Best, L., Howard, R., Kanter, M., Mellard, D., & Pearson, M. (1986, April). *Program standards and eligibility criteria for learning disabled adults in California community colleges.* Paper presented at the 64th Annual Convention of the Counsel for Exceptional Children, New Orleans.

Branden, J. P. (1989). A comparison of regression and standard score discrepancy methods for learning disabilities identification: Effects on racial representation. *Journal of School Psychology, 25*, 23–29.

Chalfant, J. C. (1984). *Identifying learning disabled students: Guidelines for decision making*. (Report No. ED 258390). East Lansing, MI: National Center for Research on Teacher Learning.

Chalfant, J. C. (1989). Diagnostic criteria for entry and exit from service: A national problem. In L. B. Silver (Ed.), *The assessment of learning disabilities* (pp. 1–25). Boston: Little, Brown.

Cone, J. E., & Wilson, L. R. (1981). Quantifying a severe discrepancy: A critical analysis. *Learning Disability Quarterly, 4*, 359–371.

Frankenberger, W., & Harper, J. (1987). States' criteria and procedures for identifying learning disabled children: A comparison of 1981/82 and 1985/86 guidelines. *Journal of Learning Disabilities, 20*, 118–122.

Glass, G. V., & Hopkins, K. D. (1984). *Statistical methods in education and psychology*. Englewood Cliffs, NJ: Prentice Hall.

Graham, S., & Harris, K. R. (1989). The relevance of IQ in the determination of learning disabilities: Abandoning scores as decision makers. *Journal of Learning Disabilities, 22*(8), 500–503.

Gregg, N. (1994). Eligibility for learning disabilities rehabilitation services: Operationalizing the definition. *Journal of Vocational Rehabilitation, 4*(2), 86–95.

Gregg, N., & Hoy, C. (1990). Identification of the learning disabled at the postsecondary level. *Journal of College Admissions, 129*, 3–34.

Hessler, G. L. (1987). Educational issues surrounding severe discrepancy. *Learning Disabilities Research, 3*, 43–49.

Jastak, S., & Wilkinson, G. S. (1984). *Wide Range Achievement Tests—Revised*. Wilmington, DE: Jastak Associates.

Kavale, K. A. (1987). Theoretical issues surrounding severe discrepancy. *Learning Disabilities Research, 3*, 12–20.

Keogh, B. K. (1983). Classification, compliance, and confusion. *Journal of Learning Disabilities, 16*, 28–29.

McNutt, G. (1986). The status of learning disabilities in the states: Consensus or controversy? *Journal of Learning Disabilities, 19*, 12–16.

Mellard, D. F. (1987). Educational issues surrounding severe discrepancy: A discussion. *Learning Disabilities Research, 3*, 50–56.

Meyen, E. (1989). Let's not confuse test scores with the substance of the discrepancy model. *Journal of Learning Disabilities, 22*(8), 482–483.

Meyers, J. (1987). The training of dynamic assessors. In C. S. Lidz (Ed.), *Dynamic assessment: An interactional approach to evaluating learning potential* (pp. 403–425). New York: Guilford Press.

National Institute on Disability and Rehabilitation Research. (1992). Certain rehabilitation research and training centers, proposed funding priorities for fiscal years 1993–1994. 57 Fed. Reg. 43,111.

Parrill, M. (1987). Developmental issues surrounding severe discrepancy. *Learning Disabilities Research, 3*, 32–41.

Reynolds, C. R. (1984–1985). Critical measurement issues in learning disabilities. *Journal of Special Education, 18*, 451–475.

Reynolds, C. R., Stowe, M. L., & Stanton, H. C. (1987). *Severe discrepancy analysis II-operations manual & software*. Bensalem, PA: Training Resources and In-Service Network.

Rothstein, L. F. (1986). Section 504 of the Rehabilitation Act: Emerging issues for college and universities. *Journal of College and University Law, 13*, 229–266.

Scruggs, T. E. (1987). Theoretical issues surrounding severe discrepancy: A discussion. *Learning Disabilities Research, 3*, 21–23.

Seigel, L. S. (1988a). Definitional and theoretical issues and research on learning disabilities. *Journal of Learning Disabilities, 21*, 264–266.

Seigel, L. S. (1988b). Evidence the IQ scores are irrelevant to the definition of reading disability. *Canadian Journal of Psychology, 42*, 201–215.

Seigel, L. S. (1990). IQ is irrelevant in the definition of learning disabilities. *Journal of Learning Disabilities, 22*, 469–478.

Senguta, S. (1991). *Cognitive affective and academic achievement profiles of adolescents with depression and anxiety: A comparison between subjects with learning disabilities and behavior disorders*. Unpublished master's thesis, University of Georgia, Athens, GA.

Stanovich, K. E., Nathan, R. G., & Vala-Rossi, M. (1986). Developmental changes in the cognitive correlates of reading ability and the developmental lag hypothesis. *Reading Research Quarterly, 21*(3), 267–283.

Swanson, H. L. (1991). Operational definitions and learning disabilities: An overview. *Learning Disabilities Quarterly, 14*(4), 242–254.

Torgesen, J. K. (1987). Thinking about the future by distinguishing between issues that have resolutions and those that do not. In S. Vaughn & C. Bos (Eds.), *Research in learning disabilities: Issues and future directions* (pp. 55–68). Boston: Little, Brown.

Vogel, S. A. (1989). Models for diagnosis of adults with learning disabilities. In L. B. Silver (Ed.), *The assessment of learning disabilities* (pp. 111–134). Boston: Little, Brown.

Vygotsky, L. S. (1962). *Thoughts and language* (E. Hanfmann & G. Vakar, Trans.). Cambridge, MA: MIT Press. (Original work published 1934).

Wechsler, D. (1981). *Wechsler Adult Intelligence Scale—Revised*. New York: Psychological Corporation.

Wilson, V. L. (1987). Statistical and psychometric issues surrounding service discrepancy. *Learning Disabilities Research, 3*, 21–23.

Woodcock, R. W. (1984). A response to some questions raised about the Woodcock–Johnson. *School Psychology Review, 13*, 355–362.

Woodcock, R. W., & Johnson, M. B. (1989). *Woodcock–Johnson Psychoeducational Battery—Revised*. Allen, TX: DLM Teaching Resources.

4

Learning Disabilities Diagnosis in Postsecondary Students: A Comparison of Discrepancy-Based Diagnostic Models

JIM BRACKETT
ANNE McPHERSON

Section 504 of the Rehabilitation Act (1973, Public Law 93-112) ensures the right of all qualified individuals with disabilities to equal postsecondary educational opportunities and requires educational institutions (e.g., community colleges, 4-year colleges and universities, vocational schools, trade schools, and military schools) to accept students with disabilities. Because nearly all colleges and universities receive some form of federal aid to education, and must therefore comply with legislative mandates, the implementation of Section 504 has resulted in a growing number of adolescents and adults with learning disabilities who are entering postsecondary educational institutions (Vogel, 1987). However, the wording of Section 504 is ambiguous and leads to conflicting interpretations of legislative intent.

EDUCATIONAL NEEDS
ACROSS SEVERITY LEVELS

Equal postsecondary educational opportunities are protected only for those individuals with disabilities who are "otherwise qualified" (*Education of Handicapped Children*, 1977, pp. 22,683–22,684). The postsecondary student is responsible for informing the institution of a handicapping condition, for requesting services, and for providing documentation of the handicapping condition (at personal expense). The postsecondary institution is responsible for (1) deciphering all documentation submitted, (2) providing support services and supplementary educational aids, and (3) setting eligibility criteria that are nondiscriminatory and ensure the student's rights of equal access to educational opportunities.

Jane Jarrow, executive director of the Association on Handicapped Student Service Programs in Postsecondary Education, states that the population of individuals with learning disabilities is the "single largest contingent of students with disabilities being served on American campuses" (Jarrow, 1987, p. 46). Colleges and universities seeking to comply with the mandates of Section 504 are overwhelmed by requests for support services and find themselves unable to provide special programs and services to every student claiming to be learning disabled (Vogel, 1989). Deciding that an individual has one or more specific learning disabilities and is therefore eligible for special programs is difficult and has been problematic for years (Hammill, 1990; Kavale, 1987; Keogh, 1983; McKinney, 1987; McNutt, 1986; Reynolds, 1984–1985; Shepard & Smith, 1983; Silver, 1989; Torgesen, 1987; Vogel, 1989). Because there are no national standards for diagnostic and eligibility criteria, there is no consensus among assessment professionals concerning identification of learning disabilities (Adelman, 1992; Reynolds, 1984–1985). Indeed, there is little agreement among psychologists and educators about the interpretation of the definition of learning disabilities and eligibility criteria, as well as about which psychometric methods should be used (Keogh, 1983; McNutt, 1986; Shepard, 1983; Vogel, 1989; Ysseldyke, Algozzine, Shinn, & McGue, 1982). The increasing demands for special services are being met with minimal resources. These limited resources have made the determination of special services eligibility a critical challenge to higher education personnel and to specialists in the field of learning disabilities. Inconsistent identification procedures (Keogh, 1986), incomplete or nonexistent documentation, and misdiagnoses result in students with unidentified learning disabilities being denied the special services they need (and are entitled to), while students incorrectly identified as having learning disabilities are receiving support services inappropriate for their needs (Chalfant, 1984; McGrady, 1987; Shepard & Smith, 1983).

IDENTIFICATION:
A REVIEW OF CURRENT METHODS

Typically, students with learning disabilities present an uneven performance profile. These students demonstrate pronounced difficulties with some tasks (e.g., tasks that place demands on an affected ability) while demonstrating average to above-average success with others (e.g., tasks accessed by intact abilities). Uneven, or "discrepant," performance between cognitive and achievement tasks is evidenced by achievement skills (one or more) being significantly weaker than overall intellectual functioning (hence, a severe discrepancy between achievement and intellectual ability) (Chalfant, 1989; Keogh, 1986; Torgesen, 1987; Valus, 1986). Academic underachievement is evidence that a severe discrepancy exists between achievement and intellectual ability (Chalfant, 1989; Keogh, 1986; Torgesen, 1987; Valus, 1986).

Although such evidence is by no means conclusive, researchers confirm that most state learning disabled eligibility guidelines rely on underachievement as the primary criterion for learning disabled identification in the public schools (Chalfant, 1989; Cone & Wilson, 1981; Frankenberger & Harper, 1987; Frankenberger & Fronzaglio, 1991; Mercer, Hughes, & Mercer, 1985; McNutt, 1986). At the elementary and secondary levels, the use of a discrepancy-based diagnostic model continues to be the primary method of determining learning disabilities, even though researchers report that such models fail to differentiate students with learning disabilities from students who are underachievers, slow learners, or average achievers (Fletcher, 1992). Reynolds (1984–1985) claims that by employing various discrepancy-based models used by the states, "an astute diagnostician can qualify between 50% and 80% of a random sample of the population as having a learning disability that requires special education services" (p. 454). Methods used to quantify a severe discrepancy, operationally defined as one that occurs in 5% or less of the population (Reynolds, 1984–1985), fall into three categories. These three categories of discrepancy-based diagnostic models detect differences in (1) ability and achievement, (2) areas of cognitive functioning, or (3) performance levels across academic subject areas.

The primary objective of this chapter is to report the validity of diagnosing learning disabilities at the postsecondary level on the basis of results generated by discrepancy-based diagnostic models. The study that forms the basis of this chapter involved investigation of the following three research questions:

1. Would discrepancy-based models consistently identify learning disabilities from non-learning disabilities among a population of postsecondary students seeking learning disabilities support services?
2. Would overall ability level of the individual influence the diagnostic model's determination of learning disabilities eligibility?
3. Are discrepancy-based diagnostic models useful techniques for differentiating underachievement from learning disabilities at the postsecondary level?

Study Procedures

This study applied four current discrepancy-based diagnostic models (Cone & Wilson, 1981; McNutt, 1986) to assessment profiles of 169 college students who sought eligibility for learning disabilities support services at a large southeastern university. Diagnoses obtained by each discrepancy model were compared to the diagnosis derived from a 2-day psychoeducational assessment conducted by the University of Georgia's Learning Disabilities Adult Clinic (now known as the Learning Disabilities Center). The clinic's model of determining the presence of a learning disability included a diagnostic staff of learning disabilities specialists, clinical psychologists, and graduate student clinicians. Clinical judgment was used to interpret test results, as well as data obtained from informal assessment measures, to analyze error responses, to determine cognitive deficit patterns among test score scatter, and to evaluate writing samples. Quantitative data included results from standardized tests and informal measures. Qualitative data included information gathered from case histories, interviews, and previous records that confirmed the chronicity of learning problems. Clinical judgment and quantitative and qualitative data were incorporated into a careful study of the individual. No diagnoses were made on the basis of a single test score or discrepancy measure; rather, diagnoses were based on performance patterns of cognitive processing deficits indicative of specific learning disabilities. Criteria used in determining the presence of learning disabilities included (1) evidence of academic disability, (2) evidence of a cognitive processing deficit, and (3) evidence that any secondary or co-occurring deficit (i.e., attention deficit, social–emotional disorder, acuity deficit, insufficient or inappropriate instructional background, or cultural and environmental differences) was not the primary cause of the discrepancy.

Subjects

Subjects for this study were selected from a pool of all students between the ages of 18 and 28, who participated in the clinic's evaluation process during 4 consecutive calendar years ($n = 173$). Two students were deleted from the subject pool because of documented head injury histories; two students were deleted for lack of assessment data consistent with that utilized by the study. The 169 subjects selected for this study (65 female; 104 male) were grouped according to diagnoses determined by the University of Georgia's Learning Disabilities Adult Clinic model. Ninety-nine of these students were diagnosed as having learning disabilities; 70 students were diagnosed as not having learning disabilities. For the purposes of this study, each student was further assigned a hypothetical diagnosis (either having or not having learning disabilities) according to the discrepancy criterion set by each of the four discrepancy-based models.

Data

Categorical and qualitative data were collected from student records, providing a descriptive profile of the subjects. These data included gender, parent educational history, first college attended, student's participation in prior evaluation of learning problems, and student's status as having received special services for learning problems. Means, standard deviations, and ranges were computed for age and Verbal and Math SAT scores, as well as scaled and standard scores for the Wechsler Adult Intelligence Scale—Revised (WAIS-R), Wide Range Achievement Test—Revised (WRAT-R), and Peabody Picture Vocabulary Test—Revised. Tables 4.1 and 4.2 give these comparisons for the groups diagnosed learning disabled and non-learning disabled by the clinic model.

Instruments

This study gathered assessment data from each subject's assessment file in order to simulate four discrepancy-based diagnostic models and to provide hypothetical diagnoses under each model for each of the 169 students. The WAIS-R (Wechsler, 1981) Full Scale standard score was used as the measure of overall cognitive ability. Standard scores from WRAT-R (Jastak & Wilkinson, 1984) subtests represented three

TABLE 4.1. Background Information

	LD ($n = 99$)	Non-LD ($n = 70$)
Gender		
Female	26 (26%)	39 (56%)
Male	73 (74%)	31 (44%)
Prior evaluation for learning problems		
Yes	83 (84%)	52 (74%)
No	16 (16%)	18 (26%)
Prior service for learning problems		
None	20 (20%)	21 (30%)
Tutoring	26 (26%)	26 (37%)
Special education placement	53 (54%)	23 (33%)
Parental education history		
Mother		
High school graduate	13 (13%)	7 (10%)
Some college	20 (20%)	27 (39%)
College graduate	66 (67%)	36 (51%)
Father		
High school graduate	4 (4%)	4 (6%)
Some college	13 (13%)	9 (13%)
College graduate	82 (83%)	57 (81%)
UGA first college attended		
Yes	51 (52%)	32 (46%)
No	42 (42%)	33 (47%)
Not reported	6 (6%)	5 (7%)

TABLE 4.2. Age, SAT, PPVT-R, WAIS-R, and WRAT-R Summaries

	LD population				Non-LD population			
	n	Mean	*SD*	Range	n	Mean	*SD*	Range
Age	99	20.7	2	18–28	69	20.3	2	18–26
SAT	76				62			
Verbal		433	96	250–670		421	68	220–540
Math		453	103	240–710		443	90	280–690
Total		886				864		
PPVT-R	99	100.9	13.6	63–141	70	100.9	10.9	75–127
WAIS-R	99				70			
Verbal		104.2	12.0	80–146		102.8	10.4	78–127
Performance		104.6	13.3	76–133		101.7	11.0	66–129
Full Scale		105.0	11.6	82–132		102.6	10.4	76–131
WRAT-R	90				70			
Reading		97.8	12.1	69–124		104.3	11.3	68–126
Spelling		90.2	12.4	68–119		100.2	10.4	56–118
Arithmetic		96.6	12.3	70–124		98.0	12.9	75–133

measures of achievement. These particular measures were chosen in order to simulate typically occurring identification procedures and do not represent endorsement on the part of the investigators as proper diagnostic procedure.

The WAIS-R consists of two major scales, Verbal and Performance, that combine to yield a Full Scale standard score ($M = 100$, $SD = 15$). Reliability coefficients, based on a formula for computing the reliability of a composite group of tests, range from .95 to .97 for the Verbal standard score, from .88 to .94 for the Performance standard score, and from .96 to .98 for the Full Scale standard score (Sattler, 1988). Six Verbal scale subtests have such items as defining vocabulary words and answering commonsense questions as well as factual questions. Five Performance scale subtests include such items as constructing puzzles and abstract designs, as well as identifying missing parts of a picture.

The WRAT-R, an instrument frequently reported by current studies as the achievement measure employed to document learning disabled samples, is an individually administered achievement test that contains three subtests (i.e., Reading, Spelling, Arithmetic) and requires approximately 20 to 30 minutes to administer.

The Reading subtest, which requires the individual to pronounce a list of unrelated words visually presented, typically measures an individual's ability to recognize and express familiar vocabulary words and to sound out unfamiliar words phonetically. Reading comprehension is not evaluated by this subtest. The Spelling subtest, a paper-and-pencil task that requires the individual to write single words from oral dictation, typically measures an individual's acquired spelling skills. The Arithmetic subtest is a timed paper-and-pencil task that requires the individual to perform addition, subtraction, multiplication, and division problems and to solve some geometric, trigonometric, logarithmic, and calculus operations. This task typically measures an individual's acquired mathematical calculation skills under timed conditions. Mathematical reasoning is not measured.

Discrepancy-Based Models

The ability–achievement discrepancy model determines the amount of disparity between a student's assessed level of intellectual functioning and assessed academic achievement (Woodcock, 1984). One and one-third standard deviations, or 20 standard score points (for both instruments, $M = 100$, $SD = 15$), between a student's WAIS-R Full Scale score and at least one WRAT-R subtest score constituted the identifying criterion (severe discrepancy between ability and achievement) for the existence of a learning disability.

The intra-achievement discrepancy model evaluates divergent achievement performance within and between academic achievement areas (Woodcock, 1984). In an effort to maintain a consistency among discrepancy criteria, this study used a simple standard score discrepancy of one and one-third standard deviations, or 20 standard score points, among WRAT-R subtest scores to constitute the level of severity needed to represent the intra-achievement discrepancy-based model criterion.

The regression equation discrepancy model also measures ability and achievement discrepancies but includes a mathematical correction to adjust for the regression toward the mean phenomenon (Reynolds, 1984–1985). The identifying criterion for the regression equation discrepancy model employed by this study was derived as follows from the "Model 3" formula suggested by the report of the U.S. Department of Education, Special Education Programs, Work Group on Measurement Issues in the Assessment of Learning Disabilities (Reynolds, 1984–1985):

1. Determine the standard error of estimate between the WAIS-R Full Scale and each WRAT-R subtest:

$$SE_{est} = SD \sqrt{1 - r_{xy}^2}$$

where r_{xy}^2 is the correlation between WAIS-R Full Scale score and the WRAT-R Reading (.73), Spelling (.74), and Arithmetic (.65).

2. Compute the difference between the WAIS-R Full Scale score and each WRAT-R score. If the difference is equal to or greater than the corresponding SE_{est} compute the Predicted Achievement score.

3. Compute the Predicted Achievement score:

Let X = achievement; Y = ability.
$\bar{X} = b_0 + b_1 (Y)$
where
$$b_1 = r_{x,y} \frac{SD_X}{SD_Y}$$

$b_0 = \bar{X} - b_1 Y$
$\bar{X} = 100(1 - r_{xy}) + r_{xy}(y)$

4. Determine a severe discrepancy. To build a 95% confidence

interval around each obtained achievement score, compute 1.65 times the corresponding SE_{est}. A severe discrepancy is determined at the point at which the discrepancy score between the Predicted Achievement score and the Actual Achievement score is more than, or equal to, $1.65SE_{est}$.

The intracognitive discrepancy model evaluates divergent cognitive performance within and between tests and subtests considered measures of distinct cognitive processes (Woodcock, 1984). For this study, intracognitive discrepancies were determined according to a statistical table adapted from Table 9 of the *WAIS-R Manual* (Wechsler, 1981). This table presents critical values for WAIS-R subtest deviations from average performance. A critical value is the magnitude of the smallest difference between a subtest scaled score and the overall averaged scaled score that is significant at the .05 level. The information in the critical values table was used to identify particular subtest scores significantly higher or lower than the individual's own average performance. A student was considered to meet the intracognitive discrepancy criterion when at least one critical value was obtained between subtest scaled scores and the score representing the mean of all 11 subtest scaled scores.

Findings

Table 4.3 shows the number and percentage of diagnostic agreements for both populations between the clinic model and each of the discrepancy-based models. Overall, diagnostic agreement was weak among the discrepancy-based models themselves, as well as between the clinical model and the four discrepancy-based models. The strongest percentage of diagnostic agreement with clinical diagnoses was achieved by the regression equation and ability–achievement models (i.e., 83%/86% when identifying non-learning disabled students). The intra-achievement model demonstrated the weakest percentage of diag-

TABLE 4.3. Agreement between Clinic Model and Four Discrepancy Models

Clinic model	Ability–ach. n (%)	Intracog. n (%)	Intra-ach. n (%)	Regression eq. n (%)
LD population	51 (52%)	66 (67%)	43 (43%)	53 (54%)
Non-LD population	60 (86%)	39 (56%)	48 (69%)	58 (83%)

	Clinic	RE	I-A	IC	A–A
Clinic	1				
Regression equation	.386	1			
Intra-achievement	.136	.258	1		
Intracognitive	.237	.076	.041	1	
Ability–achievement	.382	.9	.302	.183	1

FIGURE 4.1. Diagnosis correlation matrix for five diagnostic models.

nostic agreement (i.e., 43% when identifying students with learning disabilities).

The correlation among the four discrepancy-based models and the clinic model was determined by comparing discrepancy-based models to each other. Figure 4.1 displays the resulting correlation matrix. Results indicate that substantial variability in the learning disabled diagnosis can take place when different models are used. Other than the high correlation between the two models detecting uneven ability–achievement performance (ability–achievement and regression equation), there is a weak degree of agreement among the discrepancy-based models and the clinic model. Because the only difference between the two models measuring discrepant ability–achievement performance lies in the additional computations employed by the regression equation model, their strong correlation ($r = .9$) reflects the impact that accounting for regression effects and test error can have on diagnosis.

IMPLICATIONS FOR CHANGE

Postsecondary Learning Disabled Populations and High School Learning Disabled Populations

In all but the most unusual of circumstances, postsecondary students with learning disabilities have completed some form of secondary education; most in this study even received special learning disabilities services at the secondary level (see Table 4.1). It does not follow, however, that the postsecondary student with learning disabilities identified by the clinic model is in any sense representative of the typical secondary student with learning disabilities. The qualitative differences in profiles of secondary students with learning disabilities and the postsecondary students with learning disabilities (as identified by the clinic model) are the unavoidable result of two systemic factors present in most secondary environments. First, the most accepted criterion of learning disabilities at precollege levels—the determination of a discrepancy between ability and achievement—does not adequately differentiate students with learning disabilities from underachievers who do not have learning disabilities. Second, underachievement at the secondary level is virtually the only reason a student would ever be referred for learning disabilities testing. In short, underachievers typify the secondary learning disabled population, whereas students with performance patterns of cognitive processing deficits indicative of specific learning disabilities typify the postsecondary students with learning disabilities identified by the clinic model.

The results of this study suggest that the disparities that occur when discrepancy regimens are applied to secondary assessment also occur when discrepancy regimens are applied to postsecondary assessment. Overall, the weak associations between the clinic model diagnoses and corresponding diagnoses from the four discrepancy-based models support research findings that standardized test performance of students with learning disabilities often does not differ from that of students described as low achievers (Berk, 1982; Cone & Wilson, 1981; Kavale, 1987; Shepard & Smith, 1983; Vogel, 1989; Ysseldyke et al., 1982). Results of this study indicate that discrepancy-based models are unable to consistently differentiate students with learning disabilities from low achievers based on standardized test results (WAIS-R, WRAT-R).

Weaknesses of the Four Discrepancy Models

Studied in the context of determining learning disabilities of postsecondary students who seek learning disabilities support services, the diagnostic model used profoundly affects numbers and types of students identified. In this regard, the findings of this investigation confirm the findings of Best, Howard, Kanter, Mellard, and Pearson (1986), Chalfant (1984), McGrady (1987), McKinney (1987), Reynolds (1984–1985), and Torgesen (1987). Reynolds (1984–1985) claims that the use of various discrepancy-based models, coupled with the results of a 2-hour psychoeducational evaluation, have yielded great disparities in the types and numbers of children identified as having learning disabilities.

At best, the finding of severe discrepancies between ability and achievement marks *potential* individuals with learning disabilities.

Major weaknesses of the ability–achievement discrepancy model appear to be the tendency to overidentify students with above-average intelligence scores and the tendency to underidentify students with below-average intelligence scores. Because the regression equation discrepancy model takes into account the correlation between ability and achievement, as well as regression effects, it is considered more statistically sound than the simple standard score ability–achievement discrepancy model and the best available method for measuring underachievement (McKinney, 1987; Reynolds, 1984–1985; Sattler, 1988). Nonetheless, this model demonstrates weaknesses similar to those of the ability–achievement discrepancy model—overidentifying the above-average student and underidentifying the below-average student.

A major value of detecting severe discrepancies within and between areas of cognition is the focus on cognitive processing components of learning disabilities. However, the limited capacity of standardized instruments to assess isolated cognitive processes creates a major weakness in intracognitive discrepancy models. Although analyses of WAIS-R subtests typically report measures of distinct cognitive abilities, such abilities may not emerge by individual subtests but rather in combination with other subtests. For example, a combination of WAIS-R Similarities, Arithmetic, and Comprehension subtests can yield information about verbal reasoning; similarly, a combination of WAIS-R Picture Completion, Block Design, and Object Assembly subtests can yield information about nonverbal reasoning (Sattler, 1988). Hence, intracognitive profiles, critical to learning disabilities diagnoses, cannot be determined by computing discrepancies between single test and subtest scores.

Severe discrepancies within and between academic achievement areas can be valuable clues to clinical detectives who unravel diagnostic mysteries. Nonetheless, as the results of this study indicate, the presence of intra-achievement discrepancies is not a reliable indicator of learning disabilities, nor is the absence of such a discrepancy a valid indicator of no learning disabilities. Considerable variations in academic skills can exist among average achieving students; likewise, students with learning disabilities can successfully complete many school tasks but experience difficulty with specific subtasks. The intra-achievement discrepancy model is limited to achievement areas measured by the subtests used in its computations. For example, WRAT-R subtests lack content validity in the areas they are commonly employed to measure: reading (e.g., reading comprehension), writing (e.g., written expression), and arithmetic (e.g., mathematical reasoning).

FUTURE DIRECTIONS

The growing number of postsecondary students with learning disabilities who seek special services presents an urgent need to develop an appropriate diagnostic model that (1) determines whether a student is eligible for learning disabilities services and (2) provides information to college counselors and (learning disabilities) specialists charged with developing and justifying the necessary accommodations for these students (e.g., descriptive information about learning problems and characteristics that could interfere with performance and achievement, as well as information about learning strengths and strategies that can contribute to the student's success in college).

The results of this investigation of diagnostic models indicate that substantial variability in learning disabilities diagnosis exists when different assessment models are used. The lack of a uniform definition of learning disabilities and criteria for operationalizing that definition has resulted in a variety of diagnostic models. Therefore, research is needed to develop a primary theoretical model, with clearly stated and understood criteria, for coherent diagnosis and evaluation of individuals with learning disabilities.

The scarcity of standardized, reliable, and valid diagnostic instruments for the assessment of adults with learning disabilities further confounds the assessment of postsecondary students (Vogel, 1987). Research is needed to develop new tests and techniques designed to provide a greater range of information about the ways individuals learn—the ways individuals receive, store, integrate, and express information.

The discrepancy-based models investigated in this study did not consistently determine the presence of learning disabilities in a group of postsecondary students. When compared to an extensive clinical model, these discrepancy-based models failed to differentiate adequately students with learning disabilities from non-learning disabled underachievers. Further, these discrepancy-based models identified different types of students with learning disabilities and without. These findings show the need for differential diagnosis in order to explore ways that learning disabilities interfere with performance and achievement.

The results of this study support the notion that discrepancy-based models should not provide the sole criteria for diagnosing learning disabilities. Discrepancy-based models focus exclusively on test scores. Although norm-referenced tests are powerful tools, indispensable for clinical and psychoeducational assessment (Sattler, 1988), their results should never be interpreted in isolation (Algozzine & Ysseldyke,

1986; Berk, 1982; Blalock, 1987; Carlisle & Johnson, 1989; Chalfant, 1984; Cone & Wilson, 1981; Cruickshank, 1989; Johnson, 1987; Kavale, 1987; Mather & Healey, 1989; Reynolds, 1984–1985; Sattler, 1988; Silver, 1989; Vogel, 1989). More research is needed to investigate combinations of norm-referenced tests and subtests that may prove to be reliable and valid quantitative indicators of cognitive and achievement patterns indicative of specific learning disabilities.

Although these discrepancy-based models do detect aspects of underachievement, only the clinical assessment model incorporates case history and background information with clinical investigations and interpretations of error patterns that are indicative of processing strengths and weaknesses. Therefore, the clinical assessment model provides information that is essential to the development and facilitation of instructional strategies and curriculum modifications, needed to discriminate between the students with learning disabilities and the underprepared or low-ability students, and adequate to produce the greatest possible understanding of the student's learning strengths and weaknesses and provides safeguards for including culturally and language minority populations.

Appropriate learning disabilities diagnostic evaluations must do the following: (1) analyze an individual's performance on many different assessment tools investigating areas of psychology, academic achievement, language, and cognitive processing (e.g., perception, memory, conceptualization, attention); (2) incorporate the individual's background information (e.g., history of physical, behavioral, and academic developmental milestones); (3) incorporate instructor observations of classroom performance; (4) employ the expertise of several professionals who work together as a multidisciplinary team; and (5) generate an understandable explanation of the individual's strengths and weaknesses, as well as provide the individual with strategies to become a self-learner.

The transition period from adolescence to adulthood should be a developmental milestone for all youth. Although adulthood may be defined in various terms, few people would argue against an adult being self-supporting, capable of functioning in the community without supervision, and behaving in ways that are neither threatening nor unacceptable to others (Clark & Kolstoe, 1990). Obtaining and maintaining a good job is a standard of adult status, inexorably enmeshed in the individual's sense of independence and self-esteem, and postsecondary education programs are becoming a necessary step toward adult status. Effective postsecondary support services cannot be provided to the student identified as having learning disabilities unless the nature of the qualifying disability has been determined. By itself, the documentation of underachievement does not provide this determination. Without postsecondary support services, the developmental milestone of adulthood for individuals with learning disabilities signifies little more than legal passage to majority.

REFERENCES

Adelman, H. S. (1992). LD: The next 25 years. *Journal of Learning Disabilities, 25*, 17–22.

Algozzine, B., & Ysseldyke, J. E. (1986). The future of the LD field: Screening and diagnosis. *Journal of Learning Disabilities, 19*(7), 394–398.

Berk, R. A. (1982). Effectiveness of discrepancy score methods for screening children with learning disabilities. *Learning Disabilities, 1*(2), 12–24.

Best, L., Howard, R., Kanter, M., Mellard, D., & Pearson, M. (1986, April). *Program standards and eligibility criteria for learning disabled adults in California community colleges.* Paper presented at the 64th Annual Convention of the Council for Exceptional Children, New Orleans.

Blalock, J. W. (1987). Intellectual levels and patterns. In D. J. Johnson & J. W. Blalock (Eds.), *Adults with learning disabilities: Clinical studies* (pp. 47–66). Orlando, FL: Grune & Stratton.

Carlisle, J., & Johnson, D. J. (1989). Assessment of school age children. In L. B. Silver (Ed.), *The assessment of learning disabilities* (pp. 73–110). Boston: Little, Brown.

Chalfant, J.C. (1984). *Identifying learning disabled students: Guidelines for decision making.* Burlington, VT: Northeast Regional Resource Center, Trinity College.

Chalfant, J. C. (1989). Diagnostic criteria for entry and exit from service: A national problem. In L. B. Silver (Ed.), *The assessment of learning disabilities* (pp. 1–25). Boston: Little, Brown.

Clark, G. M., & Kolstoe, O. P. (1990). *Career development and transition education for adolescents with disabilities.* Boston: Allyn & Bacon.

Cone, T. E., & Wilson, L. R. (1981). Quantifying a severe discrepancy: A critical analysis. *Learning Disability Quarterly, 4*, 39–371.

Cruickshank, W. M. (1989). Challenges for the future. In L. B. Silver (Ed.), *The assessment of learning disabilities* (pp. 161–166). Boston: Little, Brown.

Education of handicapped children; Implementation of Part B of the Education of the Handicapped Act (1977, August 23). 20 Fed. Reg. Part II. Washington, DC: U.S. Office of Education.

Fletcher, J. M. (1992). The validity of distinguishing children with language and learning disabilities according to discrepancies with IQ: Introduction to the special series. *Journal of Learning Disabilities, 25*, 546–548.

Frankenberger, W., & Fronzaglio, K. (1991). A review of states' criteria for identifying children with learning disabilities. *Journal of Learning Disabilities, 24*, 495–500.

Frankenberger, W., & Harper, J. (1987). States' criteria and procedures for identifying learning disabled children: A comparison of 1981/82 and 1985/86 guidelines. *Journal of Learning Disabilities, 20*, 118–123.

Hammill, D. D. (1990). On defining learning disabilities: An emerging consensus. *Journal of Learning Disabilities, 23*, 74–84.

Jarrow, J. (1987). Integration of individuals with disabilities in higher education: A review of the literature. *Journal of Postsecondary Education and Disability, 5*(2), 38–57.

Jastak, S., & Wilkinson, G. S. (1984). *Wide Range Achievement Test—Revised*. Wilmington, DE: Jastak Associates.

Johnson, D. J. (1987). Nonverbal disorders and related learning disabilities. In D. J. Johnson & J. W. Blalock (Eds.), *Adults with learning disabilities: Clinical studies* (pp. 219–232). Orlando, FL: Grune & Stratton.

Kavale, K. A. (1987). Theoretical issues surrounding severe discrepancy. *Learning Disabilities Research, 3*, 12–20.

Keogh, B. K. (1983). Classification, compliance, and confusion. *Journal of Learning Disabilities, 16*, 28–29.

Keogh, B. K. (1986). Sampling issues in learning disabilities research: Markers for the study of problems in mathematics. In G. Pavlidis & D. Fisher (Eds.), *Dyslexia: Its neuropsychology and treatment* (pp. 9–22). New York: Wiley.

Mather, N., & Healey, W. (1989). Deposing aptitude achievement discrepancy as the imperial criterion for learning disabilities. *Learning Disabilities: A Multidisciplinary Journal, 1*(2), 40–48.

McGrady, H. J. (1987). Eligibility: Back to basics. In S. Vaughn & C. Bos (Eds.), *Research in learning disabilities: Issues and future directions* (pp. 105–120). Boston: Little, Brown.

McKinney, J. D. (1987). Research on the identification of learning disabled children: Perspectives on changes in educational policy. In S. Vaughn & C. Bos (Eds.), *Research in learning disabilities: Issues and future directions* (pp. 215–238). Boston: Little, Brown.

McNutt, G. (1986). The status of learning disabilities in the states: Consensus or controversy? *Journal of Learning Disabilities, 19*, 12–16.

Mercer, C. D., Hughes, C., & Mercer, A. R. (1985). Learning disabilities definitions used by state education departments. *Learning Disability Quarterly, 8*, 45–55.

Rehabilitation Act of 1973, Public Law 93-112, 87 Stat. 355 (1973).

Reynolds, C. R. (1984–1985). Critical measurement issues in learning disabilities. *Journal of Special Education, 18*, 451–475.

Sattler, J. (1988). *Assessment of children* (3rd ed.). San Diego: Author.

Shepard, L. (1983). The role of measurement in educational policy: Lessons from the identification of learning disabilities. *Educational Measurement: Issues and Practice, 2*(3), 4–8.

Shepard, L., & Smith, M. (1983). An evaluation of the identification of learning disabled students in Colorado. *Learning Disability Quarterly, 6*, 115–127.

Silver, L. B. (1989). *The assessment of learning disabilities*. Boston: Little, Brown.

Torgesen, J. K. (1987). Thinking about the future by distinguishing between issues that have resolutions and those that do not. In S. Vaughn & C. Bos (Eds.), *Research in learning disabilities: Issues and future directions* (pp. 55–68). Boston: Little, Brown.

U.S. Department of Education. (1984). *Sixth annual report to Congress on the implementation of Public Law 94–142; Education for All Handicapped Children Act.* Washington, DC: Office of Special Education.

Valus, A. (1986). Achievement potential discrepancy status of students in LD programs. *Learning Disability Quarterly, 9*(3), 200–205.

Vogel, S. A. (1987). Gender differences in cognitive abilities of learning-disabled females and males. *Annals of Dyslexia: An Interdisciplinary Journal of the Orton Dyslexia Society, 37,* 142–165.

Vogel, S. A. (1989). Adults with language learning disorders: Definition, diagnosis, and determination of eligibility for postsecondary and vocational rehabilitation services. *Rehabilitation Education, 3,* 77–90.

Wechsler, D. (1981). *Wechsler Adult Intelligence Scale—Revised.* New York: Psychological Corporation.

Woodcock, R. W. (1984). A response to some questions raised about the Woodcock–Johnson. *School Psychology Review, 13,* 355–362.

Ysseldyke, J. E., Algozzine, B., Shinn, M., & McGue, M. (1982). Similarities and differences among low achievers and students labeled learning disabled. *Journal of Special Education, 16,* 73–85.

5

Sociocultural Issues Affecting the Identification and Service Delivery Models for Adults with Learning Disabilities

JOVITA M. ROSS-GORDON

Discussing sociocultural issues that have an impact on assessment and delivery of services to adults with learning disabilities is a challenging task. This is largely true because an understanding of the sociocultural dimensions of adult learning disabilities depends on literature drawn from at least three educational subdisciplines: learning disabilities, adult and continuing education, and multicultural education. Neither educational field brings universally agreed-on definitions. Sources that incorporate concepts and data derived from cross-disciplinary perspectives are atypical. Authors writing about the individual with learning difficulties are unlikely to take a perspective that considers both the learner's social status as an adult and the impact of sociocultural dimensions such as race, class, and gender on identification and intervention.

Such a discussion is nonetheless very timely. Patton and Polloway (1992) cite the growing percentage of articles in the *Journal of Learning Disabilities* on adults with learning disabilities. Gajar (1992) attributes this growing interest in part to the simultaneous development of several trends. Among these is the emergence of relevant legislation providing an incentive for provision of services (Education for All Handicapped Children Act, 1975; Education of the Handicapped Act Amendment, 1983; Individuals with Disabilities Educational Act, 1990; Carl D. Perkins Vocational and Applied Technology Education Act, 1984; Americans with Disabilities Act, 1990). Continuing, she points to advocacy from the National Joint Committee on Learning Disabilities (as evidenced by its 1987 position paper), the imperative from the U.S. Department of Education's Office of Special Education and Rehabilitation Services for the development of transition planning and services, and the emergence of adult literacy as a national priority. Ryan and Price (1992) suggest that the growing number of adults with learning disabilities who seek assistance from educational, vocational, and social service agencies has prompted a keen interest on the part of postsecondary instructors and service providers in the needs of this population—including both individuals who have received public school services under the provisions of Public Law 94-142 (Education for All Handicapped Children Act, 1975) and others who are diagnosed as adults. For example, such professional interest is evident in the sizable interest group on learning disabilities within the recently formed National Association for Adults with Special Learning Needs, an organization founded in 1988 with much of its initial membership emerging from the American Association for Adult Continuing Education. Ryan and Price (1992) delineate issues and propose solutions for the overlapping categories of adult basic education, transition, higher education, vocational education, and employment. Yet their excellent article, like other recent overviews on the adult with learning disabilities (Gajar, 1992; Patton & Polloway, 1992; Polloway, Smith, & Patton, 1988), gives relatively little attention to sociocultural dimensions of assessment and service provision to adults with learning disabilities.

Increasing attention to multicultural issues in basic education (Banks & McGee Banks, 1989; Giroux, 1992; Sleeter, 1991), higher education (Schoem, Frankel, Zuñiga, & Lewis, 1993; Tierney, 1993), adult education (Cassara, 1990; Neufeldt & McGee, 1990; Ross-Gordon, Martin, & Briscoe, 1990; Hayes & Colin, 1994), and workplace human resources development (Morrison, 1992) suggests that we would be remiss in omitting a similar consideration of multicultural issues as we develop appropriate multidisciplinary approaches to the study of adults with learning disabilities. The imperative for such attention arises partially from the demographic patterns emerging in the United States, as well as from changing patterns of participation in postsecondary education and the work force by women. Population projections indicate a population that will be nearly evenly divided between whites and persons of color by the year 2050 (Day, 1992). Harry (1992) notes that during the 1980s, the number of people of Asian origin in the United States increased by 79.5%, those of Hispanic origin by 38.7%, Native Americans by 21.6%, blacks by 14.4%, and whites by 7% (Harry, 1992, p. 9). Likewise, the increasing participation of women in the work force (Alsalam, Fischer, Ogle, Rogers, & Smith, 1993) and rising participation in postsecondary education by women (Snyder & Hoffman, 1993), along with evidence suggesting that females with learning disabilities may face more limited employment opportunities (Karpinski, Neubert, & Graham, 1992; Lichtenstein, 1993), suggests that gender differences need to be included within our examination of multicultural issues.

In an effort to address this void, this chapter provides an overview of the literature on selected dimensions critical to our examination of the sociocultural issues relative to identification and service provision for adults with learning disabilities. It begins with a discussion of some of the sociocultural dimensions of one of the fundamental debates within the field of learning disabilities—specifically debates regarding the definition and origins of learning disabilities. Because much of the literature that has thus far focused on the sociocultural issues relevant to this chapter has been directed to children and adolescents, the next section of the literature review examines the critical issues raised with regard to identification and intervention efforts with girls and minority youth at the elementary and secondary levels and in higher education programs aimed at young adults. Next, the literature review shifts to focus on adults. After a brief review of relevant findings from general literature on adults with learning disabilities and outcomes studies, the discussion turns to issues related to assessment and intervention provisions for adults. After providing an overview of the literature, I next present a set of ideas for the design of assessment and intervention strategies that take into account many of the issues raised in this chapter. Finally, I provide a chapter summary and suggestions for future directions.

REVIEW OF THE LITERATURE

Relationship to Fundamental Definitional Issues in the Field of Learning Disabilities

Several issues that have plagued the field of learning disabilities since its inception are inextricably linked to sociocultural considerations. One set of issues relates to our conceptualization of the nature of learning disabilities and their presumed origins.

Hammill (1990) argues for a generally accepted conceptual definition of learning disabilities and discusses 11 definitions that have attained varying levels of acceptance during the history of the field. Four definitions have developed since 1977 (Association for Children with Learning Disabilities, 1986; Interagency Committee on Learning Disabilities, 1987; National Joint Committee on Learning Disabilities, 1981; United States Office of Education, 1977) are said to be professionally viable today and to reflect relative consensus. Examination of the table Hammill (1990) provides to compare elements across definitions reveals that these definitions presume disabilities in the areas of language or academic skills, reflecting a discrepancy between presumed ability and achievement levels and related to presumed central nervous system (CNS) dysfunction. Most allow for learning disabilities to exist concomitant to, although not as a primary result of, other handicapping conditions (although the officially approved version of the Learning Disabilities Association of America definition is silent on the matter of coexisting conditions). Given that these definitions share an assumption of underlying CNS dysfunction, they are rooted in a fundamentally biological model of learning disabilities. Although the presumed neurological origins have traditionally been hypothesized on the basis of psychological tests of processing abilities (Hammill, 1993) or neuropsychological tests (McCue, 1994), recent neurobiological and neuroanatomic research has provided accumulating evidence of observable neurological characteristics of individuals with learning disabilities (Bigler, 1992).

While accepting a presumed neurological basis of at least certain learning disabilities, some theorists emphasize the interactions of biological and environmental factors in the manifestation of learning disabilities. Hallahan (1992), in speculating on the causes for the dramatic increase in prevalence of learning disabilities over the last 20 years, speculates that inappropriate diagnoses by educators and psychologists anxious to provide special education placement for otherwise unserved problem learners may provide only a partial explanation. Hallahan (1992) suggests that such sociocultural factors as substance abuse and prenatal conditions associated with poverty may account for an increase in the prevalence of CNS dysfunction; moreover, postnatal environmental conditions associated with poverty and changing social supports and demands within working and middle-class families may also contribute to learning disabilities or mediate the effects of CNS dysfunction.

Adelman (1989), on the other hand, conceptualizes learning disabilities on a continuum with varying causation, reflecting an interaction of biological and environmental conditions. Although admitting to the likelihood that some individuals have neurologically based learning disabilities and are hence likely to exhibit learning problems in any environment (Type III), Adelman suggests that others, personally predisposed to learning disabilities, will only exhibit them under particular environmental conditions (Type II). Finally, he posits that some learning disabilities are entirely an outgrowth of a learning environment that is inadequate or hostile. In a related vein, Spekman, Herman, and Vogel (1993) call for the development of appropriate research models to study the risk factors and protective factors that influence the resilience of individuals identified as learning disabled.

Others have extended the analysis of the environmental dimensions of learning disabilities to examine how the educational category has been socially constructed, defined, and utilized. Carrier (1987) asserts that the emergence of the term and category "learning disabilities" reflected a "softening" or reorientation from earlier work by Strauss, Lehtinen, and others under the rubric of "brain injury." He posits that a variety of sociopolitical forces coalesced to produce this category, including the movement of special education away from a medical model to a more educational one, the growth of behavioral psychology, the development of psychoeducational diagnostic tests, and the advocacy of parents and professionals for the legal legitimization of the category through the Children with Specific Learning Disabilities Act of 1969. He especially points to the role of middle-class parents in this evolution, as they found in learning disabilities an explanation for their children's unexplained underachievement and a way to obtain special educational services (which would presumably lead to educational cures) without placement in more stigmatizing classes for students with mental retardation or emotional disorders. Christine Sleeter (1987), a leading figure in multicultural education, particularly emphasizes the role of classroom teachers in the determination of who comes to be labeled "learning disabled." She suggests that in schools the "real" child with learning disabilities is one with learning needs a teacher feels unequipped to handle; most often it is a child who has difficulty in reading and who exhibits behavioral problems in class. She sees such a pattern as inextricably linked to the dependence on literacy skills (especially in upper grades) for traditional classroom routines in highly controlled teaching–learning environments that provide for little individualization and allow for little student power in the classroom.

> What all this means is that learning disabilities is [*sic*] a by-product of the political purpose of schooling. That purpose (not the only purpose, but still an important one) is to instill in the young a

relatively standardized body of knowledge that accepts white wealthy male privilege and dominance. In the primary grades students are expected to develop literacy skills and behavioral patterns required to learn school knowledge. Those who do not make the expected progress are seen as either handicapped or "at risk." (Sleeter, 1987, p. 83)

Focusing on the inability of professionals to agree on what constitutes learning disabilities besides underachievement, Sleeter argues that professionals have focused on the wrong thing: "deficits in children rather than problems in the social structure and its system of education" (1987, p. 83–84). She cites Kavale and Forness (1985) in arguing that although a small percentage may have neurological deficiencies, those who are labeled as having learning disabilities are for the most part "normal" but have not experienced success in the regular classroom because their best learning modalities do not coincide with the classroom emphasis on reading and writing. If a variety of modalities were encouraged and student interest played a role in selection of content, she contends that varying levels of literacy would be less of a problem.

Similarly, Poplin and Phillips (1993) discuss the sociocultural aspects of language and literacy, especially as these relate to the placement of students from diverse cultures in special education. They call for a broader professional understanding of the various cultural norms regarding acquisition and social uses of spoken and written language.

> The unselfconsciousness of our assumptions about language, culture, normality, and ultimately, what constitutes a worthwhile life, has in essence, produced the category of learning disabilities . . . Once we see the larger sociocultural and sociopolitical contexts inherent in our work, we, as learning disability specialists well aware that difference is not always detrimental, find ourselves in difficult positions. Positions that require us to (a) speak up about the difference between different and disability; (b) become more aware of other world views about intelligence, language, and literacy; and (c) defend the rights of all children—different, disabled or both—to receive an appropriate education. (Poplin & Phillips, 1993, p. 253)

Gerald Coles (1987, 1989) articulated many of the concerns about definitions and identification of learning disabilities posed by Carrier (1987), Sleeter (1987), Poplin and Phillips (1993), and others in *The Learning Mystique: A Critical Look at "Learning Disabilities,"* a book that stimulated the publication of an issue of the *Journal of Learning Disabilities* in 1989 which focused on the presentation of Coles's critique and responses by a number of writers within the field. Essentially, Coles presents an analysis of the evidence supporting the theory of neurological dysfunction as the basis of learning disability and finds it unconvincing to date. He concludes:

> The numbers have not been estimated, but there is a modicum of evidence suggesting a very small portion of the children identified as learning disabled do have some degree of neurological dysfunction that may interfere with learning and academic achievement. Research shows, however that the actual extent of the problem is quite small compared to the millions of children who have been diagnosed as learning disabled. It is quite difficult to understand, therefore, why this diagnosis should have produced the pedagogical and psychological extravaganza we have seen in recent years. (Coles, 1989, p. 269)

Finding no surprise in the existence of persistent academic failure, like Sleeter (1987), Coles questions rather the almost exclusive attribution of this failure to what is happening inside the learner's head and is concerned that reliance on such explanations may hinder the pursuit of other explanations and development of preventative strategies. He calls for greater attention to the processes of learning and proposes an alternative theory of "interactivity," which incorporates elements of the constructs interaction and activity.

> The interactivity theory of LD [learning disabilities] proposes that while various features of an individual (including neurology), groups, and institutions, and social, economic, and cultural forces each have their own characteristics, identity, activity, degree of influence and interdependencies, at the same time they all combine to create the processes and products of learning and disabled learning. One might think of this interactivity as a "polyphony," a musical term for melodic parts that are both independent and interdependent. (Coles, 1989, p. 273)

Although several of the authors responding to Coles's propositions posed significant concerns about the accuracy of his claims (Galaburda, 1989), the thoroughness and comprehensiveness of his analysis (Mann, 1989; Rourke, 1989; Stanovich, 1989), and the political nature of his work (Rourke, 1989), his work has also been praised for its effort to broaden the perspectives on learning disabilities to consider its larger sociocultural contexts (Adelman, 1989; Miller, 1990; Stanovich, 1989).

Identification and Placement of Minority Children and Girls

One of the sociocultural concerns that has been voiced loudly by those concerned with special education of younger students has been the disproportionate placement of minority youth in special education programs. In introducing this topic, it is valuable to stop and consider the use of the term "minority," a term criticized by some because of its implicit negative connotations and its increasing inaccuracy in describing the actual numerical proportions of subpopulations (for instance, "minority" students are already in the numerical majority in many urban school districts). Harry (1992) provides an excellent discussion of the meaning of race, ethnicity, and minority status relative to education in U.S. society, drawing on statistical evidence and such theoretical work as that of Ogbu (1978) to detail and speculate on explanations for the relative educational disadvantage of certain groups in U.S. society—particularly African Americans, Native Americans, and Hispanics. With regard to conventions of statistical reporting, a reflection of the official meanings of race and ethnicity, Harry (1992) observes:

> In the United States, the use of the term minority essentially represents an attempt to categorize by race, not by culture. Yet the specifics of race are only important on one dimension: whether one is White or not. This is evident in the OCR's annual survey of elementary and secondary schools . . . The survey first distinguishes between five possible classifications, based on geographic and/or racial features, and then, for the purposes of summary tables, condenses the original five categories into two—White and minority. The racial category White comprises the majority group, and to be other than White is to be a member of the minority group. (p. 5)

Harry notes that this preoccupation with race as a marker of majority or minority status results in such appended phrases as "Black (not of Hispanic origin)," "White (not of Hispanic origin)," and Hispanic . . . "regardless of race."

In discussing the overrepresentation of minority students in special education, Harry observes that examining data at the national level sometimes obliterates differences. Her presentation of enrollment data from seven states by racial or ethnic group and across categories of exceptionality indicates that minority students tend to be overrepresented in states in which they account for a substantial amount of the population and to be underrepresented or proportionally represented in states in which their numbers are small. She suggests that disproportionate placement of minority students in special education may be related to cultural bias, albeit subtle, in assessment practices or to prereferral classroom practices that may include a school climate that tolerates or promotes racial or cultural prejudice, cultural incongruity in instruction and curriculum, and problems related to the match between a child's language competence and the language of instruction.

Harry is only one of many who have examined the sociocultural dimensions of special education identification and placement. Although concerns about overrepresentation due to cultural biases in identification and placement have been most frequently raised relative to placement in classes for students with mental retardation or severe emotional disorders, concerns about both underrepresentation and overrepresentation have been raised with regard to placement in classes for students with learning disabilities. Collins and Camblin (1983) warn that the application of the exclusion clause can lead to underrepresentation of blacks and other minorities in learning disabilities classes, with poor children likely to be excluded when their learning problems are seen as arising from deprived backgrounds and blacks likely to be excluded on the basis of IQ scores, which may underestimate actual ability levels. Maheady, Towne, Algozzine, Mercer, and Ysseldyke (1983), on the other hand, suggest that once classes for students with mild retardation were no longer a socially desirable placement for black students their overrepresentation in classes for students with learning disabilities quickly emerged. Whereas Fradd and Hallman (1983) and Geisinger (1992) attempt to identify the psychometric weaknesses that lead to biased assessment of bilingual students and Cummins (1989) decries regular and special education practices that lead to disempowerment and labeling of bilingual students, Ochoa, Pacheco, and Omark (1988) are equally concerned about the possibility that students with limited English proficiency may be underserved due to a failure to link bilingual and special education. In introducing a special issue on cultural pluralism in *Learning Disability Quarterly*, Poplin and Wright (1983) gave several reasons for the importance of the topic to those in the field. They noted that many minority-culture children are placed in special education in response to cultured, linguistic, and/or racial differences when their culturally based language or behaviors are treated as deviant. For those who do have legitimate handicaps, Poplin and Wright (1983) noted that understanding cultural pluralism is important in avoiding problems associated with discrimination in referral and assessment. Finally, they remarked on the virtual nonexistence of programs that combine bicultural and bilingual education with special education. Their discussion is intended to encourage learning disabilities professionals to participate in professional development aimed at enhancing their understanding of cultural differences as a way to better serve students.

A separate body of literature raises questions about differences in the rates of identification and placement of girls in programs for students with learning disabilities. Vogel (1990) notes that males are found in school-identified samples disproportionate to females at rates ranging from 3:1 to 15:1. After examining a large body of literature to look at differences between males and females in intellectual, language, visual–motor, and academic abilities for normally achieving children and those with learning disabilities she noted that girls included in the primarily school-identified samples had lower IQs, more severe cognitive deficits, and more severe academic deficits in reading and math, although generally performing better than boys with learning disabilities on written language measures. She questions whether such girls indeed represent the full range of girls with learning disabilities. Citing evidence that teachers are more likely to place a priority on the referral of boys suspected of having learning disabilities than on girls presenting the same profile, she suggests that teacher attitude may play a significant role in the identification of learning disabilities among females. This concern is supported by the findings of Hassitt and Gurian (1984) from a study of boys and girls in a clinic-served population. Only 33% of 171 girls in the sample had received school services, as compared to 53% of the 198 boys in the sample. Also notable was the fact that 78% of the girls (vs. 48% of the boys) were described in terms associated with learned helplessness (passive, anxious, withdrawn).

Adults with Learning Disabilities

It seems evident that although relatively little attention has been paid to multicultural dimensions of assessment and intervention with adults with learning disabilities, the issues raised regarding special education programs for children have considerable relevance to practice with adults. The preceding discussion, along with the following discussion of adult outcomes, should indicate that whether or not adults are likely to have been diagnosed, whether they are likely to have held a diagnosis as having learning disabilities rather than some other label, the quality of regular and special education they are likely to have received, including its responsiveness to their cultural and linguistics characteristics, and the adult outcomes they are likely to experience can all be seen as influenced by race or ethnicity, class, and gender. Diagnosis and intervention related to learning difficulties do not take place in a vacuum, unaffected by the sociocultural and political factors that impinge upon educational effectiveness, whether for children or for adults. Likewise for adults, variables related to employment and successful adjustment within the community can be seen as influenced by race, class, and gender.

General Literature on Adults with Learning Disabilities

A number of publications in the last decade have provided a broad picture of the continuing problems faced by individuals with learning disabilities once they reach adulthood and an understanding of the broader scope with which learning disabilities must be conceptualized during adulthood—they are no longer primarily an academic matter at this stage in life (Clitheroe, 1988; Gajar, 1992; Gerber & Reiff, 1994; Johnson & Blalock, 1987; Patton & Polloway, 1992; Ross-Gordon, 1989). Works such as those by Johnson and Blalock (1987), Gerber and Reiff (1994), and Smith (1991) give us a picture of the academic, cognitive, social, and vocational problems faced by clinical populations of adults with learning disabilities, as well as their potential strengths (Ginsberg, Gerber, & Reiff, 1994; Smith, 1991). Gajar (1992) reviews the status of existing research on adults with learning disabilities and calls for expansion of the amount, foci, and methodological diversity of research on issues related to postsecondary education, employment, and community adjustment of adults with learning disabilities. The National Joint Committee on Learning Disabilities (1986) identified a number of concerns related to adult learning disabilities and made recommendations for research and program development; Ryan and Price (1992) more precisely delineate concerns and recommendations as they relate specifically to education and training arenas in which those with learning disabilities are likely to seek services (adult basic education, transition service, higher education, employment training, vocational education, and psychosocial counseling). Clitheroe (1988) offers results from a survey asking both adults and service providers what they see as the critical needs of adults with learning disabilities and reveals that the affected individuals show a much greater concern for social skills, coping, and independent living issues. Patton and Polloway (Patton & Polloway, 1992; Polloway et al., 1988) have been particularly diligent in reminding us that different issues come into play as individuals reach the developmental stages of adulthood, and they suggest that adaptation to life events will be mediated by a number of factors. This last suggestion is borne out by emerging research on resilience (Spekman et al., 1993) and successful learning disabled adults (Gerber, Ginsberg, & Reiff, 1992).

Despite the call for more comprehensive models of understanding learning disabilities in adulthood, scant attention is paid to the impact of race, class, and gender on the status, needs, and recommended provisions for adults with learning disabilities. Even in an article such as that by Wiener and Siegel (1992), encompassing both multicultural issues in learning disabilities and issues of adult learning disabilities within the Canadian context, these domains of concern tend to be dealt with separately, leaving it up to the reader to infer that the multicultural issues associated with youth services still have relevance for adults. The variable of gender has received a limited amount of attention, as in articles by Buchanan and Wolf (1986) and Vogel and Walsh (1987). Buchanan and Wolf (1986) note with curiosity that women in their clinic-based adult learning disabled sample exhibited poorer functioning in several areas, including the Reasoning Abilities cluster of the Wechsler Adult Intelligence Scale—Revised (WAIS-R) and the Woodcock–Johnson achievement test in reading and mathematics. Given the self-referred population from which the sample was drawn, they speculate that societal demands may cause males to seek help more readily; many of the women served were unmarried, self-supporting, and/or heads of households. They also suggest that lower availability of remedial services in school for females may have contributed to a lower level of understanding of their learning problems and hence a decreased likelihood to seek help. In addition to reporting that a greater proportion of females were excluded from their study of college learning disabled on the basis of IQ criteria, Vogel and Walsh (1987) reported different cognitive ability patterns for males and females. The hierarchy of scores for males most closely resembled research on samples of younger individuals with learning disabilities, typically predominantly male. They question "whether much of what we know about learning disabilities is only describing the LD male portion of the population" (p. 161).

Adult Outcomes of Younger Students with Learning Disabilities

A fairly large proportion of the literature on adults with learning disabilities has been devoted to studies of adult outcomes of individuals diagnosed during childhood as having learning disabilities. Both White (1992) and Horn, O'Donnell, and Vitulano (1983) raise a number of methodological issues regarding this research (e.g., not using control groups or not controlling for severity of learning disabilities), and Polloway et al. (1988) warn us against an emphasis on looking at adults with learning disabilities in terms of problems persisting from childhood. Nonetheless, this body of literature does raise significant questions regarding the role of race, class, and gender in the likelihood of positive outcomes.

One of the sociocultural variables that appears to be of importance is gender. Although Goodman (1987) found that the outcomes of middle-class girls with learning disabilities were similar to those of their sisters without learning disabilities with regard to educational attainment, occupational level, family life, and need for psychosocial counseling, other follow-up studies have suggested that girls do not experience comparable outcomes to those of boys, particularly with regard to employment. Sitlington, Frank, and Carson (1992), in a 1-year follow-up of the adult adjustment of high school graduates with mild disabilities, included 737 individuals with learning disabilities. Females with learning disabilities were found to be receiving lower wages, prompting White (1992) to suggest that their low level of participation in postsecondary training is especially problematic. Similarly, follow-up studies of dropouts have found girls to be more disadvantaged in the area of employment. Karpinski et al. (1992) studied rural students with mild disabilities at 21 and 28 months after graduation or dropout. They found that across the graduates and dropout groups, young women were employed at half the rate (49%) of males (91%) and received lower wages when surveyed 21 months after school departure; gender differences were less pronounced but still present at 28 months (78% employment rate for males, 58% for females). Intensive case studies of several dropouts, conducted by Lichtenstein (1993), point in the same direction; the girls received lower wages while in high school and afterward. Although these findings regarding lower wages for young women should come as no great surprise given the fact that women as a group receive lower wages— approximately 70% as high as those of men at each level of educational attainment (Snyder & Hoffman, 1993)—we are certainly reminded by these data that our intervention efforts aimed at postsecondary vocational education and training may be especially critical for women.

Additional findings from follow-up studies of both high school completers and dropouts suggest that family socioeconomic status is another sociocultural variable that has an apparent influence on adult outcomes. O'Connor and Spreen (1988) analyzed follow-up data on 226 subjects divided into three groups, one with definite neurological impairment, one with soft signs of neurological impairment, and one with no signs of neurological impairment. Father's education predicted enrollment in academic college courses, employment in the last 5 years, and the subject's occupation. Mother's education predicted the first and last of these variables. Father's employment predicted 16% of the variance in the subject variables (college attendance, grade completed, school program, employed last 5 years, current salary, and longest job salary). Father's education explained 20% of the variance; mother's education did not produce a significant R^2. Although the strongest predictor of outcomes was adult IQ at age 25, contributing 44% of the variance in the outcome variables, parental socioeconomic status variables contributed more of the variance than severity of neurological status at age 20.

Werner (1993) reports relevant findings from the Kauai longitudinal study, which has traced the development of 22 children with learning disabilities and 22 matched control children from a multiracial cohort of 698 from birth to adulthood, with the most recent follow-up at the age of 32. The current focus of the research project is on the study of factors related to risk and resilience, with inclusion of a wide range of personal and environmental variables for this group of individuals identified by age 10 as having learning problems. Parental education was positively linked to more positive parent–child interactions in the first and second year of life, to more emotional support provided for the offspring during early and middle childhood, to infants' health and physical status by age 2, to competence at age 10, to better problem-solving skills, and to fewer absences from school due to repeated illnesses. Ratings of adult adaptation at age 32 were examined to identify protective factors that predicted success despite the risk associated with the learning disability. Gender differences were observed for a number of predictive variables. Protective factors for girls included a sociable temperament in infancy and young adulthood, mothers who had graduated from high school, the model of a mother who was gainfully employed, the absence of behavioral problems in middle adulthood, high self-esteem, and an internal locus of control at age 18. For men, at least average intelligence and problem-solving skills were more strongly associated with a successful transition into adulthood. The strongest positive buffers were the sources of emotional support on which they could rely after they left home (support of a spouse or mate, siblings, and elders). It should be noted, however, that parental competence and sources of support in the childhood home made less of a direct impact in adulthood than individual competencies and degree of self-esteem and self-efficacy.

Assessment of Adult Learning Disabilities

Much of the research and theoretical work described thus far has focused on a population who have had learning disabilities identified prior to adulthood. Patton and Polloway (1982) remind us that those concerned with assessment of adults with learning disabilities must take into account two distinct populations—those identified and probably served during school years and those not identified before adulthood. Each group presents particular evaluation challenges. As Patton and Polloway note, the evaluation records of those identified earlier frequently do not follow them as they move on into postsecondary education, the workplace, and adult-serving agencies. Such adults may in fact be anxious to create distance from the learning disabled label and may resist efforts to uncover this past. If evaluation information is available, judgments must still be made about its current accuracy and its relevance to current needs and purposes.

Previously unidentified adults with learning disabilities pose a different set of challenges with regard to assessment. They have shown up in a number of places, including adult basic education programs, job-training programs, higher education, and the workplace. The first critical question relates to whether a diagnosis and associated labeling are needed. Coles (1980) and Slate and Jones (1994) warn against the use of questionable assessment procedures to create labels that have potentially negative effects—including stigmatization, segregation, damage to self-concept, an emphasis on strengths and weaknesses, and the creation of self-fulfilling prophesies. They note, along with others (McCue, 1994; Ross, 1987; Travis, 1979; Vogel, 1989), that the existence of reliable and valid assessment instruments normed on adult populations is limited. Likewise, Ross-Gordon (1989) provides one caveat: that assessment be used only insofar as it seems to provide a means for helping the adult to live more fully. Examples include situations for which diagnosis determines eligibility for resources and support services that are not otherwise available to the individual and situations in which it is likely to provide direction in working with the adult to determine future goals, select appropriate educational and career development programs, and develop strategies for an individualized intervention plan. Gibbons et al. (1991), speaking out on people with dyslexia identified during adulthood, supply another rationale for diagnosis during adulthood: providing the individuals with an explanation of the learning difficulties that have haunted them all their lives. Yet, the reservations of Coles (1989) and Slate and Jones (1994) should be taken seriously, especially given the state of affairs with regard to adult assessment and the current emphasis on inclusive educational models. We are reminded as well of the controversy over cultural bias in standardized tests and evaluation procedures, discussed earlier in the chapter. Professionals should move cautiously before replicating now-questioned practices from special education in the arena of adult education. For instance, Shaw et al. (1994) described three levels of support for learning disabled students and note that many students can operate satisfactorily utilizing existing support services, while others cannot. Likewise, Ross-Gordon (1989) suggests that a comprehensive service model within adult basic education should provide specialized remediation and compensation support directly to some students, whereas others might be served through increased staff development and teacher support.

Several authors have offered comprehensive models for evaluation of adults (Hoy & Gregg, 1984a; Johnson, 1987; McCue, 1994; Vogel, 1989). All call for evaluation procedures that integrate information from several sources, including interviews with adults (and sometimes significant others) to learn the individual's history, the use of formal and informal testing, and behavioral observation. Distinct emphases can also be found, to some extent related to the context for which individuals are being evaluated. For instance, Hoy and Gregg (1984a), writing in an adult basic education context, emphasize the analysis of errors to lead to an instructional plan, whereas McCue, writing primarily from the context of evaluation for Rehabilitation Services Administration eligibility, emphasizes the importance of neuropsychological assessment and functional assessment to determine the employment-related impact of the learning disabilities. Less linked to any particular context is the concern that the evaluation process with adults involve them in a significant way (Ross-Gordon, 1989; Vogel, 1989), whether in describing their strengths and weaknesses based on personal experience or in setting goals for the outcome of the evaluation process. It should be noted here, as well, that some have argued against the use of traditional assessment procedures with adults suspected of having learning disabilities, as exemplified by Slate and Jones's (1994) arguments in favor of curriculum-based measurement as more directly linked to intervention planning.

Of critical importance for the purposes of this chapter is the lack of attention to sociocultural issues relevant to the assessment process in the foregoing discussions on evaluation of either unidentified or previously identified adults. A number of issues discussed earlier in this chapter with regard to special education of younger students might indeed be raised. With regard to those already identified, the possibility of mislabeling must be especially considered when working with minority adults who have been served as children in programs for the retarded or emotionally disturbed. For women, the absence of previous identification and service must be interpreted in the context of evidence that boys are more likely to be identified and served in school-based learning disabilities programs while only the most severe girls may be referred and served. Finally, with regard to evaluation of previously unidentified adults, we need to examine the dimension of test bias at the same time that we are working to identify a larger pool of psychometrically sound evaluation instruments for use with adults. Camara's (1992) discussion of fairness and fair use in employment tests, with a focus on Hispanic adults, suggests that many of the same concerns about test bias that have been raised with regard to identification and placement of minority youth have relevance to adult assessment in a variety of arenas, including the workplace.

Interventions with Adults

In addition to issues related to assessment, sociocultural dimensions are relevant to our growing efforts to accommodate the needs of adults with learning disabilities in postsecondary education settings and the workplace.

Remedial Adult Education: Literacy, Adult Basic Education, and General Education Development Preparation. Data from the Office of Special Education and Rehabilitation Services indicate that 56.9% of students with learning disabilities exiting the school system in 1988–1989 graduated with a diploma or certificate; the remainder dropped out (26.7%), reached maximum age (1.3%), or left for other reasons (15%) (Snyder & Hoffman, 1993). Data from the National Longitudinal Transition Study of Special Education Students indicate that reported graduation rates among former students with learning disabilities were similar for males and females (60.7% and 62.3%, respectively), as well as for blacks and whites (61.1% and 63.1%, respectively) (Valdes, Williamson, & Wagner, 1990). Hispanic youth with learning disabilities lagged behind whites and blacks with only 42.2% reporting graduation as the basis for school departure. Blacks (7.9%) and Hispanics (10.2%) were at least three times as likely as whites (2.9%) to have left school due to suspension or expulsion, putting them in the category some have referred to as pushouts. Family income also seems to be linked with likelihood of graduation; approximately 50% of those from families with incomes under $25,000 graduated whereas approximately 75% of those with incomes of $25,000 and over did so. Among participants in this national longitudinal follow-up study of recent graduates, 20% of blacks, 14.5% of whites, and 17.7% of Hispanics had participated in postsecondary education (vocational courses, 2-year, or 4-year college) within the last year; this took the form of participation in college for only 2.9% of blacks, 6.8% of whites, and 11% of Hispanics. Minskoff (1994) cites Wagner's (1989) data, which indicated that only 16.7% of 245 students had participated in postsecondary education within 1 to 2 years after leaving high school, compared to 56% of the general population. Despite the significant attention to the college-going population in the literature on learning disabilities, only 8.7% of the individuals in that study had gone on to college. Minskoff suggests that college is likely to be a feasible option only for those with reasonably mild learning disabilities and reasonably high IQs. Those with the greatest academic skill deficits may find themselves in need of further remedial education as they seek access to a variety of postsecondary employment and training opportunities. Yet, one of the contexts for intervention in which there has been little research and relatively little description of practice-related issues is that of adult basic education (ABE), General Education Development (GED), and literacy programs.

The earliest attention to the topic of learning disabilities in ABE programs appears to be reflected in a spate of articles around 1980, most appearing in the journal *Adult Literacy and Basic Education* after Travis led off the discussion with his 1979 article, "An Adult Educator Views Learning Disabilities." Several of these articles focused most on assessment and identification issues, such as Coles's query, "Can ABE Students Be Identified as Learning Disabled?" (1980)—an early exposition of the arguments he later used to challenge the field of learning disabilities in *The Learning Mystique.* O'Donnell and Wood (1981) critiqued the London Procedure, a diagnostic tool gaining popularity at the time for identification of learning disabled students in ABE programs. Other articles during that era proposed remediation procedures for teaching reading to those with learning disabilities (Bowren, 1981; Gold, 1981; Idol-Maestas, 1981). Hamilton (1983) took a rare perspective of proposing that adult education philosophy espousing the benefits of involving adults in the educational planning process be adhered to with this population as with any other. His discussion is also rare for its mention of the sociocultural dimensions of identifying language-related learning disabilities—noting that usage, for example, of black dialect cannot in and of itself be taken as an indicator of learning disabilities, given its cultural origins. Hoy and Gregg (1984a, 1984b) published a series of booklets intended for staff development use by ABE instructors. The first of these booklets focused on defining learning disabilities and assessment, whereas others were devoted to assessment and remediation for the specific domains of reading, written language, mathematics, and vocational education.

The interest in adult learning disabilities and literacy seems to have experienced a recent resurgence, especially following public policy initiatives placing greater interest and funding support in the area of adult literacy. For instance, Ross and Smith (1990) surveyed ABE professionals in an attempt to understand how they defined learning disabilities, how they viewed learning disabilities, what knowledge they had, and what services related to learning disabilities they either knew of or wanted. Their findings, based on a single state, suggest that while administrators, teachers, and counselors in the ABE system hold positive attitudes toward students with learning disabilities, there are gaps in their knowledge of learning disabilities and the ways they define learning disabilities only partially match those typically used in the assessment of learning disabilities. These staff members expressed great interest in staff development activities related to learning disabilities, and the availability of such programs has increased since the time of the study. Just as this study identified potential communication challenges between providers of ABE and those trained in learning disabilities, a study conducted by the Learning Disabilities Association of Canada (Alderson-Gill & Associates, 1989) likewise pointed to distinctions in perspectives between experts from a literacy background and those from a learning disabilities background. Learning disabilities professionals tended to view literacy programs with skepticism about their ability to serve clients with learning disabilities, and literacy professionals questioned the necessity for and wisdom of potentially damaging labeling. As Anderson (1994) suggests, adult illiterates exhibit learning difficulties for a variety of reasons— including those in the "traditional learning disabled group," those who used to be labeled "educable mentally retarded," those who have had inadequate educational opportunities, dropouts and push-outs, slow learners, students from poor-quality schools, English as a Second Language (ESL) students, and unwed mothers. It may be that professionals and tutors accustomed to working with such a heterogeneous group of students with learning difficulties are less committed to labeling for a variety of reasons, including the difficulty and questionable benefits of assigning a single label, the potential negative impact of labeling, and the lack of a direct link between particular labels and particular instructional strategies. Common to both literacy and learning disabilities experts, however, were core principles for serving the adult with learning disabilities and many tried-and true techniques and materials. All emphasized the importance of a trusting and adult-to-adult, client–teacher relationship and attempting to meet the specific needs expressed by adults with learning disabilities through the use of a variety of techniques and materials, with preference for materials relevant to adults' life situations.

Another form of remedial education available for adults with learning disabilities is found in GED programs. The Tests of General Education Development (commonly referred to as the GED) were first developed in 1941 to provide returning World War II veterans with an opportunity to earn a high school credential. The test is intended to measure outcomes and concepts of a 4-year program of high school education in the core content areas of U.S. and Canadian high school curricula. Given the high rate of dropout among students with learning disabilities, participation in GED programs would seem to be a viable option for many who will otherwise have difficulty gaining access to many jobs and postsecondary educational opportunities. Yet, Miller, Rzonca, and Snider (1991) failed to include participation in ABE (presumably including GED education) in their statewide follow-up study of postsecondary education participation by Iowa special education graduates and terminators because fewer than 10 of the 250 individuals surveyed were participating in this form of postsecondary education.

GED programs are generally offered within the community in conjunction with ABE programs (serving those who function below the high school level academically) and ESL programs, most often sponsored by either school districts or community colleges, depending on the state's predominant organizational pattern. Kutner et al. (1992) report that as many as 90% of ABE and ESL teachers are employed part time on an hourly basis and, depending on the state's certification requirements (if they exist), are likely to lack specific academic preparation in adult education; many are full-time teachers in secondary or elementary classroom with K–12 certification accepted in the states that require any certification. This 30-month study examining the training needs of teachers and volunteers in ABE and ESL identified several pedagogical needs, including knowledge of adult learning, diagnosis of student needs and ability, identification and teaching of students with learning disabilities, and awareness of different cultures. Although many adults who failed to thrive in or complete a high school curriculum for a variety of personal, education, and environmental reasons may succeed in such programs, individuals with learning disabilities may require different educational practices than those typically found in such programs. Increased student awareness of available programs, as is likely to occur through transition planning, may increase the level of participation in ABE and GED programs. Based on Kutner et al.'s (1992) findings, staff development would seem to be essential if the teachers and volunteers in such programs are to become aware of possible ways to modify teaching–learning practices for students with learning disabilities, including those students with diverse cultural backgrounds. The 58% increase in requests for special testing accommodations based on specific learning disabilities between 1992 and 1993 alone suggests that the awareness level of GED staff regarding learning disabilities is changing (Baldwin, 1994). The Pennsylvania study by Ross and Smith (1990), as well as a growing demand for staff development programs on learning disabilities, suggests that teachers in this sector are eager to learn more.

Such changes, as well as increasing dialogue between secondary special educators and professionals in adult basic and literacy education, seem essential to the economic well-being of the large segment of the learning disabled population who have not completed high school. Otherwise they are likely to remain locked into unemployment and underemployment in low-skill, low-paying jobs. This picture is exacerbated by race, class, and gender. For example, recent graduates are more likely to be employed than recent dropouts within each ethnic category, although employment levels are greatest for whites, followed by Hispanics, followed by blacks, whether comparisons are made within the group of graduates or dropouts (Alsalam et al., 1993). Likewise, recent graduates from high-income families enjoy higher employment levels than those from middle-income families, followed by those from low-income families; for dropouts, the rankings are preserved between those from middle-income and those from lower-income families, although at lower levels of employment (too few cases of dropouts from high-income families to justify their inclusion in this set of rankings) (Alsalam et al., 1993). Finally, the effects of gender must be factored in. The earnings penalty of not finishing high school (average earnings of dropouts compared to earnings of those finishing high school and not continuing on to college) is greater for young women—an average of 30% and 32% for white and black males, respectively; 37% and 47% for white and black females, respectively (Alsalam et al., 1993). The positive effect of the diploma or GED completion on income (reported for the 25–33 age group) is most observable for women who complete high school or earn the GED before age 20; their level of employment rises by 13% and 17%, respectively.

The intersect of literacy, learning disabilities, and cultural difference was addressed directly in only one identified reference. Chapman, Vaillancourt, and Dobbs (1980) describe a project creating a handbook on learning disabilities for ESL teachers along with a screening test. They describe conditions under which a teacher might suspect a student is having out-of-the-ordinary difficulty with second language acquisition and caution that the screening test is invalid if administered other than by a fluent speaker of both English and the student's native language. Although not specifically addressing a population with learning disabilities, emerging literature focusing on access and retention of nonmajority students in literacy programs is also likely to be valuable to the reader. For instance, Denny (1992) discusses the sociocultural factors, including experiences with racism and limited expectations that literacy can make a difference in their lives, that contribute to the underrepresentation of native-born African Americans in adult literacy programs. She also offers suggestions to help programs effectively recruit and retain such students, including creating an awareness that literacy skills can be relevant in their lives (as in setting a role model for their children) and setting expectations for participation that acknowledge the complexities of their lives. Cumming (1992) argues that the "challenge for literacy educators of minority populations is to create unique, participatory educational programs that address and capitalize on the cultural values, interests, and aspirations of local minority communities" (p. 2). She cites elements of successful programs including (1) location of classes within ethnic neighborhoods and at local centers with reputations for community service; (2) instructors who are themselves members of minority populations, including recycling successful learners back into the program as mentors or teachers; (3) participatory approaches to program planning, development, and evaluation that include learners themselves; and (4) ongoing liaisons with community workers and bridges to other programs.

Higher Education. Shaw et al. (1994) list eight factors related to the increase in college participation by those with learning disabilities: (1) more available and effective services during the K–12 school years; (2) increasing emphasis on education in the least restrictive environment, giving more students exposure to a mainstream classes; (3) the fact that 50% of students with learning disabilities graduate; (4) increasing awareness of options for college attendance; (5) federal requirements on transition; (6) increasing availability of technological support; (7) a shift in high school learning disabilities programs from an emphasis on remedial content to learning strategy and metacognitive approaches; and (8) the impact of Section 504 of the Rehabilitation Act (1973). They note that prospective college students should be aware there is a continuum of services at the college level, from none to loosely coordinated services (primarily using existing college resources) with a contact person, to centrally coordinated services administered by an learning disabilities coordinator, to the full-range, data-based program with a full-time learning disabilities director and support staff. As they suggest, it seems critical that both students and those assisting them in selecting appropriate educational options have a sense of the services that will be available and the prospective student needs regarding level and types of support.

For the purpose of this chapter, attention to the topic of college participation is relatively brief, with least attention to the discussion of 4-year college programs. This omission is deliberate, given the attention devoted to this topic elsewhere and the relatively small proportion of individuals with learning disabilities for whom this is likely to be the most appropriate postsecondary education option. Mellard (1994) devotes particular attention to the discussion of the community college. Reviewing various studies on rates of dropout and the work of Fairweather and Shaver (1991) on outcomes for students with learning disabilities participating in various forms of postsecondary education and training, Mellard notes that the vocational orientation of the community college makes it an especially appealing option to enable individuals to improve their employability. Other attributes that, he suggests, make it an attractive option include (1) local access, convenient for those who find it necessary to continue to live at home; (2) a wide variety of course offerings; (3) community responsiveness in the type of curriculum offered; (4) integration with agencies and services in the community, facilitating transition; (5) an instructional orientation that is tolerant of variation in students' instructional interests and needs, including options for associate degrees, vocational certificates, noncredit or remedial courses, and enrichment-type adult education; (6) community representativeness in terms of participation by persons diverse in age, ethnic, social, and academic background; and (7) relatively low costs. The last two factors seem especially relevant to the focus of this chapter. If participation choices by individuals with learning disabilities are likely to resemble those of minority students in the general population, the community college may for a variety of reasons be a more likely selection for postsecondary education than the 4-year college. Hispanics, blacks, and Native Americans are enrolled at higher levels in 2-year versus 4-year institutions; this is especially true for Hispanics whose participation rate in 2-year institutions is double that in 4-year colleges (Alsalam et al., 1993).

Very little literature on college-attending adult students with learning disabilities deals specifically with sociocultural issues. Vogel, Hruby, and Adelman (1993) studied 107 students with learning disabilities who entered college between 1980 and 1988 to ascertain distinctions between graduates and nongraduates. Several of the distinguishing variables seem to have little particular link to sociocultural dimensions. They note, for instance, that whereas females outnumbered males at this women's college, in the sample, and among graduates, there were almost twice as many male nongraduates (29%)

as female nongraduates (17%). They suggest that the finding that graduates were significantly older than nongraduates can be understood in relation to the gender difference between the two groups; many of the women enrolled in this college are non-traditional-age students. A second set of findings related to educational interventions suggest a link to socioeconomic status. Although there was no significant difference between the proportion of graduate and nongraduate students receiving private tutoring, the mean number of months of tutoring was almost four times as great (42 months) for graduates than for nongraduates (11 months). Vogel et al. (1993) suggest that the extended tutoring relationship, combining elements of teacher, mentor, friend, and role model, may be an especially important contributor to adult resilience. Similarly, they find such a relationship to be an important one for those college students who develop a strong relationship with the learning disabilities specialist.

A faculty handbook developed for faculty members at tribally controlled colleges is one of only two sources located that specifically addresses access issues for culturally diverse college students with learning disabilities. The authors of the document acknowledge that the document focuses on a discussion of learning disabilities and appropriate accommodations by students and faculty, on the assumption that the faculty members for whom the handbook is intended are likely "to understand the cultures of those tribes better than we" (Dodd & Rose, 1991, p. 2). A conference paper by Heggoy and Grant (1989) also focuses on minority college students with learning disabilities. They studied an unspecified number of students obtaining services through a college learning disabilities program to ascertain differences in the profiles of minority and nonminority students. All students had a grade point average of 2.0 or better, met regular admissions standards, had not been previously identified, and ranged in age from 18 to 30 years. For both groups they note that their sample uncharacteristically included 50% females and exhibited relatively "flat" profiles, despite academic major choices that tended to be more performance-oriented and difficulties in the use of listening, speaking, reading, writing, reasoning, or mathematical abilities manifest in multiple failures in classroom work or on the Regents tests required of college students in the state. They concluded that more differentiated evaluations were needed to identify the underlying patterns of strengths and weaknesses in information processes. Trend differences between minority and nonminority students included age (minorities older), number of postsecondary institutions attended, and reason for evaluation. Minority students, 84% of whom were black, were more typically referred after repeated failure on the Regents tests—averaging five attempts and enrollment in remedial courses at least four times. Heggoy and Grant (1989) raise the question of cultural biases affecting the test results, as was possible with the WAIS-R scores which were on average lower for minority students. The repeated failures, despite remedial courses, raise questions about both the effectiveness of these courses with this population and the factors contributing to the infrequency with which referrals for assessment were made even in the face of such failure. They note that nonminority students were more likely to be referred for classroom failure. This limited evidence, along with Vogel et al.'s (1993) work on factors contributing to success or resilience among college students with learning disabilities, suggests that there is much work to be done in this area.

Vocational Adjustment. Considerable emphasis has been given to the study and discussion of the adjustment of the adult with learning disabilities in the vocational arena. Biller (1985) earlier reported the mixed conclusions of follow-up studies looking at employment success of the learning disabled—of 15 studies reviewed, he concluded that 4 failed to provide enough data to evaluate the effect of learning disabilities on occupational attainment, 6 did not support the conclusion that learning disabilities negatively affected attainment, and 5 supported the belief that learning disabilities restrict education or occupational attainment. According to Biller's review, a variety of studies suggest some degree of success with gaining employment (Fafard & Haubrich, 1981; Fourqurean, Meisgeier, Swank, & Williams, 1991) and even paint a picture of the highly successful adult with learning disabilities (Ginsberg et al., 1994; Goodman, 1987; Rawson, 1968), but the general picture is one of individuals with learning disabilities working in low-skilled, entry-level jobs (Fourqurean et al., 1991; Siegel & Gaylord-Ross, 1991; White, Alley, Deshler, Schumaker, Warner, & Clark, 1982) with which they may be dissatisfied (Fafard & Haubrich, 1981).

Studies of young adults soon after departure from high school suggest a few variables that influence relative employment success. Fourqurean et al. (1991) found math ability, employment during high school, and frequency of parental participation in individual education plan (IEP) meetings to be predictive of job stability, along with the control variables of gender (males were more consistently employed) and mode of exit (graduates more consistently employed than school leavers). Math ability and parental participation in IEP meetings also predicted job status (unemployed, unskilled, or skilled work) along with gender (women both more likely to be unemployed and more likely to be engaged in skilled work). Fourqurean et al. (1991)

hypothesized that the parental involvement variable (admittedly measured through a somewhat simplistic indicator) would covary with socioeconomic status, although they also acknowledge that theirs was a primarily white, middle-class sample in suburban area with an abundance of entry-level jobs. They did not discuss the finding with regard to gender or their reason for including it as a control variable, although these findings are, in part, consistent with more negative employment outcomes discussed earlier in this chapter. Although not discussed, the higher likelihood of women being in skilled occupations may relate to the fact that hairdressing or cosmetology was one of the two most frequently mentioned occupations among their 75% female sample; it also was counted among the skilled jobs.

Siegel and Gaylord-Ross (1991) interviewed former students, parents, and current or former employers in their survey of ecological factors associated with job success. Based on interview responses, they derived indices for each of four variables of interest, which were then correlated with a rating for each subject on employment success; the latter ratings were assigned by one of the authors based on data and checked for reliability with ratings by a school professional who knew 26 of the 41 subjects. Marginal relationships with job success were found for social acceptance (on the job), work rationalization (ratings of the work ethic of the subject and employer and similarity between), and special services used to support the employment. A significant relationship was found between job success and job match and accommodation, to which they argue that assistance with accommodation may be essential given the likelihood that many will not find an immediate job match. No relationship was found between job success and income index derived to denote family income. Their sample was ethnically diverse and one that varied greatly in family income. Authors' discussions of sampling challenges from both these studies illustrate the difficulty of conducting follow-up studies with similar populations; Siegel and Gaylord-Ross initially wound up with 31 available participants (15%) from a randomly selected pool of 208; Fourqurean et al. (1991), with their middle-class suburban sample, were somewhat more successful in locating and gaining participation from 43% of an original sample of 284. Obviously, we must wonder about the characteristics of those who could not be located or were unwilling to participate, and Siegel and Gaylord-Ross suggest we may need to look for methodologies that facilitate greater participation levels.

Ginsberg et al. (1994) deliberately sought to identify those among the most vocationally successful of individuals with learning disabilities. They hoped to identify alterable patterns and ingredients of success that distinguished between these adults who demonstrated high and moderate levels of success with the notion that ideas might surface for interventions with the less successful. Using a nomination process yielding 211 nominations from organizations and experts throughout North America who were familiar with learning disabilities (Gerber et al., 1992), Ginsberg et al. (1994) identified 46 individuals as highly successful and 25 as moderately successful. Their criteria for success were fairly traditional: (1) income (those in the highly successful group ranging from $30,000 to over $100,000), (2) job classification, (3) prominence in field, (4) job satisfaction, and (5) educational level (26 of the highly successful had doctoral or professional degrees, as did 3 of the moderately successful; 1 from the highly successful group and 16 from the moderately successful group held master's degrees). Thus, their sample was a highly select one. Although they do not report distribution by race, women constituted 30% of the highly successful group and 36% of the moderately successful. Based on inductive analysis of extended interviews, they determined that the key factor distinguishing the most successful was control—the amount of control they sought and maintained over their lives. Distinctions, sometimes subtle, were also found between the two groups on several internal decision factors (a burning desire to succeed, strong goal orientation, and a reframing process accepting the learning disability) and external manifestations of adaptability (persistence, goodness of fit between strengths and work requirements, learned creativity for developing compensatory strategies, and social ecologies—willingness to draw on a variety of social support systems without being dependent). Such personal factors seem consistent with factors found to relate to resilience in a more ethnically diverse sample in the Kauai longitudinal study discussed earlier (Werner, 1993). Some of these characteristics may be more challenging to acquire for individuals growing up in lower socioeconomic status environments, where the lack of available rewards may delay the start of a cycle of success and where support systems may not be as strong; likewise, girls, more often socialized into patterns of learned helpfulness, may have to work harder to attain a sense of control over their lives (Parsons, 1982). Vocational rehabilitation services available through local agencies of the Rehabilitation Services Administration (RSA) offer at least one option for improving the vocational adjustment of individuals with learning disabilities. Dowdy, Smith, and Nowell (1992) provide a clear discussion of RSA definitions, diagnostic categories, and eligibility criteria for serving individuals under RSA guidelines, as well as pointing out some of the issues surrounding judgments regarding the severity of an employment-related handicap in individuals often presumed by vocational rehabilitation (VR) counselors to have primarily academic deficits. They point out that only 50% of clients with learning disabilities are determined to be severely handicapped, whereas 70% of other clients are; yet, they paint a picture of an environment that is changing with the development of learning disabilities guidelines and increasing experience and staff development of counselors. A special issue of the *Journal of Rehabilitation* (Kopp, Miller, & Mulkey, 1984) suggests that this topic has drawn the concern of VR personnel. Yet, Smith's (1992) data from a survey of Learning Disabilities Association members regarding awareness of, utilization of, and satisfaction with VR services suggest there is still progress to be made.

PROPOSED IDEAS

The foregoing discussion has concentrated on a description of the status quo. A number of issues have been raised, pointing to a need for change as a number of professional groups increasingly turn to the question of how best to serve the needs of adults with learning disabilities. At this point, it seems reasonable to offer some ideas that may prove useful as we examine how to incorporate sociocultural considerations while we develop assessment and intervention approaches that are appropriate for the adult segment of the life span. These propositions are discussed first in terms of changes under the responsibility and control of professionals and policymakers. It is important to keep in mind, even while reviewing this list, that it is the learner who must remain central to our efforts. Presented next are those ideas aimed at the learners themselves, for as adults, they are essential partners in this transformation process.

Policy, Programmatic, and Professional Changes

1. Reconceptualize our focus on postsecondary education, with its inherent emphasis on the formal educational opportunities that represent only a limited range of the postschool learning of individuals with learning disabilities, to a broader view of adult education that encompasses formal education, nonformal education, and informal learning.[1] Individuals with learning disabilities, like other adults, are likely to engage in each of these as they go about the business of adapting to adult life needs and circumstances.

2. Incorporate knowledge and theory regarding adult learning and development. Patton and Polloway (1992) have reminded us that adult life poses developmental tasks distinct from those on which we

have focused in discussions of children with learning disabilities. Such tasks extend beyond the academic domain into the personal, social and familial, and occupational domains that are often more deeply interconnected with the sociocultural concerns central to this chapter. In addition, theoretical conceptions of adult learning (Brookfield, 1986; Knowles & Associates, 1984; Mezirow, 1991) offer perspectives that will add to our ability to understand the needs for self-direction and immediately useful knowledge that our clients bring, as well as understanding the need for capitalizing on their experiences and creating experiences that challenge them to think critically.

3. Work with policymakers and other education and rehabilitation professionals to expand the availability of programs aimed at individuals with learning disabilities. Work to ensure that these programs are accessible to those often in greatest need—women, minorities, and those of the lowest socioeconomic status.

4. Involve individuals from underrepresented groups in developing approaches to recruitment, eligibility evaluation, and program delivery that maximally consider and address the particular learner characteristics and needs of these groups.

5. Develop approaches that encompass multiple levels of service, address multiple dimensions of adult lives, and coordinate the efforts of multiple agencies.

a. With regard to levels of service, the needs of many adults with undiagnosed learning problems and mild to moderate learning disabilities may be addressed through adult education opportunities to address staff development needs of professionals who serve them. These professionals include college faculty, VR counselors, teachers and tutors in adult literacy and basic education programs, and employers. Direct assistance to such professionals should be viewed as a second option, ancillary to the conventional option of providing evaluation and instruction directly to individuals with learning disabilities (Ross & Smith, 1990; Ross-Gordon, 1989).

b. The work of Clitheroe (1988) and others suggests that adults with learning disabilities place equal or greater importance on skills related to coping, independent living, and social interaction than they do on academic and vocational skills. Indeed, satisfactory academic and vocational success beyond the secondary level depends on successful performance in these sociocultural domains as well. For individuals with diverse cultural backgrounds and learning disabilities, learning to operate bilingually and biculturally may pose a particular challenge. Hence, educational and vocational programs should be planned with adequate attention to these concerns, which are often relegated to the counseling domain.

c. Because the needs of adults with learning disabilities intersect the missions of a variety of organizations and agencies, it is essential that mechanisms be developed for increasing the effectiveness with which these organizations interact. Developing and updating lists of contact persons in each organization, examining and developing articulation policies across agencies (such as those which relate to learning disabilities eligibility), and maintaining communication channels are essential. Personal introductions to contact people will help ease the transition as adults move from one setting to another.

6. Staff development on issues related to multiculturalism, including gender issues, is needed to help learning disabilities professionals who serve adults become more aware of the kinds of issues raised throughout this chapter that have an impact on appropriate assessment, development, and delivery of effective intervention programs.

Enhancing Personal Capacity of Individuals with Learning Disabilities

1. Greater familiarity with literature on adult learning and on multicultural education is likely to convince the reader of the importance of empowerment-oriented approaches to the adult education of individuals who are socially marginalized *and* have learning disabilities. Cummins (1989) has already touted the value of empowering minority students in special education programs at the elementary and secondary levels; his message is equally pertinent for those who must learn to cope in an adult world where they may be doubly affected by virtue of their race, class, or gender as well as their learning disabilities.

2. Adults with learning disabilities, whatever their race, class, or gender, need to be assisted in developing an understanding of their own personal weaknesses and, equally important, strengths. A number of authors cited here have also mentioned the work of Howard Gardner (1983) on multiple intelligence. Only when adults with learning disabilities are in touch with their own special talents as well as their limitations can they begin to play the active role appropriate for adult learners in setting goals for their future learning.

3. As they begin to set goals based on self-awareness, an awareness of the breadth of educational and training options available to enable them to pursue personal and economic improvement goals is

essential. Miller et al. (1991) have presented evidence that students' choices regarding postsecondary education are significantly influenced by their familiarity with given options, often through direct contact with representatives of the involved agencies. It is essential that opportunities for such contact be expanded, and that prospective students' or trainees' perspectives not be constricted by professionals operating under limiting assumptions about which kinds of opportunities are appropriate for women, minorities, or working-class individuals.

4. Finally, individuals with learning disabilities from all backgrounds and of varying ability and skill levels need to learn skills for self-advocacy (Ryan & Price, 1992; Smith, 1992). These skills are even more essential for individuals who, due to personal and cultural characteristics, may be assumed to be less capable by some within the educational and work worlds.

SUMMARY

This volume and other recent publications attest to the growing interest in adults with learning disabilities; not yet apparent is the attention to multiculturalism and other sociocultural dimensions reflected in other segments of education. Demographic and social trends related to educational participation and employment suggest that these dimensions will of necessity take on importance in relationship to our study of adults with learning disabilities.

The literature review began with a discussion of the debate that strikes to the very heart of the field of learning disabilities. Several critics (Carrier, 1987; Coles, 1987, 1989; Sleeter, 1987; Poplin & Phillips, 1993) have called our attention to the sociopolitical context within which the field of learning disabilities emerged and the sociocultural context within which individuals are labeled as having learning disabilities. Their arguments support emerging models of learning disabilities, which look beyond the biological source of learning problems in the individual to, or alternatively at, environmental causes of learning problems or factors mediating their manifestation. Similarly, literature on placement of minority children and girls into special education programs for those with mild disabilities challenges the notion that such placement occurs in a social vacuum uncorrupted by biases of either referring teachers or "objective" tests.

The remainder of the chapter focused specifically on literature related to adults with learning disabilities. First, we are reminded that the concerns of adults with learning disabilities are inherently linked more closely to sociocultural contexts by nature of the extension of their needs beyond the academic and into the vocational and social arenas. Although dimensions of race, class, and gender are seldom the focus of discussion in literature on adults with learning disabilities, a closer examination reveals a number of issues. Outcome studies show that family socioeconomic status and gender have an impact on adult outcomes related to postsecondary education participation, employment, and income; at least one study (Werner, 1993) suggests that different factors are predictive of adult success for girls and boys. Otherwise comprehensive discussions of adult evaluation, especially critical for the previously unidentified, pay attention to the lack of availability of standardized tests appropriately normed on adult samples but neglect to mention the measurement issue of culturally biased tests. A review of literature on interventions in the domains of remedial education (literacy, ABE, GED preparation) and higher education and on factors related to employment success indicated that sociocultural issues likewise play a minor role in the discussion, although research findings point with some frequency to the importance of race, gender, family socioeconomic status, and previous educational attainment as influential variables on both the forms of postsecondary education elected and the success experienced in the world of employment. With increasing awareness of these factors, educators may be able to more effectively recruit and serve the individuals often in greatest need of postsecondary education and training.

FUTURE DIRECTIONS

Several directions for the future are suggested by the preceding discussion. These will be organized in terms of primary emphasis on research, assessment, or intervention.

Research

Research is needed in a number of areas. We need to know more about how outcomes of those with learning disabilities diagnosed during childhood are influenced by sociocultural dimensions including race, class, and gender. This may lead to suggestions valuable for special education of youth, because data on employment and adult education participation tell us that those who fail to complete high school are less likely to continue their education as adults and to have lucrative employment. We also need to know much more about factors associated with resilience and success—what helps individuals defy the odds to become successful adults when their personal characteristics and life situations are associated with less positive outcomes? The debate over the impact of labeling should also be investigated through qualitative research exploring the meaning of the "learning disabled" label to people who have been identified during youth and adulthood—what do they see as benefits and disadvantages? Are such labels perceived differently by particular cultural groups, as Harry's (1992) work suggests is true in families of children labeled for special education purposes? Finally, research is needed as we develop new assessment and intervention approaches designed to be more appropriate for adulthood. Is access to various forms of education and training available to all? Are certain approaches effective for recruiting and involving different groups of learners?

Assessment

Appropriate approaches to evaluation of adults need to take into account issues of bias introduced by tests or referring parties. Evaluators need to understand the cultural and linguistic differences that may influence response patterns. In some settings, such as adult literacy and basic education, learners' past negative experiences with assessment and the more general test anxiety experienced by many adults must be considered when deciding the scope and timing of evaluation. Failure to consider such factors may lead to premature program dropout for some or may yield results that do not accurately reflect the individual's performance capability.

Intervention

Several dimensions seem especially critical here. First, interdisciplinary and cross-agency cooperation seems imperative if a full range of professionals and agencies, including those most experienced in working with adults from nonmajority cultures, are to become involved in improving opportunities for education and training. In addition to the typical educational, training, counseling, and vocational rehabilitation agencies, it will be valuable to interact with churches and community-based organizations that serve minority communities. Doing so can increase the likelihood that individuals are aware of opportunities and are likely to take advantage of them. Second, it is essential that various professionals responsible for intervention have the benefit of staff developmental opportunities to increase their understanding of multiculturalism and of the needs and characteristics of adults with learning disabilities. Providing this form of adult education to those who have an impact on the design and delivery of education and training programs will decrease the likelihood that women, minorities, or poor individuals are negatively influenced by diminished expectations on the part of professionals or culturally insensitive instruction or counseling. Finally, programs that are successful with minority adults exhibit a number of common characteristics that symbolize recognition and respect for the cultural habits and learning styles that learners bring (Cumming, 1992; Ross-Gordon et al., 1990). In essence, much work remains to be done as we expand our efforts to serve adults with learning disabilities to ensure that all are equitably served. The task is not insurmountable, but the time is right for change.

NOTES

1. Apps (1988), cites Philip Coombs in defining nonformal, informal, and formal education. Formal education refers to education provided by institutions normally associated with schooling, from preschools through universities. It generally results in some form of credit and credential. Nonformal education, like formal, is organized, sponsored educational activity, although offered outside the established formal education system by such organizations as the military and the workplace. Often it is short term and specific in its purpose. Informal education is that truly lifelong process that recognizes that we learn from our daily experiences at work, with our families, in our homes, and in our communities. It "is neither organized nor planned, yet it contributes to our lifelong learning" (Apps, 1988, p. 18).

REFERENCES

Adelman, H. S. (1989). Beyond the learning mystique: An interactional perspective on learning disabilities. *Journal of Learning Disabilities*, 22(5), 301–304, 328.

Alderson-Gill & Associates. (1989). *Study of literacy and learning disabilities*. Ottawa, Ontario: Learning Disabilities Association of Canada.

Alsalam, N., Fischer, G. E., Ogle, L. T., Rogers, G. T., & Smith, T. M. (1993). *The condition of education, 1993*. Washington DC: National Center for Education Statistics.

Americans with Disabilities Act of 1990, 42 U.S.C.A. §§ 12101 et seq. (West 1993).

Anderson, C. W. (1994). Adult literacy and learning disabilities. In P. J. Gerber & H. B. Reiff (Eds.), *Learning disabilities in adulthood: Persisting problems and evolving issues* (pp. 121–129). Boston: Andover Medical.

Apps, J. W. (1988). *Higher education in a learning society.* San Francisco: Jossey-Bass.

Association for Children with Learning Disabilities. (1986, October). ACLD description: Specific learning disabilities. *ACLD Newsbriefs,* pp. 15–16.

Baldwin, J. (1994). *Who took the GED? GED 1993 statistical report.* Washington, DC: American Council on Education, GED Testing Service.

Banks, J. A., & McGee Banks, C. A. (Eds.). (1989). *Multicultural education: Issues and perspectives.* Boston: Allyn & Bacon.

Bigler, E. P. (1992). The neurobiology and neuropsychology of adult learning disorders. *Journal of Learning Disabilities, 25*(8), 488–506.

Biller, E. F. (1985). *Understanding and guiding the career development of adolescents and young adults with learning disabilities.* Springfield, IL: Charles C. Thomas.

Bowren, F. F. (1981). Teaching the learning disabled adult to read. *Adult Literacy and Basic Education, 5*(3), 179–184.

Brookfield, S. (1986). *Understanding and facilitating adult learning: A comprehensive analysis of principles and effective practice.* San Francisco: Jossey-Bass.

Buchanan, M., & Wolf, J. S. (1986). A comprehensive study of learning disabled adults. *Journal of Learning Disabilities, 19*(1), 34–38.

Camara, W. J. (1992). Fairness and fair use in employment testing: A matter of perspective. In K. F. Geisinger (Ed.), *Psychological testing of Hispanics* (pp. 215–231). Washington, DC: American Psychological Association.

Carl D. Perkins Vocational and Applied Technology Education Act of 1984, Public Law 98-524, 98 Stat. 2435 (1984).

Carrier, J. G. (1987). The politics of early learning disability theory. In B. M. Franklin (Ed.), *Learning disability: Dissenting essays* (pp. 45–66). London: Falmer Press.

Cassara, B. B. (1990). *Adult education in a multicultural society.* London: Routledge.

Chapman, J. B., Vaillancourt, B., & Dobbs, C. S. (1980). *Learning disabilities and the adult student of English as a second language.* Palatine, IL: William Rainey Harper College. (ERIC Document Reproduction Service No. ED 329 137)

Clitheroe, H. C. (1988). *A needs assessment for learning disabled adults.* Irvine, CA: Rehabilitation Center for Brain Dysfunction, Inc. (ERIC Document Reproduction Service No. ED 302 011)

Coles, G. S. (1980). Can ABE students be identified as learning disabled? *Adult Literacy and Basic Education, 4*(3), 170–181.

Coles, G. S. (1987). *The learning mystique: A critical look at learning disabilities.* New York: Pantheon.

Coles, G. S. (1989). Excerpts from the learning mystique: A critical look at learning disabilities. *Journal of Learning Disabilities, 22*(5), 267–273, 277.

Collins, R., & Camblin, L. D. (1983). The politics and science of learning disabilities classification. Implications for Black children. *Contemporary Education, 54*(2), 113–118.

Coombs, P. H., with Prosser, R. C., & Ahmed, M. (1973). *New paths to learning for rural children and youth.* New York: International Council for Educational Development.

Cumming, A. (1992). *Access to literacy for language minority adults.* [ERIC digest]. Washington, DC: National Clearinghouse on Literacy Education. (ERIC Document Reproduction Service No. ED 350 886)

Cummins, J. (1989). A theoretical framework for bilingual special education. *Exceptional Children, 56*(2), 111–119.

Day, J. D. (1992). *Population projections of the United States by age, sex, race, and Hispanic origin: 1992 to 2050.* Washington, DC: U.S. Bureau of the Census.

Denny, V. H. (1992). Access to literacy programs: Perspectives of African American adults. *Theory into Practice, 31*(4), 337–341.

Dodd, J. M., & Rose, P. M. (1991). *Faculty handbook: Students with learning disabilities.* Flaggstaff, AZ: Northern Arizona University, American Indian Rehabilitation Research and Training Center.

Dowdy, C. A., Smith, T. E. C., & Nowell, C. H. (1992). Learning disabilities and vocational rehabilitation. *Journal of Learning Disabilities, 25*(7), 442–447.

Education for All Handicapped Children Act of 1975, Public Law 94-142, 89 Stat. 773 (1975).

Education of the Handicapped Act Amendment of 1983, Public Law 98-109, 97 Stat. 1357 (1983).

Fafard, M., & Haubrich, P. (1981). Vocational and social adjustment of learning disabled young adults: A follow-up study. *Learning Disability Quarterly, 4*(2), 122–130.

Fairweather, J. S., & Shaver, D. M. (1991). Making the transition to postsecondary education and training. *Exceptional Children, 57,* 265–270.

Fourqurean, J. H., Meisgeier, C., Swank, P., & Williams, R. B. (1991). Correlates of postsecondary employment outcomes for young adults with learning disabilities. *Journal of Learning Disabilities, 24*(7), 400–405.

Fradd, S., & Hallman, C. C. (1983). Implications of psychological and educational research for assessment and instruction of culturally and linguistically different students. *Learning Disability Quarterly, 6*(4), 468–478.

Gajar, A. (1992). Adults with learning disabilities: Current and future research priorities. *Journal of Learning Disabilities, 25*(8), 507–519.

Galaburda, A. M. (1989). Learning Disability: Biological, societal, or both? A response to Gerald Coles. *Journal of Learning Disabilities, 22*(5), 278–282, 286.

Gardner, H. (1983). *Frames of mind, the theory of multiple intelligences.* New York: Basic Books.

Geisinger, K. F. (1992). Fairness and selected psychometric issues in the psychological testing of Hispanics. In K. F. Geisinger (Ed.), *Psychological testing of Hispanics* (pp. 17–42). Washington, DC: American Psychological Association.

Gerber, P., Ginsberg, R., & Reiff, H. (1992). Identifying alterable patterns in employment success for highly successful adults with learning disabilities. *Journal of Learning Disabilities, 25*(8), 475–487.

Gerber, P. J., & Reiff, H. B. (1994). *Learning disabilities in adulthood: Persisting problems and evolving issues.* Boston: Andover Medical.

Gibbons, J., Hannigan, B., Harris, C., Russell, L., White, R., & Williams, E. (in collaboration with J. Oddleifson). (1991). Adult dyslexics speak out about dyslexia. *Connections: A Journal of Adult Literacy, 4*, 31–33. (ERIC Document Reproduction Service No. ED 333 205)

Ginsberg, R., Gerber, P. J., & Reiff, H. B. (1994). Employment success for adults with learning disabilities. In P. J. Gerber & H. B. Reiff (Eds.), *Learning disabilities in adulthood: Persisting problems and evolving issues* (pp. 204–213). Boston: Andover Medical.

Giroux, H. (1992). *Border crossings, cultural works and the politics of education.* New York: Routledge.

Gold, P. C. (1981). The Dl-LEA: A remedial approach for nonreaders with a language deficiency handicap. *Adult Literacy and Basic Education, 5*(3), 185–192

Goodman, N. C. (1987). Girls with learning disabilities and their sisters: How are they faring in adulthood? *Journal of Clinical Child Psychology, 16*(4), 290–300.

Hallahan, D. P. (1992). Some thoughts on why the prevalence of learning disabilities has increased. *Journal of Learning Disabilities, 25*(8), 523–528.

Hamilton, E. (1983). Language and reading comprehension: A strategy for planning programs with learning-disabled adults. *Adult Literacy and Basic Education, 7*(3), 129–137.

Hammill, D. D. (1990). On defining learning disabilities: An emerging consensus. *Journal of Learning Disabilities, 23*(2), 74–84.

Hammill, D. D. (1993). A brief look at the learning disabilities movement in the U. S. *Journal of Learning Disabilities, 26*(5), 295–310.

Harry, B. (1992). *Cultural diversity, families, and the special education system.* New York: Teachers College Press.

Hassitt, I. D., & Gurian, A. (1984, August). *The learning disabled girl: A profile.* Paper presented at the Annual Convention of the American Psychological Association, Toronto, Canada. (ERIC Document Reproduction Service No. ED 250 872)

Hayes, E., & Colin, S. A. J. III. (Eds.). (1994). *Confronting racism and sexism.* (New Directions for Adult and Continuing Education No. 61). San Francisco: Jossey-Bass.

Heggoy, S., & Grant, D. (1989, February.). *Issues in the identification of minority college students with learning disabilities.* Paper presented at the meeting of the International Conference of the Association for Children and Adults with Learning Disabilities, Miami Beach, FL. (ERIC Document Reproduction Service No. ED 317 009)

Horn, W. F., O'Donnell, J. P., & Vitulano, L. A. (1983). Long term follow-up studies of learning disabled persons. *Journal of Learning Disabilities, 16*(9), 542–555.

Hoy, C. A., & Gregg, K. N. (1984a). *Appraisal and assessment of learning disabilities, including a special bibliography. Academic assessment and remediation of adults with learning disabilities. A resource series for adult basic education teachers.* Athens, GA: Clarke County Board of Education. (ERIC Document Reproduction Service No. ED 285 356)

Hoy, C. A., & Gregg, K. N. (1984b). *Description and definition of learning disabilities. Academic assessment and remediation of adults with learning disabilities: A resource series for Adult Basic Education teachers.* Athens, GA: Clarke County Board of Education. (ERIC Document Reproduction Service No. 285 354)

Idol-Maestas, L. (1981). Increasing the oral reading performance of a learning disabled adult. *Learning Disability Quarterly, 4*(3), 294–301.

Individuals with Disabilities Education Act of 1990, Public Law 101-476, 104 Stat. 1142 (1990).

Interagency Committee on Learning Disabilities. (1987). *Learning disabilities: A report to the U.S. Congress.* Bethesda, MD: National Institutes of Health. (ERIC Document Reproduction Service No. ED 294 358)

Johnson, D. J. (1987). Principles of assessment and diagnosis. In D. J. Johnson & J. W. Blalock (Eds.), *Adults with learning disabilities: Clinical studies* (pp. 9–30). Orlando: FL: Grune & Stratton.

Johnson, D. J., & Blalock, J. W. (Eds.). (1987). *Adults with learning disabilities: Clinical studies.* Orlando, FL: Grune & Stratton.

Karpinski, M. J., Neubert, D. J., & Graham, S. (1992). A follow-along study of postsecondary outcomes for graduates and dropouts with mild disabilities in a rural setting. *Journal of Learning Disabilities, 26*(6), 386–385.

Kavale, K. A., & Forness, S. R. (1985). *The science of learning disabilities.* San Diego, CA: College Hill Press.

Knowles, M. S., & Associates. (1984). *Andragogy in action.* San Francisco: Jossey-Bass.

Kopp, K. H., Miller, J., & Mulkey, S. W. (1984). Rehabilitation of adults with learning disabilities [Special Issue]. *Journal of Rehabilitation 50*(2).

Kutner, M., Sherman, R., Webb, L., Hermann, R., Tibbetts, J., Hemphill, D., Tardy, D., & Jones, E. (1992). *Study of ABE/ESL instructor training approaches. Phase I, technical report.* Washington, DC: Pelavin Association; San Francisco, CA: San Francisco State University.

Lichtenstein, S. (1993). Transition from school to adulthood: Case studies of adults with learning disabilities. *Exceptional Children, 59*(4), 336–347.

Maheady, L., Towne, R., Algozzine, B., Mercer, J., & Ysseldyke, J. (1983). Minority overrepresentation: A case for alternative practices prior to referral. *Learning Disability Quarterly, 6*(4), 448–456.

Mann, V. (1989). The learning mystique: A fair appraisal, a fruitful new direction? *Journal of Learning Disabilities, 22*(5), 283–286.

McCue, M. (1994). Clinical diagnostic and functional assessment of adults with learning disabilities. In P. J. Gerber & H. B. Reiff (Eds.), *Learning disabilities in adulthood: Persisting problems and evolving issues* (pp. 55–71). Boston: Andover Medical.

Mellard, D. F. (1994). Services for students and learning disabilities in the community colleges. In P. J. Gerber & H. B. Reiff (Eds.), *Learning disabilities in adulthood: Persisting problems and evolving issues* (pp. 130–140). Boston: Andover Medical.

Mezirow, J. (1991). *Transformative dimensions of adult learning*. San Francisco: Jossey-Bass.

Miller, J. L. (1990). Apocalypse or renaissance or something in between? Toward a realistic appraisal of the learning mystique. *Journal of Learning Disabilities, 23*(2), 86–91.

Miller, R. J., Rzonca, C., & Snider, B. (1991). Variables related to the type of postsecondary education experience chosen by young adults with learning disabilities. *Journal of Learning Disabilities, 24*(3), 188–91.

Minskoff, E. H. (1994). Post-secondary education and vocational training: Keys to success for adults with learning disabilities. In P. J. Gerber & H. Reiff (Eds.), *Learning disabilities in adulthood: Persisting problems and evolving issues* (pp. 111–120). Boston: Andover Medical.

Morrison, A. M. (1992). *The new leaders: Guidelines on leadership diversity in America*. San Francisco: Jossey-Bass.

National Joint Committee on Learning Disabilities. (1981). *Learning disabilities: Issues on definition*. Unpublished manuscript. (Available from the Orton Dyslexia Society, 8600 LaSalle Road, Chester Building, Suite 382, Baltimore, MD) (Reprinted in *Journal of Learning Disabilities, 20*, 107–108).

National Joint Committee on Learning Disabilities. (1986). Adults with learning disabilities: A call to action. *Learning Disability Quarterly, 9*(2), 164–168.

National Joint Committee on Learning Disabilities. (1987). Adults with learning disabilities: A call to action. *Journal of Learning Disabilities, 20*, 172–174.

Neufeldt, H. G., & McGee, L. (Eds.). (1990). *Education of the African American adult: An historical overview*. New York: Greenwood Press.

Ochoa, A. M., Pacheco, R., & Omark, D. R. (1988). Addressing the learning disability needs of limited-English proficient students: Beyond language and race issues. *Learning Disability Quarterly, 11*(3), 257–264.

O'Connor, S. C., & Spreen, O. (1988). The relationship between parents' socioeconomic status and education level, and adult occupational and educational achievement of children with learning disabilities. *Journal of Learning Disabilities, 21*(3), 148–53.

O'Donnell, M. P., & Wood, M. (1981). Adult learning problems: A critique of the London procedure. *Adult Literacy and Basic Education, 5*(4), 243–249.

Ogbu, J. U. (1978). *Minority education and caste: The American system in cross-cultural perspective*. New York: Academic Press.

Parsons, J. E. (1982). Sex differences in attributions and learned helplessness. *Sex Roles. A Journal of Research, 8*(4), 421–432.

Patton, J. R., & Polloway, E. A. (1982). The learning disabled: The adult years. *Topics in Learning and Learning Disabilities, 2*(3), 79–83.

Patton, J. R., & Polloway, E. A. (1992). Learning disabilities: The challenges of adulthood. *Journal of Learning Disabilities, 25*(7), 410–415, 447.

Polloway, E., Smith, J. D., & Patton, J. R. (1988). Learning disabilities: An adult development perspective. *Learning Disability Quarterly, 11*(3), 265–272.

Poplin, M., & Phillips, L. (1993). Sociocultural aspects of language and literacy: Issues facing educators of students with learning disabilities. *Learning Disability Quarterly, 16,* 245–254.

Poplin, M. J., & Wright, P. (1983). The concept of cultural pluralism: Issues in special education. *Learning Disability Quarterly, 6*(4), 367–71.

Rawson, M. (1968). *Developmental language disability: Adult accomplishments of dyslexic boys.* Baltimore: Johns Hopkins University Press.

Ross, J. M. (1987). Learning disabled adults: Who are they and what do we do with them? *Lifelong Learning, 11*(3), 4–7, 11.

Ross, J. M., & Smith, J. O. (1990). Adult basic educator's perceptions of learning disabilities. *Journal of Reading, 33*(5), 340–347.

Ross-Gordon, J. M. (1989). *Adults with learning disabilities: An overview for the adult educator.* (Information Series No. 337). Columbus, OH: ERIC Clearinghouse on Adult, Career, & Vocational Education. (ERIC Document Reproduction Service No. ED 315 664)

Ross-Gordon, J. M., Martin, L. G., & Briscoe, D. B. (1990). *Serving culturally diverse populations.* (New Directions for Adult and Continuing Education No. 48). San Francisco: Jossey-Bass.

Rourke, B. P. (1989). Cole's learning mystique: The good, the bad, and the irrelevant. *Journal of Learning Disabilities, 22*(5), 274–277.

Ryan, A. G., & Price, L. (1992). Adults with learning disabilities in the 1990s. *Intervention in School and Clinic, 28*(1), 6–15, 18–20.

Schoem, D., Frankel, L., Zuñiga, S., & Lewis, E. (1993). *Multicultural teaching in the university.* Westport, CN: Praeger.

Shaw, S. F., Mcguire, J. M., & Brinckerhoff, L. C. (1994). College and university programming. In P. J. Gerber & H. B. Reiff (Eds.), *Learning disabilities in adulthood: Persisting problems and evolving issues* (pp. 141–151). Boston: Andover Medical.

Siegel, S., & Gaylord-Ross, R. (1991). Factors associated with employment success among youths with learning disabilities. *Journal of Learning Disabilities, 24*(1), 40–47.

Sitlington, P. L., Frank, A. R., & Carson, R. (1992). Adult adjustment among high school graduates with mild disabilities. *Exceptional Children, 59*(3), 221–233.

Slate, J. R., & Jones, C. H. (1994). Learning from problems in special education II: Labeling of and intervening with adults with learning disabilities. *Journal of the National Association for Adults with Special Learning Needs, 4*(1), 26–34.

Sleeter, C. E. (1986). Learning Disabilities: A social construction of a special education category. *Exceptional Children, 53*(1), 46–54.

Sleeter, C. (1987). Literacy, definitions of learning disabilities, and social control. In B. M. Franklin (Ed.), *Learning disabilities: Dissenting essays* (pp. 67–87). London: Falmer Press.

Sleeter, C. (Ed.). (1991). *Empowerment through multicultural education.* Albany: State University of New York Press.

Smith, J. O. (1992). Falling through the cracks: Rehabilitation services for adults with learning disabilities. *Exceptional Children, 58*(5), 451–460.

Smith, S. L. (1991). *Succeeding against the odds: How the learning disabled can realize their promise.* New York: Jeremy P. Tarcher/Perigree Books.

Snyder, T. D., & Hoffman, C. M. (1993). *Digest of education statistics, 1993.* Washington, DC: National Center for Education Statistics.

Spekman, N. J., Herman, K., & Vogel, S. (1993). Risk and resilience in individuals with learning disabilities: A challenge to the field. *Learning Disabilities Research and Practice, 8*(1), 59–65.

Stanovich, K. E. (1989). Learning disabilities in a broader context. *Journal of Learning Disabilities, 22*(5), 287–291, 297.

Tierney, W. G. (1993). *Building communities of difference: Higher education in the 21st century.* Westport, CN: Bergin & Garvey.

Tomlinson, S. (1982). *The sociology of special education.* London: Routledge and Kegan Paul.

Travis, G. (1979). An adult educator views learning disabilities. *Adult Literacy and Basic Education, 8*(8), 16–18.

United States Office of Education. (1977). Definition and criteria for defining students as learning disabled. 42 *Fed. Reg.* 65,083. Washington, DC: U.S. Government Printing Office.

Valdes, K. A., Williamson, C. L., & Wagner, M. M. (1990). *The national longitudinal transition study of special education students. Statistical almanac, Volume 2: Youth categorized as learning disabled.* Menlo Park, CA: SRI International. (ERIC Document Reproduction Service No. ED 324 894)

Vogel, S. A. (1989). Special considerations in the development of models for diagnosis of adults with learning disabilities. In L. B. Silver (Ed.), *The assessment of learning disabilities: Preschool through adulthood.* (pp. 111–134) Boston: Little, Brown.

Vogel, S. A. (1990). Gender differences in intelligence, language, visual motor abilities, and academic achievement in students with learning disabilities. A review of literature. *Journal of Learning Disabilities, 23*(1), 44–52.

Vogel, S. A., Hruby, P. J., & Adelman, P. B. (1993). Educational and psychological factors in successful and unsuccessful college students with learning disabilities. *Learning Disabilities Research and Practice, 8*(1), 35–43.

Vogel, S. A., & Walsh, P. C. (1987). Gender differences in cognitive abilities of learning disabled females and males. *Annals of Dyslexia, 37,* 142–165.

Wagner, M. (1989). *Youth with disabilities during transition: An overview of descriptive findings from the National Longitudinal Transition Study.* Menlo Park: CA: SRI International.

Werner, E. (1993). Risk and resilience in individuals with learning disabilities: Lessons learned from the Kauai longitudinal study. *Learning Disabilities Research and Practice, 8*(1), 28–34.

White, W. J. (1992). The postschool adjustment of persons with learning disabilities. Current status and future projections. *Journal of Learning Disabilities, 25*(7), 448–456.

White, W. J., Alley, G. R., Deshler, D. D., Schumaker, J. B., Warner, M. M., & Clark, R. C. (1982). Are there learning disabilities after high school? *Exceptional Children, 49*(3), 273–274.

Wiener, J., & Siegel, L. (1992). A Canadian perspective on learning disabilities. *Journal of Learning Disabilities, 25*(6), 340–350.

6

Neurobiological Research Specific to the Adult Population with Learning Disabilities

CYNTHIA A. RICCIO
GEORGE W. HYND

A diagnosis of a learning disability typically requires normal intelligence, a significant discrepancy between measured ability and achievement, and the absence of other conditions that may produce the observed delay. Although some adults have learned to compensate for their disability (e.g., Flowers, 1993; Gross-Glenn, Jallad, Novoa, Helgren-Lempesis, & Lubbs, 1990), developmental learning disabilities are believed to be stable and to persist into adulthood (e.g., Flowers, 1993; Gross-Glenn et al., 1990). In particular, adults with a childhood history of reading disability (dyslexia) continue to show deficits in phonological aspects of reading and often concurrently demonstrate poor spelling (Pennington, Lefly, Van Orden, Bookman, & Smith, 1987). These deficits are often manifested in poor nonword reading (Gross-Glenn et al., 1990; Pennington et al., 1987). Further, there is evidence that adults with dyslexia who eventually are able to master the reading process do so by adopting different strategies than those used by individuals without a childhood history of dyslexia (Gross-Glenn et al., 1990; Olson, 1985). Also, they frequently demonstrate weaknesses in the automaticity (speed) with which they are able to apply phonological skills (Lefly, 1991).

Historically, it has been presumed that these deficits result from a disruption in underlying neurological systems (Hynd & Cohen, 1983; Hynd, Marshall, & Gonzalez, 1991). Although the notion that learning disabilities may be attributable to deficient neurological processes continues to elicit controversy (e.g., Shaywitz, Escobar, Shaywitz, Fletcher, & Makuch, 1992), indications of heritable forms of learning disability (Pennington et al., 1991; Smith, Kimberling, Pennington, & Lubs, 1983; Smith, Pennington, Kimberling, & Ing, 1990) would support a neurobiological etiology. In this regard, the study of brain–behavior relations is viewed as important in improving the diagnosis and treatment of learning disabilities (Leonard et al., 1993). Until recently, the behavioral evidence for the presumed neurological origins of specific learning disability has been predominantly correlative (Golden, 1982; Hynd & Willis, 1988). With improved technology, advances have been made in the understanding of the brain–behavior relationships in learning disabilities.

The majority of neuropsychological and neurobiological investigations have focused on learning disability specific to reading or dyslexia, whereas less attention has been paid to learning disabilities in mathematics. Thus, this chapter focuses on studies of brain structure and function in adults with reading disabilities as they relate to neurobiological models. Consistent with the terminology used in neurophysiological and neurological arenas, the term "dyslexia" will be used throughout the text.

STUDIES OF BRAIN MORPHOLOGY

Cerebral Asymmetry

Postmortem and neuroimaging studies (summarized in Tables 6.1 and 6.2) have provided direct evidence as to how neurological substrates differ in the brains of adults with dyslexia. Consistent with research on children with dyslexia (e.g., Hynd, Semrud-Clikeman, Lorys, Novey, & Eliopulos, 1990), variations in cerebral asymmetry have been reported for adults with dyslexia (e.g., Galaburda & Kemper, 1979; Galaburda, Sherman, Rosen, Aboitiz, & Geschwind, 1985). Both computed tomography (CT) and postmortem studies (Geschwind & Levitsky, 1968; Rubens, Mahuwold, & Hutton, 1976) document that about 66% of normal brains are asymmetric (left greater than right), favoring the left planum temporale (see Figure 6.1).

Normal asymmetry (left greater than right) has also been found in the anterior speech region (Falzi, Perrone, & Vignolo, 1982), auditory cortex (Galaburda, Sanides, & Geschwind, 1978), and posterior thalamus (Eidelberg & Galaburda, 1982). In contrast to other regions of the brain, however, in 75% of normal brains, the volume of the right frontal region exceeds that of the left (Duara et al., 1991; Weinberger, Luchins, Morihisa, & Wyatt, 1982).

CT and magnetic resonance imaging (MRI) studies have provided evidence that ties deviations in these normal patterns of asymmetry to the dyslexic syndrome (Hier, LeMay, Rosenberger, & Perlo, 1978; LeMay, 1981; Rosenberger & Hier, 1980; Rumsey et al., 1986). Dyslexics would appear to have a higher incidence of symmetrical or reversed posterior asymmetry than is found in control populations with only 10% to 50% of dyslexic brains showing the left greater than right asymmetry (Hier et al., 1978; Rumsey et al., 1986). Evidence suggests that the symmetry found in the brains of dyslexics is not due to a smaller left but to a larger right hemisphere and is possibly the result of reduced neuronal loss in the right hemisphere (Galaburda et al., 1985). Figure 6.2 provides a comparison of MRIs for an adult without dyslexia and one with dyslexia.

TABLE 6.1. Postmortem Brain Studies of Adult Dyslexics

Study	Subjects	Neuropathological findings
Galaburda & Kemper (1979)	$n = 1$	Polymicrogyria in left posterior sylvian area; neurons in cell-free layer of left auditory cortex; minute cellular abnormalities throughout the left hemisphere; thalamic abnormality; symmetrical plana.
Galaburda et al. (1985)	$n = 3$	Focal dysplasias in all three subjects, predominantly in the left temporal, left frontal, and right frontal areas; symmetrical plana in all three subjects; thalamic abnormality in two of three subjects; enlarged thymus in one subject; polymicrogyria in anterior left temporal lobe in one subject.
Humphreys, Kaufman, & Galaburda (1990)	$n = 3$	Focal ectopias in all three subjects in differing areas (bilateral frontal and left temporal, throughout both hemispheres, and primarily in the right hemisphere); symmetrical plana in all three subjects; vascular malformation in left frontal region in two of three subjects.
Livingstone et al. (1991)	$n = 4$	Disorganization in subcortical pathways, specific to the lateral geniculate of the thalamus.

Note. Modified and updated from Hynd, Marshall, and Gonzalez (1991).

TABLE 6.2. Brain Imaging Studies of Adults with Dyslexia

Study	Subjects	Type	Neuropathological findings
Hier et al. (1978)	24 dyslexics	CT	Subjects with reversed posterior asymmetry had lower Verbal IQ; 67% had symmetry or reversed (L < R) posterior asymmetry.
Rosenberger & Hier (1980)	53 dyslexics	CT	42% of dyslexics had reversed asymmetry (L < R) of posterior region; asymmetry index correlated with Verbal–Performance IQ discrepancy ($r = .38, p < .02$).
LeMay (1981)	27 dyslexics; 317 controls	CT	33% of dyslexics had normal (L > R) posterior asymmetry compared to 70% of right-handed controls.
Rumsey et al. (1986)	10 dyslexics	MRI	90% of dyslexics showed symmetry of posterior regions.
Parkins, Roberts, Reinarz, & Varney (1987)	44 dyslexics; 254 controls	CT	Concluded that reversed posterior asymmetries are not characteristic of right-handed dyslexics; left-handed dyslexics evidence more symmetry.
Larsen et al. (1990)	19 dyslexics; 19 controls	MRI	70% of dyslexics evidenced symmetry of the planum temporale as compared to 30% of the controls; associated with significant phonological coding deficits.
Duara et al. (1991)	21 dyslexics; 29 controls	MRI	Reversed asymmetry in the mid-posterior/angular gyrus region of dyslexics; splenium of corpus callosum larger in dyslexics, especially in females; genu in female dyslexics larger.
Leonard et al. (1993)	9 dyslexics; 10 relatives; 12 controls	MRI	Group with dyslexia had exaggerated asymmetries of temporal and parietal banks; differences due to significant shift of right planar tissue from temporal to parietal bank.

Note. Modified and updated from Hynd, Marshall, and Gonzalez, (1991).

Regions of Language Processing

Differences in brain morphology as well as brain function have been found in subjects with dyslexia specific to those regions of the brains implicated in language processing (e.g., Flowers, Wood, & Naylor, 1991; Wood, Flowers, Buchsbaum, & Tallal, 1991). In particular, stud-

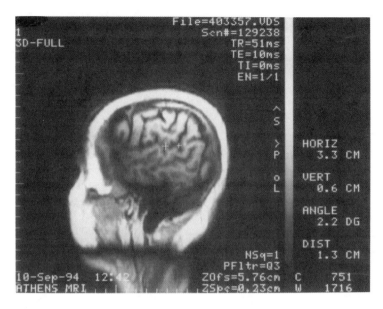

FIGURE 6.1. Sagittal view of the brain as shown on lateral sagittal MRI scan. The temporal bank of the left planum temporale is marked as being the region between the two crosshatches. As can be seen in this scan, the planum temporale is 1.3 cm long.

ies completed in the last decade have, with some consistency, implicated a left hemisphere functional deficit for dyslexia (Flowers, 1993) with anomalous neural organization as well as atypical symmetry of the right and left hemispheres. Following the dual-route model of reading development (Frith, 1985), dysfunction of the left hemisphere would be consistent with residual phonological deficits (Gross-Glenn et al., 1990; Lefly, 1991).

Based on the importance of the central language centers (Geschwind, 1974; Geschwind & Galaburda, 1985), a number of studies have focused on the morphology of these centers in particular. Consistent with results of Galaburda et al. (1985), findings in a recent study using MRI demonstrate evidence of significantly greater right planum temporale surface area in subjects with dyslexia, whereas no differences were found in the left hemisphere planum as compared to normals (Wood & Flowers, 1991, cited in Flowers, 1993). In contrast, Galaburda et al. (1985) visually inspected the plana in dyslexics at autopsy and concluded that the plana were bilaterally larger in area.

The results of Leonard et al. (1993) conflicted somewhat with identified differences in symmetry of structure as characteristic of

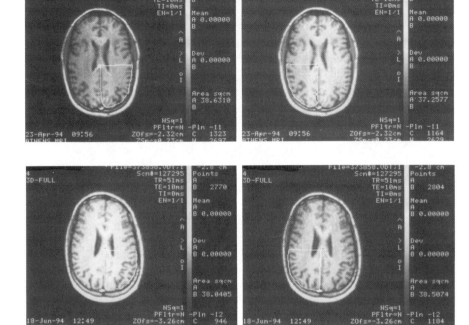

FIGURE 6.2. By convention MRI images are viewed from the bottom of the brain looking up. Consequently right and left are reversed. MRI of normal adult male (top) with posterior asymmetry (L > R); left posterior = 38.6310 cm²; right = 37.2577 cm². MRI of dyslexic adult male (bottom) with posterior symmetry (L = R); left = 38.5074 cm²; right = 38.0405 cm².

dyslexia in adults. Using MRI and different methods of measurement, they found that the group with dyslexia had exaggerated asymmetries of the temporal and parietal banks. Results indicated that the differences were due to a significant shift of right planar tissue from the temporal to the parietal bank (Leonard et al., 1993).

The area of the plana is not the only area in which differences in symmetry were found. Using MRI, Duara et al. (1991) investigated neuroanatomical differences specific to the midposterior segment that would correspond to the angular gyrus in 21 dyslexics and 29 control subjects. Results indicated that in contrast to the relatively symmetrical findings in this area for controls, the group with dyslexia exhibited asymmetry (right greater than left). Based on this and other findings, Duara et al. (1991) suggested that anatomical differences in the region of the angular gyrus are also implicated in dyslexia. Taken together, these findings would provide support for the neuroanatomical components of the Wernicke–Geschwind model (Mayeux & Kandel, 1985).

Cytoarchitectonic Studies

Autopsy studies have further identified the presence of a disproportionate clustering of cellular abnormalities (focal dysplasias) in the left planum temporale in those subjects with a history of dyslexia as compared to normal subjects (Galaburda et al., 1985) In addition, cortical anomalies have been found in the left inferior frontal and right frontal regions in adults with dyslexia (Galaburda et al., 1985). A higher incidence of cerebral anomalies (e.g., missing or duplicated gyri bilaterally in the planum and parietal operculum) have also been identified (Leonard et al., 1993). In another autopsy study, Livingstone, Rosen, Drislane, and Galaburda (1991) identified disorganization in the subcortical pathways, specific to the lateral geniculate nucleus of the thalamus. Thus, cytoarchitectonic studies support the finding of a higher than normal incidence of numerous focal dysplasias preferentially involving the left frontal, left perisylvian, and right frontal regions (Galaburda & Kemper, 1979; Galaburda et al., 1985; Humphreys, Kaufman, & Galaburda, 1990) as well as bilaterally in the temporal and parietal lobes (Leonard et al., 1993) with preliminary evidence of subcortical differences (Livingstone et al., 1991).

STUDIES OF BRAIN FUNCTION

Through the use of positron emission tomography (PET) and regional cerebral blood flow (rCBF) (summarized in Table 6.3), in addition to the information obtained from CT, MRI, and postmortem studies, more is now known about brain functioning relative to the reading process in dyslexia (Gross-Glenn et al., 1986; Gross-Glenn et al., 1991). In resting states or with nondemanding tasks, no differences were found on cerebral flow or electroencephalogram patterns (Fein et al., 1986; Rumsey et al., 1987; Yingling, Galin, Fein, Peltzmann, & Davenport, 1986). This may, however, be due to the subtlety of the neural anomalies that are thought to underlie dyslexia (Gross-Glenn et al., 1991).

Activation during Cognitive Functions

Results of initial PET and rCBF studies of cognitive functions (e.g., serial word reading) indicate that reading depends on neural activity in a widely distributed set of specific brain regions (Gross-Glenn et al., 1991; Hynd, Hynd, Sullivan, & Kingsbury, 1987; Petersen, Fox, Posner, Mintun, & Raichle, 1989). For example, in comparing patterns of rCBF in two variants of reading disability (surface and deep

TABLE 6.3. Studies of Brain Function in Adults with Dyslexia

Study	Subjects	Method	Neuropathological findings
Gross-Glenn et al. (1986)	25 dyslexics; 25 controls	PET	Bilaterally decreased levels of regional cerebral glucose in dyslexics during reading.
Hynd et al. (1987)	2 dyslexics; 2 controls	rCBF	Differing patterns of activation evidenced for normals, the dyslexic with phonological deficits, and the dyslexic with impaired sight word vocabulary.
Rumsey et al. (1987)	14 dyslexics; 14 controls	rCBF	Dyslexic group showed increased hemispheric asymmetry (L > R) on semantic classification and reduced anteroposterior gradient on line orientation as compared to controls.
Flowers et al. (1991)	*Study 1:* 69 controls *Study 2:* 33 dyslexics; 27 borderline; 23 controls	rCBF	Childhood reading ability found to be inversely correlated with focal activation in more posterior, temporoparietal area of cortex.
Gross-Glenn et al. (1991)	25 dyslexics; 25 controls	PET	Decreased or no asymmetry in activation of the frontal and occipital lobes; reversed or no asymmetry in the lingual lobule; no difference from normal on temporoparietal activation.
Wood et al. (1991)	10 dyslexics; 10 controls	PET	Metabolism in left caudate of dyslexics correlated with left inferior parietal lobule rather than with the left temporal lobe.
Rumsey et al. (1992)	14 dyslexics; 14 controls	PET	Dyslexic men failed to activate left temporoparietal cortex on rhyme detection; no significant difference from controls during rest or attentional testing.
Rumsey et al. (1994)	15 dyslexics; 20 controls	PET	At rest, dyslexics showed reduced blood flow in left parietal region near angular/supramarginal gyri; during syntactic processing, both groups demonstrated activation of the left middle to anterior temporal and inferior frontal regions.

dyslexia), differing patterns were identified depending on the nature of the reading disability (Hynd et al., 1987). Specifically, the adult dyslexic who demonstrated significant deficits in sight word recognition and a reliance on phonological processing exhibited less activation in the right posterior cortex as compared to normals. In contrast, the dyslexic who demonstrated deficits in phonological processing exhibited less activation bilaterally as compared to normals (Hynd et al., 1987). Although the sample size was small, the preliminary investigation of Hynd et al. (1987) implicated significant interaction of the right and left hemispheres in normal reading.

In a study using transcranial magnetic stimulation (TMS), Coslett and Monsul (1994) found that TMS of the right hemisphere disrupted oral reading, further demonstrating involvement of the right hemisphere in reading. Other studies have found notable differences, particularly in the occipital- and frontal-lobe regions when PET studies have compared adults with dyslexia to adults with no history of childhood dyslexia on single-word reading tasks (Gross-Glenn et al., 1991). These differences will be reviewed briefly by area.

Prefrontal Region

Oral reading requires a temporal synthesis of information from several sensory modalities as well as a sequential integration of oculomotor and articulatory activity. The prefrontal cortex receives processed information from visual, auditory, and somatosensory cortices. Furthermore, there is evidence from both monkey and human studies that this region has an important role in cross-modal and temporal integration of ongoing behavior (Fuster, Bauer, & Jervey, 1985). Normal readers tended toward higher right than left prefrontal activity; however, prefrontal activity was symmetrical for dyslexics (Gross-Glenn et al., 1991). Of some interest, this finding of left less than right (L < R) asymmetry anteriorly for activation in normals and symmetry in dyslexics corresponds to the L < R asymmetry in normals and symmetry (L = R) in dyslexics as reported in a morphological (MRI) study by Hynd et al. (1990).

Temporoparietal Regions

Using an auditory phonological task (rhyme detection) with PET, Rumsey et al. (1992) found that adults with severe developmental dyslexia failed to activate the left temporoparietal regions activated by controls. On the rhyming task, control subjects demonstrated activation in the left parietal region near the angular gyrus, the left middle temporal region (e.g., Wernicke's region), the left posterior frontal regions, the right middle temporal, and right parietal area. In contrast, dyslexic subjects showed significantly less activation than controls in the left parietal and left middle temporal, greater activation in the left rolandic region, and decreased blood flow in the left posterior frontal and right anterior regions relative to resting state. Based on rCBF studies, the left temporal blood flow has been found to be significantly positively correlated with single-word and paragraph reading, spelling, nonword reading, and rapid naming while the angular gyrus flow has been found to be significantly negatively correlated with oral and silent reading comprehension (Flowers, 1993). Thus, studies using rCBF data and language-related tasks provide evidence for a significant relationship between left temporal and parietal blood flow and childhood-diagnosed dyslexia regardless of whether the reading difficulties have been remediated or persist (Flowers et al., 1991).

Insular Region

The left insular region has historically been associated with language disturbance. The relative importance of the insular region in dyslexia is implicated in PET studies of regional cerebral glucose metabolism (rCMRglc) in which dyslexics show bilaterally decreased levels of rCMRglc during reading as compared to normals (Gross-Glenn et al., 1986).

Caudate and Parietal Areas

Wood et al. (1991) used PET with a cognitive-challenge task consisting of a continuous performance auditory phonemic discrimination task. The adults with a childhood history of dyslexia did more poorly on this task than normals. Of particular interest, however, was the finding that in subjects with dyslexia, metabolism in the left caudate was not highly or uniformly correlated with other brain regions as it was with normal subjects. The linkage in the dyslexics appeared to be with the left inferior parietal lobule, while in the normals the left caudate metabolism correlated best with the left temporal lobe. This finding would suggest that the differences that underlie reading difficulties may be longstanding (Wood et al., 1991).

Occipital Lobe

It has also been determined that single-word reading results in bilateral metabolic activation of lateral extrastriate regions in normals but not in dyslexics (Gross-Glenn et al., 1991). In normal adults, there appears to be a tendency toward asymmetry of metabolic activity in the occipital lobe favoring the left hemisphere as a whole as well as in the lingual lobule. In contrast, adults with a childhood history of dyslexia showed little asymmetry over the occipital lobe and asymmetry of activity in the lingual lobule favoring the right hemisphere (Gross-Glenn et al., 1991). These findings correspond well with the reduced structural posterior asymmetry that has been observed in CT, MRI, and postmortem studies of dyslexics' brains (Galaburda & Kemper, 1979; Galaburda et al., 1985; Hier et al., 1978).

ELECTROPHYSIOLOGICAL STUDIES

Although numerous childhood electrophysiological studies have been conducted (e.g., Duffy, Denckla, Bartels, & Sandini, 1980; Harter, Diering, & Wood, 1988), fewer studies have been done with adults with dyslexia. One study, however, replicated the child visual evoked potential (EP) data with adults (Naylor, Wood, & Flowers, 1990). In particular, results indicated a fairly generalized bilateral attenuation of wave form amplitude which was independent of reading improvement from childhood to adulthood. This would further suggest an enduring brain profile that may underlie early reading problems (Flowers, 1993).

Using EPs and focusing on callosal function, Markee, Moore, Brown, and Theberge (1994) found that their sample of 21 adults with dyslexia demonstrated significantly slower interhemispheric transfer times than did the group of 21 controls, particularly for P1 and N1 wave form components. The dyslexic group made significantly more errors on the letter-matching task and were slower than the controls. The conclusion reached was that callosal dysfunction may be a significant contributor to at least some forms of reading disability (Markee et al., 1994).

In another study, Livingstone et al. (1991) found absent or slowed event related potentials (ERPs) to low contrast, pattern-reversal stimuli in four subjects with dyslexia. These results, unlike other studies, implicated slowed visual processing in at least some individuals with a childhood history of reading difficulty, thus reaffirming the widely distributed functional system involved in reading.

DISCUSSION

Results of PET scan studies suggest that neural activity accompanying reading in adult dyslexics differs from that of normals in the lingual regions as well as in the prefrontal region. Differences in these regions would not be predicted based on lesion sites known to be associated with acquired dyslexia (Benson & Geschwind, 1969; Dejerine, 1891, 1892), suggesting a pathophysiology that is quite separate from that for acquired dyslexia (Gross-Glenn et al., 1991).

At the same time, however, research indicates consistency in patterns of structural anomalies and functional differences in children and adults with dyslexia. Furthermore, genetic studies suggest a continuity between children and adults with reading disabilities particularly as related to phonological deficits (Pennington et al., 1987). Taken together, these findings support presumed morphological differences in this population and, thus, a neurobiological basis for dyslexia (Hynd & Semrud-Clikeman, 1989).

Both adults and children with dyslexia consistently have been found to have smaller regions in language areas (left planum, bilateral insular regions, and right anterior region). The fact that there were no significant differences found in total brain area and the identification of focal dysplasias in the left planum temporale (Galaburda et al., 1985) suggest that this regional variation in the morphological features of the brain in dyslexics is due to a more specific deviation in brain ontogeny (Hynd & Semrud-Clikeman, 1989). Results support the notion that the mechanism of corticogenesis, and possibly the processes associated with the elimination of unwanted cells, is implicated in dyslexia. Specifically, these studies would seem to implicate some deviation in normal patterns of neuronal migration and maturation during the fifth to seventh month of fetal gestation (Hynd et al., 1990).

In summarizing the neurophysiological and neurological literature, it is clear that there is no unitary neurological factor but rather a combination of structural or functional differences (Semrud-Clikeman, Hynd, Novey, & Eliopulos, 1991). The number of possible combinations results in a somewhat heterogeneous group when referring to adults with dyslexia as a whole. The variation in impaired processes as well as recent neurophysiological research would support the conceptualization that reading involves a widely distributed functional system, with any impairment or developmental deficit in the system resulting in distinct patterns of reading failure (Duffy, Denckla, Bartels, Sandini, & Kiessling, 1980; Hynd & Hynd, 1984). The interactive activation model of reading development (e.g., Adams, 1990; Chase & Tallal, 1991) would be consistent with this conceptualization.

Additional investigation into the familial transmission of dyslexia as well as continued investigation into the brain–behavior relationships is needed. As more is learned about the nature of the various forms of dyslexia, predictability, and thus early intervention, will be facilitated. In this regard, investigation of the compensatory processes utilized by adults with a childhood history of dyslexia is needed.

ACKNOWLEDGMENT

This work was supported in part by a grant (R01-HD26890-02) awarded to the second author (G. W. H.) from the National Institute of Child Health and Human Development (NICHHD), National Institutes of Health (NIH).

REFERENCES

Adams, M. J. (1990). *Beginning to read: Thinking and learning about print.* Cambridge, MA: MIT Press.

Benson, D. F., & Geschwind, N. (1969). The alexias. In P. J. Vinken & G. W. Bruyn (Eds.), *Handbook of clinical neurology* (Vol. 4). Amsterdam: North-Holland.

Chase, C. H., & Tallal, P. (1991). Cognitive models of developmental reading disorders. In J. E. Obrzut & G. W. Hynd (Eds.), *Neuropsychological foundations of learning disabilities* (pp. 199–240). San Diego, CA: Academic Press.

Coslett, H. B., & Monsul, N. (1994). Reading with the right hemisphere: Evidence from transcranial magnetic stimulation. *Brain and Language, 46*, 198–211.

Dejerine, J. (1891). Sur un cas de cécité verbale avec agraphie, suivi d'autopsie. *Mémoires de la Société de Biologie, 3*, 197–201.

Dejerine, J. (1892). Contribution à l'étude anatomopathologique des différentes variétés de cécité verbale. *Comptes Rendus des Séances de la Société de Biologie, 4*, 61–90.

Duara, R., Kushch, A., Gross-Glenn, K., Barker, W., Jallad, B., Pascal, S., Loewenstein, J. A., Sheldon, J., Rabin, M., Levin, B., & Lubs, H. (1991). Neuroanatomic differences between dyslexic and normal readers on magnetic resonance imaging scans. *Archives of Neurology, 48*, 410–416.

Duffy, F. H., Denckla, M. B., Bartels, P. H., & Sandini, G. (1980). Dyslexia: Regional differences in brain electrical activity by topographical mapping. *Annals of Neurology, 7*, 412–420.

Duffy, F. H., Denckla, M. B., Bartels, P. H., Sandini, G., & Kiessling, L. S. (1980). Dyslexia: Automated diagnosis by computerized classification of brain electrical activity. *Annals of Neurology, 7*, 421–428.

Eidelberg, D., & Galaburda, A. M. (1982). Symmetry and asymmetry in the human posterior thalamus: I. Cytoarchitectonic analysis in normal persons. *Archives of Neurology, 39*, 325–332.

Falzi, G., Perrone, P., & Vignolo, L. A. (1982). Right left asymmetry in anterior speech region. *Archives of Neurology, 39*, 239–240.

Fein, G., Galin, D., Yingling, C. D., Johnstone, J., Davenport, L., & Herron,

J. (1986). EEG spectra in dyslexic and control boys during resting conditions. *Electroencephalography and Clinical Neurophysiology, 63*, 87–97.

Flowers, D. L. (1993). Brain basis for dyslexia: A summary of work in progress. *Journal of Learning Disabilities, 26*, 575–582.

Flowers, D. L., Wood, F. B., & Naylor, C. E. (1991). Regional cerebral blood flow correlates of language processes in reading disability. *Archives of Neurology, 48*, 637–643.

Frith, U. (1985). Beneath the surface of developmental dyslexia. In K. E. Patterson, J. C. Marshall, & M. Coltheart (Eds.), *Surface dyslexia* (pp. 301–329). London: Erlbaum.

Fuster, J. M., Bauer, R. H., & Jervey, J. (1985). Functional interactions between inferotemporal and prefrontal cortex in a cognitive task. *Brain Research, 330*, 299–307.

Galaburda, A. M., & Kemper, T. L. (1979). Cytoarchitectonic abnormalities in developmental dyslexia: A case study. *Annals of Neurology, 6*, 94–100.

Galaburda, A. M., Sanides, F., & Geschwind, N. (1978). Human brain: Cytoarchitectonic left–right asymmetries in the temporal speech region. *Archives of Neurology, 35*, 812–817.

Galaburda, A. M., Sherman, G. F., Rosen, G. D., Aboitz, F., & Geschwind, N. (1985). Developmental dyslexia: Four consecutive patients with cortical anomalies. *Annals of Neurology, 18*, 222–233.

Geschwind, N. (1974). The development of the brain and the evolution of language. In N. Geschwind (Ed.), *Selected papers on language and the brain* (pp. 122–146). Dordrecht, The Netherlands: D. Reidel.

Geschwind, N., & Galaburda, A. (1985). Cerebral lateralization: Biological mechanisms, associations, and pathology. *Archives of Neurology, 43*, 428–459.

Geschwind, N., & Levitsky, W. (1968). Human brain: Left–right asymmetries in temporal speech region. *Science, 161*, 186–187.

Golden, G. S. (1982). Neurobiological correlates of learning disabilities. *Annals of Neurology, 12*, 409–418.

Gross-Glenn, K., Duara, R., Barker, W. W., Loewenstein, D., Chang, J. Y., Yoshii, F., Apicella, A. M., Pascal, S., Boothe, T., Sevush, S., Jallad, B. J., Novoa, L., & Lubs, H. A. (1991). Positron emission tomographic studies during serial word-reading by normal and dyslexic adults. *Journal of Clinical and Experimental Neuropsychology, 13*, 531–544.

Gross-Glenn, K., Duara, R., Yoshii, F., Barker, W. W., Chang, J. Y., Apicella, A., Boothe, T., & Lubs, H. A. (1986). PET-scan studies during reading in dyslexic and non-dyslexic adults. *Neuroscience Abstracts, 15*, 371.

Gross-Glenn, K., Jallad, B., Novoa, L., Helgren-Lempesis, V., & Lubbs, H. A. (1990). Nonsense passage reading as a diagnostic aid in the study of adult familial dyslexia. *Reading and Writing: An Interdisciplinary Journal, 2*, 161–173.

Harter, M. R., Diering, S., & Wood, F. B. (1988). Separate brainpotential characteristics in children with reading disability and attention deficit disorder: Relevance-independent effects. *Brain and Cognition, 7*, 54–96.

Hier, D. B., LeMay, M., Rosenberger, P. B., & Perlo, V. P. (1978). Developmental dyslexia: Evidence for a subgroup with a reversal of cerebral asymmetry. *Archives of Neurology, 35,* 90–92.

Humphreys, P., Kaufman, W. E., & Galaburda, A. M. (1990). Developmental dyslexia in women: Neuropathological findings in three patients. *Annals of Neurology, 28,* 727–738.

Hynd, G. W., & Cohen, M.J. (1983). *Dyslexia: Neuropsychological theory, research, and clinical differentiation.* New York: Grune & Stratton.

Hynd, G. W., & Hynd, C. R. (1984). Dyslexia: Neuroanatomical/neurolinguistic perspectives. *Reading Research Quarterly, 19,* 482–495.

Hynd, G. W., Hynd, C. R., Sullivan, H. G., & Kingsbury, T. B. (1987). Regional cerebral blood flow in developmental dyslexia: Activation during reading in a surface and deep dyslexic. *Journal of Reading Disabilities, 20,* 294–300.

Hynd, G. W., Marshall, R. M., & Gonzalez, J. (1991). Learning disabilities and presumed central nervous system dysfunction. *Learning Disability Quarterly, 14,* 283–296.

Hynd, G. W., & Semrud-Clikeman, M. (1989). Dyslexia and brain morphology. *Psychological Bulletin, 106,* 447–482.

Hynd, G. W., Semrud-Clikeman, M., Lorys, A. R., Novey, E. S., & Eliopulos, D. (1990). Brain morphology in developmental dyslexia and attention deficit disorder/hyperactivity. *Archives of Neurology, 47,* 919–926.

Hynd, G. W., & Willis, W. G. (1988). *Pediatric neuropsychology.* Orlando, FL: Grune & Stratton.

Larsen, J. P., Hoien, T., Lundberg, I., & Odegaard, H. (1990). MRI evaluation of the size and symmetry of the planum temporal in adolescents with developmental dyslexia. *Brain and Language, 39,* 289–301.

Lefly, D. L. (1991). Spelling error and reading fluency in compensated adult dyslexics. *Annals of Dyslexia, 41,* 143–162.

LeMay, M. (1981). Are there radiological changes in the brains of individuals with dyslexia? *Bulletin of the Orton Society, 31,* 135–140.

Leonard, C. M., Voeller, K. K. S., Lombardino, L. J., Morris, M. K., Hynd, G. W., Alexander, A. W., Andersen, H. G., Garofalakis, M., Honeyman, J. C., Mao, J., Agee, F., & Staab, E. V. (1993). Anomalous cerebral structure in dyslexia revealed with magnetic resonance imaging. *Archives of Neurology, 50,* 461–469.

Livingstone, M. S., Rosen, G. D., Drislane, F. W., & Galaburda, A. M. (1991). Physiological and anatomical evidence for a magnocellular defect in developmental dyslexia. *Neurobiology, 88,* 7943–7947.

Markee, T. W., Moore, L. H., Brown, W. S., & Theberge, D. C. (1994, February). *Bilateral field advantage and evoked potential interhemispheric transfer time in dyslexic adults.* Paper presented at the 22nd Annual Meeting of the International Neuropsychological Society, Cincinnati, OH.

Mayeux, R., & Kandel, E. R. (1985). Natural language, disorders of language, and other localizable disorders of cognitive functioning. In E. R. Kandel & J. H. Schwartz (Eds.), *Principles in neural science* (2nd ed., pp. 688–703). New York: Elsevier.

Naylor, C. E., Wood, F. B., & Flowers, D. L. (1990). Physiological correlates of reading disability. In G. T. Pavlidis (Ed.), *Perspectives on dyslexia* (Vol. 1, pp. 141–162). Chichester, England: Wiley.

Olson, R. K. (1985). Disabled reading processes and cognitive profiles. In D. B. Gray & J. F. Kavagh (Eds.), *Biobehavioral measures of dyslexia* (pp. 215–243). Parkton, MD: York Press.

Parkins, R., Roberts, R. J., Reinarz, S. J., & Varney, N. R. (1987, January). *CT asymmetries in adult developmental dyslexics.* Paper presented at the annual convention of the International Neuropsychological Society, Washington, DC.

Pennington, B. F., Gilger, J. W., Pauls, D., Smith, S. A., Smith, S. D., & DeFries, J. C. (1991). Evidence for major gene transmission of developmental dyslexia. *Journal of the American Medical Association, 266,* 1527–1534.

Pennington, B., Lefly, D., Van Orden, G., Bookman, M., & Smith, S. D. (1987). Is phonology bypassed in normal or dyslexic development? *Annals of Dyslexia, 37,* 62–89.

Petersen, S. E., Fox, P. T., Posner, M. I., Mintun, M., & Raichle, M. E. (1989). Positron emission tomographic studies of the processing of single words. *Journal of Cognitive Neuroscience, 1,* 153–170.

Rosenberger, P. B., & Hier, D. B. (1980). Cerebral asymmetry and verbal intellectual deficits. *Annals of Neurology, 8,* 300–304.

Rubens, A. B., Mahuwold, M. W., & Hutton, J. T. (1976). Asymmetry of the lateral (sylvian) fissures in man. *Neurology, 26,* 620–624.

Rumsey, J. M., Andreason, P., Zametkin, A. J., Aquino, T., King, A. C., Hamberger, S. D., Pikus, A., Rapoport, J. L., & Cohen, R. M. (1992). Failure to activate the left temporoparietal cortex in dyslexia. *Archives of Neurology, 49,* 527–534.

Rumsey, J. M., Berman, K. F., Denckla, M. D., Hamberger, S. D., Kruesi, M. J., & Weinberger, D. R. (1987). Regional cerebral blood flow in severe developmental dyslexia. *Archives of Neurology, 44,* 1144–1150.

Rumsey, J. M., Dorwart, R., Vermess, M., Denckla, M. B., Kruesi, M. J. P., & Rapoport, J. L. (1986). Magnetic resonance imaging of brain anatomy in severe developmental dyslexia. *Archives of Neurology, 43,* 1045–1046.

Rumsey, J. M., Zametkin, A. J., Andreason, P., Hanahan, A. P., Hamberger, S. D., Aquino, T., King, A. C., Pikus, A., & Cohen, R. M. (1994). Normal activation of frontotemporal language cortex in dyslexia as measured with oxygen 15 positron emission tomography. *Archives of Neurology, 51,* 27–38.

Semrud-Clikeman, M., Hynd, G. W., Novey, E. S., & Eliopulos, D. (1991). Dyslexia and brain morphology: Relationships between neuroanatomical variation and neurolinguistic tasks. *Learning and Individual Differences, 3,* 225–242.

Shaywitz, S. E., Escobar, M. D., Shaywitz, B. A., Fletcher, J. M., & Makuch, R. (1992). Evidence that dyslexia may represent the lower tail of a normal distribution of reading ability. *New England Journal of Medicine, 326,* 145–150.

Smith, S., Kimberling, W. J., Pennington, B., & Lubs, H. A. (1983). Specific reading disability: Identification of an inherited form through linkage analysis. *Science, 219,* 1345–1347.

Smith, S., Pennington, B., Kimberling, W. J., & Ing, P. S. (1990). Familial dyslexias: Use of genetic linkage data to define subtypes. *Journal of the American Academy of Child and Adolescent Psychiatry, 29,* 204–213.

Weinberger, D. R., Luchins, D. J., Morihisa, J., & Wyatt, R. J. (1982). Asymmetrical volumes of the right and left frontal and occipital regions of the human brain. *Neurology, 11,* 97–100.

Wood, F. B., Flowers, D. L., Buchsbaum, M., & Tallal, P. (1991). Investigation of abnormal left temporal functioning in dyslexia through rCBF, auditory evoked potentials, and positron emission tomography. *Reading and Writing: An Interdisciplinary Journal, 4,* 81–95.

Yingling, C. D., Galin, D., Fein, G., Peltzmann, D., & Davenport, L. (1986). Neurometrics does not detect "pure" dyslexics. *Electroencephalography and Clinical Neurophysiology, 63,* 426–430.

7

Assessing Adults with Learning Disabilities

ROBIN HAWKS

Learning disabilities were once thought of as a childhood disorder. However, more current research has documented the persistent nature of this disability. It appears that at least a portion of the learning disabled population remains disabled into adulthood (McCue, Shelly, & Goldstein, 1986). In perhaps one of the most compelling studies, researchers found that learning disabilities not only persist into adulthood, but they worsen in adulthood (Gerber et al., 1990).

In 1981, the Rehabilitation Services Administration (RSA) identified specific learning disabilities as a medically recognizable disability, and adults with learning disabilities became eligible for vocational rehabilitation services. In a policy directive dated March 5, 1985, the RSA adopted the following definition of learning disabilities for vocational rehabilitation purposes:

> A specific learning disability is a disorder in one or more of the central nervous system processes involved in perceiving, understanding and/or using concepts through verbal (spoken or written) language or nonverbal means. This disorder manifests itself with a deficit in one or more of the following areas: Attention, reasoning, processing, memory, communication, reading, writing, spelling, calculation, coordination, social competence and emotional maturity.

This definition of learning disabilities is a component of Section 504 of the Rehabilitation Act and, therefore, affects individuals with learning disabilities who are being served by vocational rehabilitation institutions as well as such others as colleges and universities. The recognition of learning disabilities as a disorder that persists into adulthood provides the impetus for development of adolescent and adult-based psychological assessment procedures. It would seem efficacious to assess adults with learning disabilities to determine the current status of the disability. In addition, assessment assists in identifying the presence of a learning disability and provides an understanding of the individual's strengths and weakness to promote effective treatment planning. An assessment procedure is necessary and the measures utilized must approximate the RSA definition of learning disabilities.

REVIEW OF THE LITERATURE

The office of Special Education and Rehabilitation Services has established the successful transition of individuals with learning disabilities from school to adult life as a national priority (Haring, Lovett, & Smith, 1990). Between 250,000 and 300,000 students with disabilities leave the public school each year (Will, 1984). However, the outcome data on this population suggest that the impact of learning disabilities on adults has significance for the personal, occupational, and emotional adjustment of the individual, as well as for the social, economic, and judicial systems of society (Spreen, 1988). Research suggests that individuals with learning disabilities as a group tend not to do well after leaving school (Rojewski, 1989). Few individuals with disabilities make a successful transition from school to the work world without exacting "significant societal and personal costs" (Posthill & Roffman, 1991). These outcomes would suggest that current practice needs to be enhanced or altered if the individual is to make a successful entry into the adult world.

Numerous problems have been associated with the manifestation of learning disabilities in adolescents and adults. Adults with learning disabilities report having significant academic problems with reading, spelling, arithmetic, written composition, and handwriting (Hoffmann et al., 1987). In addition, problems with memory, coordination, social skills, self-esteem, and lack of vocational preparation are also reported to be prevalent among adults with learning disabilities (Hoffmann, et al., 1987). Difficulties with planning, problem solving, and language also have a negative impact on adult adjustment within this population (Reiff & deFur, 1992). Unfortunately, individuals with learning disabilities exhibit minimal awareness of their strengths and weaknesses (Reiff & deFur, 1992). Therefore, comprehensive assessment procedures designed to identify individual strengths and weaknesses across a deficit class structure should lead to improved treatment, thereby improving the academic, social, and vocational outcomes for individuals with disabilities. Within the college environment, comprehensive evaluations are completed for the purpose of creating a current profile of students' strengths and weaknesses (Dalke & Schmitt, 1987). Students with learning disabilities are the fastest-growing disability group on college campuses; 14.3% of all disabled freshmen have learning disabilities and the majority of students do not have documentation of their learning disability (Gregg & Hoy, 1990).

The idea of comprehensive assessment is one that appears repeatedly in the literature (e.g., McCue, 1984). A comprehensive approach to diagnosis may be more psychometrically sound. Lewis and Lorion (1988) suggest that a combination of valid indicators is preferable to one that relies exclusively on a single index. A test battery that taps a broad range of functions, enhances clinical utility, and helps identify the nature and extent of cognitive impairments that accompany the learning disability (Taylor, 1988). Implied in the process of comprehensive assessment is the suggestion that the types of psychological assessment procedures employed reflect the needs and characteristics of the population.

There is a paucity of literature regarding assessment batteries for adults with learning disabilities. Assessment measures designed specifically for adults with learning disabilities are practically nonexistent (Johnston, 1984). Much of the literature regarding adults with learning disabilities focuses on the need for comprehensive assessment, outcome data, or specific problem areas (e.g., language). The sheer breadth of these problems clearly suggests the need to develop a comprehensive assessment approach to measure the manifestation of the disability.

Development of the Model Diagnostic Battery

Despite the recognition of learning disabilities in the adult population, systematic procedures for assessment are lacking (Malcolm, Polatajko, & Simons, 1990). In an effort to address the lack of adult-based assessment procedures, the National Institute on Disability and

Rehabilitation Research awarded the Virginia Department of Rehabilitation Services a 4-year grant to study the learning disabled population. One of the objectives of the Research and Demonstration Project for Improving Vocational Rehabilitation for Adults with Learning Disabilities was to develop a model diagnostic battery (MDB) for assessing adults with learning disabilities. Giving significant consideration to the needs of the population and the guidelines set forth in the definition, the MDB was developed as a comprehensive neuropsychoeducational battery. The battery consists of deficit classes and subclasses to be measured and instruments that correspond to the proposed classes (see Table 7.1). These deficit classes are closely tied to the 12 characteristics of learning disabilities described in the RSA definition.

The MDB was developed within the general guidelines of Gresham's (1983) work on a multimethod approach to multifactored assessment. The MDB is a comprehensive battery yielding multitest scores. Mayes and Vance (1992) suggest that this type of approach to assessment makes a differential diagnosis possible. Each deficit area of the MDB not only has multiple test measures but also includes record review, clinical interview, and behavioral observation methods of measuring the deficits. Chalfant and King (1976) have suggested

TABLE 7.1. Deficit Classes and Subclasses of the Model Diagnostic Battery

Deficit class	Subclass
Cognitive processing	Perception
	Memory
	Attention
	Reasoning
Academics	Reading
	Mathematics
	Written expression
Language	Receptive
	Expressive
Psychological adjustment	Social skills
	Self-control
	Self-direction
	Self-esteem
Balance and coordination	Motor skills
Vocational skills	Job-seeking
	Interests

that the clinical judgment of a competent professional is useful in identifying learning disabilities. Clinical judgment is even more important when it is used to support or refute the results of standardized tests.

The following is a brief discussion of each of the six deficit classes proposed in the MDB. Each class corresponds to the RSA definition of learning disabilities.

Cognitive Processing (Attention, Memory, Reasoning, and Processing)

A number of studies have considered the impact of cognitive processing deficits. In 1983, the Rehabilitation Services Administration found that adults with learning disabilities have significant discrepancies between Verbal and Performance IQ, with Performance being reported as the higher of the two. Szuhay and Newill (1980) also found similar discrepancy on the Wechsler Adult Intelligence Scale—Revised (WAIS-R). They also reported significant subtest variability and signs of neurological impairment on neuropsychological batteries. Blalock (1982) reported that her population of adults with learning disabilities demonstrated problems in visual–motor skills, attention, and lack of organization and reasoning. Results of a survey conducted by the Vocational Committee of the Association for Children and Adults with Learning Disabilities (ACLD) suggest that almost half the subjects had difficulty in visual perception, hyperactivity, and distractibility. The results of these studies would indicate that cognitive processing deficits exist in this population and, therefore, should be assessed.

Academics (Reading, Calculation, Writing, and Spelling)

Study results support the existence of an academic deficit classification. In a study of adults with learning disabilities, the mean grade level for reading, spelling, and arithmetic was fourth and fifth grade (RSA, 1983). The ACLD (1982) survey revealed that assistance in spelling and reading ranked in the top 10 needs expressed. Follow-up studies suggest that adults continue to have academic problems, with reading being the most prevalent (Silver & Hagin, 1964; Gottesman, 1979; Major-Kingsley, 1982). Ninety percent of the subjects in Blalock's study (1982) were diagnosed with reading problems. Nonexperimental literature (Brown, 1980; Patton & Polloway, 1982; Institute on Rehabilitation Issues, 1982) has also highlighted the persistent academic problems of persons with learning disabilities (Steidle et al., 1985).

Speech and Language (Communication)

Johnson (1980) describes adults with learning disabilities as having persistent language problems in phonemic discrimination, short-term auditory memory, sequencing, word retrieval, multiple word meanings, and language rules. Blalock (1982) found that of 80 subjects with learning disabilities, 63 had problems in auditory perception, comprehension, and expression of ideas (Steidle et al., 1985).

Medical/Coordination (Coordination)

Problems with tactile perception and motor skills have been reported by Brown (1980). The 1982 report from the Institute on Rehabilitation Issues also cited generalized motor deficits in the learning disabled population; however, no seriously debilitating medical problems appear to be attributed to this population. Szuhay and Newill (1980) report that even allergies are no more common in this population than in the general population (Steidle et al., 1985).

Psychological Adjustment (Social Competence and Emotional Maturity)

Social and emotional problems of adults with learning disabilities have been reported in follow-up studies (Balow & Blomquist, 1965; Hechtman & Weiss, 1983). Depression and poor self-esteem were found in Major-Kingsley's (1982) follow-up study of children with learning disabilities. Building self-esteem, overcoming dependence, and improving social relationships were identified as 3 of the top 10 needs found in the ACLD (1982) survey. In general, White, Schumaker, Warner, Alley, and Deshler (1980) found that adults with learning disabilities were significantly less satisfied with their quality of life. Severe problems with social perception and loneliness were reported by Siegel (1974) and Kronick (1981). Therefore, as the RSA (1983) has suggested, "the combination of emotional, personal, and independent living related problems indicates that perhaps the disabling condition of learning disabilities is not so much in academics or intellectual dimensions as in psychosocial considerations" (cited in Steidle et al., 1985).

Vocational Skills

Levinson (1993) suggests that school psychologists can contribute to the planning process by "considering the vocational implications of the assessment data gathered as part of a psychoeducational assessment" (p. 249). Without guidance, individuals with learning disabilities appear unlikely to engage in systematic career planning (Hutchinson, Freeman, Downey, & Kilbreath, 1992). Career counseling, vocational training, and help with obtaining and keeping a job were the top 10 needs expressed in the ACLD (1982) survey. Patton and Polloway (1982) describe the following vocational characteristics of the adult with learning disabilities: below-average career success, poor work habits and work skills, problems in getting and keeping a job, and numerous job changes. The nature of these vocational deficits in adults with learning disabilities is unclear. Nevertheless, assessment in this area appears warranted (Steidle et al., 1985).

Although the studies reviewed are quite different in methodology and specific subpopulation studied, there appears to be evidence from the literature to support the existence of the proposed classification system. This deficit structure serves as the basis for the MDB developed with the express purpose of creating a battery for use with adults with learning disabilities (Steidle et al., 1987).

The subjects in the preliminary study were 141 unemployed adults who had been diagnosed as learning disabled by the Virginia Department of Rehabilitation Services. The mean age was 20.31 (*SD* = 3.64). The group was 78% male, which is consistent with the literature regarding the prevalence of males in the learning disabled population (Selz & Reitan, 1979). Seventy-four percent of the sample were white, and 95% unmarried. Full Scale IQ was generally in the average range with Verbal IQ lower than Performance IQ on the WAIS-R. The mean grade completed was 10.68. These sample characteristics are similar to those reported by McCue (1984; McCue et al., 1986). A discriminate function analysis was conducted to discriminate learning disabilities from non-learning disabilities on each of the deficit areas of the MDB and to determine the order in which each instrument was able to predict deficit area (Hawks et al., 1990). Due to space constraints, readers are referred to the original research for detailed results. Readers are cautioned that this procedure was used for exploratory purposes and can only be interpreted within those limitations.

Further research on the MDB will need to be conducted to determine whether independent samples from the same population yield similar predictive results. In addition, at the time of press, a factor-analytic study is being conducted to confirm the deficit class structure and the structure's correspondence to the RSA characteristics of learning disabilities. The MDB is viewed as an initial attempt to use explicit rules for determining test deficits, deficits in specific subclasses, and the decision as to whether a particular individual has a learning disability. Much of the research has been muddled because of different definitions and diagnostic procedures. Explicit criteria and utilization of tests with predictive power for the construct being measured should contribute to overcoming such problems.

In conclusion, the MDB deficit structure provides a conceptual framework from which to further explore assessment procedures for adults. The MDB serves to directly link identification (learning disabilities characteristics) with assessment procedures.

PROPOSED IDEAS

The Testing Process

Learning disabilities are complex to diagnose; therefore, a comprehensive test battery is necessary to fully understand the psychological processes of the individual to be assessed. The MDB is being proposed as an effective and useful assessment procedure. Each instrument in the battery provides the interpreter with information specific to all possible deficit areas. To illustrate the utility of this large battery, one might liken it to a zoom lens used first by photographers to view the vista from a wide angle and then to zero in on their subject. By zooming in, the observer can view the subject's characteristics more specifically. To treat the person with learning disabilities effectively, one must first understand the specific manifestation of the disorder. The MDB provides the interpreter with this focused perspective and thereby links assessment to treatment. I currently use the test instruments listed in Table 7.2 as the typical battery administered to adults with learning disabilities. Although I am not proposing these instruments as definitive for assessing adults with learning disabilities, the examiner needs to choose instruments carefully to ensure that the 12 characteristics listed in the RSA definition are assessed. The instruments listed in Table 7.2 are currently being validated as to their factor structure and results are not available at the time of press.

TABLE 7.2. Test Measures of the Model Diagnostic Battery

Bender Visual–Motor Gestalt Test
Benton Visual Form Discrimination Test
Emotional Problem Solving Scale (EPS) or
    Minnesota Multiphasic Personality Inventory (MMPI)
Informal writing sample
Preliminary Diagnostic Questionnaire (PDQ)
Perceptual Memory Task (PMT)
Rey Auditory Verbal Learning Test
Seashore Rhythm Test
Self-Directed Search (SDS)
Wechsler Adult Intelligence Scale—Revised (WAIS-R)
Woodcock–Johnson Psychoeducational Battery—Revised (WJR)
Clinical interview
Behavioral observations

The Clinical Interview

Critical to the assessment process is the use of a clinical interview to establish rapport, gain valuable insight into the individual's background, and introduce the client to the upcoming battery. The Learning Disabilities Adult Clinical Interview (Hawks, 1994) is a semistructured interview designed to elicit information from clients in a number of different areas. Both facts and opinions are gathered on education, social and family history, medical status, psychological adjustment, cognitive skills, and vocational history and interests. A good clinical interview can be expected to take between 45 minutes and 1 hour. The interview may be helpful observationally as an indicator of the client's memory and verbal organizational skills and in identifying sensitive areas the client may have difficulty discussing. Excerpts from the clinical interview are found in Table 7.3.

The Assessment Report

Once the administration of the instruments has been completed, a written report is generated that details the results and makes appropriate recommendations. The recommendations section of the report is perhaps the most critical and the most neglected. Examiners tend to focus on diagnosis to the exclusion of a well-developed set of recommendations. Although assessment is scientifically based, the interpretation and report writing are best described as an art. I developed the following recommendations format to facilitate the expansion of this section. If assessment and treatment are to be truly linked in a meaningful manner, the recommendations part of the as-

TABLE 7.3. Clinical Interview Excerpts: Categories and Sample Questions

Educational history

What was your hardest subject?
What was your easiest subject?
How do you think you learn best? (visual/auditory/demonstration)
How are your reading skills?
Is it sometimes difficult for you to understand things, even though you can read all the words?

Social history

Do any of your family members have a learning disability or other related problems?
Did your parents complete high school?
    Father (Yes/No)   Mother (Yes/No)
Tell me about your friends. How many friends do you have?
What do you do with your friends?
Do you consider yourself (Social/A loner)?

Medical

Did you have any serious illnesses or high fevers as a child?
    (Yes/No) Explain
Have you ever had a head injury? (Yes/No)
How old were you?
Did you pass out?
For how long?
Did you notice anything different about yourself afterward, for example, dizziness, memory, attention, temper?

Psychological adjustment

How well do you get along with other people—your friends and coworkers?
How easily do you make new friends?
Cognitive processes
How good are you at judging the distance from place to place?
    For example: Between cities, from___to___,__miles
    Wall to wall in the examiner's office, __Feet

Vocational

Tell me about your goals.

sessment report is the opportunity for the examiner to make this connection.

Vocational/Educational Plan

This section describes educational needs. Recommendations for vocational training, college, and school placement are described. The types or range of occupations that seem appropriate should be discussed.

Learning Style

The way in which the individual learns best is identified in this section. For example, if test results suggest better developed perceptual skills and memory and attention tests yield better results in the visual area, these results may indicate a visual learning style. Techniques for capitalizing on individual strengths are described, for example:

> "Mr. Jones appears to learn more efficiently when presented with visual information; therefore, it is recommended that demonstration learning or charts and diagrams be utilized when possible; furthermore, it is recommended that the use of verbal instructions be limited."

Compensatory and Remedial Strategies

Compensatory strategies should be utilized when the deficit area cannot be remediated or in the interim before remediation can be achieved. Deficit areas that appear amenable to remediation should be identified. The type of program suggested should also be discussed. For example, a report on a college student with poor note-taking strategies may include the following:

> "When taking notes either from lecture or text, John should fold rule-lined paper from the right side to the left red margin line. Questions about the notes can then be written to the left of the red line. When studying or reviewing, John can fold over the paper so that only the questions are exposed. This will provide a review technique to assist with recall. He can also use green, yellow, and pink highlighters to code the questions according to how well he knows the material. For example, material he knows well should be coded in green to signify go. Yellow (caution) is used for material that needs some review. A pink highlighter is used for questions that need frequent review. Notes can also be

mind-mapped. For example, the major concept can be placed in the center of a page. Superordinate and subordinate ideas shoot off in rays from the center idea. This strategy helps to provide a visual picture of the information."

Emotional Status

Emotional issues that may have an impact on treatment or vocational potential should be addressed. Therapy recommendations should be identified here. For example, is the individual depressed and in need of counseling or a medication evaluation? Perhaps emotional issues are impeding the process of making vocational choices or progressing in college. These issues can be identified during the assessment process and treatment recommendations should follow.

Prognosis

The individual's potential for future accomplishment should be discussed. Expectations for the individual if the treatment is successful are described.

Diagnosis

Use of the *Diagnostic and Statistical Manual of Mental Disorders,* fourth edition (DSM-IV; American Psychiatric Association, 1994), is helpful particularly if eligibility for services requires such a diagnosis. Learning disorders are coded on Axis II of DSM-IV.

This assessment report format structures the results and provides the consumer with clear and understandable recommendations.

Giving Feedback on Test Results

Generating a report does not end the examiner's assessment responsibilities. The results of the assessment must be shared with the individual with learning disabilities. Sharing feedback with clients is generally a difficult task. The examiner must work at not using professional jargon and statistical terms which those outside the field of testing will not understand. This task is even more crucial for sharing feedback with clients with learning disabilities. The very nature of their problem means they will often have difficulty understanding many abstract terms and concepts. Thus, above all, it is essential that simple, concrete terms are employed in providing feedback about test results. In addition, a warm and friendly atmosphere needs to be provided.

The typical client will more than likely feel anxious about receiving such feedback. Some individuals may even be intimidated by the process. The client will be helped by a supportive attitude and should be encouraged to ask questions if feedback seems unclear.

To begin the feedback session, the clinician will want to give brief, simple explanations about the purpose and nature of the tests that were administered. He or she may want to make statements similar to the following:

> "These tests help to find out more about your skills or abilities to do different tasks, what your interests are in school or at work, and how well you should be able to do in school or at work. We also wanted to find out if you have any problems doing certain kinds of work and to learn more about your personality, the way you react to situations, the way you cope with problems, and the way you feel about things in your life."

With these introductory statements, the examiner may proceed to explain the results of the various tests on the client's level. Consideration should be given to the client's strengths and weaknesses as the clinician provides feedback. For example, if a client is weak in verbal abilities, drawings, charts, or the bell curve may be used in explaining some of the results. Encourage questions or feedback from the client frequently throughout the session.

To conclude the session, facilitate the client's reaction to the overall feedback session. It is especially important to conclude with recommendations for treatment and remediation. It will be helpful to review and accentuate the client's strengths and use this as a way of presenting a positive view of his or her future. The examiner will also want to consider exploring resources for helping the client to gain access to recommended treatment, remediation, or both. It is also beneficial to express appreciation for the client's cooperation and to encourage him or her to call later for further questions or assistance.

In general, persons with learning disabilities, present the informer (person interpreting results to the client) with many concerns. The following issues should be addressed by the informer:

1. The person with learning disabilities sometimes operates under the misunderstanding that the disability will end in adulthood. However, learning disabilities are a lifelong disorder. The individual will need assistance in facing this reality. This reality may be difficult for some to accept and the informer needs to be sensitive to this issue.

2. Learning disabilities are perceived as being primarily academic in nature. However, it would appear that this disability manifests itself within the demands of the institution. Once a person leaves the public school system and enters adulthood, the institution becomes the work world. The informer must assist the client in understanding how his or her disability may affect his or her career option or choices.

3. Clients with language disabilities may have difficulty comprehending test results. The informer should take care to ensure that the client has a clear understanding by asking the client to repeat periodically a summary of his or her understanding of the feedback.

4. The term "learned helplessness" has been used as a way to describe the client's nonparticipation in decision-making processes. Therefore, the informer should engage the client in a didactic interaction regarding his or her thoughts and beliefs about the test results. Gaining the client's active participation in treatment planning may help to develop self-advocating skills.

5. All clients should be asked whether they have a learning disability and what kind of learning disability they have. Research and Demonstration Project participants were asked what it means to have a learning disability. Few of these clients understood their disability. Common answers were: "It means I'm slow"; "I have trouble in school"; or "I don't think I have a learning disability." The results of the MDB provide the foundation for subsequent work to be done with the client. If the client does not understand the manifestation of the disability, how may we expect him or her to affect change, and compensate or remediate the disability?

FUTURE DIRECTIONS

The need to develop adult-based assessment procedures has been well established. Overall, assessment of adults with learning disabilities involve three components: testing, report writing, and giving feedback.

The testing itself involves the use of a comprehensive battery designed to assess characteristics identified in the RSA definition of learning disabilities. Connecting the assessment to the definition of learning disabilities is essential if the diagnosis and treatment recommendations are to be meaningful when considering the eligibility of persons with learning disabilities for services. Preliminary research on the six deficit class structures of the MDB suggests that the MDB is a useful assessment procedure.

Furthermore, it is critical that a report be generated that will have utility for the professionals providing services to the individual with learning disabilities. The report-writing format I proposed encourages expansive recommendations focusing on vocational planning, learning style, remedial and compensatory strategies, emotional status, and diagnosis.

It is equally important that adults with learning disabilities be provided with test results to increase their understanding of the disability and to allow the individual to effectively participate in future planning.

In summary, effective assessment involves a clear and explicit definition on which to base the choice of instrumentation and direct treatment recommendations.

The purpose of this chapter is to inspire the reader to think about the complexity and importance of assessing adults with learning disabilities. If done properly, assessment can provide needed direction in an individual's life. Assessment also provides objective measures and ensures that individuals with learning disabilities do not fall victim to capricious decision making. However, assessment practices need to be refined, and further research is needed.

REFERENCES

American Psychiatric Association. (1994). *Diagnostic and statistical manual of mental disorders* (4th ed.). Washington, DC: Author.

Association for Children and Adults with Learning Disabilities Vocational Committee Survey of LD Adults. (1982). Preliminary report. *ACLD Newsbriefs*, pp. 10–13.

Balow, B., & Blomquist, M. (1965). Young adults ten to fifteen years after severe reading disability. *Elementary School Journal, 66*, 44–48.

Blalock, J. (1982). Persistent auditory language deficits in adults with learning disabilities. *Journal of Learning Disabilities, 15*, 604–609.

Brown, D. (1980). *Steps to independence for people with learning disabilities*. Washington, DC: Closer Look.

Chalfant, J. C., & King, F. S. (1976). An approach to operationalizing the definition of learning disabilities. *Journal of Learning Disabilities, 9*, 34–49.

Dalke, C., & Schmitt, S. (1987). Meeting the transition needs of college bound students with learning disabilities. *Journal of Learning Disabilities, 20*, 176–180.

Gerber, P. J., Schnieders, D. A., Paradise, L. V., Reiff, H. B., Ginsberg, R. J.,

& Popp, P. A. (1990). Persisting problems of adults with learning disabilities: Self-reported comparisons from their school-age and adult years. *Journal of Learning Disabilities, 23,* 570–573.

Gottesman, R. L. (1979). Follow-up of learning disabled children. *Learning Disability Quarterly, 2,* 60–69.

Gregg, N., & Hoy, C. (1990). Identifying the learning disabled. *The Sound of College Admissions, 129,* 30–33.

Gresham, F. (1983). Multimethod approach to multifactored assessment: Theoretical rationale and practical application. *School Psychology Review, 12,* 26–34.

Haring, K. A., Lovett, D. L., & Smith, D. D. (1990). A follow-up study of recent special education graduates of learning disabilities programs. *Journal of Learning Disabilities, 23,* 108–113.

Hawks, R. (1994). *Learning disabilities clinical interview.* Unpublished manuscript, Virginia Center for Learning Potential, Mt. Sidney.

Hawks, R., Minskoff, E. H., Sautter, S., Shelton, K. L., Steidle, E. F., & Hoffmann, F. J. (1990). A model diagnostic battery for adults with learning disabilities in vocational rehabilitation. *Learning Disabilities, 1,* 94–101.

Hoffmann, F. J., Sheldon, K. L., Minskoff, E. H., Sautter, S. W., Steidle, E. F., Baker, D. B., Bailey, M. B., & Echols, L. D. (1987). Needs of the learning disabled adult. *Journal of Learning Disabilities, 20,* 43–52.

Hutchinson, N. C., Freeman, J. G., Downey, K. H., & Kilbreath, L. (1992). Development and evaluation of an instructional module to promote career maturity for youth with learning disabilities. *Canadian Journal of Counseling, 26,* 290–299.

Institute on Rehabilitation Issues. (1982). *Rehabilitation of clients with specific learning disabilities* (NIHR Office of Special Education Grant No. G008200023). Little Rock: University of Arkansas Press.

Johnson, D. J. (1980). Persistent auditory disorders in young dyslexic adults. *Bulletin of the Orton Society, 30,* 268–276.

Johnston, C. L. (1984). The learning disabled adolescent and young adult: An overview and critique of current practices. *Journal of Learning Disabilities, 17,* 386–391.

Kronick, D. (1981). *Social development of learning disabled persons.* San Francisco: Jossey-Bass.

Levinson, E. M. (1993). *Transdisciplinary vocational assessment: Issues in school based programs.* Brandon, VT: Clinical Psychology Publishing.

Lewis, R. D., & Lorion, R. P. (1988). Discriminative effectiveness of the Luria–Nebraska Neuropsychological Battery for LD adolescents. *Learning Disability Quarterly, 11,* 62–70.

Malcolm, C. B., Polatajko, H. J., & Simons, J. (1990). A descriptive study of adults with suspected learning disabilities. *Journal of Learning Disabilities, 23,* 518–520.

Major-Kingsley, S. (1982). Learning disabled boys as young adults: Achievement, adjustment, and aspirations. *Dissertation Abstracts International, 43,* 3289.

Mayes, L. D., & Vance, H. B. (1992). Using three different types of assessment data for diagnostic purposes. *Psychological Reports, 70,* 83–88.

McCue, M. (1984, May). Assessment and rehabilitation of learning disabled adults. *Rehabilitation Counseling Bulletin,* 281–290.

McCue, M., Shelly, C., & Goldstein, G. (1986). Intellectual, academic and neuropsychological performance levels in learning disabled adults. *Journal of Learning Disabilities, 19,* 233–236.

Patton, J. R., & Polloway, E. A. (1982). The learning disabled: The adult years. *Topics in Learning and Learning Disabilities, 2,* 79–88.

Posthill, S. M., & Roffman, A. J. (1991). The impact of a transitional training program for young adults with learning disabilities. *Journal of Learning Disabilities, 24,* 619–629.

Rehabilitation Services Administration. (1983). *A study of case processing issues and demographic characteristics of persons with learning disabilities being served by three state vocational rehabilitation agencies within Region III.* Philadelphia: Author.

Rehabilitation Services Administration. (1985). *Operational definition of specific learning disabilities for VR purposes* (Program Policy Directive, RSA-PPD-85-7). Philadelphia: Author.

Reiff, H. B., & deFur, S. (1992). Transition for youth with learning disabilities: A focus on developing independence. *Learning Disability Quarterly, 15,* 237–249.

Rojewski, J. W. (1989). A rural based transition model for students with learning disabilities: A demonstration. *Journal of Learning Disabilities, 22,* 613–620.

Selz, M., & Reitan, R. M. (1979). Rules for neuropsychological diagnosis: Classification of brain function in older children. *Journal of Consulting and Clinical Psychology, 47,* 258–264.

Siegel, E. (1974). *The exceptional child grows up: Guidelines for understanding and helping the brain-injured adolescent and young adult.* New York: Dutton.

Silver, A. A., & Hagin, R. A. (1964). Special reading disability: Follow-up studies. *American Journal of Orthopsychiatry, 34,* 95–102.

Spreen, O. (1988). Prognosis of learning disabilities. *Journal of Consulting and Clinical Psychology, 56,* 836–842.

Steidle, E. F., Hawks, R., Bailey, M. B., Minskoff, E. H., Pondel, B., & Hoffmann, F. J. (1987). *The evaluation and revision of the Model Diagnostic Battery* (Research Report 21). Fishersville, VA: Woodrow Wilson Rehabilitation Center.

Steidle, E. F., Sautter, S. W., Sheldon, K. L., Minskoff, E. H., Boyd, T. M., & Hoffmann, F. J. (1985). *Methodology: Development of the standard and model diagnostic batteries* (Research Report 3). Fishersville, VA: Woodrow Wilson Rehabilitation Center Project for Improving Vocational Rehabilitation for Adults with Learning Disabilities.

Szuhay, J. A., & Newill, B. (1980). A survey of adult learning disabled clients in Pennsylvania. *Field Investigation and Evaluation of Learning Disabilities* (Vol. 3). Scranton, PA: University of Scranton Press.

Taylor, H. G. (1988). Neuropsychological testing: Relevance for assessing children's learning disabilities. *Journal of Consulting and Clinical Psychology, 56,* 795–800.

White, W. J., Schumaker, J. B., Warner, M. M., Alley, G. R., & Deshler, D. D. (1980). *The current status of young adults identified as learning disabled during their school career* (Research Report 21). Lawrence: University of Kansas Institute for Research and Learning Disabilities.

Will, M. (1984). *OSERS programming for the transition of youth with disabilities: Bridges from school to work life.* Washington, DC: Office of Special Education and Rehabilitation Services, U.S. Department of Education.

8

Psychological Comorbidity in Adults with Learning Disabilities

STEPHEN R. HOOPER
J. GREGORY OLLEY

As many of the chapters in this volume attest, the area of adult learning disabilities presents a variety of challenges and new frontiers for clinicians and researchers. Given the plethora of issues confronting the definition of learning disabilities in childhood (Fletcher, Francis, Rourke, Shaywitz, & Shaywitz, 1992), how does one define significant learning disabilities in adulthood? Should the definition be multidimensional in its description, essentially encompassing various subtypes of learning problems, or will a unidimensional description suffice? If multidimensional conceptualizations are asserted, will the adult subtype descriptions be similar to ones evolved in the childhood subtyping literature (Feagans, Short, & Meltzer, 1991; Hooper & Willis, 1989; Rourke, 1985)? Do the specific learning profiles and subtypes manifested in childhood continue into adulthood, or are these profiles altered with the impact of time and life experiences? What is the impact of these profiles on adult outcomes (e.g., vocations, educational attainment, and leisure activities)? What comorbid conditions might be present and are their manifestations similar to their appearance during childhood?

The intent of this chapter is not to provide definitive answers to the above questions but, more specifically, to address what psychological conditions might be co-occurring with learning disabilities in adult-hood. The need to address these co-occurring issues is paramount with respect to understanding the impact of learning problems that extend into the adult years. Further, given the research efforts on children with learning problems and co-occurring social–emotional difficulties (e.g., Bruck, 1986; Rourke, 1989), the adult field can benefit from what has been learned from these clinical and research perspectives. For example, the adult with specific learning problems may require more time to process information, and, consequently, this deficit or inefficiency may take time away from social activities. Understanding the interactions between learning and social–emotional functioning is crucial to facilitating the adjustment of adults with learning disabilities.

This chapter provides an overview of the literature in this domain, with a particular emphasis on adult outcome studies in which social and emotional variables were assessed. Given the presumed neurological involvement for most learning disabilities, much of the discussion will be devoted to neurobiological foundations for the co-existence of specific learning disabilities and the psychosocial manifestations that might be observed in adulthood. One key neurobiological model, the nonverbal learning disabilities model, is described, and proposed areas for continued study are presented.

NEUROBIOLOGICAL CONCEPTUALIZATIONS FOR COMORBIDITY

A number of theoretical positions have been posited to explain psychopathology during childhood, adolescence, and adulthood. These positions have included psychoanalytical (Freud, 1956), developmental (Achenbach, 1985), behavioral (Bandura, 1969), and cognitive-behavioral (Meichenbaum, Bream, & Cohen, 1985) perspectives. Another theoretical conceptualization that has been advanced in recent years involves the neurobiological basis of emotional expression and psychopathology (Gainotti, 1989), and, given the presumed central nervous system dysfunction inherent in most learning disabilities (Interagency Committee on Learning Disabilities, 1987), this conceptualization is especially pertinent to examining psychological comorbidity in adults with learning disabilities. Within this theoretical perspective, psychopathology is believed to originate from neuroanatomical, neurophysiological, or neuroendocrine dysfunction via acquired or neurodevelopmental etiological mechanisms. More recently, neuropsychological factors also have been implicated in the manifestation of psychopathology in children and adults.

In general, the presence of brain dysfunction in childhood appears to be associated with a greater risk for the development of a psychiatric disorder, far more so than with other physical handicaps (Brown, Chadwick, Shaffer, Rutter, & Traub, 1981; Esser, Schmidt, & Woerner, 1990; Rutter, Chadwick, & Shaffer, 1983; Shaffer, 1978). Moreover, the effects appear to persist and impede the child's long-term adjustment in many important areas, particularly with respect to the manifestation of social isolation and internalizing symptoms (Breslau & Marshall, 1985).

A number of mechanisms have been suggested whereby brain dysfunction may lead to psychopathology, although evidence as to the relative merits of these mechanisms is uncertain (Rutter, 1977, 1983), and they certainly are not mutually exclusive in their contributions. These mechanisms include (1) behavioral disruption that arises directly from abnormal brain activity; (2) heightened exposure to failure, frustration, and social stigma due to associated disabilities; (3) the possible effects of brain damage or anomalous neurodevelopment on subsequent temperament and personality development; (4) adverse family reactions ranging from overprotection to scapegoating; (5) the individual's own reaction to being handicapped and its effect on his or her actual capacity to cope and compete; and (6) possible adverse effects from treatments themselves (e.g., lack of or poor treatment for specific learning problems) that may restrict normal activities and socialization. Thus, the effects may be direct or indirect. They also may be conceptualized as transactional and dynamic.

Direct effects, for example, would be seen in the case of learning difficulties arising from frontal lobe damage or dysfunction resulting in pronounced impulsivity, social disinhibition, and poor judgment (Price, Daffner, Stowe, & Mesulam, 1990). Another example might be seen in the case of right hemisphere dysfunction in which an individual would be prone to a variety of internalizing symptoms and social interaction problems. In other cases, however, brain dysfunction may play more of an *indirect* role in the manifestation of psychosocial difficulties in individuals. Here, the learning disabilities set the stage for other factors to come into play which, themselves, act to produce emotional or behavioral disturbances and perhaps aggravate existing functional difficulties (Tramontana & Hooper, 1989).

For example, a learning disability may render an individual more likely to encounter frustration and failure in school and vocational endeavors, and perhaps even in selected leisure activities. There also may be compounded difficulty in those areas of performance that have become anxiety laden and aversive. Parents, teachers, spouses, and employers may come to view the individual as lazy, apathetic, or otherwise difficult, thereby, generating expectations and subsequent behaviors that would only serve to perpetuate the existing problems. The latter example represents a transactional effect, namely, the differential reinforcement elicited from significant others by the adult with learning problems and the "cycle of failure" perpetuated by this process (Kinsbourne & Caplan, 1979). Indeed, empirical evidence from the childhood literature confirms that teacher interactions with students with learning disabilities differ both quantitatively and qualitatively from interactions with non-learning disabled students (Bryan, 1974; Chapman, Larsen, & Parker, 1979; Dorval, McKinney, & Feagans, 1982).

For example, students with learning disabilities are more likely to be criticized and ignored in academic interactions and to be excluded from nonacademic interactions by their teachers than students who are not learning disabled. Further, based on data showing correlations between teacher ratings of students and student ratings of classmates, Bruck (1986) suggested that negative teacher perceptions of learning disabled students may be communicated to the classmates of those students. Although such questions have yet to be explored for adults with learning disabilities, it would seem that the existence or ongoing occurrence of these dynamics would be plausible for adults with learning disabilities, perhaps with more devastating effects (e.g., losing a job, poor job performance, divorce, and ineffective parenting).

Last, the effects of a long-standing learning disability on behavior are likely to be dynamic rather than static. Just as the primary symptoms of learning disabilities may change over time, so, too, they may vary in terms of their developmental significance and the reactions they elicit from others, as well as the individual. The pattern of behavioral disturbance itself may vary so that, for example, instead of the hypersensitivity, defiance, and misconduct reported during childhood, the adult may now show apathy, withdrawal, and resignation.

PROPOSED NEUROBIOLOGICAL MODELS

A number of neurobiological models have been proposed for understanding the interrelationship between neurological dysfunction and emotional functioning. These models are important in that they permit the examination of the nature of the comorbid association of learning problems and social–emotional manifestations. For example, Bryden (1982) and Etcoff (1986) reviewed the literature and asserted that the expression and perception of human emotions tend to be mediated by the right hemisphere. The anterior regions are primarily responsible for expression and the posterior regions, particularly the parietal region, are involved in the reception of emotional stimuli. In addition, although investigators have speculated that the perception of emotions and visual–spatial functions are mediated by the posterior regions of the right hemisphere (e.g., Rourke, 1989), other investigators hypothesize that there is a dissociation between these different functional systems (Bowers, Blonder, Feinberg, & Heilman, 1990; Etcoff, 1986). These perspectives will require ongoing study for children and adults. Issues regarding valence (i.e., positive emotions being mediated by the left hemisphere and negative emotions by the right hemisphere) persist, although it now appears certain that a simple localizationist perspective for such a complex array of functions as human emotions will have limited clinical and scientific utility.

In this regard, more complex neurobiological models comprising interactive components have been proposed (e.g., Gray, 1982; Rourke, 1989; Tucker, 1989). Each one of these models has made a unique contribution to our understanding of the interaction between neurological damage or dysfunction and emotional functioning, although here discussion is devoted exclusively to the nonverbal learning disabilities model because of its direct origin and application in learning disabilities, and because of its direct link to emotional manifestations over the life span.

Nonverbal Learning Disabilities Model

Although Rourke (1989) has popularized the nonverbal learning disabilities model, early descriptions by Johnson and Myklebust (1971) over two decades ago provided accurate descriptions of these individuals. They stated that individuals with this disorder typically were unable to comprehend the significance of many aspects of the environment, could not pretend and anticipate, and failed to learn and appreciate the implications of actions such as gestures, facial expressions, caresses, and other elements of emotion. Johnson and Myklebust (1971) noted that this disorder constituted a fundamental distortion of the total perceptual experience of the child. They labeled this "social perception disability," and Myklebust (1975) later coined the term "nonverbal learning disability." This was consistent with findings of Borod, Koff, and Caron (1983) and Ross and Mesulam (1979) in their study of right-brain-damaged adult patients. Although this link to brain damage or dysfunction was emerging in the adult literature, it remained for Denckla (1983) to make the comparison of these children with adults with right hemisphere involvement. She described this group of children as experiencing a social (emotional) learning disability.

Unlike the neurologically based models proffered by Gray (1982) and Tucker (1989), Rourke (1987, 1988a, 1989) has proposed a model that is psychometrically, instead of neurologically, derived. It is based on selected aspects of neuropsychologically based learning disability subtypes, and on a theory of differential hemispheric functioning advanced by Goldberg and Costa (1981). Relying primarily on data and speculative evidence derived from adult samples, Goldberg and Costa asserted that the right hemisphere is relatively more specialized for intermodal integration, whereas the left hemisphere is more specialized for intramodal integration. Neuroanatomically, these investigators postulated that intramodal integration may be related to a higher ratio of gray matter (i.e., neuronal mass and short nonmyelinated fibers) to white matter (i.e., long myelinated fibers) characteristic of the left hemisphere, whereas intermodal integration may be related to the lower ratio characteristic of the right hemisphere.

Rourke extended this model by applying a developmental perspective and, given his previous findings with respect to learning disability subtypes (see Rourke, 1985, 1989), extended it to account for nonverbal learning disabilities. Rourke hypothesized that involvement of the white matter of the right hemisphere (i.e., lesioned, excised, or dysfunctional white matter) interacts with developmental parameters, resulting in nonverbal learning disabilities. He reasoned that although a significant lesion in the right hemisphere may be sufficient to produce a nonverbal learning disability, it is the destruction of white matter (i.e., matter associated with intermodal functions) that is necessary to produce these types of learning disabilities. Generally, the nonverbal learning disabilities syndrome would be expected to develop under any circumstance that interferes significantly with the functioning of right hemispheric functional systems or with access to those systems (e.g., agenesis of the corpus callosum). Functionally, the characteristics of such an individual, which Rourke noted should be observable by approximately ages 7 to 9 years (Rourke, 1988b; Rourke, Young, & Leenaars, 1989), implicate neuropsychological, academic, and social–emotional and adaptive domains.

Neuropsychologically, individuals with nonverbal learning disabilities tend to present a distinct profile of strengths and weaknesses. Relative strengths include auditory perception, simple motor functions, and intact rote verbal learning. Selective auditory attention, phonological skills, and auditory–verbal memory also appear intact. Neuropsychological deficits include bilateral tactile-perception problems and motor difficulties that usually are more marked on the left than on the right side of the body, visual–spatial organization problems, and nonverbal problem-solving difficulties. Paralinguistic aspects of language also are impaired (e.g., prosody and pragmatics). Academically, these individuals evidence adequate word decoding and spelling, with most spelling errors reflecting good phonetic equivalents. Graphomotor skills eventually appear age appropriate, but are delayed early in development. Marked academic deficits tend to be manifested in mechanical arithmetic, mathematical reasoning, and reading comprehension. Academic subject areas (e.g., science) also tend to be impaired, largely due to reading comprehension deficiencies and deficits in nonverbal problem solving.

Perhaps one of the most interesting aspects associated with this syndrome is that there appears to be a strong relationship with social–emotional and adaptive behavior deficits. These individuals have great difficulty adapting to novel situations and manifest poor social perception and judgment. These difficulties, in turn, result in poor social-interaction skills. There appears to be a marked tendency for these individuals to engage in social withdrawal and social isolation as age increases; consequently, they appear to be at greater risk for such internalized forms of psychopathology as depression and anxiety. In fact, Rourke et al. (1989) and Bigler (1989) noted the increased risk that these individuals have for depression and suicide. Earlier work by Porter and Rourke (1985), and more recently by Fuerst, Fisk, and Rourke (1990), also suggests the possible linkage of this model to individuals with anxiety disorders.

Given its neuroanatomical and neuropsychological bases, this model is noteworthy, particularly as it may contribute to conceptualizations of differential diagnosis and, perhaps, to issues of severity for many individuals with learning disabilities. One of the major contributions of this model is the conjecture that social–emotional disturbances, particularly internalizing types of disorders (e.g., anxiety and depression), typically are associated with this neuropsychological pattern. Although ongoing examination of these hypotheses is required, this model provides the opportunity to study the interaction between neurological and neuropsychological interactions as they may be contributing, directly or indirectly, to manifestations of psychosocial adjustment and psychopathology.

The nonverbal learning disabilities model holds promise with respect to increasing our understanding of the comorbid conditions that can exist in individuals with learning disabilities. Exploration of other proposed neurologically based models for adult psychopathology and emotional functioning, however, also may prove fruitful in this regard. Further, it should be remembered that these neurological models reflect only one major perspective in attempting to understand the comorbid conditions that might be manifested in adulthood, and other psychosocial explanations should be considered as well.

REVIEW OF THE LITERATURE

Thus far, this chapter has presented neurobiological conceptualizations and a specific model for beginning to understand the comorbid psychological problems that might manifest in adults with learning disabilities. Given what would appear to be a solid conceptual foundation, one might expect this literature to be abundant with far-reaching speculations and conclusions. In contrast, however, there have been relatively few studies to date that have examined the social, emotional, and psychiatric outcomes in adults with learning disabilities. Further, given the many definitional issues inherent in diagnosing adult learning problems, along with the many variables that can be carried forward in individuals with learning disabilities diagnosed during the childhood or adolescent period, longitudinal methodologies seem to represent the only clear framework from which to approach the question of psychological comorbidity in this population.

At present, there have been precious few attempts to address this concern. Most of the literature describing psychological comorbidity in adults with learning disabilities is neither highly empirical nor well controlled. Most accounts are case studies (e.g., Smith, 1991), interviews with adults with learning disabilities (e.g., Gerber & Reitt, 1991), or other forms of anecdotal report (Cruickshank, Morse, & Johns, 1980). In addition, such reports have not defined their population clearly. Although the adults are referred to as learning disabled, there is typically no statement of how the diagnosis was made and no description of the likely coexisting conditions.

Although a number of longitudinal studies have been conducted in the area of learning disabilities, some of these did not follow children into the adult years (e.g., Ackerman, Dykman, & Peters, 1977; Rourke & Orr, 1977; Satz, Taylor, Friel, & Fletcher, 1978), were poorly defined with respect to the time of outcome measurement (Kline & Kline, 1975), or focused exclusively on neuropsychological (Silver & Hagin, 1964), academic (Carter, 1964), or a combination of academic and vocational outcomes (Hardy, 1968; Howden, 1967; Preston & Yarrington, 1967; Rawson, 1968; Robinson & Smith, 1962). The studies included for discussion were selected because of their longitudinal nature—wherein children and adolescents diagnosed as learning disabled were followed and reevaluated at age 18 years or older, the age at which most child services stop and adult services begin—and because of their inclusion of a formal or informal measure of social–behavioral adjustment. For discussion purposes, these studies are grouped into those primarily addressing psychosocial adjustment, psychopathology, and psychological functioning by learning disabilities subtypes.

Psychosocial Adjustment

Psychosocial adjustment difficulties frequently are assumed to be the major social–emotional manifestations of learning disabilities. The hypothesis that individuals with learning disabilities are at high risk for developing interpersonal relationship and adjustment problems has been studied extensively in children and adolescents (e.g., Bryan, 1976; Garrett & Crump, 1980; Kistner & Osborne, 1987; Pearl, 1987; Scranton & Ryckman, 1979); however, it has only begun to be examined in adulthood.

Blalock and Johnson (1987) reported a number of observations from a sample of 93 successive cases diagnosed at their Adult Learning Disabilities Center at Northwestern University. They noted that although complaints about learning problems were typical portals of entry into their clinic, about 25% of the patients described social difficulties as well. They speculated that this number likely represented an underestimate in that individuals manifesting nonverbal learning disabilities were not typically aware of their social functioning and were less likely to mention psychosocial adjustment difficulties as their primary concerns. Further, some individuals would not participate in social activities that required rhythmic gross motor skills, whereas others noted that they had no good friendships and were concerned about meeting members of the opposite gender. In general, Blalock and Johnson noted that many individuals were socially isolated and maintained low levels of self-esteem.

Similarly, Smith (1991) wrote about the experience of adults with learning disabilities based on her conversations with former students of The Lab School of Washington and with adult students in its night school. These programs serve children and adults, respectively, with severe learning disabilities. The emotional difficulties reported by Smith's populations were not the severe antisocial problems that other investigators have found for adults with attention deficits (e.g., Mannuzza, Klein, Bessler, Malloy, & LaPadula, 1993). Instead, Smith reported more frequent internalizing behaviors, such as lowered self-esteem, heightened anxiety and perceived stress, and depressive themes. Smith reported that these difficulties tended to interfere significantly with family functioning and other interpersonal relations.

Using formal interviews with adults with learning disabilities, Gerber and Reitt (1991) reported a similar association between learning disabilities and psychosocial adjustment. Their subjects described many examples of specific learning problems leading to frustration with schoolwork and difficulties understanding the subtleties of interpersonal relations. They reported being taunted by other children; feeling the disapproval of parents, teachers, and peers; and developing elaborate strategies to hide their disabilities. These concerns have been echoed by other investigators working with college students with learning disabilities (e.g., Saracoglu, Minden, & Wilchesky, 1989).

Perhaps the most frequently reported adult difficulty for people with learning disabilities has been in the area of social skills. The difficulties in social interaction of children with learning disabilities has been recognized for many years (e.g., Bryan, 1978). A review of this literature by Polloway, Smith, and Patton (1984) indicated that social skills deficits begin in childhood and persist into adulthood. They cited findings of low scores on tests of social skills and problems in such areas as affective deficits, poor social perception and related communication difficulties, and poor self-esteem. Cartledge (1989) further identified social skills problems in three areas: task-related behaviors (e.g., following directions, staying on task, attending, volunteering, and completing tasks), social communication (e.g., greeting others, conversing, listening to others, smiling and laughing, and complimenting others), and decision-making skills (e.g., use of good judgment and increased reflection). In the review by Cartledge (1989), as in other studies, attention problems tended to account for some of the identified problems.

Despite these claims, the effects of a learning disability on interpersonal relations and adult adjustment may not be uniformly negative. Smith (1991) reported that the presence of a learning disability gave some individuals (e.g., Olympic diver Greg Louganis) the determination to excel and to work harder than others to prove their worth. She also reported that some individuals with learning disabilities developed a strong sense of empathy for others which made them effective counselors and friends. Horn, O'Donnell, and Vitulano (1983) also noted that the actual vocational attainment of adults with learning disabilities does not seem to differ from that of the general population. Nonetheless, although these observations are encouraging, they do not reflect the inordinate amount of time and energy that might need to be devoted to a specific academic or vocation domain by these individuals, nor do they address the psychosocial adjustment issues inherent in this apparent success. Further, as Mannuzza et al. (1993) reported for adults with attention deficits, those with learning disabilities also may have an increased tendency to employ limited or poor coping strategies (e.g., turning to substance abuse as a method of coping).

As can be seen, the published literature in this area is generally weak from a scientific standpoint, but the commonly reported adjustment difficulties of adults with learning disabilities must be acknowledged. The etiology and prevalence of these adjustment difficulties may be unclear at present, but their effect on adult functioning can be significant for many individuals.

Psychopathology

In addition to low self-esteem and psychosocial adjustment difficulties, many individuals with learning disabilities experience more serious psychopathology and seek mental health services for their difficulties. Silver (1974) stated that learning disabilities can be total life disabilities, with many of the psychiatric problems being directly related to the underlying information processing deficits, or secondary to the frustrations of long-standing learning impediments, or both. Similar sentiments have been echoed by Peter and Spreen (1979), particularly when there is evidence of neurological deficit or dysfunction.

Along with low self-esteem and social isolation, more severe psychopathology such as anxiety, depression, and conduct disorders also has been described (Gregg, Hoy, King, Moreland, & Jagota, 1992; Herjanic & Penick, 1972; Offord & Poushinsky, 1981; Offord, Poushinsky, & Sullivan, 1978; Rosenberg & Gaier, 1977) in children and adults with learning disabilities. For example, Balow and Blomquist (1965) reported that approximately 25% of their sample of children diagnosed with reading disability showed evidence of psychopathology on the Minnesota Multiphasic Personality Inventory (MMPI) as young adults 10 to 15 years later.

In one of the most comprehensive follow-up studies conducted to date, Spreen (1988) described results from psychoeducational, neuropsychological, family history, and behavioral ratings and interviews for a large group of children diagnosed as learning disabled and a normal control group. The learning disabled group was further subdivided into those with hard neurological signs reflecting brain damage, those with soft neurological signs reflecting minimal brain dysfunction, and those showing only learning problems with no neurological signs. All the subjects were approximately 9 to 10 years old at initial assessment, about 18 years old at the first follow-up, and about 25 years old at the second follow-up.

With respect to psychological comorbidity at the first follow-up point, the two brain-impaired learning disabled groups reported less satisfaction in their lives, and they were viewed as more impulsive than the other two groups. At the second follow-up point, the groups were administered the MMPI. Group comparisons revealed that the learning disabled adults experienced more maladjustment than did their normal counterparts. Specifically, the learning disabled adults reported more depression, acting-out tendencies, social insensitivity, obsessions and compulsions, phobias, social withdrawal, and disorganized thoughts than did the normal controls. Gender differences also were noted, with females reporting more affective disruption and males describing problems with behavioral dyscontrol and thought organization. These findings were accentuated in the two brain-impaired groups.

One psychiatric diagnosis, with perhaps the highest rate of comorbidity with learning disabilities, is attention deficit hyperactivity disorder. Although the prevalence of attention-deficit disorder among children may be 3% or more (Barkley, 1990), it has been estimated that about 30% to 70% of children with learning disabilities will experience ongoing symptoms of comorbid attention-deficit disorder as they enter into adulthood (Barkley, Fischer, Edelbrock, & Smallish, in press; Bellak & Black, 1992; Weiss, Hechtman, Milroy, & Perlman, 1985). Even in anecdotal reports it is clear that many of the individuals being described have experienced significant attention problems in addition to their learning disability.

Relatedly, both learning disabilities and attention-deficit hyperactivity disorder maintain a high degree of comorbidity with other psychiatric disorders such as depression, conduct disorder, anxiety disorder, substance abuse, and Tourette's syndrome, but the impact of these comorbid psychiatric conditions on the lives of individuals with learning disabilities remains relatively unstudied. In fact, using a structured rating scale for psychopathology, some researchers (e.g., Lamm & Epstein, 1992) have reported that there are few differences between individuals with learning disabilities and normal controls. Further, Porter and Rourke (1985) found that 46% of their sample of children and adolescents with learning disabilities showed no more personality problems than did their normal counterparts; however, it remains unclear whether the other 54% continue to manifest social–emotional difficulties or whether these 46% manifest such difficulties at a later point in life.

Although not directly indicative of frank psychopathology, there appears to be a large number of individuals with learning disabilities who seek mental health services. Nearly 20 years ago, Rogan and Hartman (1976) reported that about 75% of students who had attended a special school for children with learning disabilities needed counseling services during their adulthood. Similarly, Chesler (1982) reported more than 10 years ago that at least 50% of the respondents to a survey of adults with learning disabilities wanted or needed mental health services for more severe emotional problems. About 36% of the Blalock and Johnson (1987) subjects had participated in some form of psychotherapy, while others stated a need for such services. About 4% required pharmacological treatment for depression.

Psychological Functioning by Learning Disability Subtype

The subtyping of learning disabilities in children and adolescents has received significant attention over the past two decades, with entire volumes being devoted to these studies and related classification issues (Feagans et al., 1991; Hooper & Willis, 1989; Rourke, 1985). As noted earlier, one of the key findings with respect to learning disability subtyping has been the association between the presence of a non-verbal learning disability and internalizing behavioral manifestations (Rourke, 1989; Weintraub & Mesulam, 1983), and this association apparently continues into adulthood (Blalock & Johnson, 1987; Rourke, Young, Strang, & Russell, 1986).

Although the details of this model have been described earlier, little research is available regarding the adult outcomes of this subtype, or any other learning disability subtype for that matter. Rourke et al. (1986) have reported on the adult outcomes of a small number of children who manifested different subtype patterns, including the nonverbal learning disabilities pattern. In one comparison, one individual who initially exhibited characteristics of nonverbal learning disabilities was compared to another who showed more language-based learning problems. Each subject was in his or her early 20s at the time of the follow-up neuropsychological evaluation. In addition to the expected continuation of the expected neuropsychological patterns, each case manifested distinct social–emotional features. The case with a significant language-based problem was described essentially as well adjusted and pleasant. This individual did show increased anxiety around his inability to read, but few other psychosocial or psychiatric concerns were raised. In contrast, the individual with nonverbal learning disabilities had experienced significant social difficulties, although she seemed relatively unaware of her shortcomings. She exhibited inadequate social judgment, inappropriate social behaviors, inconsistent emotional reactivity, and apparent emotional insensitivity.

As a follow-up to these case descriptions, Rourke et al. (1986) described the adult outcomes of eight individuals manifesting the nonverbal learning disabilities pattern. This small group included three males and five females with highly varied cultural backgrounds. The age at adult follow-up ranged from 17 to 48 years, with most of the subjects coming from middle-class backgrounds. Rourke et al. noted that the histories of these subjects were significant for the presence of social skills deficits, low self-esteem, and social withdrawal and isolation. Nearly all these subjects were experiencing flagrant psychopathology, with approximately 25% showing schizophrenia, 25% having a severe depression, and about 38% being prone to severe, chronic depression. Further, most of the subjects appeared to be relatively unaware of their psychiatric difficulties. In addition, despite a high degree of literacy and advanced post-high school education in this sample, all these subjects were underemployed.

Summary

In their classic review of the outcome literature in the field of learning disabilities, Schonhaut and Satz (1983) noted more than a decade ago that the link between learning disabilities and later psychosocial or psychiatric difficulties was uncertain, and this continues to be true to the present. To date, precious few studies exist that provide longitudinal data on outcomes of samples of individuals with learning disabilities, and even fewer explicitly examine the psychosocial outcomes of individuals with learning disabilities in adulthood. The studies that do exist provide clues as to the relationship between learning problems and psychosocial difficulties, but they are by no means definitive given the correlative nature of many of the findings.

What can be gleaned from this emergent literature, however, appears to be generally consistent with what is known about the social–emotional functioning of children with learning disabilities. This should come as no surprise in that many of these problems typically do not "disappear" as one progresses into the various phases of adulthood. Indeed, one might expect some of these problems to intensify for some individuals given the increased demands on independence and self-sufficiency and the lessening influences of supportive environmental structures (e.g., family and school). More specifically, it appears that individuals with learning disabilities have an increased risk for psychosocial adjustment difficulties and, perhaps, more severe forms of psychopathology. This may be most pronounced for individuals showing learning problems and comorbid attention deficits. Further, similar to the child literature, there seems to be emergent evidence that individuals showing nonverbal learning disabilities are at greater risk for manifesting affective disruption, and this will require further examination.

FUTURE DIRECTIONS

Given the relative dearth of adult outcome studies examining the link between psychosocial difficulties and manifest learning disabilities, several ideas for change are proposed. These ideas encapsulate not only research initiatives but clinical practice endeavors as well.

First, it will be important for investigators to study the relationship between learning disabilities and psychological comorbidity using longitudinal designs. Cross-sectional studies will continue to be useful with respect to describing comorbid conditions, but longitudinal methodology will lessen the need to define the adult phenotype for learning disabilities, and it will allow for control of other factors that can influence the manifestation of psychopathology. As noted earlier, there are relatively few longitudinal studies that have followed learning disabled subjects into their adult years. Of these studies, it appears that only token attention has been devoted to the issues associated with psychosocial and psychiatric comorbidity. It will be essential for investigators to design longitudinal studies on learning disabilities samples to include a priori measures of psychosocial and psychiatric status and to obtain these measures at multiple follow-up intervals during the adult years. Specific assessment strategies should be more sensitive to adult learning differences and attempt to take into account the long-term psychological effects of not knowing how to read, write, or perform arithmetic.

Second, it will be essential for definitions of learning disabilities to be operationalized in a clear manner and for the samples utilized to be well marked from the time of diagnosis through adulthood. A well-developed marker system has been proposed by Keogh, Major-Kingsley, Omori-Gordon, and Reid (1982), and such a system would serve the adult outcome literature well. A thorough marker system would allow for analysis of the influence of a multitude of variables on psychological outcomes. Further, and crucial to this literature, such a priori descriptions will permit explorations into why some individuals with learning disabilities are more resilient to developing psychosocial adjustment difficulties or psychopathology than are others.

Third, given the emergent data indicating a differential social–

emotional pattern for the nonverbal learning disabilities subtype, it will prove useful for investigators to include some means for subtyping their subjects a priori. This model is proving useful in exploring psychological comorbidity in childhood outcomes, and its conceptual merit in adulthood appears promising, although it remains unclear whether membership in selected subtypes remains constant or changes over time (Spreen & Haaf, 1986).

Fourth, it will be important for investigators to examine a wide array of variables across the brain–behavior spectrum. Neurological and neuropsychological deficiencies and dysfunctions have been linked to social–emotional problems in children and adults, and it might prove beneficial for other models (e.g., Tucker, 1989) to be examined with respect to their applicability to a learning disabled population. This also may prove useful in evaluating treatment alternatives (e.g., pharmacological treatments) for an adult population.

Finally, from a clinical perspective, it will be important for individuals working with adults with learning disabilities to be sensitive to the psychosocial difficulties as well as the learning differences that can be manifested in this population (Denckla, 1993). Any evaluation should include a personality appraisal, and these results should be compared to the obtained learning profile. Obtaining a clearer picture of the underlying cognitive processing contributing to the learning disability actually may provide avenues for intervention for a particular individual. In fact, Blalock and Johnson (1987) noted that all their adults with learning disabilities said that they preferred to work with someone who understood learning disabilities in general and their specific learning problems in particular. Increased understanding of how a particular profile affects adult functions (e.g., expectations and demands of marriage, interpersonal relationships, parenthood, vocational choices, earning a livelihood, management of a household, and leisure time) undoubtedly will prove therapeutic for this population. Relatedly, the treatment issues may be more pervasive in adulthood as they may extend into marriage relationships, parenthood, vocational issues and unemployment or underemployment, and selection of leisure activities (Bender, 1994).

Given the above ideas for change, the future holds much promise with respect to the investigation into the psychological comorbidity of adults with learning disabilities. Although the field of adult learning disorders truly is in its early stages, many of the pitfalls encountered by investigators studying childhood learning disabilities and their associated conditions can be avoided; however, understanding the long-term impact of these learning problems also will prove challenging, especially with respect to psychological comorbidity.

ACKNOWLEDGMENT

This work was supported in part by grants awarded to the Center for Development and Learning from the Maternal and Child Health Bureau (MCJ-379154-02-0) and the Administration on Developmental Disabilities (90DD0207).

REFERENCES

Achenbach, T. M. (1985). *Assessment and taxonomy of child and adolescent psychopathology.* Beverly Hills, CA: Sage.

Ackerman, P. T., Dykman, R. A., & Peters, J. E. (1977). Learning disabled boys as adolescents: Cognitive factors and achievement. *Journal of the American Academy of Child Psychiatry, 16,* 296–313.

Balow, B., & Blomquist, M. (1965). Young adults ten to fifteen years after severe reading disability. *Elementary School Journal, 66,* 44–48.

Bandura, A. (1969). *Principles of behavior modification.* New York: Holt, Rinehart & Winston.

Barkley, R. A. (1990). *Attention-deficit hyperactivity disorder: A handbook for diagnosis and treatment.* New York: Guilford Press.

Barkley, R. A., Fischer, M., Edelbrock, C. S., & Smallish, L. (in press). The adolescent outcome of hyperactive children diagnosed by research criteria: I. An 8-year prospective follow-up study. *Journal of the American Academy of Child and Adolescent Psychiatry.*

Bellak, L., & Black, R. B. (1992). Attention-deficit hyperactivity disorder in adults. *Clinical Therapeutics, 14,* 138–147.

Bender, M. (1994). Learning disabilities: Beyond the school years. In A. J. Capute, P. J. Accardo, & B. K. Shapiro (Eds.), *Learning disabilities spectrum: ADD, ADHD, and LD* (pp. 241–253). Baltimore: York Press.

Bigler, E. D. (1989). On the neuropsychology of suicide. *Journal of Learning Disabilities, 22,* 180–185.

Blalock, J. W., & Johnson, D. J. (1987). Primary concerns and group characteristics. In D. J. Johnson & J. W. Blalock (Eds.), *Adults with learning disabilities: Clinical studies* (pp. 31–45). New York: Grune & Stratton.

Borod, J. C., Koff, E., & Caron, H. S. (1983). Right hemispheric specialization for the expression and appreciation of emotions: A focus on the fact. In E. Perecman (Ed.), *Cognitive processing in the right hemisphere* (pp. 83–110). New York: Academic Press.

Bowers, D., Blonder, L., Feinberg, T., & Heilman, K. (1990). Emotional versus object imagery: Differential impact of right versus left hemisphere lesions. *Journal of Clinical and Experimental Neuropsychology, 12,* 84–93.

Breslau, N., & Marshall, I. A. (1985). Psychological disturbance in children with physical disabilities: Continuity and change in a 5-year follow-up. *Journal of Abnormal Child Psychology, 13,* 199–216.

Brown, G., Chadwick, O., Shaffer, D., Rutter, M., & Traub, M. (1981). A prospective study of children with head injuries: III. Psychiatric sequelae. *Psychological Medicine, 11,* 63–78.

Bruck, M. (1986). Social and emotional adjustments of learning disabled children: A review of the issues. In S. J. Ceci (Ed.), *Handbook of cognitive, social, and neuropsychological aspects of learning disabilities* (Vol. 1, pp. 361–380). Hillsdale, NJ: Erlbaum.

Bryan, T. H. (1974). Peer popularity of learning disabled children. *Journal of Learning Disabilities, 7,* 621–625.

Bryan, T. H. (1976). Peer popularity of learning disabled children: A replication. *Journal of Learning Disabilities, 9,* 307–311.

Bryan, T. H. (1978). Social relationships and verbal interactions of learning disabled children. *Journal of Learning Disabilities, 11,* 58–66.

Bryden, M. P. (1982). *Laterality: Functional asymmetry in the intact brain.* New York: Academic Press.

Carter, R. P. A. (1964). *A descriptive analysis of the adult adjustment of persons once identified as disabled readers.* Unpublished doctoral dissertation, Indiana University, Bloomington.

Cartledge, G. (1989). Social skills and vocational success for workers with learning disabilities. *Rehabilitation Counseling Bulletin, 33,* 74–79.

Chapman, R. B., Larsen, S. C., & Parker, R. M. (1979). Interactions of first grade classroom teachers with learning disabled students. *Journal of Learning Disabilities, 12,* 225–230.

Chesler, B. (1982). ACLD vocational committee survey on LD adults. *ACLD Newsbrief,* No. 145.

Cruickshank, W. M., Morse, W. C., & Johns, J. (1980). *Learning disabilities. The struggle from adolescence toward adulthood.* New York: Syracuse University Press.

Denckla, M. B. (1983). The neuropsychology of social–emotional learning disabilities. *Archives of Neurology, 40,* 461–462.

Denckla, M. B. (1993). The child with developmental disabilities grown up: Adult residuals of childhood disorders. *Neurological Clinics, 11,* 105–125.

Dorval, B., McKinney, J. D., & Feagans, L. (1982). Teacher interaction with learning disabled children and average achievers. *Journal of Pediatric Psychology, 17,* 317–330.

Esser, G., Schmidt, M. H., & Woerner, W. (1990). Epidemiology and course of psychiatric disorders in school-age children: Results of a longitudinal study. *Journal of Child Psychology, Psychiatry, and Allied Disciplines, 31,* 243–263.

Etcoff, N. L. (1986). The neuropsychology of emotional expression. In G. Goldstein & R. E. Tarter (Eds.), *Advances in clinical neuropsychology* (Vol. 3, pp. 127–179). New York: Plenum Press.

Feagans, L. V., Short, E. J., & Meltzer, L. J. (Eds.). (1991). *Subtypes of learning disabilities: Theoretical perspectives and research.* Hillsdale, NJ: Erlbaum.

Fletcher, J.M., Francis, D. J., Rourke, B. P., Shaywitz, S. E., & Shaywitz, B.

A. (1992). Validity of discrepancy-based definitions of reading disabilities. *Journal of Learning Disabilities, 25,* 555–561.

Freud, A. (1956). *Normality and pathology in childhood.* New York: International Universities Press.

Fuerst, D. R., Fisk, J. D., & Rourke, B. P. (1990). Psychosocial functioning of learning disabled children: Relations between WISC Verbal IQ–Performance IQ discrepancies and personality subtypes. *Journal of Consulting and Clinical Psychology, 58,* 657–660.

Gainotti, G. (1989). Features of emotional behavior relevant to neurobiology and theories of emotions. In G. Gainotti & C. Caltagirone (Eds.), *Emotions and the dual brain* (pp. 9–27). New York: Springer-Verlag.

Garrett, M. K., & Crump, W. D. (1980). Peer acceptance, teacher references, and self-appraisal of social status among learning-disabled students. *Learning Disability Quarterly, 3,* 42–48.

Gerber, P. J., & Reitt, H. B. (1991). *Speaking for themselves: Ethnographic interviews with adults with learning disabilities.* Ann Arbor: University of Michigan Press.

Goldberg, E., & Costa, L. D. (1981). Hemisphere differences in the acquisition and use of descriptive systems. *Brain and Language, 14,* 144–173.

Gray, J. A. (1982). *The neuropsychology of anxiety: An enquiry into the functions of the septo-hippocampal system.* Oxford, England: Oxford University Press.

Gregg, N., Hoy, C., King, M., Moreland, C., & Jagota, M. (1992). The MMPI-2 profile of adults with learning disabilities in University and rehabilitation settings. *Journal of Learning Disabilities, 25,* 386–395.

Hardy, M. E. (1968). *Clinical follow-up study of disabled readers.* Unpublished doctoral dissertation, University of Toronto.

Herjanic, B., & Penick, E. (1972). Adult outcome of disabled child readers. *Journal of Special Education, 6,* 397–410.

Hooper, S. R., & Willis, W. G. (1989). *Learning disability subtyping. Neuropsychological foundations, conceptual models, and issues in clinical differentiation.* New York: Springer-Verlag.

Horn, W., O'Donnell, J., & Vitulano, L. (1983). Long-term follow-up studies of learning disabled persons. *Journal of Learning Disabilities, 16,* 542–555.

Howden, M. E. (1967). *A nineteen-year follow-up study of good, average and poor readers in the fifth and sixth grades.* Unpublished doctoral dissertation, University of Oregon, Eugene.

Interagency Committee on Learning Disabilities. (1987). *Learning disabilities: A report to the U.S. Congress.* Bethesda, MD: National Institutes of Health. (ERIC Document Reproduction Service No. ED 294 358)

Johnson, D. J., & Myklebust, H. R. (1971). *Learning disabilities.* New York: Grune & Stratton.

Keogh, B. K., Major-Kingsley, S., Omori-Gordon, H., & Reid, H. P. (1982). *A system of marker variables for the field of learning disabilities.* Syracuse, NY: Syracuse University Press.

Kinsbourne, M., & Caplan, P. J. (1979). *Children's learning and attentional problems*. Boston: Little, Brown.

Kistner, J., & Osborne, M. (1987). A longitudinal study of LD children's self-evaluations. *Learning Disability Quarterly, 10*, 258–266.

Kline, C., & Kline, C. (1975). Follow-up study of 211 dyslexic children. *Bulletin of the Orton Society, 25*, 127–144.

Lamm, O., & Epstein, R. (1992). Specific reading impairments: Are they to be associated with emotional difficulties? *Journal of Learning Disabilities, 25*, 605–615.

Mannuzza, S., Klein, R. G., Bessler, A., Malloy, P., & LaPadula, M. (1993). Adult outcomes of hyperactive boys: Educational achievement, occupational rank, and psychiatric status. *Archives of General Psychiatry, 50*, 565–576.

Meichenbaum, D. H., Bream, L. A., & Cohen, J. C. (1985). A cognitive-behavioral perspective of child psychopathology: Implications for assessment and training. In R. J. McMahon & R. D. Peters (Eds.), *Childhood disorders: Behavioral–developmental approaches* (pp. 36–52). New York: Brunner/Mazel.

Myklebust, H. R. (1975). Nonverbal learning disabilities: Assessment and intervention. In H. R. Myklebust (Ed.), *Progress in learning disabilities* (Vol. 3, pp. 85–121). New York: Grune & Stratton.

Offord, D. R., & Poushinsky, M. F. (1981). School performance, IQ and female delinquency. *International Journal of Social Psychiatry, 27*, 53.

Offord, D. R., Poushinsky, M. R., & Sullivan, D. (1978). School performance, IQ, and delinquency. *British Journal of Criminology, 18*, 110–127.

Pearl, R. (1987). Social cognitive factors in learning- disabled children's social problems. In S. J. Ceci (Ed.), *Handbook of cognitive, social, and neuropsychological aspects of learning disabilities* (Vol. 2, pp. 273–294). Hillsdale, NJ: Erlbaum.

Peter, B. M., & Spreen, O. (1979). Behavior rating and personal adjustment scales of neuropsychologically and learning handicapped children during adolescence and early adulthood: Results of a follow-up study. *Journal of Clinical Neuropsychology, 1*, 75–91.

Polloway, E. A., Smith, J. D., & Patton, J. R. (1984). Learning disabilities: An adult development perspective. *Learning Disability Quarterly, 7*, 179–186.

Porter, J. E., & Rourke, B. P. (1985). Socioemotional functioning of learning-disabled children: A subtypal analysis of personality patterns. In B. P. Rourke (Ed.), *Neuropsychology of learning disabilities: Essentials of subtype analysis* (pp. 257–280). New York: Guilford Press.

Preston, R. C., & Yarrington, D. J. (1967). Status of fifty retarded readers 8 years after reading clinic diagnosis. *Journal of Reading, 11*, 122–124.

Price, B. H., Daffner, K. R., Stowe, R. M., & Mesulam, M. M. (1990). The compartmental learning disabilities of early frontal lobe damage. *Brain, 113*, 1383–1393.

Rawson, M. (1968). *Developmental language disability: Adult accomplishments of dyslexic boys*. Baltimore: Johns Hopkins Press.

Robinson, H. M., & Smith, H. D. (1962). Reading clinic: Ten years after. *Elementary School Journal, 63,* 22–27.

Rogan, L., & Hartman, L. (1976). *A follow–up study of learning disabled children as adults. Final Report.* Evanston, IL: Cove School Research Office.

Rosenberg, B., & Gaier, E. (1977). The self-concept of the adolescent with learning disabilities. *Adolescence, 12,* 490–497.

Ross, E. D., & Mesulam, M. M. (1979). Dominant language functions of the right hemisphere? *Archives of Neurology, 36,* 144–149.

Rourke, B. P. (Ed.). (1985). *Neuropsychology of learning disabilities: Essentials of subtype analysis.* New York: Guilford Press.

Rourke, B. P. (1987). Syndrome of nonverbal learning disabilities: The final common pathway of white-matter disease/dysfunction. *The Clinical Neuropsychologist, 1,* 209–234.

Rourke, B. P. (1988a). Socio-emotional disturbances of learning disabled children. *Journal of Consulting and Clinical Psychology, 56,* 801–810.

Rourke, B. P. (1988b). The syndrome of nonverbal learning disabilities: Developmental manifestations in neurological disease, disorder, and dysfunction. *The Clinical Neuropsychologist, 2,* 293–330.

Rourke, B. P. (1989). *Nonverbal learning disabilities: The syndrome and the model.* New York: Guilford Press.

Rourke, B. P., & Orr, R. R. (1977). Prediction of the reading and spelling performances of normal and retarded children: A four-year follow-up. *Journal of Abnormal Child Psychology, 5,* 9–20.

Rourke, B. P., Young, G. C., & Leenaars, A. A. (1989). A childhood learning disability that predisposes those afflicted to adolescent and adult depression and suicide risk. *Journal of Learning Disabilities, 22,* 169–175.

Rourke, B. P., Young, G. C., Strang, J. D., & Russell, D. L. (1986). Adult outcomes of central processing deficiencies in childhood. In I. Grant & K. M. Adams (Eds.), *Neuropsychological assessment of neuropsychiatric disorders* (pp. 244–267). New York: Oxford University Press.

Rutter, M. (1977). Brain damage syndromes in childhood: Concepts and findings. *Journal of Child Psychology and Psychiatry, 18,* 1–21.

Rutter, M. (1983). Issues and prospects in developmental neuropsychiatry. In M. Rutter (Ed.), *Developmental neuropsychiatry* (pp. 577–598). New York: Guilford Press.

Rutter, M., Chadwick, O., & Shaffer, D. (1983). Head injury. In M. Rutter (Ed.), *Developmental neuropsychiatry* (pp. 83–111). New York: Guilford Press.

Saracoglu, B., Minder, H., & Wilchesky, M. (1989). The adjustment of students with learning disabilities to university and its relationship to self-esteem and self-efficacy. *Journal of Learning Disabilities, 22,* 590–592.

Satz, P., Taylor, H. G., Friel, J., & Fletcher, J. M. (1978). Some developmental and predictive precursors of reading disabilities: A six year follow-up. In A. L. Benton & D. Pearl (Eds.), *Dyslexia: An appraisal of current knowledge* (pp. 315–347). New York: Oxford University Press.

Schonhaut, S., & Satz, P. (1983). Prognosis for children with learning disabilities: A review of follow-up studies. In M. Rutter (Ed.), *Developmental neuropsychiatry* (pp. 542–563). New York: Guilford Press.

Scranton, T., & Ryckman, D. (1979). Sociometric status of learning disabled children in an integrative program. *Journal of Learning Disabilities, 12,* 402–407.

Shaffer, D. (1978). "Soft" neurological signs and later psychiatric disorder: A review. *Journal of Child Psychology and Psychiatry, 19,* 63–65.

Silver, A. A., & Hagin, R. A. (1964). Specific reading disability: Follow-up studies. *American Journal of Orthopsychiatry, 34,* 95–102.

Silver, L. B. (1974). Emotional and social problems of children with developmental disabilities. In R. E. Weber (Ed.), *Handbook on learning disabilities* (pp. 97–120). Englewood Cliffs, NJ: Prentice Hall.

Smith, S. L. (1991). *Succeeding against the odds: Strategies and insights from the learning disabled.* Los Angeles: Jeremy P. Tarcher.

Spreen, O. (1988). *Learning disabled children growing up. A follow-up into adulthood.* New York: Oxford University Press.

Spreen, O., & Haaf, R. G. (1986). Empirically derived learning disability subtypes: A replication attempt and longitudinal patterns over 15 years. *Journal of Learning Disabilities, 19,* 170-180.

Tramontana, M. G., & Hooper, S. R. (1989). Neuropsychology of child psychopathology. In C. R. Reynolds & E. Fletcher-Janzen (Eds.), *Handbook of child neuropsychology* (pp. 87–106). New York: Plenum Press.

Tucker, D. M. (1989). Neural substrates of thought and affective disorders. In G. Gainotti & C. Caltagirone (Eds.), *Emotions and the dual brain* (pp. 225–234). New York: Springer-Verlag.

Weintraub, S., & Mesulam, M. M. (1983). Developmental learning disabilities of the right hemisphere: Emotional, interpersonal, and cognitive components. *Archives of Neurology, 40,* 463–468.

Weiss, G., Hechtman, L., Milroy, T., & Perlman, T. (1985). Psychiatric status of hyperactives as adults: A controlled prospective 15-year follow-up of 63 hyperactive children. *Journal of the American Academy of Child Psychiatry, 24,* 211–220.

9

Cognitive Functioning Profiles of the Adult Population with Learning Disabilities

CINDY A. DARDEN
ANNA W. MORGAN

The U.S. Department of Education (1987) reported a 135% increase in students classified with specific learning disabilities over a 10-year period. This population should be a major concern of the professionals who focus on identification and service to adults with disabilities (Ross, 1987), as a number of studies have indicated that testing scores, cognitive profiles, and academic shortcomings persist throughout the life span (Bowen & Hynd, 1988; Haig & Patterson, 1980; McCue, Shelly, & Goldstein, 1986; Reiff & Gerber, 1992).

Adults with learning disabilities reveal a need to understand why they have difficulties (Johnson & Blalock, 1987). They have difficulties with such basic life skills as financial management (Siegel, 1974) and interpersonal relationships (indicating that their disorder has an impact on social relationships) (Gajar, 1992). This population has been shown to be less likely to pursue postsecondary education. These adults also have lower-paying jobs with concomitant lower social status and higher reported job dissatisfaction than do their peers (Miller, Snider, & Rzonca, 1990).

Professionals, legislators, adults with learning disabilities, and the population at large should have a common interest. If those who suffer with learning disabilities are accurately identified, and if the information provided promotes understanding and drives appropriate interventions and accommodation, these adults will be able to perform as fully as possible within our society. This is the least costly possibility in terms of human potential, tax dollars, litigation, and time.

Thus, increased knowledge concerning the uniqueness of cognitive functioning of this population is a worthy goal. This chapter reviews the current knowledge concerning cognitive processing in adults with learning disabilities and outlines the current needs in regard to this population that can be addressed by focusing on their cognitive processes. We focus on the roles that research, clinical practice, and service practitioners can play.

REVIEW OF THE LITERATURE

In an effort to understand complex phenomena, definitions, models, and taxonomies are designed, tested, confirmed, or refuted. "Learning disabilities" is such a phenomenon. Theory development and research are being conducted at each level of this identification process. Central to this work is an understanding of cognitive processing. Keogh (1994) identifies two critical current issues: defining the basic nature of a learning disability and establishing robust guidelines and assessment procedures to identify those with learning disabilities.

Basic Nature of Learning Disabilities

The fields of psychology, neurology, and education have not always defined the primary characteristics of learning disabilities in the same way; however, most assert that central nervous system dysfunction plays a major role (Interagency Committee on Learning Disabilities, 1987). According to Feagans and McKinney (1991), the majority of definitions of learning disabilities provide for deficits in cognitive processes that affect school learning, even though difficulty exists in the attempt to determine the processes that are present and how to measure them.

Several approaches have been used to demonstrate that a learning disability is a distinct pathological entity (Hagen, Kamberelis, & Segal, 1991). Some researchers have focused on discrepancies between the Verbal and Performance scales on intelligence tests, whereas others have investigated intelligence achievement discrepancies. Some have focused on differential patterns of information processing (Speece, 1987; Torgesen, 1988), whereas others have attempted to document abnormal neurological functioning and to demonstrate maturational delay (Rourke, 1985).

Many works have been devoted to developing single-factor theories of learning disabilities (Satz, Rardin, & Ross, 1971); some of these focus on such neurological causality as poor intersensory integration (Birch & Belmont, 1965) and delayed development in cerebral dominance (Orton, 1928, 1937; Satz et al., 1971). Others focus on such processing areas as visual–perceptual deficits (Frostig, 1964; Kephart, 1971; Lyle & Goyen, 1975), auditory–perceptual deficits and associated language inefficiencies (Stanovich, 1988), inefficient attention (Dyckman, Ackerman, Clements, & Peters, 1971; Hynd, Obrzut, Hynd, & O'Connor, 1978), and deficient memory skills (Brainerd, Kingma, & Howe, 1986; Cohen & Netley, 1981; Nelson & Warrington, 1980; Torgesen, 1988).

Due to a variety of methodological problems, convergent validity has seldom been achieved in most research programs and none of the single-factor theories has been able to explain the broad spectrum of learning deficiencies (Willis, Hooper, & Stone, 1992). Several investigators have proposed that the search for specific underlying causes is too simplistic given the complexities of the central nervous system (Hynd & Hynd, 1984; Olson, Kliegl, Davidson, & Foltz, 1985). Even a cursory review of the literature shows that instead of becoming more precise, definitions of learning disabilities have become more nebulous and criteria for assessment more varied (Coles, 1987).

Models of Identification

No national standards or criteria for diagnosis of learning disabilities exist for the adult population. Standards are needed to ensure that institutions do not inadvertently or deliberately discriminate against individuals seeking accommodation or placement. Keogh (1994) identifies five reasons for identification: eligibility, planning for services, assessing outcomes, research, and advocacy. Different professionals are involved with each of these functions and require different information. Those who determine eligibility, as the gatekeepers within the field, usually determine the basic information that will be obtained concerning an adult's cognitive functioning. Thus, determining which model to utilize becomes a primary question that has an impact well beyond establishing eligibility.

Researchers have proposed several models for the diagnosis of learning disabilities. All incorporate the notion of depressed achievement. The achievement-only model proposed by Siegel (1990) bases diagnosis on achievement measures alone. Although the model allows for liberal eligibility, it provides no information on cognitive processing and fails to identify those with superior ability who are only able to perform within the average range of achievement. It is also a less useful model with adults in that academic achievement is not always the primary referral issue.

Intelligence in the average range, along with displayed discrepant achievement, has been a frequently used criterion for learning disabilities (Critchley, 1970). The failure of psychometric and etiological classification procedures to provide useful indexes has led to an overreliance on the IQ–achievement score discrepancy formula as the principal index. Discrepancy criteria have the advantage of providing a more objective index of underachievement in light of ability but present a host of methodological, conceptual, and practical problems (Feagans & McKinney, 1991; Siegel, 1990). The *Diagnostic and Statistical Manual of Mental Disorders*, fourth edition (DSM-IV; American Psychiatric Association, 1994), is the categorization system most likely to be used with the adult population in rehabilitation and mental health agencies. It identifies three learning disorders: reading, mathematics, and disorder of written language, using a discrepancy model. Although DSM-IV acknowledges that abnormalities in cognitive processing may precede or be associated with the disorder, cognitive processing deficits are not addressed.

Others advocate the use of the regression model because it is the most statistically sound (Feagans & McKinney, 1991). Although this model well provides for empirical research, it is somewhat limited in the information it provides about the individual and is impractical in clinical settings (Feagans & McKinney, 1991).

Models that incorporate identification of specific cognitive processing deficits that affect achievement are also prevalent (Geib, Guzzardi, & Genova, 1981; Hoy & Gregg , 1994; Johnson & Blalock, 1987). These models use a variety of instrumentation, from as little as an analysis of the subtests of an intelligence measure (Leonard, 1991) to an intensive clinical model such as that utilized by Johnson and Blalock (1987) and the model recently proposed by Hoy et al. (Chapter 3, this volume).

The model by Hoy et al. uses both quantitative and qualitative data gathered from psychological assessment in the cognitive, social and emotional, achievement, and oral language domains in conjunction with a thorough history of the client and the clinical observations and expertise of a multidisciplinary team. This process allows for the inclusion of students at either end of the range of cognitive abilities and attempts to explain how cognitive deficits influence the client's manipulations of his or her environment (e.g., spelling, directionality, reading, social cue interpretation, and financial management skills). This model purports to fill the need for a model that not only determines eligibility but provides information to drive the interventions planned. Its major disadvantages are that it is not as psychometrically objective as is needed for some levels of research, and it is a time- and personnel-costly model.

The choice of methods has been shown to be critical as evidenced by the lack of consistency in both the number of individuals identified and which individuals are identified by different models (Brackett & McPherson, Chapter 4, this volume; Feagans & McKinney, 1991; Hoy et al., 1994). Each of these models depends on assessment instrumentation for identification of the disorders. Thus, much of what we know about the cognitive processing of adults with learning disabilities is within the framework of the best known and most widely used instruments.

Intelligence Tests and Cognitive Functioning

Researchers have been interested in adult intelligence for the past 70 years (Jones & Conrad, 1933; Lorge, 1936; Miles & Miles, 1932; Wiloughby, 1927). According to Kaufman (1990), an adequate understanding of the expected fluctuations in an individual's cognitive abilities from adolescence to older adulthood is needed. Understanding the normal and pathological development of cognitive abilities of adults is essential for diagnostic efforts.

The intelligence score has served as the watermark measure of ability and as the most solid predictor of success that we have. Intelligence measures have come under a great deal of scrutiny, and even litigation; however, they have stood the test of time (Kaufman, 1990). Standardized intelligence measures continue to show high intercorrelation among themselves as well as with standardized achievement measures and more practical measures of achievement (i.e., success in college). This predictive value may be lessened if learning disabilities are present. Leonard (1991) concluded that the Wechsler Adult Intelligence Scale—Revised (WAIS-R; Wechsler, 1981) was not predictive of success at the postsecondary level even though the Comprehension and Similarities subtests were significantly correlated with grade point average.

The Wechsler scales have been the most utilized instruments in the assessment of learning disabilities. Cognitive processing profiles have been examined through focusing on subdivisions of the Wechsler instruments.

Two- and Three-Factor-Analytic Profiles

The Wechsler instruments comprise three scales, with the Verbal and Performance scales derived through factor analysis. Kaufman's (1990) review of the literature on significant differences between these two scales in relation to adults with learning disabilities determined that a Performance greater than Verbal profile (P > V) often exists, with the exception of college students. Apparently college students typically evidence the opposite pattern: V > P by as much as 10 points or evidence no V–P difference. Johnson and Blalock (1987) found that their group (including both college and noncollege) did not exhibit the typical profile of P > V. Rather, an equal number exhibited the reverse pattern.

The three-factor design (Verbal Comprehension, Perceptual Organization, and Freedom from Distractibility) has been used for the past 40 years. Kaufman (1990) suggested that for many individuals with learning disabilities the Perceptual Organization factor is the best evidence for intellectual potential. He also reminded clinicians that the third factor, Freedom from Distractibility, has a greater impact on the Verbal and Full Scale scores for adults because Digit Span is figured into adults' scores but not into children's scores.

ACID Profile

One of the most familiar profiles associated with learning disabilities is the ACID (Arithmetic, Coding [or Digit Symbol], Information, and Digit Span) profile, whose subtests are posited to be the lowest. Kaufman (1990) stated that, in general, this pattern persists in adulthood, but in the individual case, it may not be true. This is substantiated by Johnson and Blalock's (1987) examination of 93 adults with learning disabilities which found weaknesses on Arithmetic, Coding, and Digit Span (ACD), but strength on Information as a group. When the authors examined each case, even these three subtests (ACD) were within the lowest scores of only 11 of the 93 cases. The authors suggested that these subtests are sensitive to a number of deficit areas. Thus, in group analysis, they are frequently identified but are not diagnostic in individual cases.

Bannatyne's Model

Bannatyne (1974) rationally derived four categories: Verbal Conceptualization, Spatial and Sequential Abilities, and Acquired Knowledge.

Evidence suggests that adults with learning disabilities perform poorly on the Sequential and Acquired Knowledge groupings and highest on Spatial ability, with the exception of college students for whom Verbal Conceptualization has emerged as highest in a number of studies (Kaufman, 1990). In some studies the two have been equally high and in other studies Acquired Knowledge has failed to emerge as a weakness.

Johnson and Blalock's (1987) study found that Verbal Conceptualization was highest and Sequential Ability was lowest, confirming sequential ability as problematic but not spatial ability as a strength. Ten subjects demonstrated the clear pattern expected: Spatial > Verbal > Acquired Knowledge > Sequential; however, even within these 10, the learning problems experienced were different. The authors concluded that this system should not be used diagnostically.

Classification Systems

Recently, attempts have been made to develop subtypes of learning disabilities (e.g., Feagans & Applebaum, 1986). The goal of this research is to classify the heterogeneous population of those with learning disabilities into homogeneous subgroups for practical and scientific purposes (Kavale, 1990).

Approaches to the classification of those with learning disabilities have ranged from clinical inferential to statistical analytical approaches. Typically naturalistic observation is followed by theory development and then empirical research. However, this is not a linear process. Once empirical research begins, observation and theory development do not end. Rather, all three occur simultaneously, either in isolation from one another, resulting in competing taxonomies, or in unison, resulting, it is hoped, in a more accurate classification system. The state of development in the field of learning disabilities includes loosely developed systems derived from all three approaches.

Empirical Subtyping

Kavale and Nye (1985–1986) reported on a meta-analysis of 1,400 studies, comparing groups of individuals with learning disabilities with non-learning disabled individuals across 38 variables. None distinguished the two groups clearly. Kavale (1990) stated that although discrete descriptors have been made, a unified conceptualization of learning disabilities has not yet materialized.

Kavale (1990) stated the commonalities in subtyping research as follows: similar areas of functioning are being assessed, with from two to seven subtypes typically emerging, and the majority of studies focus on the macrolevel of distinctions. Speece (1990) suggested that a broad exploratory approach is appropriate at this point to ensure that legitimate subtypes are not overlooked or eliminated prematurely. In Forness's review of the literature (1990), he drew from the work of Weller and Strawser (1987) to summarize the subtypes that have established the highest level of consensus in the field as non-learning disabilities pattern (discrepancy in grade achievement, but not in light of intellectual potential), production deficits (inefficient cognitive strategies), verbal and nonverbal organization disorders, and global disorders (multiple deficits in processing).

Problems in subtyping research include (1) test unreliability, (2) methodological and statistical limitations, and (3) lack of focus on the predictive ability of subtypes (Forness, 1990; Shafrir & Siegel, 1994). Kavale (1990) states that the field of subtyping is too method driven and warns that classification needs to have a theoretical base to be meaningful. Forness (1990) and Kavale (1990) both call for subtyping to become more contextual by including such other interactive factors as temperament, motivation, teacher competence, and so on.

Clinical Subtyping

In clinical practice and research, learning disabilities are often categorized by the academic area that the disabilities affect: reading, written language, and mathematics. Another common way to categorize is by the cognitive process that is impaired: auditory processing or visual processing. Classification by processing area appears to occur both theoretically and rationally. Other categories are designated because of a particular exceptionality (e.g., gifted individuals with learning disabilities). Academic, cognitive processing, and special population classifications are discussed here.

Academic Classifications. Academic classification developed in the school system and has generalized to other settings. Categories typically include reading, written language, and arithmetic, with reading the most well researched. This research has included the examination of the differences between poor readers and good readers and among poor readers with discrepant and those who are nondiscrepant IQ as well as comprehensive investigations. Shafrir and Siegel (1994) found significant differences between adults with and without reading disabilities in phonological processing and short-term memory. The evidence is mixed for differences between poor readers who are discrepant and those who are nondiscrepant in reading achievement and IQ score. Studies by Bloom, Wagner, Reskin, and Bergman (1980), Fredman and Stevenson (1988), Siegel (1988), and Taylor, Satz, and Friel (1979) did not find significant discrepancy group differences in a variety of component reading and cognitive skills.

Johnson (1987) reviewed the literature related to reading disabilities and suggested that both visual and auditory processing problems affect reading, as do both simultaneous and sequential processing deficits. When reading was affected by processing problems, the population was classified as oral expressive language, visual processing, and multisensory deficient. These results were similar to those reported by Bruck (1990), who found that deficits in phonological processing and pseudoword reading documented during childhood persisted into adulthood, as well as to results of recent research by Siegel (1993) reporting phonological deficits in adults with learning disabilities. Other research reports memory deficits in readers with disabilities (Baker, Ceci, & Hermann, 1987; Swanson, 1986; Wagner & Torgesen, 1987).

In Gregg's (1992) review of the history of written language disorders, she stated that these disorders are the result of a breakdown in the cognitive system, although which processes have an impact in certain ways is not clear. Written language likely depends on visual–spatial and linguistic processes. Research on the cognitive processes involved in producing written text has focused on microtasks of writing (e.g., spelling) rather than macrotasks (e.g., organization and sense of audience) (Gregg, 1992). Johnson (1987) and Gregg (1992) both stated that different cognitive processing deficits are likely to affect different aspects of written language, and both list speculative characteristic behaviors of selected cognitive deficits on written text. Gregg (1992) concluded that the empirical support for the existence of these deficits is weak and additional research is needed.

Blalock (1987) summarized disturbances in mathematics documented in the literature, concluding that both verbal and nonverbal deficits have been found to affect functioning in mathematics, with verbal and visual–spatial deficits most often identified. Shafrir and Siegel (1994) found that adults diagnosed with an arithmetic disability only performed in the average range in phonological processing but exhibited deficits in visual–spatial functioning. Kosc (1974, 1981) suggested six types of dyscalculia and Badian (1983) suggested four types. Deficits in mathematics are thought to be less common than deficits in reading and written language.

Theoretical Classifications. Theoretical taxonomies can be used to drive diagnosis and also as frameworks to understand cognitive processing. The Horn–Cattell model (Horn & Cattell, 1966, 1967) of fluid and crystallized intelligence is a theoretical model of particular interest in investigating adults with learning disabilities. A primary interest in this model is in interpreting age-related changes in intelligence across the adult life span. Horn and McArdle (1980) created divisions for the WAIS-R. Two cognitive instruments have been developed that utilize this theory as a primary theoretical base. The Woodcock–Johnson Psychoeducational Battery (Woodcock & Johnson, 1989), breaks the crystallized and fluid abilities into more specific processes. It also provides a norm-based interpretation for aptitude and achievement and intracognitive discrepancies. The Kaufman Adolescent and Adult Intelligence Test (KAIT; Kaufman & Kaufman, 1993) was developed with Horn and Cattell as its primary theoretical base but also includes the Luria–Golden (Golden, 1981; Luria, 1980) definition of planning ability and Piaget's Formal Operations stage (Inhelder & Piaget, 1958; Piaget, 1972) in its development.

There are several additional models of cognitive classification. One of these is Osgood's Psycholinguistic Approach (Kirk, McCarthy, & Kirk, 1968). Kaufman (1990) suggested that an advantage of this approach is that the examiner should be able to pinpoint the channel or level of organization that is defective (i.e., auditory–vocal or visual–motor) as well as the specific process that is deficient (i.e., reception, association, or expression). Dean's (1983) Individual Ability Profile is a useful example of a more detailed system, with 12 categories specified, including general ability, abstract thought, remote memory, social comprehension, and visual–motor speed. Guilford's (1967) Structure-of-Intellect model includes four operations (cognition, memory, evaluation, and convergent–production), three content areas (semantic, figural, symbolic), and products (how the stimuli is organized). Kaufman (1990) stated that using this model is sometimes the only way to make sense out of fluctuations in an individual's subtest profile. Rapaport's Clinical Model (Mayman, Schafer, & Rapaport, 1951; Rapaport, Gill, & Schafer, 1945–1946) stresses the importance of such factors as the influence of personality, environmental stimulation, cultural issues, and psychopathology on the maturation and expression of intelligence. Its strength with adults lies in its emphasis on context.

Rational Classifications. Rational classifications are derived from observed phenomena in any number of related fields. For example, in biogenetics, research has focused on group factors of specific cognitive abilities, especially verbal, spatial, memory, and perceptual speed factors (Plomin, 1991).

The field of special education has contributed a great deal of observational insights. Hoy and Gregg (1994) have suggested a framework for thinking about learner characteristics and tasks characteristics that takes into account content-specific skills, the stage of learning of the student in relation to the sensory modality utilized in the transmission of information, and the basic learning abilities of the student. They discuss two basic styles of processing information—successive and simultaneous—and divide cognitive processes into lower- and higher-order functions. Selective attention, perception, memory, and visual–motor integration are the lower-order processes, and symbolization/representation, conceptualization/reasoning, speed of processing, and automaticity are the higher-order processes. Hoy and Gregg (1994) provide a useful discussion about how the processing areas create difficulties in specific academic areas.

Research on Processing Areas

Particular processing deficits frequently discussed in psychological reports, academic remediation plans, and some controlled research projects include auditory processing; visual processing, including attention, perception, and memory; and higher-order cognition, including abstract reasoning and conceptualization skills.

An example of this research is found in Elliott and Busse's (1987) research project on auditory processing utilizing experimental test procedures, as standardized instruments to measure these processes in adults are lacking. Many of the subjects showed poorer than normal performance for detection of pure tones and syllables, for syllable identification thresholds, for discriminating differences between syllables, and in sentence understanding, suggesting poor auditory discrimination skills. A majority of the subjects were found to have some oral language, auditory processing, or metalinguistic problems. The discussion identified problems in auditory reception (perception, discrimination), comprehension, memory, and auditory expression resulting in difficulty in reading decoding skills, expressive language, and writing, particularly spelling.

Level of Severity

Hoy et al. (1994) found differences in overall ability level of those diagnosed with learning disabilities in a rehabilitation versus college setting, underscoring the heterogeneity of adults with learning disabilities and highlighting the importance of considering severity in the assessment of adults. Geib et al. (1981) stated that despite the person's cognitive ability, his or her learning disability will prevent gaining information from the environment, such as the media, instructions, and directions of operation on appliances, tools, and so on.

Categorization by special populations also occurs. This has been particularly true for populations of individuals with varying ability levels and varying severity levels of learning disabilities. Three groups are of particular interest: nonverbal, college, and gifted individuals.

Nonverbal Learning Disabilities

Rourke, Young, and Leeners (1989) have identified a particularly severe syndrome of deficits in neurological functioning referred to as nonverbal learning disabilities. This disorder may predispose those afflicted to adolescent and adult depression and suicide risk. Johnson and Myklebust (1967) have offered a definition of this disability as deficits in the ability to understand nonverbal particulars of daily living, while such other cognitive abilities as verbal abilities are in the average-to-above-average range. Difficulties learning from observation, perceptual–motor deficits (spatial orientation, body image, facial recognition, interpretation of gesture), visual–motor difficulties, and deficits in the analysis, synthesis, and organization of nonverbal information are speculated to be distinguishing features (Myklebust, 1975; Rourke, 1985).

Analysis of the WAIS-R profile in 18 adults revealed significant discrepancies between Verbal and Performance scales (Verbal > Performance by 15+ points; Johnson, 1987). The author suggested that the Performance scale is most affected by this disability, but the Verbal scale is also affected. Individuals with nonverbal learning disabilities do not display apparent difficulties with language syntax or the development of vocabulary (Rourke, 1985), resulting in their cognitive abilities frequently being misinterpreted because of their relatively strong verbal skills (Jackson, 1988), despite their experiencing more difficulties in daily living than those with verbal disabilities. These adults exhibit a pattern of reliance on others, underemployment, poor emotional and social functioning, and low self-esteem (Rourke, Young, Strang, & Russell, 1986).

College Students with Learning Disabilities

As already discussed, college students with learning disabilities do not fit the typical profiles of adults with learning disabilities on analyses with the WAIS-R. The WAIS-R is not as predictive of success (Leonard, 1991) for this group, but high verbal skills are typically identified in those who do succeed, with Full Scale, Verbal, and Performance scores typically within the average-to-above-average range with Verbal higher than Performance scores.

In a recent investigation of college students, with and without learning disabilities (Morgan, Sullivan, Darden, & Gregg, 1994), it was found that the three scales of the KAIT were highly correlated with the scales on the WAIS-R, and that the subjects performed comparably well on the Crystallized and Verbal scales. However, both groups performed significantly poorer on the Fluid than they performed on the Performance Scale. Thus, it was suggested that the Fluid Scale captures abilities that are distinct. No specific profile for students with learning disabilities emerged in this initial study.

Gifted Adults with Learning Disabilities

Barton and Starnes (1988) in their review of the literature concerning those classified as gifted and learning disabled concluded that no pattern has materialized regarding this group. Individual studies have identified differences that are noteworthy. Most studies report Verbal–Performance splits on Wechsler instruments, but magnitude and direction differ.

Schiff, Kaufman, and Kaufman (1981) observed greater Verbal–Performance discrepancies for students with learning disabilities in the superior IQ range than for students with learning disabilities in the average IQ range. They found the gifted students scored highest on subtests of the Verbal Comprehension factor and fared most poorly on sequencing tasks. In the Ferri, Gregg, and Heggoy (in press) study, almost half the sample exhibited at least a 15-point difference between the two factors. Highest WAIS-R subtest scaled scores were in Comprehension and Block Design. Fox (1981) found Verbal–Performance discrepancies greater than or equal to 15 points in 50% of their sample, with similar results in strengths and weaknesses to other studies.

Ferri, et al. (in press) state that the population of those with learning disabilities who are also gifted is difficult to assess because the presence of a learning disability may be masked by high intelligence and resulting compensatory mechanisms, and the individual's giftedness may be overlooked due to the interference of his or her learning problems. In their study of this population in a college setting, 25% were not diagnosed with learning disabilities until college. Barton and Starnes (1988) suggested that this is not a homogeneous group and recommend further study of smaller groups within the larger gifted and learning disabled group.

FUTURE DIRECTIONS

Implications for Service Providers

How do we interpret what we learn about the cognitive functioning of adults with learning disabilities in a way that is relevant within their social context? How do our procedures apply to postsecondary education, job choice and modification, life skills issues (i.e., decision making and personal relationships), and identity maturity?

Geib et al. (1981) stress the importance of considering developmentally appropriate needs of adults in establishing interventions. An interactive model taking into consideration the adult development, cognitive functioning, temperament, social environment, and the content and organization of the task at hand is an ecologically sound approach.

Hoy and Gregg (1994) are proponents of task analysis. They suggest that when low scores are determined on standardized instruments, the examiner should analyze these data and work samples and make process observations in an effort to understand how the learning disability affects academics. These researchers suggest an interactive model in service provision as well.

Task analysis is also applicable to vocational development. Gerber, Ginsberg, and Reiff (1992) studied highly successful adults with learning disabilities and identified several factors that they believe to be critical to their success, including goodness of fit and the adequacy of the social ecology. Goodness of fit within an occupation may be difficult to determine for the adult with learning disabilities due to the differences in his or her cognitive processing and lack of knowledge as how to equate strengths and weaknesses in vocational terminology. The *Employment Assessment Process Job Analysis/Job Value* manual, a guide used by vocational rehabilitation counselors in job placement of clients with physical, mental, and psychological disorders, including learning disabilities, establishes a number and letter codes indicative of worker trait factors (e.g., temperament), general educational development (based on IQ) in three areas, and level of aptitude in nine areas (e.g., verbal, numerical, spatial, and eye–hand coordination). Many of these aptitudes are equivalent to the cognitive processing areas typically identified by psychoeducational assessment. Identification offers the possibility of using what is known about job demands in combination with what is known about an individual's cognitive processing profile to provide career counseling that would emphasize goodness of fit between the person and the environment.

The cognitive processing deficit model is quite useful in explaining the disability to the client; understanding can aid the client in developing a metacognitive awareness of his or her strengths and weaknesses. Awareness enables the individual to develop immediate compensatory mechanisms and promotes independence. This awareness of cognitive functioning is needed so that the adult with learning disabilities will be able to adapt to an ever-changing environment. Academic, vocational, or psychological therapy, or all three, may be needed to facilitate this development.

There is increasing evidence that those with learning disabilities have difficulties beyond the intellectual arena. Social learning theory purports that social competence is learned behavior. A person must be able to convert social knowledge into behaviors, accurately self-evaluate performance and outcomes, and adjust his or her behavior accordingly to be perceived as competent (Bandura, 1978; Bellack & Morrison, 1982; Ladd & Mize, 1983). This process suggests that social–cognitive deficits may be due in part to cognitive processing deficits.

Neuroses and functional psychoses may result from failure to develop one's life skills (Kazdin, 1979). Kelly (1982) suggests that psychological adjustment can be conceptualized with socially skillful functioning as a prerequisite. A neglected area of research has been the emotional or psychological disturbances that might characterize those diagnosed with learning disabilities.

Most theories of development have in some way been equated with cognitive development (Dupont, 1979; Erikson, 1950; Gilligan, 1982; Havighurst, 1953; Kohlberg, 1970; Loevinger, 1976; Piaget, 1929; Selman, 1977; Super, 1953), implying that deficits in cognitive functioning can impair ego development and, in turn, affective, vocational, and moral development. The senior author (C.D.) has more than 5 years of experience providing in-depth therapy to young adults with learning disabilities and believes that their cognitive impairments often interfere with the successful accomplishment of developmental tasks. This area is largely unresearched.

Assessment Models and Instrumentation

When examining adults, it is important to remember that the needs of group research and individual diagnostics differ. Group research designs typically require powerful empirical data, whereas individual diagnostic and remediative functions produce the best results when psychometric information is combined and weighted with clinical observation, experience, and judgment.

There are several problem areas in assessment: (1) within the cognitive correlate framework, traditional psychometric measures administered in isolation provide little insight into the nature of cognitive mechanisms (Swanson & Ransby, 1994); (2) many instruments lack normative data for the adult population, are simply upper extensions of instruments designed for children, or both; (3) within the adult population, achievement is inadequately defined and assessed, particularly for those who are no longer in the academic arena; (4) there is a lack of consensus in the field regarding qualitative data used in the assessment process; and (5) criteria for assessing the adult population are difficult to determine.

There is growing consensus for the use of a comprehensive model. Kaufman (1990) discussed the potentially different interpretations of diagnostic information, concluding that good clinical judgment is essential to the process. Nontraditional, holistic, flexible assessment practices that include task analysis are being promoted (Ferri et al., in press; Geib et al., 1981; Hoy & Gregg, 1994).

Our experiences using both the discrepancy and the clinical model (e.g., Hoy et al., 1994) have led us to believe that a cognitive processing deficit paradigm utilizing a clinical assessment model offers the most ecologically sound approach to assessment of learning disabilities in adults. Such a paradigm uses the predictive value of the best researched intelligence measures in conjunction with a holistic examination of the adult within his or her environment. This model can be used to establish eligibility, but it also provides ample information to service providers (academic, vocational, psychological) to determine interventions. It provides researchers a plethora of data. It represents the true heterogeneity of the group and respects the individual by providing clients with a framework to understand their own cognitive functioning.

Research

Knowledge in the area of cognitive functioning of adults with learning disabilities is limited. Neither psychometric research with adult intelligence measures nor cluster-analytical subtyping research has provided clinical profiles with adequate diagnostic or predictive validity. Continued research in the areas of psychometrics, empirical subtyping, and clinical investigation is recommended. Several other areas need to be examined. The group of young adults who are currently swarming to postsecondary settings will continue to age. Although there have been many studies regarding the relationship between cognitive abilities and the aging process (Birren & Schaie, 1985; Kausler, 1982; Poon, 1980), none has investigated what occurs in the cognitive functioning of adults with learning disabilities as they enter midlife and later adulthood. We need to consider these individuals in light of the natural aging process and in relation to their cognitive deficits and compensatory mechanisms. Siegel (1988) stated the need for empirical research documenting the impact of remediation on intelligence measures. We also need studies investigating aptitude and treatment interactions and the connection between cognitive processing and social, emotional, and ego development.

Classification Systems

Kavale (1990) reminds us that classifications are arbitrary structural arrangements. The parable of the four blind men and the elephant (Taylor, 1951) is appropriate. In this parable, four blind men feel an elephant's leg, tail, ear, and body, respectively, and conclude it is like a log, a rope, a fan, and something without beginning or end. The phenomenon called learning disabilities is complex and is being examined by various fields at different levels. Exploration from each of these groups at each level can provide a unique perspective. We only run into difficulties when we, like the blind men, believe that what we observe is "truth and sole truth." Paradigms are meant to help organize and communicate knowledge; they are also meant to be revised and, at times, rejected as new information is revealed. Our best course is to continue our study of the cognitive processing of adults with learning disabilities from each of these perspectives, but in a circular model in which each group of researchers and practitioners shares its knowledge and insights with each of the other groups. Too much is at stake for the adults with learning disabilities to allow our classification efforts to become a competition.

REFERENCES

American Psychiatric Association. (1994). *Diagnostic and statistical manual of mental disorders* (4th ed.). Washington, DC: Author.
Anastasi, A. (1986). *Psychological testing* (6th ed.). New York: Macmillan.
Badian, N. (1983). Dyscalculia and nonverbal disorders of reading. In H. Myklebust (Ed.), *Progress in learning disabilities* (Vol. 5, pp. 235–264). New York: Grune & Stratton.
Baker, J. G., Ceci, S. J., & Hermann, N. D. (1987). Semantic structure and processing: Implications for the learning disabled child. In H. L. Swanson (Ed.), *Memory and learning disabilities* (pp. 83–110). Greenwich, CT: JAI Press.

Bandura, A. (1978). The self system in reciprocal determinism. *American Psychologist, 33,* 344–358.

Bannatyne, A. (1974). Diagnosis: A note on recategorization of the WISC scaled scores. *Journal of Learning Disabilities, 7,* 272–274.

Barton, J., & Starnes, W. (1988). Identifying distinguishing characteristics of gifted and talented/learning disabled students. *Roeper Review, 12,* 23–29.

Bellack, A. S., & Morrison, R. L. (1982). Interpersonal dysfunction. In A. S. Bellack, M. Hersen, & A. E. Kazdin (Eds.), *International handbook of behavioral modification and therapy* (pp. 717–747). New York: Plenum Press.

Birch, H., & Belmont, L. (1965). Auditory–visual integration, intelligence, and reading ability in school children. *Perceptual and Motor Skills, 20,* 295–305.

Birren, J. E., & Schaie, K. W. (1985). *Handbook of the psychology of aging* (2nd ed.). New York: Van Nostrand Reinhold.

Blalock, J. (1982). Persistent auditory language deficits in adults with learning disabilities. *Journal of Learning Disabilities, 15,* 604–609.

Blalock, J. (1987). Intellectual levels and patterns. In D. Johnson & J. Blalock (Eds.), *Young adults with learning disabilities: Clinical studies* (pp. 47–65). Orlando, FL: Grune & Stratton.

Bloom, A., Wagner, M., Reskin, L., & Bergman, A. (1980). A comparison of intellectually delayed and primary reading disabled children on measures of intelligence and achievement. *Journal of Clinical Psychology, 36,* 788–790.

Bowen, S., & Hynd, G. W. (1988). Do children with learning disabilities outgrow deficits in selective auditory attention? Evidence from dichotic listening in adults with learning disabilities. *Journal of Learning Disabilities, 21,* 623–631.

Brainerd, C. J., Kingma, J., & Howe, M. L. (1986). Long term memory development and learning disability: Storage and retrieval loci of disabled/nondisabled differences. In S. Ceci (Ed.), *Handbook on cognitive, social, and neuropsychological aspects of learning disabilities* (pp. 161–184). Hillsdale, NJ: Erlbaum.

Bruck, M. (1990). Word recognition skills of adults with childhood diagnoses of dyslexia. *Developmental Psychology, 26,* 439–454.

Cohen, R., & Netley, C. (1981). Short-term memory deficits in reading disabled children, in the absence of opportunity for rehearsal strategies. *Intelligence, 5,* 69–76.

Coles, G. (1987). *The learning mystique.* New York: Pantheon Books.

Critchley, M. (1970). *The dyslexic child* (2nd ed.). Springfield, IL: Charles C. Thomas.

Dean, R. S. (1983). *Manual: Report on individual evaluation for use with WAIS/WAIS-R.* Orlando, FL: Psychological Assessment Resources.

Dupont, H. (1979). Affective development: Stage and sequence. In R. L. Mosher (Ed.), *Adolescents' development and education* (pp. 163–183). Berkeley, CA: McCutchan.

Dyckman, R. A., Ackerman, P., Clements, S. D., & Peters, J. E. (1971). Specific learning disabilities: An attention deficit syndrome. In H. R. Myklebust (Ed.), *Progress in learning disabilities* (pp. 55–60). New York: Grune & Stratton.

Elliott, L. L., & Busse, L. L. (1987). Auditory processing by learning disabled young adults. In D. J. Johnson & J. W. Blalock (Eds.), *Adults with learning disabilities: Clinical studies* (pp. 107–129). New York: Grune & Stratton.

Erikson, E. H. (1950). *Childhood and society* (2nd ed.). New York: Norton.

Feagans, L. V., & Appelbaum, M. (1986). Language subtypes and their validation in learning disabled children. *Journal of Educational Psychology, 78,* 358–364.

Feagans, L. V., & McKinney, J. D. (1991). Subtypes of learning disabilities: A review. In L. V. Feagans, E. J. Short, & L. J. Meltzer (Eds.), *Subtypes of learning disabilities* (pp. 3–31). Hillsdale, NJ: Erlbaum.

Ferri, B., Gregg, N., & Heggoy, S. (in press). *A descriptive analysis of adults demonstrating a gifted/learning disabled profile.*

Forness, S. R. (1990). Subtyping in learning disabilities: Introduction to the issues. In H. L. Swanson & B. Keogh (Eds.), *Learning disabilities: Theoretical and research issues* (pp. 195–200). Hillsdale, NJ: Erlbaum.

Fox, L. (1981). Identification of the academically gifted. *American Psychologist, 36,* 1103–1111.

Fredman, G., & Stevenson, J. (1988). Reading processes in specific reading retarded and reading backward 13-year-olds. *British Journal of Developmental Psychology, 6,* 97–108.

Frostig, M. (1964). *The Frostig program for the development of visual perception; Teacher's guide.* Chicago, IL: Follett.

Gajar, A. (1992). Adults with learning disabilities: Current and future research priorities. *Journal of Learning Disabilities, 25,* 507–519.

Geib, B., Guzzardi, L., & Genova, P. (1981). Intervention for adults with learning disabilities. *Academic Therapy, 16,* 317–325.

Gerber, P., Ginsberg, R., & Reiff, H. (1992). Identifying alterable patterns in employment success for highly successful adults with learning disabilities. *Journal of Learning Disabilities, 25,* 475–487.

Gilligan, C. (1982). *In a different voice: Psychological theory and women's development.* Cambridge MA: Harvard University Press.

Golden, C. J. (1981). The Luria–Nebraska Children's Battery: Theory and formulation. In G. W. Hynd & J. E. Obrzut (Eds.), *Neuropsychological assessment and the school-age child: Issues and procedures* (pp. 277–302). New York: Grune & Stratton.

Gregg, N. (1992). Expressive writing disorders. In S. R. Hooper, G. W. Hynd, & R. E. Mattison (Eds.), *Developmental disorders diagnostic criteria and clinical assessment* (pp. 127–172). Hillsdale, NJ: Erlbaum.

Guilford, J. P. (1967). *Psychometric methods.* New York: McGraw-Hill.

Hagen, J. W., Kamberelis, G., & Segal, S. (1991). A dimensional approach to cognition and academic performance in children with medical problems or learning difficulties. In L. V. Feagans, E. J. Short, & L. J. Meltzer (Eds.), *Subtypes of learning disabilities* (pp. 53–82). Hillsdale, NJ: Erlbaum.

Haig, J. M., & Patterson, B. H. (1980). *An overview of adult learning disabilities.* Paper presented at the 13th annual meeting of the Western College Reading Association, San Francisco.

Havighurst, R. J. (1953). *Human development and education.* New York: Longmans/Green.

Horn, J. L., & Cattell, R. B. (1966). Refinement and test of the theory of fluid and crystallized intelligence. *Journal of Educational Psychology, 57,* 253–270.

Horn, J. L., & Cattell, R. B. (1967). Age differences in fluid and crystallized intelligence. *Acta Psychologica, 26,* 107–129.

Horn, J. L., & McArdle, J. J. (1980). Perspectives on mathematical/statistical model building (MASMOB) in research on aging. In L. W. Poon (Ed.), *Aging in the 1980's: Psychological issues* (pp. 503–541). Washington, DC: American Psychological Association.

Hoy, C., & Gregg, N. (1994). *Assessment: The special educator's role.* Pacific Grove, CA: Brooks/Cole.

Hoy, C., Gregg, N., Jagota, M., King, M., Moreland, C., & Manglitz, E. (1994). Relationship between the Wechsler Adult Intelligence Scale—Revised and the Woodcock–Johnson Test of Cognitive Ability—Revised among adults with learning disabilities in university and rehabilitation settings [WJ-R Monograph]. *Journal of Psychoeducational Assessment,* 54–63.

Hynd, G. W., & Hynd, C. R. (1984). Dyslexia: Neuroanatomical/neurolinguistic perspectives. *Reading Research Quarterly, 19,* 482–498.

Hynd, G. W., Orbzut, J. E. , Hynd, C. R., & O'Connor, J. (1978). Attentional deficits and word attributes preferred by learning disabled children in grades 2, 4, and 6. *Perceptual and Motor Skills, 47,* 643–652.

Inhelder, B., & Piaget, J. (1958). *The growth of logical thinking from childhood to adolescence.* New York: Basic Books.

Interagency Committee on Learning Disabilities. (1987). *Learning disabilities: A report to the U.S. Congress.* Bethesda, MD: National Institutes of Health. (ERIC Document Reproduction Service No. ED 294 358)

Jackson, R. F. (1988). *Adults with nonverbal learning disabilities and their roles in achieving independence: A qualitative study.* Unpublished doctoral dissertation, University of Georgia, Athens.

Johnson, D. J. (1987). Principles of assessment and diagnosis. In D. J. Johnson & J. W. Blalock (Eds.), *Adults with learning disabilities: Clinical studies* (pp. 9–30). Orlando, FL: Grune & Stratton.

Johnson, D. J., & Blalock, J. W. (1987). Summary of problems and needs. In D. J. Johnson & J. W. Blalock (Eds.), *Adults with learning disabilities: Clinical studies* (pp. 277–296). Orlando, FL: Grune & Stratton.

Johnson, D. J., & Myklebust, H. R. (1967). *Learning disabilities: Educational principles and practices.* New York: Grune & Stratton.

Jones, H. E., & Conrad, H. S. (1933). The growth and decline of intelligence: A study of a homogeneous group between the ages of ten and sixty. *Genetic Psychology Monographs, 13*, 223–298.

Kaufman, A. S. (1990). *Assessing adolescent and adult intelligence.* Boston: Allyn & Bacon.

Kaufman, A. S., & Kaufman, N. L. (1977). *Clinical evaluation of young children with the McCarthy Scales.* New York: Grune & Stratton.

Kaufman, A. S., & Kaufman, N. L. (1993). *Manual for the Kaufman Adolescent and Adult Intelligence Test (KAIT).* Circle Pines, MN: American Guidance Service.

Kausler, D. H. (1982). *Experimental psychology and human aging.* New York: Wiley.

Kavale, K. A. (1990). A critical appraisal of empirical subtyping research in learning disabilities. In H. L. Swanson & B. Keogh (Eds.), *Learning disabilities: Theoretical and research issues* (pp. 215–230). Hillsdale, NJ: Erlbaum.

Kavale, K. A., & Nye, C. (1985–1986). Parameters of learning disabilities in achievement, linguistics, neuropsychological, and social/behavioral domains. *Journal of Special Education, 19*, 443–458.

Kazdin, A. E. (1979). Sociological factors in psychopathology. In A. S. Bellack & M. Hersen (Eds.), *Research and practice in social skills training* (pp. 41–73). New York: Plenum Press.

Kelly, J. A. (1982). *Social-skills training: A practical guide for interventions.* New York: Springer.

Keogh, B. K. (1994). A matrix of decision points in the measurement of learning disabilities. In G. L. Lyon (Ed.), *Frames of reference for the assessment of learning disabilities: New views on measurement issues* (pp. 15–26). Baltimore: Paul H. Brookes.

Kephart, N. C. (1971, February). *The relationship of measured perceptual processes to school learning.* Paper presented at the Annual Meeting of the American Educational Research Association, New York.

Kirk, S. A., McCarthy, J. J., & Kirk, W. D. (1968). *Examiner manual: Illinois Test of Psycholinguistic Abilities.* Urbana: University of Illinois Press.

Kohlberg, L. (1970). *Moral development.* New York: Holt, Rinehart & Winston.

Kosc, L. (1974). Developmental dyscalculia. *Journal of Learning Disabilities, 7*, 165–178.

Kosc, L. (1981). Neuropsychological implications of diagnosis and treatment of mathematical learning disabilities. *Topics in Learning and Learning Disabilities, 1*, 19–30.

Ladd, G. W., & Mize, J. (1983). Social skills training and assessment with children: A cognitive–social learning approach. In C. W. LeCroy (Ed.), *Social skills training for children and youth* (pp. 61–74). New York: Haworth Press.

Leonard, F. (1991). Using Wechsler data to predict success for learning disabled college students. *Learning Disabilities Practice, 6*, 17–24.

Loevinger, J. (1976). *Ego development: Conceptions and theories*. San Francisco: Jossey-Bass.

Lorge, I. (1936). The influence of test upon the nature of mental decline as a function of age. *Journal of Educational Psychology, 27,* 100–110.

Luria, A. R. (1980). *Higher cortical functions in man* (2nd ed.). New York: Basic Books.

Lyle, J. G., Goyen, J. D. (1975). Effect of speed of exposure and difficulty of discrimination on visual recognition of retarded readers. *Journal of Abnormal Psychology, 84,* 673–676.

Mayman, M., Schafer, R., & Rapaport, D. (1951). Interpretation of the WAIS in personality appraisal. In H. H. Anderson & G. L. Anderson (Eds.), *An introduction to the projective techniques* (pp. 541–580). New York: Prentice Hall.

McCue, P. M., Shelly, C., & Goldstein, G. (1986). Intellectual, academic, and neuropsychological performance levels in learning disabled adults. *Journal of Learning Disabilities, 19,* 233–241.

Miles, C. C., & Miles, W. R. (1932). The correlation of intelligence scores and chronological age from early to late maturity. *American Journal of Psychology, 44,* 44–78.

Miller, R., Snider, B., & Rzonca, C. (1990). Variables related to the decision of young adults with learning disabilities to participate in postsecondary education. *Journal of Learning Disabilities, 23,* 349–354.

Morgan, A. W., Sullivan, S. A. , Darden, C. A., & Gregg, N. (1994, March). *Measuring intelligence of college students with learning disabilities: A comparison of results obtained on the Wechsler Adult Intelligence Scale— Revised (WAIS-R) and the Kaufman Adolescent and Adult Intelligence Test (KAIT)*. Paper presented at the annual meeting of the National Association of School Psychologists, Seattle, WA.

Myklebust, H. R. (1975). Nonverbal learning disabilities. In H. R. Myklebust (Ed.), *Progress in learning disabilities* (Vol. 3, pp. 85–121). New York: Grune & Stratton.

Nelson, H. E., & Warrington, E. K. (1980). An investigation of memory functions in dyslexic children. *British Journal of Psychology, 71,* 487–503.

Olson, R., Kliegl, R., Davidson, B. J., & Foltz, G. (1985). Individual and developmental differences in reading disability. In T. G. Waller (Ed.), *Reading research: Advances in theory and practice* (Vol. 4, pp. 1–64). New York: Academic Press.

Orton, S. (1928). Specific reading disability–strephosymbolia. *Journal of the American Medical Association, 90,* 1095–1099.

Orton, S. (1937). *Reading, writing and speech problems in children*. New York: Norton.

Piaget, J. (1929). *The child's conception of the world*. New York: Harcourt, Brace.

Piaget, J. (1972). Intellectual evolution from adolescence to adulthood. *Human Development, 15,* 1–12.

Plomin, R. (1991). A behavioral genetic approach to learning disabilities and their subtypes. In L. V. Feagans, E. J. Short, & L. J. Meltzer (Eds.), *Subtypes of learning disabilities: Theoretical perspectives and research* (pp. 83–109). Hillsdale, NJ: Erlbaum.

Poon, L. W. (Ed.). (1980). *Aging in the 1980s: Psychological issues.* Washington, DC: American Psychological Corporation.

Rapaport, D., Gill, M., & Schafer, R. (1945–1946). *Diagnostic psychological testing.* Chicago: Year Book.

Reiff, H. B., & Gerber, P. J. (1992). Learning to achieve: Suggestions for adults with learning disabilities. *Journal of Postsecondary Education and Disability, 10,* 11–23.

Ross, J. M. (1987). Learning disabled adults: Who are they and what do we do with them? *Lifelong Learning: An Omnibus of Practice and Research, 11,* 4–7, 11.

Rourke, B. P. (Ed.). (1985). *Neuropsychology of learning disabilities: Essentials of subtype analysis.* New York: Guilford Press.

Rourke, B. P., Young, G. C., & Leeners, A. A. (1989). A childhood learning disability that predisposes those afflicted to adolescent and adult depression and suicide risk. *Journal of Learning Disabilities, 22,* 169–175.

Rourke, B. P., Young, G. C., Strang, J. D., & Russell, D. L. (1986). Adult outcomes of childhood central processing deficiencies. In I. Grant & K. M. Adams (Eds.), *Neuropsychological assessment of neuropsychiatric disorders* (pp. 244–267). New York: Oxford University Press.

Satz, P., Rardin, D., & Ross, J. (1971). An evaluation of a theory of specific developmental dyslexia. *Child Development, 42,* 27–46.

Schiff, M. M., Kaufman, A. S., & Kaufman, N. L. (1981). Scatter analysis of WISC-R profiles for learning disabled children with superior intelligence. *Journal of Learning Disabilities, 14,* 400–404.

Selman, R. L. (1977). A structural-developmental model of social cognition: Implications for intervention research. *The Counseling Psychologist, 6,* 3–6.

Shafrir, U., & Siegel, L. S. (1994). Subtypes of learning disabilities in adolescents and adults. *Journal of Learning Disabilities, 27,* 123–134.

Siegel, L. S. (1974). *The exceptional child grows up.* New York: Dutton.

Siegel, L. S. (1988). Evidence that IQ scores are irrelevant to the definition and analysis of reading disability. *Canadian Journal of Psychology, 42,* 201–215.

Siegel, L. (1990). IQ and learning disabilities: RIP. In H. L. Swanson & B. Keogh (Eds.), *Learning disabilities: Theoretical and research issues* (pp. 111–128). Hillsdale, NJ: Erlbaum.

Siegel, L. S. (1993). Phonological processing deficits as the basis of a reading disability. *Developmental Review, 13,* 246–257.

Speece, D. L. (1987). Information processing subtypes of learning disabled readers. *Learning Disabilities Research, 2,* 91–102.

Speece, D. L. (1990). Methodological issues in cluster analysis: How clusters become real. In H. L. Swanson & B. Keogh (Eds.), Learning disabilities: Theoretical and research issues (201–213). Hillsdale, NJ: Erlbaum.

Stanovich, K. E. (1988). *The right and wrong places to look for the cognitive focus of reading disability*. Paper presented at the meeting of the Orton Dyslexia Society, New York.

Super, D. E. (1953). A theory of vocational development. *American Psychologist, 8*, 185–190.

Swanson, H. L. (1986). Do semantic memory deficiencies underlie learning disabled readers' encoding processes? *Journal of Experimental Child Psychology, 41*, 461–488.

Swanson, H. L., & Ransby, M. (1994). The study of cognitive processes in learning disabled students. In S. Vaughn & C. Bos (Eds.), *Research issues in learning disabilities: Theory, methodology, assessment, and ethics* (pp. 246–275). New York: Springer-Verlag.

Taylor, A. (1951). *English riddles from oral tradition*. Berkeley: University of California Press.

Taylor, H. G., Satz, P., & Friel, J. (1979). Developmental dyslexia in relation to other childhood reading disorders: Significance and clinical utility. *Reading Research Quarterly, 15*, 84–101.

Torgesen, J. K. (1988). Studies of children who perform poorly on memory span tasks. *Journal of Learning Disabilities Quarterly, 21*, 605–612.

U. S. Department of Education. (1987). *Annual evaluation report, Fiscal year 1987*. Washington, DC: Author.

Wagner, R. K., & Torgesen, J. K. (1987). The nature of phonological processing and its causal role in the acquisition of reading skills. *Psychological Bulletin, 101*, 192–212.

Wechsler, D. (1981). *Manual for the Wechsler Adult Intelligence Scale—Revised (WAIS-R)*. San Antonio, TX: Psychological Corporation.

Weller, C., & Strawser, S. (1987). Adaptive behavior of subtypes of learning disabled individuals. *Journal of Special Education, 21*, 101–116.

Willis, W., Hooper, S., & Stone, J. (1992). Neuropsychological theories of learning disabilities. In N. Singh & I. Beale (Eds.), *Current perspectives in learning disabilities: Nature, theory, and treatment* (pp. 201–245). New York: Springer-Verlag.

Wiloughby, R. R. (1927). Family similarities in mental-test abilities. *Genetic Psychology Monographs, 2*, 239–277.

Woodcock, R. W., & Johnson, M. B. (1989). *Manual for the Woodcock–Johnson Psychoeducational Battery—Revised (WJ-R)*. Allen TX: DLM Teaching Resources.

10

Social and Affective Adjustment of Adults with Learning Disabilities: A Life-Span Perspective

CHERI HOY
ELAINE MANGLITZ

The field of learning disabilities is often identified as beginning roughly 30 years ago when Kirk popularized the term in 1963. By many standards it is considered a relatively new field of scholarly inquiry. Another relatively new field, life-span developmental psychology, also began approximately 30 to 40 years ago (Smolak, 1993). It is time for the two fields to be welded as a means for examining characteristics of adults with learning disabilities and the effectiveness of services offered to this population. Early studies of adults with learning disabilities often used follow-up approaches to examine adult characteristics (Balow & Blomquist, 1965; Rawson, 1968; Silver & Hagin, 1964). Later studies (Blalock, 1981; Buchanan & Wolf, 1986; Fafard & Haubrich, 1981) frequently used similar descriptive techniques, often without a control group of nondisabled adults for comparison. Despite this weakness, these studies provided important documentation that learning disabilities continued to have an impact on the lives of adults. These studies helped establish that learning disabilities were not just academic problems which faded into the background once the individual left school. In particular, these studies focused on the social and affective difficulties adults with learning disabilities encountered as they tried to assume adult roles.

By the mid-1980s and early 1990s, the population of students first served for learning disabilities in public schools under the mandate of the Education for All Handicapped Children Act (Public Law 94-142), passed in 1975, were leaving school and trying to establish themselves in adult roles. There was an awareness of the continuing impact of learning disabilities, as this first wave of individuals who received public service under Public Law 94-142 experienced the frustrations of assuming adult responsibilities, as well as the realization that services for adults would also be needed. Service providers and researchers working with this adult population quickly realized that it was not appropriate to view these consumers as merely children with learning disabilities who had grown up (Patton & Polloway, 1992). The pluralistic and multidirectional nature of adulthood needed to be considered. The deficit view of people with learning disabilities, which so often drove services for children, needed to be replaced with the understanding that many adults with learning disabilities possess positive traits that can be used in conjunction with the wider options available to adults (Patton & Polloway, 1982).

Early follow-up studies left little doubt about the persistence of learning disabilities into adulthood. However, predicting which adults would make the adjustment to adult roles was more difficult. Methodological problems and vague subject descriptions contributed to the problem of sorting out the inconsistent results often obtained. A few factors did emerge as influencing adult adjustment. These factors included the type and severity of the disability, measured intelligence, family socioeconomic status, and gender.

Type of learning disability, its severity, and the individual's measured intelligence are three factors that often emerge as affecting adult adjustment. Research has suggested that individuals with severe language problems (Spreen, 1988a, 1988b) or with severe nonverbal learning disabilities (Rourke, Young, Strang, & Russell, 1986) tend to have poorer outcomes than do adults with less severe or other types of learning disabilities. Often individuals with severe language or nonverbal learning disabilities are identified at younger ages. Yet, despite early intervention, many of these individuals experience more problems as adults. The variable of measured intelligence, although sometimes related to severity or type of learning disabilities, is also often identified as a factor in the quality of adult adjustment. Critical reviewers of follow-up studies have consistently found that adults with learning disabilities who have average or above-average intelligence as measured by individually administered standardized tests tend to have better adjustment outcomes than do adults with scores in the low-average range (Bruck, 1987; Horn, O'Donnell, & Vitulano, 1983; Rourke et al., 1986; Schonhaut & Satz, 1983; Spreen, 1988a, 1988b; Vogel & Forness, 1992).

Family socioeconomic status also emerged from critical reviews of follow-up studies as having a significant bearing on adult adjustment. Individuals from higher socioeconomic levels tended to have better adult outcomes than did adults from lower socioeconomic levels. Family financial resources often govern the amount and quality of private educational and therapeutic support individuals receive. Those with the means to obtain this support on a frequent basis tend to have more positive adult adjustment.

A final variable described by critical reviewers of follow-up studies was gender. Reviewers found that when this variable was considered in follow-up studies, females tended to have a poorer prognosis than did males even when the females' disabilities were less severe. It is unclear why this occurs. Referral bias, timely intervention, and environmental expectations have been suggested as contributing to this finding.

Whenever adult adjustment is considered, it is important to keep in mind the dynamic nature of the affective and environmental interaction and its impact on functioning and quality of life. Life demands change not only from adolescence to adulthood but also across the adult years. Spekman, Goldberg, and Herman (1993) point out that "some individuals may be able to cope with and manage their LD better at some stages than at others" (p. 14). This observation has been supported by research. Bruck (1985) found that adults with learning disabilities in the 21-to-29 age range seemed to have better adjustment than do adults with learning disabilities between 17 and 20 years of age. In a longitudinal study, Werner (Werner & Smith, 1992; Werner, 1993) also found that by age 30, 75% of adults with learning disabilities and nondisabled adults had made a successful adaptation to life demands. This was not the case for adolescent and younger adults with learning disabilities who had more problems and more contacts with public service agencies than did their nondisabled peers. Life demands are also multidimensional. Merriam and Clark (1991) found that for some nondisabled adults, patterns of satisfaction with work and interpersonal relationships are parallel. However, for large segments of the populations, divergent or fluctuating patterns of satisfaction with these two domains are more common.

As we review the literature on the social and affective adjustment of adults with learning disabilities, it is important to keep in mind the several themes summarized above. Adults with learning disabilities are not just children who have grown up. There are qualitative as well as quantitative changes that make the adult life stage very different. Patterns of functioning and adjustment of children with learning disabilities cannot merely be generalized to adults. Factors beyond the individuals' control often influence adult outcomes. Research has shown that these factors include type and severity of the disability, measured intelligence, family socioeconomic status, and gender. Finally, adult functioning and quality of life are not static. Reaching adulthood is merely the continuation of a dynamic interaction of affective and environmental variables. It is not the permanent "destination" as we may have envisioned it during childhood. Adjustment and satisfaction at one point in time, or the lack of it, do not guarantee that a similar state will exist during another period of the adult years.

REVIEW OF THE LITERATURE

Life-span developmental psychology provides an important theoretical framework from which to view the research on adults with learning disabilities. Without such a perspective we run the risk of focusing on a limited dimension of the adults—their deficits. A deficit perspective has driven much of the literature on children and adolescents with learning disabilities. Because of a certain level of deficit that affects school learning, students with learning disabilities are eligible for services within an environment that seems to have discouragingly little flexibility. There are few self-selected options. This situation is dramatically different in adulthood. Employers seek skills that can be used effectively in various situations. Adults also can choose environments in which their disabilities will have the least impact. A brief review of the literature on adult development and quality of life provides the background from which the literature on the social and affective adjustment of adults with learning disabilities is considered.

Adult Development and Quality of Life

Such early theorists in developmental psychology as Piaget and Vygotsky used a stage approach to discuss important changes in the life of children. Similarly, the stage approach was initially a popular way to conceptualize adult development. Erikson (1963, 1968) was one of the first to extend a developmental theory from childhood through adulthood with his eight stages of psychosocial development. Each of Erikson's stages consists of an important psychological conflict. The manner in which the individual resolves or fails to resolve that stage-associated conflict influences subsequent development. Erikson's first four stages cover the childhood years. The fourth stage, identity versus role confusion, is associated with adolescence. The last three stages, intimacy versus isolation, generativity versus stagnation, and ego integrity versus despair, cover the adult years. Taking a slightly different approach, Havighurst (1972) and Levinson (1978) both tended to examine the roles associated with various ages in adulthood. Although the age ranges varied somewhat, both models of adult development focused on such tasks as exploring options, finding a mate, settling down and beginning a family, helping teenage children and aging parents, assuming civic responsibilities, adjusting to changes in one's own health, and adapting to retirement. Gould's (1972) seven developmental stages of adult life suggest a dynamic struggle to leave one stage and master the goals of the next. His stages imply more self-questioning and self-awareness than seem to be inherent in models developed by either Havighurst or Levinson. Finally, Schaie's (1977–1978) model of adult development focuses exclusively on cognitive development, much as Piaget's work examined childhood cognitive development. Schaie's model traces the change from learning for the sake of learning to more goal-oriented, problem-solving behavior. The stages in this model consider the integration of various goals in problem solving and the increasing selectivity in solving problems.

Critics of childhood- and adulthood-stage theories express concerns about the rigid, stepwise nature of the stages. Such stages seem to suggest that it is difficult or detrimental to skip stages and that optimal development depends on the successful mastery or resolution of previous stages. Adults with learning disabilities deal with the issues depicted in stage models, but frequently not at the same time as nondisabled individuals. Full independence and self-sufficiency may come later, whereas learning to cope with failure might develop earlier. Baltes and his colleagues (Baltes, 1987; Baltes & Goulet, 1970; Baltes & Willis, 1977; Hetherington & Baltes, 1988), Loevinger (1976), and Gilligan (1982) were all critical of adult-stage models and the age- or time-related changes associated with them. Models developed by Loevinger and Gilligan attempted to separate from the issues of age and gender. Loevinger (1976) conceptualized a process of moving from an impulsive, childlike state through self-protection, conformism, and autonomy toward a capacity to cope with deeper problems. Gilligan (1982) focused on a process of moral development. Baltes and his colleagues argue that development is lifelong change shaped by biology, environment, and cultural events. Although many of these changes are normative with respect to age (e.g., childbirth and menopause) or sociopolitical events (e.g., war and economic depression), others are nonnormative (e.g., divorce and traumatic injuries). These pluralistic factors influence the intensity and duration of change at any given age. Robertson (1988) makes a distinction between simple change and change that denotes growth. He writes "that growth involves some kind of significant transformation of the self" (p. 18). Such a transformation involves a gain and loss process (Hetherington & Baltes, 1988; Robertson, 1988). At important transformation points, individuals are likely to experience resistance to leaving the familiar old world, grieving over the loss of the familiar, and a sense of courage at risking the loss and facing the unfamiliar.

From the perspective of life-span developmentalists, development is a continuously evolving process that varies in intensity and duration; is influenced by biological, environmental, and cultural variables; and includes feelings of both gain and loss during important transformations. When subgroups of adults are studied, it is important to keep in mind that adjustment and quality of life are subject to change. Merriam and Clark (1991) note, "The study of adulthood is characterized by the tension between uncovering commonalities of experience and at the same time preserving the uniqueness of the individual" (p. 53). This tension must be kept in mind as we examine the research on the social and affective characteristics of adults with learning disabilities.

Another equally important consideration as we examine the social and affective characteristics of adults with learning disabilities is quality of life. This concept is very difficult to define. Taylor and Bogdan (1990) emphasize the subjectivity of the concept, noting that what seems enhancing to one person's quality of life may actually detract from another's. Parmenter (1988) includes the balance or discrepancy between an individual meeting his or her needs and having a certain social validation. Goode (1990) also includes the notion of meeting normative expectations as a factor in quality of life. Others have focused on the notions of sense of well-being and personal satisfaction as important in defining quality of life (Coulter, 1990; Karen, Lambour, & Greenspan, 1990; Stark & Goldsbury, 1990). Key elements across various definitions of quality of life are the subjectivity, the notion of control over one's environment, and having one's needs met while satisfying expectations of society and one's culture (Halprin, 1993). Dennis, Williams, Giangreco, and Cloninger (1993) add the elements of the fluid and temporal nature of quality-of-life factors.

Given that there is no single agreed-on definition and that quality of life is subjective, it may seem too difficult to examine. To simplify research in this area, researchers have tried to enumerate components of life quality and then examine each component. Edgar (1987) listed seven components which should be included: safety, pleasantness, friends and companions, self-esteem, fun, accomplishments or productivity in what we do, and excitement. Halprin (1993) considers three broad areas in the study of quality of life: physical and material well-being, performance of adult roles, and personal fulfillment. Within the broad area of physical and material well-being, Halprin (1993) includes basic necessities such as food, clothing and shelter, safety, health, and financial security. In the area of performance of adult roles, Halprin (1993) incorporates the notions of cultural and societal expectations through employment, citizenship, leisure, education, relationships, and spiritual fulfillment. Halprin's area of personal fulfillment deals with happiness, satisfaction, and a general sense of well-being. Components such as those listed by Edgar or Halprin have been used in research to examine the quality of life of individuals with disabilities. However, in much of this work the nature of the disability was unspecified or the population was primarily individuals with mental retardation (Brown, Bayer, & MacFarlane, 1988; Donegan & Potts, 1988; Edgerton, 1990; Miller, 1984; Parmenter, 1988; Rosen, 1986; Schalock & Bogale, 1990). Halprin (1993) reviewed 41 follow-up studies published in refereed journals between 1975 and 1990. Of the studies he reviewed, all reported employment outcomes, three quarters addressed financial security, and approximate half reported educational attainment. Halprin pointed out that the most glaring omission in the studies was reports on personal fulfillment. Quality-of-life issues and Halprin's findings must be considered when we examine the literature on adults with learning disabilities and their social and affective adjustment.

Social and Affective Adjustment of Adults with Learning Disabilities

Studies of adults with learning disabilities have been growing in popularity since the early study by Robinson and Smith (1962). These early studies (Balow & Blomquist, 1965; Preston & Yarington, 1967; Rawson, 1968) tended to follow clinic- or private school-identified poor readers into adulthood. Reviews of follow-up studies began appearing in the early 1980s (Horn et al., 1983; Schonhaut & Satz, 1983). These early works examined a host of adult adjustment variables but often focused on achievement, education, and employment. Later adult studies (Blalock, 1981; Bruck, 1985; Buchanan & Wolf, 1986; Fafard & Haubrich, 1981; Gerber & Reiff, 1991; Jaklewicz,

1982; Reiff & Gerber, 1994; Rogan & Hartman, 1990; Saracoglu, Minden, & Wilchesky, 1989; Spekman, Goldberg, & Herman, 1992; Spreen, 1988a, 1988b) and critical reviews of these studies examined the social or affective domain more specifically (Hoy, 1994; Vogel & Forness, 1992). Hoy (1994) divided the adult studies that addressed social and affective characteristics into four broad categories: descriptive studies without control groups, descriptive studies with control groups, studies of adults in different service settings, and studies that use success as a variable. Descriptive studies without a control group (Blalock, 1981; Blalock & Johnson, 1987; Balow & Blomquist, 1965; Buchanan & Wolf, 1986; Fafard & Haubrich, 1981; Rogan & Hartman, 1990) help document that adults with learning disabilities do experience social and affective difficulties. These difficulties include a negative attitude about life, little sense of control over life, moodiness, a poor self-image, and parental concern for social adjustment and independence. Without a control group it is difficult to determine whether these are common problems all adults face. It is also important to note that these studies tended to consider adults with learning disabilities in a generic sense rather than subdivide the group based on different age groups within the adult life span.

Studies that include a control group help determine whether identified problems are general adult life problems or problems specific to the subpopulation of adults with learning disabilities (Bruck, 1985; Jaklewicz, 1982; Saracoglu et al., 1989; Spreen, 1988a, 1988b; Stephens, 1989; Werner, 1993). These studies reveal that, compared to a nondisabled adult group, the adults with learning disabilities had fewer social contacts, received more counseling, and had a higher incidence of emotional adjustment difficulties, higher levels of anxiety and fear, and generally lower self-esteem. With the exception of Bruck (1985) and Werner (1993), the studies tended to examine the adjustment of young adults at or below the age of 25. It is unclear whether these problems, which seem to differentiate the two groups, persist into later years of adulthood. The work of Bruck (1985) and Werner (1993) sheds important light on the persistence of problems. Bruck (1985) found that younger adults with learning disabilities (17–20 years of age) experienced poorer adjustment than did older adults with learning disabilities (21–29 years of age). Similarly, Werner (1993) found group differences when her participants were 17 to 18 years of age. By the time adults with learning disabilities and their matched controls reached their early 30s there was little difference in terms of their successful adaptation to marriage, family life, and work demands. These two studies reinforce the need to use a life-span perspective in the study of adult adjustment.

Studies of adults with learning disabilities suggest the importance of considering environmental demands. Two studies examined the profiles from the Minnesota Multiphasic Personality Inventory—Revised of adults with learning disabilities in college and rehabilitation settings (Gregg, Hoy, King, Moreland, & Jagota, 1992; Gregg et al., 1992). Compared to a nondisabled group of college students, both the rehabilitation consumers and college students with learning disabilities had profiles of higher anxiety characteristic of extreme long-term stress. The clients in the rehabilitation setting demonstrated feelings of social isolation, poor self-esteem, self-doubt, and restlessness. The college students with learning disabilities tended to have profiles suggesting feelings of fear, obsessive thoughts, lack of self-confidence, self-doubt, and extreme self-criticism. There were no differences between the college students with learning disabilities and the rehabilitation consumers in the area of social introversion. These studies support previous research that young adults with learning disabilities experience more social and affective problems than do nondisabled young adults. They also suggest that environmental expectations may have a role in the types of problems these young adults face, which will have to be explored further in research. These two studies tell us nothing about the adjustment of the two populations of young adults with learning disabilities later in life. A longitudinal study of these two groups would be important. If the findings of Bruck (1985) and Werner (1993) apply to populations from different settings, the working hypothesis of improved adjustment by the mid-thirties would guide the follow-up work.

Hoy's (1994) fourth category of studies examining the social and affective characteristics of adults with learning disabilities used success as a variable. Several studies in the last decade have focused on a description of the successful and unsuccessful continuum of adults with learning disabilities and can provide information about the social and affective adjustment of these adults. Some of the studies have used a population drawn exclusively from the postsecondary setting in which successful college completion or occupational status, or both, is the primary criterion for success, whereas others have focused on individuals from various walks of life and have used broader definitions of success. Definitions of successful and unsuccessful in each of these studies, their findings, and any emergent common themes or patterns identified are addressed in more detail because of their important implications for changes in the field.

In one of the earliest studies conducted, Rawson (1968) reported on the educational and occupational status of 20 men identified as dyslexics who had been students at a private school. Eighteen of the

20 men had completed college and achieved occupational status commensurate with the high socioeconomic level of their parents. This sample came from upper-middle-class families, had a mean IQ on the Stanford–Binet of 130, and had attended a private school that provided individualized instructions. In fact, Rawson (1968) identified the intensive, one-on-one instruction as the most important school experience leading to the success of the students.

Bruck (1987) conducted a follow-up study of 101 individuals with learning disabilities; half were between the ages of 17 and 21 years and half were between 22 and 29. The sample had average IQ and came primarily from middle-class families. The group had received special services in schools and private tutoring, and their families had received assistance in understanding their children's learning disabilities. Of the 58% of the 101 who had entered college, 31% were still in college at the time of the follow-up study (Bruck, 1987). Bruck (1987) identified motivational factors, a willingness to persist to obtain their degree, and a realistic understanding of their learning disabilities as factors contributing to the success of these students. In addition to the motivational factors, Bruck (1987) also reported IQ level and socioeconomic status as the two best predictors of educational attainment.

Vogel, Hruby, and Adelman (1993) recently conducted a study that looked specifically at identifying factors that may enhance the chances of successful college completion. They focused particularly on individuals' history of educational interventions and psychological supports in an effort to identify factors that may facilitate academic attainment. The group of 107 students was divided into those who completed their bachelor's degree and those who were dismissed or who dropped out because of academic failure (Vogel et al., 1993). From the results obtained in their study, the authors identified several characteristics and experiences that may be important in the enhancement of college success, including the availability and use of private tutoring throughout the school years; relationship with a tutor or mentor, motivation, and determination to persist at obtaining a college degree; and availing oneself of psychological support and counseling when needed (Vogel et al., 1993).

Rogan and Hartman (1990) completed a follow-up study of 68 adults who attended a private school for students with learning disabilities. These same students had participated in a previous follow-up study in 1974–1976. Rogan and Hartman (1990) divided the group of 68 adults into three subgroups: 28 who had completed college or graduate school, 26 who were high school graduates, and 12 who had attended self-contained special education classes in high school.

Data were collected by means of a questionnaire, interview, and standardized psychological and achievement tests (Rogan & Hartman, 1990). Successful individuals in this group were judged as those who had found relatively secure and satisfying occupations, had made a move toward independent living, and had cultivated a variety of interests (Rogan & Hartman, 1990). Possible factors contributing to a successful outcome included the relatively early age at which the learning disability was recognized, the intensive and effective intervention during the early school years, parental understanding and support, and the use of counseling or therapy when needed by the student (Rogan & Hartman, 1990). Rogan and Hartman (1990) emphasized in their study that their sample was mainly from middle- or upper-middle-class families for whom education and career success were important. These families had the means to provide such necessary services for their children as private tutoring, and they did so.

Gerber and Reiff (1991) conducted in-depth interviews with 71 adults with learning disabilities. The sample was then divided into two subgroups: those who were highly successful and those who were moderately successful. Success was defined in the study by educational attainment, job classification and satisfaction, and career attainment and eminence. Gerber and Reiff (1991) identified a set of several characteristics and behaviors that described the successful adults. They reported that the successful adults had the ability to reframe their learning disability into a positive experience which consisted of recognizing, accepting, and understanding their disability. These adults were goal-oriented, highly motivated and determined, and willing to take risks to achieve their goals. They were able to identify environments in which they could utilize their strengths and compensate for their weaknesses and were also adept at finding mentors and building support networks to contribute to their success (Gerber & Reiff, 1991).

Spekman et al. (1992) conducted a follow-up study on 50 young adults (ages 18 to 25) who had been enrolled in a private school for children with learning disabilities. The sample was divided into two groups: successful and unsuccessful. Individuals were defined as successful if they described themselves as achieving a level of education, employment, social life, and life satisfaction that was commensurate with their self-perceptions, capabilities, and aspirations (Spekman et al., 1992). Data were collected using information from case histories, parent ratings, in-depth interviews, and current testing; the groups were compared quantitatively and qualitatively. Specific attention was paid whether certain variables in past and current experiences of these young adults with learning disabilities differentiated between those who were identified as successful and those who were not. Spekman

et al. (1992) identified several themes that characterized the successful adults, including a high level of self-awareness, acceptance and
understanding of their learning disability, the ability to establish and
use mentors or support systems, perseverence, emotional stability, and
the ability to set and obtain goals.

In summary, several common themes emerged from the studies
to date that have focused on characteristics of successful and unsuccessful adults. In the studies that focused on the college population
and the definition of success as degree attainment, the variables of
socioeconomic status and higher ability level, especially higher verbal
abilities, emerged along with themes related to motivation, availability and use of one-on-one instruction, and use of support systems as
needed. With regard to the Gerber and Reiff (1991) and the Spekman
et al. (1992) studies, which used broader definitions of success, the
common themes of self-awareness, acceptance and understanding of
one's learning disability, goodness of fit between ability and environment, use of support systems, perseverance, and ability to set and
attain goals emerged as patterns that differentiated the successful from
the unsuccessful adults. It is evident that many of these factors influencing success are from the social and affective domain.

Most of the studies discussed above sampled individuals primarily from middle- to upper-middle-class families who are at least of
average intelligence and do not address the difficulties facing adults
with learning disabilities who are more severe within these socioeconomic classes or those who are in the working- or lower-class environments. Definitions of success and the abilities needed to achieve
that success may be different for those individuals. This hypothesis
will have to be explored through further research with these populations. Likewise, most of the studies explore the attainment of success
among individuals under the age of 30, with the exception of the work
by Rogan and Hartman (1990), Gerber and Reiff (1991), and Werner
(1993). Again, it will be important to examine successful adult adjustment at later stages of adulthood through longitudinal studies.
However, longitudinal studies need to consider success from a quality-of-life perspective with special attention to personal satisfaction.

Risk/Resilience Factors in Interpreting the Literature

Closely related to the identification of patterns of success in adults
with learning disabilities has been the research on the identification
of factors of risk and resilience in the population of adults with learning disabilities. In fact, several authors discuss risk and resilience in
conjunction with factors contributing to success or lack of success

(Spekman et al., 1992; Vogel et al., 1993). Many of the characteristics associated with the successful adults are now viewed as "protective" factors, which can serve to ameliorate or buffer the impact of risks assumed to be associated with learning disabilities (Spekman, Goldberg, & Herman, 1993). In a broad sense, risk factors are generally defined as negative or potentially negative conditions that impede or threaten normal development and increase the likelihood of a negative outcome; protective factors are those that increase the likelihood of a positive developmental outcome despite exposure to risk (Keogh & Weisner, 1993).

In general, the risk and resilience literature has focused on life experiences and consequences that place individuals at risk, including poverty, severe perinatal stress, family discord, maternal mental illness, and other such factors. Several research studies and clinical reports also reveal that there are many individuals who even under the most adverse circumstances are able to develop and maintain healthy personalities and become successful, satisfied adults (Werner, 1990). Several researchers in the field of learning disabilities have considered the constructs of risk and resilience relative to the field of learning disabilities. Spekman, Goldberg, and Herman (1993) stress the fact that individuals with learning disabilities are at risk for a variety of negative outcomes throughout their lives, citing such difficulties as elevated high school dropout rates, underemployment, job difficulties, prolonged dependence on others, and ongoing self-esteem and emotional difficulties as examples of these negative outcomes. However, these authors also propose that little is currently known about the nature of learning disabilities themselves as a risk factor. Many of the negative outcomes associated with a learning disability do not differentiate those with learning disabilities from other at-risk groups (Spekman, Goldberg, & Herman, 1993). The relationship of specific difficulties in the heterogeneous population of individuals with learning disabilities to outcome measures of success has not been researched. Several authors stress the importance of research that considers the context in which individuals with learning disabilities develop, as well as individual patterns of strengths and weaknesses, in order to better understand the complex influences of a learning disability on an individual's life and adjustment (Spekman, Goldberg, & Herman, 1993; Spekman, Herman, & Vogel, 1993). All dimensions of a learning disability that make the experience of risk unique, such as the type and severity of a learning disability, the age at identification, the multiplicity of problems, and chronicity, may play a part in the impact of a learning disability on the life of an individual (Spekman, Goldberg, & Herman, 1993). Likewise, variables such as personality, temperament, and social circumstances affect the individual with a learning disability as they do all of us and lead to complex interactions between factors of risk and resilience. Keogh and Weisner (1993) also emphasize the importance of understanding the larger ecological and cultural context around children and families when attempting to assess the risk and protective factors of an individual or group. Little is known about the interactive nature of risk and resilience in the lives of individuals considered at risk, including those with learning disabilities. The presence of protective factors is assumed to buffer the effects of the risk associated with a learning disability; however, it is not clear whether the absence of protective qualities actually increases risk (Spekman, Herman, & Vogel, 1993). Likewise, the absence of a risk condition does not necessarily imply the presence of a protective factor; protection is not necessarily the "flip side" of risk (Keogh & Weisner, 1993). The relationship between risk and protective factors may also depend on the nature of the factors being considered, including those factors that are alterable versus unalterable, continuous versus categorical, and within the individual or external to the individual in the family, school, or community (Spekman, Herman, & Vogel, 1993). As Keogh and Weisner (1993) suggest, the next step in understanding the combined and interactive effects of factors of risk and resilience on the lives of individuals with learning disabilities may be understanding the interactive nature of risk and protection.

Research on models of risk and resilience that offer ways to operationalize and assess risk and protection factors for individuals with learning disabilities has just begun. However, several researchers have suggested strategies and overall guiding principles for intervention in the lives of individuals with learning disabilities that take into account the research to date on risk and resilience. Some of these guiding principles include the importance of assessing both risk and protective factors, the necessity of viewing the individual with a learning disability as a total individual who develops and interacts within a holistic, ecocultural context, and the importance of a developmental orientation and life-span perspective when assessing factors related to risk and resilience (Spekman, Goldberg, & Herman, 1993; Spekman, Herman, & Vogel, 1993).

Summary

Most studies on adults with learning disabilities have focused on young adults, with the exception of the work by Rogan and Hartman (1990), Bruck (1987), Gerber and Reiff (1991), and Werner (1993). These studies support the need for a life-span approach to understanding the impact of a learning disability at various periods of development. Many of the characteristics of successful adults also appear to be the factors identified as protective in the risk and resilience literature. However, success in many of the studies is often narrowly defined in terms of employment or educational attainment. Quality of life, especially personal satisfaction and fulfillment, is often not addressed in the studies that discuss success and the characteristics that lead to success. More frequent use of counseling and a smaller circle of friends may reduce stress and enhance an individual's quality of life, yet these are often factors associated with poor adjustment and lack of success. This example represents somewhat of a mismatch between what is currently considered adaptive for adults with learning disabilities and what may actually be protective and positive when a life-span approach and more attention to quality of life are considered.

PROPOSED IDEAS FOR CHANGE

Several patterns or themes have surfaced through the review of the literature on the social and affective characteristics of adults with learning disabilities in conjunction with the background information provided on adult development and quality of life that suggest ideas for change in relation to this population. This section discusses those themes broadly and conceptually, with more specific details of the proposals for change presented in the following section on future directions in the field.

One theme that has emerged from the information currently available on the social and affective characteristics of adults with learning disabilities is the need to reframe what is currently known about these adults through a developmental or life-span perspective. This theme emerges from the literature on adults with disabilities and the kinds of difficulties they have in educational, employment, and social areas and from information on successful adaptation and risk and resilience. As mentioned earlier, these adults are not just children grown up. The demands they face and the environments they can choose are qualitatively different from those they faced as children or adolescents. In addition, patterns of functioning and quality of life among adults are not static, one-dimensional states. The life-span developmental perspective suggests ways to approach and structure research and interventions with adults somewhat differently from how they have been structured in the past. It takes into account research within the adult development literature that postulates that change is normal and indeed necessary for growth to occur. Longitudinal, within-setting, and within-age group studies offer ways to address issues related to the different demands faced by adults with learning disabilities and the characteristics important for obtaining success within various sociocultural environments.

Another theme that has emerged from a review of the research on the social and affective characteristics of adults with learning disabilities is the need for more consumer involvement in research, intervention planning, and evaluation of services. It is important that the adults with learning disabilities themselves define such terms and constructs as success, risk and resilience, and quality of life. The consumers' own construction of meaning of these terms can direct those involved in planning and research. Otherwise, those who interact with these adults run the risk of setting up programs and conducting research that is not relevant or pertinent to the difficulties they face. Involving consumers in the various phases of research, program planning, program evaluation, and establishment of policy are, in general, ways to ensure a more relevant and valid connection between the lives of adults with learning disabilities and the various programs and services offered to assist them.

Closely related to the themes described above is the need for service providers, professionals, and researchers to reframe as positive much of the information available on the social and affective characteristics of adults with learning disabilities. These adults possess many strengths that enable them to achieve in many different environments, and compensate for their weaknesses and deficits. For example, research shows that many adults with learning disabilities have been involved in therapy, which is often viewed as negative. However, as much of the literature on successful adults with learning disabilities shows, the ability to identify and use support systems and mentors is one characteristic of those adults who are successful and can be viewed as a strength rather than a weakness. It represents a double standard to provide and suggest services for adults and then to view the use of those services as a negative characteristic. Refocusing on the strengths and protective factors of adults with learning disabilities, while not ignoring the more negative social and affective characteristics identified in the literature, may lead to more appropriate interventions and more optimal outcomes for adults with learning disabilities.

The ecocultural context of the individual with a learning disability also suggests proposals for change in the field. Individuals with learning disabilities should be viewed as total individuals who develop and interact within a context and who affect and are affected by that context (Spekman, Goldberg, & Herman, 1993). Indeed, the meaning of a disability itself is affected by the meaning constructed around the behaviors exhibited within the various cultural contexts that exist, including but not limited to the school, family, and community environments. A learning disability does not exist as an isolated, within-person phenomenon but extends to all areas of individual development and beyond the individual (Spekman, Goldberg, & Herman, 1993). Keogh and Weisner (1993) assert that it is necessary to assess the ecocultural context, including the interpretations and meanings that caregivers and the community ascribe to such constructs as risk, resilience, success, and intervention itself as we attempt to assess, predict, and intervene in the lives of individuals with learning disabilities. It is also important to keep in mind that cultural contexts change for individuals, as do definitions of success, quality of life, and the developmental tasks appropriate for different age groups to achieve growth and transformation.

In summary, all the themes identified above are closely related and hinge on the recognition of the dynamic nature of the affective and environmental interaction and its impact on functioning and quality of life. The principles that seem pertinent to guiding change, as well as the more specific suggestions in the next section, are increased consumer involvement at all levels of research, planning, and intervention and recognition of the contextual and temporal nature of constructs such as success, risk, resilience, and quality of life. None of these constructs is static, absolute, or one-dimensional, and the most relevant and valid information about them can be gathered from the people who grow up and continuously live with a learning disability.

FUTURE DIRECTIONS

The review of the literature has highlighted the need for more longitudinal studies with adults with learning disabilities, similar to those conducted by Rogan and Hartman (1990) and Werner and Smith (1982/1989, 1992). Many of their study participants who were judged to be vulnerable at age 20 were found to be more successful at 30. Likewise, Spekman et al. (1992) have suggested that further follow-up with their young adults who are now in their 30s might reveal a different pattern of success and satisfaction with their lives. These studies, as well as the focus on a developmental and life-span perspective, bring to the forefront the importance of multiple points of measurement. Individuals often achieve varying degrees of success across such areas as personal and career domains and across life stages.

An understanding of the characteristics underlying successful adaptation across these domains and life stages could add to the research base and have an impact on intervention planning and service delivery for adults with learning disabilities.

Given the heterogeneity of the adult population with learning disabilities, the literature also suggests that within-setting studies be conducted, with the knowledge that the unique characteristics and demands of the setting may affect the manifestations of social and affective characteristics of adults with learning disabilities. Research with adults with learning disabilities is relevant in a number of settings, including community, employment, and postsecondary settings, and variables that increase the probability of successful movement between and within settings need to be identified (Gajar, 1992). Within-setting studies are compatible with the ecocultural perspective discussed earlier, as the context of the different settings studied would influence the expectancies and requirements for success and adaptation.

Regardless of the type of study conducted, it is suggested that research samples be clearly described using a variety of demographic and other variables (Keogh & Weisner, 1993). Factors such as family socioeconomic status, gender, age, and severity level have been shown to affect outcomes and have also been related to the constructs of risk, resilience, and success in other high-risk groups (Spekman, Herman, & Vogel, 1993). Information on how these variables affect the individuals' own construction of meaning of success and risk and resilience might also be of interest. It is likely that an individual's socioeconomic status, gender, or age may affect what one considers to be success, as well as what factors one considers to be risks. As the meaning of these constructs may differ among individuals in relation to the variables mentioned above, the particular risk or protective factors may vary in impact and importance and should be considered in the context of the individual's own interpretation. Researchers' description of samples and selection criteria can provide professionals with data to make informed interpretations and to translate research findings into practice (Spekman, Herman, & Vogel, 1993).

Studies investigating such constructs as success, risk, resilience, and quality of life that are socially mediated and vary within the contexts assessed should attempt to obtain input from consumers themselves on the definitions of these constructs. As has been discussed, these constructs are temporal, contextual, and vary with societal norms and expectations, as well as with developmental age and gender. Qualitative and participatory research designs can allow consumer input into the development of research questions and the interpretation and ownership of the research. Several researchers have discussed the strengths of qualitative and participatory research designs for research with adults with learning disabilities. Reiff, Gerber, and Ginsberg (1993) contend that listening to insiders' perspectives lends a critical dimension to the discussion and may be essential for understanding and defining learning disabilities in adulthood. They further state that the experiences and perspectives of adults with learning disabilities present subjective but unimpeachable social validity and can lend insights that are unavailable to the outside observer (Reiff et al., 1993). Bos and Richardson (1994) have recently commented on the fact that qualitative research is the smallest base of research in learning disabilities yet is gaining acceptance as a means of studying the complex issues that arise when attempting to understand learning disabilities from a contextualist perspective. They stress the need for the greater use of qualitative methodologies to investigate difficult questions regarding policy, identification, and service delivery for individuals with learning disabilities (Bos & Richardson, 1994). Qualitative designs, in conjunction with quantitative studies, or as part of longitudinal and within-setting designs, can address issues related to the themes of consumer involvement, a life-span perspective, and the ecocultural context and can possibly lead to meaningful insights to inform intervention for adults with learning disabilities.

Pertinent to the discussion of research designs is our need to predict outcome based on information about possible relationships between past variables and different outcome measures. As Spekman, Herman, and Vogel (1993) discuss, the issue is related to whether outcomes are even possible to predict accurately at either the group or the individual level. Research aimed at predicting outcomes has revealed that relationships do exist between certain past characteristics, such as poverty, family discord, or good self-esteem and the availability of supports, and a variety of outcome measures (Spekman et al., 1993). However, the ability to predict accurately for any individual is less clear. Group research may define the parameters of what is true for an individual but may have less validity when predicting outcomes for a specific individual. Some researchers have argued against trying to use extant research to make predictions at the individual level and have noted that the dynamic processes involved in human development are so complex that we may be unable to predict successfully for any individual what the outcome will be. Arguments such as these emphasize the importance of deciding how our research will be used and whether to include consumer input in the research process.

As discussed throughout this chapter, much of the research reviewed on the social and affective characteristics of adults with learning disabilities has revealed strengths that these adults have that enable them to cope and obtain success. Many of the characteristics of successful adults and the protective factors associated with the risk and resilience literature are virtually identical, including self-awareness, the proactive orientation of these adults, and the ability and decision to use family support systems and mentors. Even though it is important to continue to expand research in these areas, we already have a wealth of information to use in planning interventions and evaluating programs for adults with learning disabilities. We need to be attuned to these proactive patterns and strengths and foster them and at the same time be cognizant that patterns can change across the life span and within different contexts.

REFERENCES

Baltes, P. B. (1987). Theoretical propositions of life-span developmental psychology: On the dynamics between growth and decline. *Developmental Psychology, 23,* 611–626.

Baltes, P. B., & Goulet, L. (1970). Status and issues of a life-span developmental psychology. In L. Goulet & P. Baltes (Eds.), *Life-span developmental psychology: Research and theory* (pp. 3–21). New York: Academic Press.

Baltes, P. B., & Willis, S. (1977). Toward psychological theories of aging and development. In J. Birren & K. Schaie (Eds.), *Handbook of the psychology of aging* (pp. 128–154). New York: Van Nostrand Reinhold.

Balow, B., & Blomquist, M. (1965). Young adults ten to fifteen years after severe reading disability. *Elementary School Journal, 65,* 44–48.

Blalock, J. W. (1981). Persistent problems and concerns of young adults with learning disabilities. In W. M. Crickshank & A. A. Silver (Eds.), *Bridges to tomorrow: Vol. 2. The best of ACLD* (pp. 35–55). Syracuse, NY: Syracuse University Press.

Blalock, J., & Johnson, J. D. (1987). Primary concerns and group characteristics. In J. W. Blalock & J. D. Johnson (Eds.), *Adults with learning disabilities: Clinical studies* (pp. 31–45). Orlando, FL: Grune & Stratton.

Bos, C., & Richardson, V. (1994). Qualitative research and learning disabilities. In S. Vaughn & C. Bos (Eds.), *Research issues in learning disabilities: Theory, methodology, assessment, and ethics* (pp. 178–201). New York: Springer-Verlag.

Brown, R., Bayer, M., & MacFarlane, C. (1988). Quality of life amongst handicapped adults. In R. Brown (Ed.), *Quality of life for handicapped people: A series in rehabilitation education* (pp. 107–123). London: Croom Helm.

Bruck, M. (1985). The adult functioning of children with specific learning disabilities: A follow-up study. In I. Siegel (Ed.), *Advances in applied developmental psychology* (pp. 110–123). Norwood, NJ: Ablex.

Bruck, M. (1987). The adult outcomes of children with learning disabilities. *Annals of Dyslexia, 37,* 252–263.

Buchanan, M., & Wolf, J. S. (1986). A comprehensive study of learning disabled adults. *Journal of Learning Disabilities, 19,* 34–38.

Coulter, D. (1990). Home is the place: Quality of life for young children with developmental disabilities. In R. Schalock & M. J. Bogale (Eds.), *Quality of life: Perspectives and issues* (pp. 61–70). Washington, DC: American Association of Mental Retardation.

Dennis, R. E., Williams, W., Giangreco, M. F., & Cloninger, C. J. (1993). Quality of life as context for planning and evaluation of services for people with disabilities. *Exceptional Children, 59,* 499–512.

Donegan, C., & Potts, M. (1988). People with mental handicaps living alone in the community: A pilot study on their quality of life. *British Journal of Mental Subnormality, 34*(1), 10–22.

Edgar, E. (1987). *Early morning thoughts on the quality of life.* Unpublished manuscript, University of Washington, Seattle.

Edgerton, R. (1990). Quality of life from a longitudinal research perspective. In R. Schalock & M. J. Bogale (Eds.), *Quality of life: Perspectives and issues* (pp. 149–160). Washington, DC: American Association of Mental Retardation.

Education for All Handicapped Children Act of 1975, Public Law 94-142, *89 Stat. 773* (1975).

Erikson, E. (1963). *Childhood and society.* New York: Norton.

Erikson, E. (1968). *Identity: Youth and crisis.* New York: Norton.

Fafard, M., & Haubrich, P. A. (1981). Vocational and social adjustment of learning disabled young adults: A following study. *Learning Disability Quarterly, 4,* 122–130.

Gajar, A. (1992). Adults with learning disabilities: Current and future research priorities. *Journal of Learning Disabilities, 25,* 507–519.

Gerber, P. J., & Reiff, H. B. (1991). *Speaking for themselves: Ethnographic interviews with adults with learning disabilities.* Ann Arbor: University of Michigan Press.

Gilligan, C. (1982). *In a different voice: Psychological theory and women's development.* Cambridge, MA: Harvard University Press.

Goode, D. (1990). Thinking about and discussing quality of life. In R. Schalock & M. J. Bogale (Eds.), *Quality of life: Perspectives and issues* (pp. 41–58). Washington, DC: American Association on Mental Retardation.

Gould, R. (1972). The phases of adult life: A study in developmental psychology. *American Journal of Psychiatry, 129,* 521–531.

Gregg, N., Hoy, C., King, M., Moreland, C., & Jagota, M. (1992). The MMPI-2 profile of adults with learning disabilities in university and rehabilitation settings. *Journal of Learning Disabilities, 25,* 386–395.

Gregg, N., Hoy, C., King, M., Moreland, M., Jagota, M., & Nemati, M. (1992). Performance of adults with learning disabilities at a rehabilitation and a university setting on the MMPI-2, Harris–Lingoes and Social Introversion (SI) Scales. *Journal of Rehabilitation Education, 6,* 1–9.

Halprin, A. S. (1993). Quality of life as a conceptual framework for evaluating transition outcomes. *Exceptional Children, 59,* 486–498.

Havighurst, R. (1972). *Developmental tasks and education.* New York: McKay.

Hetherington, E. M., & Baltes, P. B. (1988). Child psychology and life-span development. In E. Hetherington, R. Lerner, & M. Perlmutter (Eds.), *Child development in a life span perspective* (pp. 1–20). Hillsdale, NJ: Erlbaum.

Horn, W. F., O'Donnell, J. P., & Vitulano, L. A. (1983). Long-term follow-up studies of learning-disabled persons. *Journal of Learning Disabilities, 16,* 542–555.

Hoy, C. (1994). Social/emotional characteristics of adults with learning disabilities: Implication for service providers. *Journal of Vocational Rehabilitation, 4,* 122–130.

Jaklewicz, H. (1982). Dyslexia: Follow-up studies. *Thalamus, 2,* 3–9.

Karen, O., Lambour, G., & Greenspan, S. (1990). Persons in transition. In R. Schalock & M. J. Bogale (Eds.), *Quality of life: Perspectives and issues* (pp. 85–92). Washington, DC: American Association of Mental Retardation.

Keogh, B. K., & Weisner, T. (1993). An ecocultural perspective on risk and protective factors in children's development: Implications for learning disabilities. *Learning Disabilities Research and Practice, 8,* 3–10.

Levinson, D. (1978). *The sessions of a man's life.* New York: Knopf.

Loevinger, J. (1976). *Ego development: Conceptions and theories.* San Francisco: Jossey-Bass.

Merriam, S. B., & Clark, M. C. (1991). *Lifeline: Patterns of work, love, and learning in adulthood.* San Francisco: Jossey-Bass.

Miller, P. (1984). Quality of life and services for people with disabilities. *Bulletin of the British Psychological Society, 37,* 218–225.

Parmenter, T. (1988). An analysis of the dimensions of quality of life for people with physical disabilities. In R. I. Brown (Ed.), *Quality of life for handicapped people: A series in rehabilitation education* (pp. 7–36). London: Croom Helm.

Patton, J. R., & Polloway, E. A. (1982). The learning disabled: The adult years. *Topics in Learning Disabilities, 2*(3), 79–88.

Patton, J. R., & Polloway, E. A. (1992). Learning disabilities: The challenges of adulthood. *Journal of Learning Disabilities, 25,* 410–415, 447.

Preston, R. C., & Yarington, D. J. (1967). Status of fifty retarded readers eight years after reading clinic diagnosis. *Journal of Reading, 11,* 122–129.

Rawson, M. (1968). *Developmental language disability: Adult accomplishments of dyslexic boys.* Baltimore: Johns Hopkins Press.

Reiff, H. B., & Gerber, P. J. (1994). Social/emotional and daily living issues for adults with learning disabilities. In P. J. Gerber & H. B. Reiff (Eds.),

Learning disabilities in adulthood: Persisting problems and evolving issues (pp. 72–81). Boston: Andover Medical.

Reiff, H. B., Gerber, P. J., & Ginsberg, R. (1993). Definitions of learning disabilities from adults with learning disabilities: The insiders' perspectives. *Learning Disability Quarterly, 16,* 114–125.

Robertson, D. L. (1988). *Self-directed growth.* Muncie, IN: Accelerated Development.

Robinson, H. M., & Smith, H. K. (1962). Reading clinic clients—ten years after. *Elementary School Journal, 63,* 22–27.

Rogan, L. L., & Hartman, L. D. (1990). Adult outcome of learning disabled students ten years after initial follow-up. *Learning Disabilities Focus, 5*(2), 91–102.

Rosen, M. (1986). Quality of life for persons with mental retardation: A question of entitlement. *Mental Retardation, 24,* 365–366.

Rourke, B. P., Young, G. C., Strang, J. D., & Russell, D. L. (1986). Adult outcomes of childhood central processing deficiencies. In J. Grant & K. M. Adams (Eds.), *Neuropsychological assessment of neuropsychiatric disorders* (pp. 244–267). New York: Oxford University Press.

Saracoglu, B., Minden, H., & Wilchesky, M. (1989). The adjustment of students with learning disabilities to the university and its relationship to self-esteem and self-efficacy. *Journal of Learning Disabilities, 22,* 590–592.

Schaie, K. W. (1977–1978). Toward a stage theory of adult cognitive development. *Journal of Aging and Human Development, 8,* 129–138.

Schalock, R., & Bogale, M. J. (Eds.). (1990). *Quality of life: Perspectives and issues.* Washington, DC: American Association of Mental Retardation.

Schonhaut, S., & Satz, P. (1983). Prognosis for children with learning disabilities: A review of follow-up studies. In M. Rutter (Ed.), *Developmental neuropsychiatry* (pp. 542–563). New York: Guilford Press.

Silver, A. A., & Hagin, R. A. (1964). Specific reading disabilities: Follow-up studies. *American Journal of Orthopsychiatry, 34,* 95–102.

Smolak, L. (1993). *Adult development.* Englewood Cliffs, NJ: Prentice Hall.

Spekman, N. J., Goldberg, R. J., & Herman, K. L. (1992). Learning disabled children grow up: A search for factors related to success in the young adult years. *Learning Disabilities Research and Practice, 7,* 161–170.

Spekman, N. J., Goldberg, R. J., & Herman, K. L. (1993). An exploration of risk and resilience in the lives of individuals with learning disabilities. *Learning Disabilities Research and Practice, 8,* 11–18.

Spekman, N. J., Herman, K. L., & Vogel, S. A. (1993). Risk and resilience in individuals with learning disabilities: A challenge to the field. *Learning Disabilities Research and Practice, 8,* 59–65.

Spreen, O. (1988a). *Learning disabled children growing up.* New York: Oxford University Press.

Spreen, O. (1988b). Prognosis of learning disability. *Journal of Consulting Clinical Psychology, 56,* 836–842.

Stark, J., & Goldsbury, T. (1990). Quality of life from childhood to adulthood. In R. Schalock & M. J. Bogale (Eds.), *Quality of life: Perspectives and issues* (pp. 71–84). Washington, DC: American Association of Mental Retardation.

Stephens, M. (1989). *Depression and focus of control in college students with learning disabilities.* Unpublished doctoral dissertation, University of Georgia, Athens.

Taylor, S., & Bogdan, R. (1990). Quality of life and the individual's perspective. In R. Schalock & M. J. Bogale (Eds.), *Quality of life: Perspective and issues* (pp. 27–40). Washington, DC: American Association on Mental Retardation.

Vogel, S., & Forness, S. R. (1992). Social functioning in adults with learning disabilities. *School Psychology Review, 21,* 375–386.

Vogel, S. A., Hruby, P. J., & Adelman, P. B. (1993). Educational and psychological factors in successful and unsuccessful college students with learning disabilities. *Learning Disabilities Research and Practice, 8,* 35–43.

Werner, E. E. (1990). Protective factors and individual resilience. In S. Meisel & J. Shonkoff (Eds.), *Handbook of early childhood intervention* (pp. 97–116). Cambridge, England: Cambridge University Press.

Werner, E. E. (1993). Risk and resilience and individuals with learning disabilities: Lessons learned from the Kauai longitudinal study. *Learning Disabilities Research and Practice, 8,* 28–34.

Werner, E. E., & Smith, R. S. (1989). *Vulnerable but invincible: A longitudinal study of resilient children and youth.* New York: Adams-Bannister-Cox. (Original work published 1982)

Werner, E. E., & Smith, R. S. (1992). *Overcoming the odds: High-risk children from birth to adulthood.* Ithaca, NY: Cornell University Press.

11

Language and Communication Disorders in Adults with Learning Disabilities

ELISABETH H. WIIG

PERSONAL PERSPECTIVES AND NEEDS

Over the years adults with learning disabilities and language and communication disorders have come to me to find "the answer." Because the language and communication disorders in adults with learning disabilities are of a heterogeneous nature and the personal contexts and demands vary, there is no single remedy for everyone. Some of my cases are memorable for their diversity and outcomes. I will share some of their personal perspectives, as they are typical of the adult needs for language and communication assessment and intervention.

"I have flunked English 101 three times. Why do I have to take that course when I do so well in the computer courses?" This complaint is a very common one.

"My wife and I are separated. We have a four-year-old son. I want my family back. My wife says I don't talk to her. I don't share my feelings. She says she'll come back if I can woo her with language." These statements came from a workshop teacher with an excellent teaching record.

"I don't know what they want from me. I did great as a pro-

grammer. Now they want me to be a manager and everyone complains." This was said by a successful computer programmer who had been promoted and whose language communication disorders emerged as barriers to his professional performance.

"My self-esteem is gone; I am always depressed. Whenever we have to present a project I designed, my colleague takes over the talking. I don't get the credit I deserve for my creativity." These comments came from a highly creative female architect with a history of language disorders and dysnomia.

Several themes emerge when adults with language-learning disabilities speak of their problems in everyday life. Many adults feel they have lost control, and say they do not understand what has gone wrong. Many emphasize that they are well trained or have performed well in the past in areas unrelated to their language disabilities. They have little awareness of how their language and communication affect their family life, peer relationships in the workplace, or interactions with consumers or authority figures. They often express that others are placing unreasonable demands on them. Practically everyone shows evidence of or expresses low self-esteem.

The assessments and interventions provided for each case illustrated have varied. They range from formal assessment and direct intervention to establishing interpersonal communication (pragmatic) skills to self-evaluation and counseling. The types of assessments and interventions are generally determined by the adult's indications of what his or her immediate and long-term goals are. We will revisit the adults quoted earlier to explore how the cases were managed, but first we need to consider professional perspectives.

DEVELOPMENTAL PATTERNS

Professionals working with adults with language and communication problems must understand that language disorder syndromes associated with learning disabilities persist into adolescence and adulthood (Bashir & Scavuzzo, 1992; Bashir, Wiig, & Abrams, 1987; Gerber, 1993; Wallach & Butler, 1984; Wiig, 1989). Furthermore, individuals with language-learning disabilities (LLD) who do not receive appropriate services may reach plateaus in linguistic and metalinguistic development that correspond to preadolescent levels and may not complete the expected transitions to metalinguistic maturity and strategic language use (Kamhi & Catts, 1988; Kamhi & Koenig, 1985; Nippold, 1993; Wiig, 1989; Wiig & Freedman, 1993). Research (Bashir & Scavuzzo, 1992; Capute, Accardo, & Shapiro, 1993; Lapadat, 1991;

Lewis & Freebairn, 1992; Nippold, 1993) consistently reminds us that LLD occur (1) in varying degrees of severity and in different syndromes (e.g., primarily expressive); (2) concomitantly with other deficits (e.g., affect disorders, nonverbal learning disabilities, and social learning difficulties); and (3) in new forms with changes in academic, vocational, and social demands.

LINGUISTIC–METALINGUISTIC DEFICITS

Language and communication disorders remain among the primary adaptive problems for many individuals with learning disabilities (Bashir et al., 1987; Wallach & Butler, 1984; Wiig, 1989). We can identify several problem areas that stand out during the transition from childhood to adolescence (Levine, 1987; Wiig, 1992). Most often, adaptive problems become evident in relation to the transition from childhood to adolescent and adult communication in context (pragmatics). To understand why pragmatic (communication) deficits assume primary status in the adolescent transitions, we must examine what the mature communicator (adolescent or adult), does automatically:

1. Adheres to principles and maxims for communication.
2. Responds to the variables that control what to say and when and how to say it.
3. Takes the conceptual and affective perspectives of listeners and audiences.
4. Follows underlying plans (scripts or schemas) and conventions for discourse or narrative.
5. Uses the linguistic (content and form) and pragmatic (use) knowledge to achieve a desired social register, to attenuate (soften messages), or to amplify (adding emphasis).

We can give a practically endless list of pragmatic difficulties observed among adults with LLD. Among them are: (1) introducing topics appropriately and maintaining them during interactions, (2) taking a listener's conceptual or affective perspective in a situation, (3) internalizing and applying rules for different forms of spoken and written expression, (4) expressing higher-level intentions appropriately (e.g., offering opinions, expressing attitudes, making persuasive arguments, or negotiating), and (5) perceiving and interpreting supportive or contradictory nonverbal communication cues (e.g., tone of voice [prosody], body language [kinesics], and use of distance [proxemics]).

Deficits in acquiring metalinguistic–metacognitive abilities, characteristic of mature communicators, contribute to the adaptive deficits. These abilities are characterized by, for example, being able to (1) analyze and talk about language, (2) use language as a tool and play with language (e.g., riddles and jokes), and (3) interpret and use double meaning and figurative expressions (e.g., jokes, sarcasm, and metaphors). Metalinguistic–metacognitive abilities are often inadequately developed in adults with LLD. Consequently, they may have problems in (1) planning for the production of statements, questions, discourse interactions, and narratives; (2) making predictions, inferences, and forming hypotheses; (3) coming up with communication options and selecting which might be most effective (strategic language use); and (4) self-monitoring, correcting, and editing speech and writing. In other words, they are not able to use language strategically for communication.

Content Deficits

In the text *The Unschooled Mind*, Gardner (1991) has focused our attention on the importance of word and concepts knowledge for adult learning and achievement. He provides examples of misconceptions or internalized pseudo-concepts that interfere with understanding and learning in academic and vocational contexts. He also indicates that misconceptions are typical, but not confined to, low-achieving college students.

Gardner (1991) and Rieber and Carton (1987) differentiate two concept categories, spontaneous concepts—developed from reflections on everyday life—and scientific concepts—originating in the structured, specialized activities of education and subject area instruction. Assessments and observations of adolescents and adults with LLD indicate that deficits in the knowledge of *scientific* concepts are common and may limit equity of access to academic or vocational training, as well as employment opportunities (Nippold, 1993; Wiig, Freedman, & Secord, 1992; Wiig & Freedman, 1993). A class of adolescents with language disorders and learning disabilities showed this pattern by insisting that "zero" means "nothing." They did not understand space or actual and historical time measurements because they did not understand the underlying scientific concepts (i.e., "zero represents an arbitrary, beginning point in quantity, quality, space or time") (Wiig & Freedman, 1993). Such deficits persist in many adults with learning disabilities and may interfere with common sense, lifelong learning, and social adjustment.

Linguistic Rule Deficits

The linguistic rules for sentences (syntax) add structure and predict-ability to social, vocational, and professional communications. Deficits in using rules for complex sentences (e.g., subordination of clauses and relative clauses) and achieving cohesion (surface structure consistency) and coherence (logical consistency) stand out among adolescents with LLD (Semel, Wiig, & Secord, 1989; Wiig & Secord, 1992). Among adults with LLD, such limitations become evident in breakdowns and inefficiencies in integrated communication (e.g., informational exchanges, conversation, and written language) in which content, form, and use parameters must be integrated and evaluated.

Knowledge of rules and conventions for communication in context (pragmatics) also tends to be deficient among adolescents and adults with LLD and pragmatic deficits that influence listening, speaking, reading, and writing assume primary focus in adulthood (Dalke, 1988; Gerber et al., 1990; Hoffmann et al., 1987; Malcolm, Polatajko, & Simons, 1990). Pragmatic deficits and communication deviances related to commitment and referent problems, language anomalies, disruptions, and contradictory, arbitrary sequences have also been observed among undiagnosed parents of children with learning disabilities (Ditton, Green, & Singer, 1987).

The pervasiveness of pragmatic deficits and communication deviance may reflect the fact that adult communication requires multiattribute and multistage decisions because communication occurs within a multidimensional system and involves risky decision making (Gilhooly, 1988). In adult interactions there is generally uncertainty about the outcome or effectiveness of any communication. Competent adults integrate conceptual (shared knowledge) and affective (emotional needs) perspectives, communication maxims, linguistic and pragmatic rules, and social–cultural conventions holistically and automatically to achieve success in communicating. The deficiencies observed among adult with LLD may result from, among other things, lack of linguistic flexibility, problems in perspective taking (conceptual or affective), or difficulties in abstracting and internalizing communication maxims and social conventions.

ORGANIZATION, PROBLEM SOLVING, CREATIVITY

Organization of spoken and written language, as well as task and time management, is often deficient in adolescents and adults with LLD. The concurrence of deficits in the organization of communication and task management may relate to underlying factors because all organized behavior is guided by plans, goals, objectives, and perspectives (Dreyfus & Dreyfus, 1986). Language provides a sequential code for organizing all tasks, internalizing scripts, and creating higher-order schemas. It is also a valuable code for guiding categorization, a productive approach to general organization, task management, and developing productive mental models (Lakoff, 1987). Therefore, deficits in the use of language for mediation and problem solving can have negative effects across domains.

Discourse and narrative production and formal spoken or written communication follow underlying plans (scripts or schemas), as do tasks, because events and experiences are structured internally into situational, cause–effect, personal, or mixed scripts (Lahey, 1988; Schank, 1982; Wiig, 1989). Higher-order schemas are abstracted and created from these scripts and become templates for actions, reactions, problem solving, imagination, and innovation (E. H. Wiig, 1989, 1992; K. M. Wiig, 1993). Adolescents and adults with learning disabilities often possess inadequate knowledge of common, academic, vocational, or culturally determined scripts. Furthermore, many do not appear to have abstracted and created the higher-order schemas that underlie strategic functioning and can relieve the burdens on immediate or working memory.

Inadequacies in acquiring and using problem-solving process may also persist among adults with LLD. Pattern recognition in linguistic and nonverbal stimuli and contexts is a prerequisite for linguistic rule learning and script and schema development. Pattern recognition and abstraction; making inferences; forming alternative hypotheses; arriving at conclusions from observations, facts, examples, or models; and extrapolating to unfamiliar or abstract contexts are inherent features of inductive and analogical reasoning. These reasoning strategies appear deficient in many adolescents with learning disabilities and deficits affect communication and metalinguistic strategy acquisition negatively (Ellis Weismer, 1985, 1992; Meltzer, 1992; Stone & Forman, 1988; Swanson, 1989; Wansart, 1990; Westby, 1984, 1985; Wiig, 1992).

Creativity, characterized by divergence in conceptualization and imaging, or both, also influences an adolescent's or adult's educational, vocational, and professional options and potential for success. Adolescents and adults with LLD often show creativity in imagery and artistic or scientific expression. However, they may have difficulties using language as a medium and tool (listening, speaking, reading, writing) for expressing this creativity.

AFFECT AND MENTAL HEALTH

Speech–language pathologists are becoming increasingly aware of the relationships among learning disabilities and mental health problems. It is now widely acknowledged that the anxieties, frustrations, and tension associated with learning disabilities and language and communication disorders may result in secondary emotional problems (Bashir et al., 1987; Lavoie, 1990). Preadolescents and adolescents with language and learning disabilities are often labeled "aggressive," "defensive," "direct," "rude," or "stubborn." Unfortunately, some of the characteristics of language disabilities, such as short-term and working memory limitations, word-finding problems, and lack of organization, logical coherence, and surface structure cohesion in dialogues or narratives are also characteristics of mood disorders.

There is evidence that some individuals with learning disabilities may be predisposed for affect disorders in the forms of depression (unipolar) or, less frequently, manic–depression (bipolar). Affect disorders often escalate during or immediately after puberty and manifestations have been observed among adults with learning disabilities (Gregg, Hoy, King, Moreland, & Jagota, 1992). Cortical and subcortical right hemisphere dysfunctions are implicated and these disorders have been linked with nonverbal learning disabilities and diagnoses of attention-deficit/hyperactivity disorder (Biederman, Newcorn, & Sprich, 1991; Joshi, 1993; Rourke, 1989; Semrud-Clikeman & Hynd, 1990). Speech–language pathologists and other professionals, who are involved in evaluating, observing, and treating adults with LLD should be aware of and watch for excessive, unpredictable mood swings and mediate medical intervention through community mental health and other resources. The *Diagnostic and Statistical Manual of Mental Disorders*, fourth edition (American Psychiatric Association, 1994) describes behavioral deviations and patterns associated with clinical depression, manic–depressive (bipolar) and schizoaffective disorders, and schizophrenia.

PROFESSIONAL PERSPECTIVES ON ASSESSMENT

Professionals increasingly take a holistic perspective of the nature and implications of LLD. This perspective emphasizes that language, cognition, and affect are interrelated and that all develop within social contexts (Luria, 1980; Vygotsky, 1962). Speech–language pathologists and other professionals apply this perspective to assessment as well as to intervention (Gerber, 1993; Shames, Wiig, & Secord, 1993; Wiig & Freedman, 1993). Traditional assessments are complemented by authentic, ecological, and ethnographic evaluations to evaluate the dynamics of language and communication disorders (Damico, 1992, 1993; Damico & Simon, 1993; Wiig, 1990; Wiig & Secord, 1991). Clinicians evaluate linguistic as well as metalinguistic abilities and strategies for language and communication and include assessment of literacy and socialization (Damico, 1993; Larson & McKinley, 1987; Miller, 1990; Nippold, 1993; Westby, 1984, 1985; Westby & Erickson, 1992).

Whereas holistic perspectives have influenced language and communication assessment of children and adolescents, they have not yet been implemented fully for adult language assessments. Traditional assessments for adults have their origin in acquired, neurogenic language disorders (e.g., aphasia and traumatic brain injury) (Ylvisaker & Feeney, 1995). Furthermore, clinicians have to choose among a limited set of adult assessment options and have realistic limitations in time for testing, staffing, program planning, client conferences, report writing, and overall program planning. This requires clinicians to consider assets and limitations of each available assessment option to be aware of areas to evaluate and syndromes that may emerge. The diagnostician may benefit from considering a generic model for adult language assessment before considering any formal or informal assessment methods. Such a model will be presented before specific methods are discussed.

A MULTIDIMENSIONAL ASSESSMENT AND PLANNING MODEL

Evaluations of adults with language and communication disorders should be multidimensional, involve the adult and significant others, identify inherent and situational variables that contribute to the problems, and take the client's "mental models" (i.e., complex collections of understandings, associations, beliefs, and goals) into account. The evaluation, therefore, becomes an interaction in which the clinician and client explore the situation and dynamics in a stepwise process captured in Figure 11.1 (Wiig, 1994).

The first step in the process is to explore the target situation through fact finding. The clinician must gain satisfactory knowledge of the situation and obtain detailed facts that describe behaviors, perceptions, and reactions. The clinician and client can engage in fact finding through conversations, interviews, observations, review of previous educational or diagnostic findings, and other appropriate means. As information is gathered, the clinician analyzes and evalu-

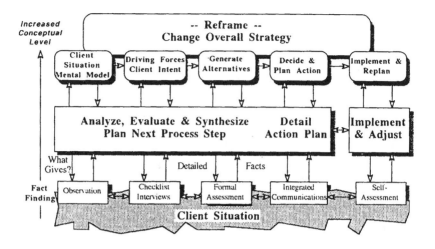

FIGURE 11.1. A model for adult language assessment and program planning. From Wiig (1994). Copyright 1994 by The Wiig Group. Reprinted by permission.

ates the information to arrive at the next conceptual level and plan what to do next, moving to the second and higher conceptual level in the process. Experienced clinicians often conduct fact finding and analysis and synthesis of the information automatically and holistically, whereas new clinicians may have to control the process consciously and after prior planning.

At the third level, the clinician begins to identify the nature of the target situation, the client's mental models, and the driving forces behind the situation. In adults with LLD, the driving forces are often inherent deficits and secondary emotional reaction to the conflicts that arise from the deficits. Later, the clinician identifies the alternatives for dealing with the situation, generates options, and decides which assessment alternatives to pursue and how to implement them. The experienced clinician may also think about how the situation may be reframed, conceptualized as a whole, and thought about in a different manner to obtain an even better approach to managing it. Input from all practical and conceptual levels is needed to implement an action plan for the client. The model I present here—guided decision making and implementation of short- and long-term management for several of my adult clients with LLD—is reflected in the client–management scenarios presented below.

Assessment Options

Among options for evaluating language abilities and disabilities in adults with learning disabilities are (1) observational checklists and interviews, (2) norm-referenced tests, (3) criterion-referenced probes, (4) integrated communication samples, and (5) self-assessment. Each of these is discussed in terms of assets, limitations, interpretations, and implications for program planning. A clinician would very rarely implement all options. Rather, a combination of options may be selected that focus on the client's presenting problems.

Checklists and Interviews

Observational checklists and interviews are a rich source of information about and validation of language and communication difficulties (Secord & Wiig, 1992; Wiig & Secord, 1992). There are published checklists designed for classroom communication skills in children and adolescents (Secord, Damico, & Wiig, 1994). Recently, Wiig and Story (1993) designed a checklist for adults for observing the functional communication demands of environmental settings (e.g., job, home, and training) and the client's ability to respond to the demands. The content is grouped according to the categories' spontaneous style, communicative awareness, and the listening-speaking environment; the focus is on dyadic–contextual communication variables.

Common to all use of checklists and interviews for fact finding are that the clinician must categorize observations. Among possible categories are (1) educational, vocational, or social relevance; (2) strengths and weaknesses; (3) use of modalities (e.g., reading, writing, listening, or speaking) or media (e.g., letter, telephone, or computer); (4) interpretation and content (semantics), form (morphology/syntax), and use (pragmatic/social conventions) parameters; (5) recall and retrieval of given information, problem solving, and going beyond the given information; and (6) metalinguistic–strategic aspects of communication. Usually, checklists identify the relative frequencies of occurrence, but it is also important to identify the degree of concern that the client or the setting have about specific difficulties. By taking both parameters into consideration, the social significance of a problem can be established. Categorized observations can assist the clinician in identifying appropriate language and communication adaptations or accommodations and areas for intervention.

Norm-Referenced Tests

There are few, if any, norm-referenced language tests for adults with LLD, or with neurogenic language disorders, who have recovered to higher levels of cognitive functioning. However, let us take a look at norm-referenced language assessment and delineate uses, abuses, assets, and limitations. Norm-referenced tests are designed to (1) obtain a first-time diagnosis, (2) determine the extent and nature of LLD, (3) establish eligibility for services or adaptations, or (4) determine eligibility for taking college entry tests without time limits (Wiig & Secord, 1991). The assets of using norm-referenced tests relate to the developmental process, knowledge of statistical characteristics (e.g., internal consistency, test–retest reliability, concurrent validity, and standard error of measurement), and availability of scores that reflect group characteristics (e.g., standard scores and percentile ranks). Currently there are relatively few norm-referenced tests that probe the transitions from linguistic skill to metalinguistic ability and strategy use. Two examples are the Test of Language Competence—Expanded (TLC-E; Wiig & Secord, 1989) and the Test of Word Knowledge (TOWK; Wiig & Secord, 1992), both standardized through age 17 years.

Among adolescents with learning disabilities, TLC-E Level 2 commonly identifies form–content deficits for interpreting ambiguities in sentences (Ambiguous Sentences); recreating sentences in response to given contexts, participants, and word choices (Recreating Sentences); interpreting figurative expressions and matching them by intent (Figurative Expressions); and identifying appropriate conjunctions and transition words in a cloze procedure (Conjunctions and Transition Words). The acquisition of memory strategies for recalling word pairs may also be deficient, indicating inadequate access to memory strategies. Inadequate metalinguistic ability and communication and strategy use affect learning, career development, and socialization negatively. This is because adolescent and adult communication demands ability to interpret ambiguities and multiple meanings (e.g., jokes, sarcasm, and idiomatic and figurative language), condense thoughts and ideas into complex sentences (e.g., using subordinated and relative clause constructions), tie thoughts and ideas together across sentence and paragraph boundaries (e.g., using transition words and phrases), and revise and repair communicative breakdowns. TOWK results suggest that many adolescents with language disabilities approach the task of acquiring new words and concepts from a holistic, rather than an analytical, perspective and form misconceptions that interfere with the transfer of word knowledge to academic and world knowledge (Gardner, 1991; Lehrer & Kittay, 1992; McKeown & Curtis, 1987).

Content deficits are likely to exist and persist in anywhere from 60% to 75% of heterogeneous samples of adolescents with learning disabilities (Wiig & Secord, 1992).

In recent practice, we have observed characteristic language deficits among adult injury-to-a-child offenders (Smith, McNamara, Wiig, & Diller, 1995). With these adults, TLC-E and TOWK were used as criterion measures and all performances were judged against the criterion for maturation by referring to standard scores for age 17. The patterns are indicative of generative language deficits with shared features that are as follows:

1. Receptive word knowledge is within normal limits (e.g., synonyms and figurative usage), whereas expressive word knowledge (e.g., word definitions and multiple meanings) is significantly delayed.
2. There are significant deficits in interpreting sentence ambiguities, planning, and producing sentences with given word choices and memory strategy acquisition.
3. There are significant deficits and discrepancies in academic achievement for reading comprehension and written language.

Criterion-Referenced Probes

Criterion-referenced language and communication probes, designed to evaluate specific language and communication objectives, are a third option. These can be tailored to curriculum, vocational, or social demands for adolescent and adult communication (Silbert et al., 1981; Starlin & Starlin, 1973; Wiig, 1990; Wilson, 1980; Wolf, 1989). The content can focus on specific academic or broad or specific social or vocational training and on-the-job demands. Criterion-referenced probes can also be used to validate test results, response and error patterns, or observations; determine targets for intervention; and establish outcomes.

Criterion-referenced assessments often use one criterion for performance and judge 70% accuracy to indicate adequate acquisition of the content tested (Wilson, 1980). This is convenient, but it does not provide the power of differentiation that a variable-criterion scale gives (Silbert et al., 1981; Wiig, 1990). On this scale, 30% or less accuracy indicates a random performance level. The second lowest level can be thought of as the level of emergence or frustration. Performance between 30% and 50% accuracy indicates the level of emergence or frustration. Performance between 50% and 80% accuracy is indicative of the transition or instructional level. The mastery or independent level is reached when performance is above 80% accuracy.

Integrated Communication

Integrated communication samples, such as spontaneous language samples, provide a third alternative. The usefulness of analyzing spontaneous language samples has recently been extended beyond stage 5 (Dollaghan, 1992). Among procedures are computerized analysis of structural features (e.g., mean length of utterances, or MLU, number of words, number of different words, type or token ratio), frequency and types of disruptions (e.g., "mazes," repetitions, pauses, revisions, and orphans), disruption taxonomy analysis, and listener judgment for social impact and validation (Campbell & Dollaghan, 1992; Dollaghan & Campbell, 1992; Miller, Freiberg, Rolland, & Reeves, 1992).

Portfolio assessment provides a different option for authentic, performance-based evaluation of integrated oral or written communication. A portfolio is a collection of communication samples that reflects the performance level or efforts of a child, adolescent, or adult (Finch, 1991; Reif, 1990; Thomas, 1993; Wiggins, 1989; Wiig & Story, 1995). Portfolio samples are designed by defining (1) reasons and objectives, (2) content (e.g., topic, theme, and narrative structure), (3) representative communication tasks (narrative), (4) performance standards (general, specific, relative), and (5) evaluation methods (qualitative, quantitative) and criteria (holistic, focused holistic) (Farr & Farr, 1990; Semel et al., 1989; Warden & Hutchinson, 1992; Wigggins, 1989; Wiig & Story, 1995).

In whole language programs, portfolio samples are usually analyzed holistically, based on the premise that a student's development across dimensions of language and cognition is in phase (Wiggins, 1989). Adolescents and adults with LLD unfortunately show discrepancies in development (Westman, 1990). Purely holistic scoring of integrated communication samples from adolescents and adults may therefore result in spuriously low or high judgments. When adolescent and adult portfolio samples are scored in a focused holistic process, more representative profiles of performance emerge (Wiig & Story, 1995).

Portfolio assessment with focused holistic scoring of integrated communication samples, such as writing or giving oral reports in descriptive-, expository-, or argumentative-style essays, indicates tentative profile patterns among adolescents. Deficits in content–form–use interfaces and limitations in organization (script or schema adherence) are evident. However, organizational inadequacies or deficits often exist in the presence of excellent content–form–use interfaces, especially in those having nonverbal learning disabilities, visual–spatial deficits, and math and social learning difficulties (Rourke, 1989; Semrud-Clikeman & Hynd, 1990). Furthermore, even when an adolescent's performances on the dimensions of organization, content–form–use interfaces, or mechanics of writing or speaking are rated marginal, the level of creativity may be rated excellent. The dimension reflecting mechanics of writing is generally rated marginal or unacceptable among these students.

Focused holistic scoring of biographical accounts and narratives have provided important input for intervention with adults after traumatic brain injury (TBI) (Wiig & Story, 1995). Graded performance matrices for clients with TBI are similar to, yet different from, matrices used for students with LLD. For clients with TBI, the dimensions "organizational structure," "details and elaboration," "coherence–cohesion–conventions," and "evaluation–monitoring–revision" are considered critical (Ylvisaker & Feeney, 1995). The matrix in Table 11.1 for narrative, elicited in response to an open-topic illustration, provides an example of dimensions, performance levels, and descriptive criteria considered important.

Self-Assessment

Many educational specialists use self-assessments with late elementary- and secondary-level students and with college students and adults (Thomas, 1993). Self-assessments can be elicited for example, by using interview procedures, structured question–answer interactions or checklists, categorically focused performance accounts, anecdotal accounts, and exchanges of letters or notes. Each procedure has assets and limitations that should be considered before choosing a specific procedure.

The importance of allowing an adult to assess himself or herself cannot be minimized. A common objective is for the adult to be empowered, to take ownership and be in charge of his or her communication difficulties and their implications. Self-assessment allows the adult to describe strengths and weaknesses, implications for achievement and quality of life, emotional impact and reactions, use of coping and compensation strategies, and visions and goals for the future. The methods used for self-assessment (audiotaping an account, interviewing) should, of course, be decided in collaboration between the adult and the clinician. Self-assessments can be compared to the outcomes of other evaluations to assist in analyzing and evaluating facts,

TABLE 11.1. A matrix for Focused Holistic Scoring of Picture-Elicited Narratives

Picture Elicitation	Organizational structure	Details and elaboration	Coherence, cohesion, and conventions	Evaluation, monitoring, and revision
Good 3	A recognizable narrative structure is followed. There is a clear beginning, middle sequence, and ending.	There is a rich amount of details and elaboration to support the narrative structures and segments.	Details and descriptions are logically connected and marked in surface structure. Linguistic conventions for structure and content and use are followed.	There is little or no need for revision. If a revision is indicated, it is smooth and transitional.
Acceptable 2	There is a recognizable narrative structure with minor digressions. There is a clear beginning, middle, and ending, in spite of digressions.	There are sufficient details and elaborations to support the narrative structure and segments.	There are only a few deviations in logical connections and use of surface structure markers. There are only a few deviations (1–3) in the use of linguistic conventions. Meanings and intents are clear.	There are a few revisions. When revisions occur, they are smooth and transitional.
Marginal 1	There is evidence of narrative structure, beginning, middle, or end may be omitted, out of sequence, or marked by major digressions.	There are details and elaborations but there is not enough to support some segments.	Linguistic conventions are followed but there are many deviations in logical connection and use of surface structure markers. Logical connections exist but there are many deviations in linguistic conventions. Meanings and intents are still discernible but are ambiguous.	There are many revisions or no revisions when appropriate. When there are revisions, they are abrupt and without transitions, become tangential and verbose.
Unacceptable 0	There is little or no evidence of narrative structure. There are two or more major omissions and/or digressions. The account may give a list or series of disconnected events.	There is insufficient detail and elaboration to support most or all of the narrative structure or segments.	There are few, if any, instances of logical connections or use of surface structure markers. Linguistic conventions are not followed or there are major deviations. Meanings are unclear and intents are not discernible.	There are no revisions even though the account is tangential, off topic, or disorganized.

Note. From Wiig and Story (1993).Copyright 1993 by Wiig and Story. Reprinted by permission.

246

generating alternatives and deciding on a plan of action, and reframing to arrive at an overall strategy for management.

PROFESSIONAL PERSPECTIVES ON MANAGEMENT: FOSTERING SUCCESS

Current professional perspectives of managing language and communication disorders in adolescents and adults are also holistic. The methods chosen for intervention may include directive or nondirective counseling, experiential intervention (psychodrama, social drama, role playing), focused teaching, and participation in support groups. Regardless of the methods selected, the clinician can learn from the alterable patterns of success observed in adults with learning disabilities (Gerber et al., 1990; Gerber, Ginsburg, & Reiff, 1992). The driving forces among the successful adults were (1) control, (2) internal decisions (e.g., desire, goal orientation, and reframing), and (3) external manifestations–adaptability (e.g., persistence. goodness of fit, and learned creativity). For this group, control meant taking charge of one's life and making conscious decisions about it.

In the management of adults with LLD, the variable *control* seems to be a predictor of the length of intervention and the degree of continued success in applying what was learned. Management formats that foster taking charge of the communication difficulties, such as counseling, psychodrama or social drama, can benefit clients who show ability to control, even though that control may not be evident vis-à-vis the communication deficits. Taking control of one's life, either spontaneously or through intervention, requires internal decisions (desire, goal orientation, and reframing) that are sometimes difficult for the adult with LLD. Often the desire to succeed in the arena of communication has been eradicated by failures, rejections, or primary or secondary depression. To revive this desire, the adult must feel unconditionally accepted by and trusting of the clinician. In other words, the clinician must remain nonjudgmental, realistically reinforcing, and flexible to meet the adult's needs. Goal orientation is often unrealistic among these adults. In some cases, goals are set too high and are, therefore, never attainable, adding to the sense of failure. In other cases, the goals have been reduced to a nonparticipatory level through negative evaluations and rejections. The role of the clinician is, therefore, to assist the client in setting realistic and attainable goals for intervention. Reframing requires the ability to interpret the language-learning disability more positively and face the implications as challenges to be overcome. Counseling, experiential interventions, and continued self-assessment can be helpful in fostering the reframing because they can heighten awareness, recognition, acceptance, and understanding of the disability. These methods, combined with more traditional language, can provide the basis for establishing communication options and building communicative competence.

Management can also address the external manifestations and foster the adaptability that leads to success. Adaptability among successful adults with learning disabilities was characterized by persistence, goodness of fit with the environment, effective coping behaviors or learned creativity, and utilization of available social ecologies (e.g., support groups, personal improvement efforts, and compensation). The goodness of fit with the environment, coping behaviors and learned creativity can be improved through counseling, experiential intervention, and traditional language intervention, among others. The effective utilization of social ecologies can be supported by providing referrals to peer support groups, to rehabilitation services or personnel departments for supportive equipment or staffing, and to professional services in psychology and mental health. We will now take a brief look at intervention options.

LANGUAGE INTERVENTION OPTIONS

The pragmatic, metalinguistic–metacognitive difficulties in adults with LLD combine to create a complex set of needs for intervention that goes beyond traditional language intervention formats (e.g., clinical language therapy, language tutoring, and curriculum-related interventions) (Damico, 1992; Secord & Wiig, 1992; Wiig, 1989, 1992; Wiig & Freedman, 1993). Clinical language therapy and tutoring tend to focus on linguistic skill and repertoire building and are deficit-driven and reactive. Curriculum-related interventions are academically oriented and related to specific subjects or areas of a curriculum. These formats do not develop self-understanding, self-advocacy skills, and adaptive life skills for communication that are needed by most adults to succeed (Roffman, Herzog, & Wershba-Gershon, 1994).

Adults with pragmatic difficulties must develop insight into the specific target situation, the driving forces, and the mental models with which he or she operates. The adult must be guided to consider available options for coping with and compensating for communication difficulties that are of a high level of significance (i.e., they occur frequently and cause great concern or frustration) and develop better communication approaches or strategies. Intervention to develop coping, compensation, and communication strategies for social or vocational interactions must (1) be holistic (integrating cognition, affect, and language), (2) be interaction-oriented (pragmatic), (3) be as close to natural as possible (authentic, naturalistic, interactive), (4) be experiential, and (5) involve the adult in active problem solving (cognitive processing). Two, if not more, experiential intervention approaches meet these criteria: social drama and psychodrama.

EXPERIENTIAL INTERVENTIONS

Social Drama

Social drama uses role playing in which players present brief skits to an audience to demonstrate real-life experiences and conflicts (Wiig & McCracken, 1992). Among primary objectives, learners become aware of and express attitudes and feelings about interactive conflicts and discuss and consider what occurred, why it occurred, and what could have been done to resolve or prevent a conflict. Among benefits, the participants gain new views, deeper insights, and broadened perspectives of conflicts and become empowered to prevent or resolve similar conflicts by using appropriate coping, compensation, and communication strategies.

Social drama is developed and implemented in a process with hierarchical steps and stages. The skit, a vignette of an interaction with a main issue or conflict, is the central component of social drama. The social-drama skit has a beginning that introduces characters and settings, a middle that introduces complications and conflicts and attempts to resolve them, and a climax in which the action reaches a peak. The design urges the participants to problem-solve outcomes and resolutions. Skits are best developed in a team process in an alternating, interactive brainstorming and focusing approach. The value and outcomes of the social drama experience depend on the reality, commonality, and believability of the issues, conflicts, characters, and dialogue in a skit. To be effective, a skit must be clearly focused on a single issue or conflict, be open-ended, unfold in logical, realistic stages, be short (3 to 5 minutes), and be entertaining. Social drama can be used for intervention by regular and special educators, speech–language pathologists, learning disabilities specialists, counselors, and psychologists. Each brings a different perspective to the process (cognitive, affective, behavioral, communicative).

Cognitive processing, a technique in which a facilitator guides and supports the audience in a learning experience that leads to conflict resolution and conclusion, is the second major component of social drama. It has its origin in Bloom's taxonomy of educational objectives for the cognitive and affective domains (Bloom, Engelhart, Furst, Hill, & Kratwohl, 1956; Kratwohl, Bloom, & Masia, 1964). Among objectives for cognitive processing are to allow participants to (1) share and discuss feelings and reactions to the skit (sharing); (2) identify and discuss overt behaviors that lead to the conflict (experiencing); (3) identify and talk about probable causes for the behaviors (interpreting); and (4) come up with alternatives and strategies for coping, compensating, communicating, and preventing future conflicts (generalizing and applying). The facilitator uses three types of questions to support cognitive processing. Lead-in questions are global and open-ended to get the discussion flowing. Follow-up questions are general and open-ended to focus the discussion. Exploration questions probe for specifics to get to the heart of issues.

In work with preadolescents and adolescents in educational settings, we have used social-drama procedures in which generic skits were prewritten by a team of professionals (Wiig & McCracken, 1992). As a result of participating in a prestructured social-drama program, adolescents with LLD have been observed to (1) articulate descriptions and explanations for deficits associated with learning disabilities; (2) express an increase in compassion and understanding; (3) articulate reasonable, relevant, and realistic alternatives and behaviors; and (4) demonstrate observable improvement in social communication. Social-drama skits can also be written in collaboration between a professional and a student or client to focus on issues and conflicts of significance to the person. In work with adults, writing the skit becomes an integral part of problem identification, cognitive processing, and problem solving. When the skit has been written, it is produced by the writers, who can then follow up by rewriting the skit to reflect the adult's goals for future interactions.

Psychodrama

Psychodrama is traditionally a specialized form of psychotherapy (Moreno, 1946, 1958) that has its origin in the premise that a person plays "roles" in his or her life and in the lives of others. The objectives are similar to those of social drama, namely, to increase awareness of emotions, actions, and causes and effects and to foster personal problem solving. The principles are to make events, feelings, and driving forces "concrete" and to act them out to achieve adaptation and healing through role playing and cognitive processing.

In psychodrama no scripts or skits are written in advance. Instead, the situation (drama) unfolds, as if in real life, so that participants can translate it into action, experience it as vividly as possible, review details, and find an outlet through action rather than through words. Psychodrama techniques have been used effectively in intervention with adults with LLD (Wiig, McCracken, & McPeek, 1995). However, whereas social drama can be led by different professionals or by peer-support groups, psychodrama requires specialized training to lead sessions.

ILLUSTRATIVE SCENARIOS
A Case of English 101

"I have flunked English 101 three times. Why do I have to take that course , when I do so well in the computer courses?" This client was referred by the college's student services center. The student's language disabilities were previously diagnosed and clearly documented through formal college-level testing. The problem was how to approach intervention to improve the student's chances of passing English 101. We explored the student's learning styles and facility for learning computer languages. All pointed to the student's ability to learn a code in an explicit, formalistic, diagrammatic approach. The approach was adapted to the English 101 language, organizational, and stylistic demands. Intervention occurred in the learning center, concurrently with retaking English 101. The student finally passed this critical course by a few grade points.

The Case of the Tacit Husband

"My wife and I are separated. We have a four-year-old son. I want my family back. My wife says I don't talk to her. I don't share my feelings. She says she'll come back if I can woo her with language." This workshop teacher was a self-referral, suggested by one of his school's counselors. After on-the-job observations, self-assessment, and assessment of social pragmatic abilities, it was clear that the problems were pervasive. The client participated in daily, group-based pragmatics intervention and social-drama sessions during his summer vacation. He also saw a male speech–language pathologist for pragmatics training from a male perspective. That fall the client started to implement learned strategies for coping, compensating, and communicating and he achieved his goal of getting his wife back within a year. Follow-up indicated that his job satisfaction, job ratings, and student and staff relationships had improved, also.

The Case of the Peter Principle

"I don't know what they want from me. I did great as a programmer. Now they want me to be a manager and everyone complains." This computer programmer was referred by his company's personnel department. He had recently been promoted to unit manager, but there were staff and customer complaints about his professional performance. The personnel office identified that the programmer had a school history of LLD and that his communications in the new job were inefficient and immature. Norm-referenced assessments validated the persistence of language-based academic achievement deficits. I evaluated the client's language and communication abilities broadly. The results identified deficits in the semantic–syntactic–pragmatic interfaces of communication. Expressions of intent showed the characteristics of interpersonal communication by 9- to 11-year-olds (e.g., simple structures, directness, lack of politeness features, and problems in sequencing speech acts for complex intents or interchanges). Self-assessment by the client indicated, among other problems, that his self-esteem had suffered and he felt incompetent and unrewarded. Because the client had been a successful, highly rewarded programmer before the promotion, the option of resuming the former job was discussed and accepted by the client and the company. The company sponsored language intervention to improve pragmatic abilities and the client's employment stabilized for the long term.

The Case of the Creative Designer

"My self-esteem is gone; I am always depressed. Whenever we have to present a project I designed, my colleague takes over the talking. I don't get the credit I deserve for my creativity." This client was referred to me by a psychiatrist, who had diagnosed clinical depression and was treating the symptoms with antidepressants. The client was on leave of absence for depression with suicidal thoughts. There seemed little need for formal diagnostic assessment. The client received a graduate degree from an Ivy League school and was gainfully employed in her chosen field. The chosen management approach was nondirective counseling, in which the client described her communication difficulties, reactions, and feelings. After thorough exploration we agreed that the problems were situational and coworker-related and might best be handled in goal-oriented confrontation. We planned the confrontation with the coworker and role-played possible interactions in social-drama sessions in which skits were written and processed collaboratively. When the client felt confident she could

handle the real situation, she followed the arguments and scripts developed in counseling and practiced in role playing. The coworker relationship changed positively over time. As an aside, the antidepressant medicine reduced the client's word-finding problems and increased the automaticity of speaking.

FUTURE DIRECTIONS

The recent advances in computer technology have had a drastic, if localized, influence on educational practices and programs in schools (Thomas, Sechrest, & Estes, 1994). In the field of speech–language pathology, current technologies are being applied to the management of clients, the analysis of spontaneous language samples, scoring standardized tests, the assessment of aspects of language, and individualized intervention (Ferguson, 1993; Fitch, 1993; Long, 1991; Long & Masterson, 1993; Semel, Wiig, & Secord, 1990; Wiig & Wiig, 1993; Wynn, Seaton, & Allen, 1993). However, current microcomputer technologies have not yet had a full impact on the management of adults with LLD involved in academic or vocational training, habilitation or rehabilitation, personnel development, or social integration. Among inherent features of current microcomputer technologies are that they can provide multimedia presentations, text-to-speech and speech-to text transformation, and interactive communication, and that the user can employ the keyboard, a mouse, or a touch screen for responding. Assessment of such language and communication abilities as word knowledge, metalinguistic abilities, and integrated communication in adults with reading skills at grade 5 or above could be conducted in supervised interaction between the adult consumer and the computer (Wiig, Jones, & Wiig, in press). The adult would have the freedom of scheduling testing at a convenient time and place, or at home if the required computer capacity were available. Furthermore, checklists for adult communication and functional communication demands could be provided on disks and the respondent, whether the client or clinician, could complete the checklists by computer. It would even be possible to customize checklists, communication probes for criterion referencing, or integrated communication tasks for the problem areas and needs of the adult.

There is also a great need for improving the awareness of the nature and implications of language disabilities in adults among staff in personnel departments of major employers. Such products as reference and resource materials could be delivered in hard copy or on computer disks. They may increase awareness and make personnel departments assume greater responsibility for referring, assessing, and managing employees with language disabilities.

In the arena of research, there is a need to explore aspects of what we are now learning about the functioning of the brain. Recent research, reported in *The New York Times* (Blakeslee, 1994), points to the pervasiveness among children with dyslexia of processing deficits for rapid auditory stimuli, including speech, and implicates the medial geniculate body. Parallel research supports the findings that some persons with dyslexia and nonverbal learning disabilities may have parallel deficits in processing rapid visual stimuli and implicates the lateral geniculate body. The persistence of these basic problems and the implications for responding to adult communication demands (customer orders, work assignments, discourse in the workplace, sensitivity to nonverbal communication cues) should be explored.

In à similar vein, research on the use of neurotransmitter modifiers for controlling affect disorders should be broadened to explore the effects on neurological manifestations of language disabilities (e.g., word-finding deficits [dysnomia] and working memory deficits). It has been documented that the link between depression and memory deficits is mediated by attentional capacity (Ellis & Hertel, 1993; Williams, Watts, McLeod, & Matthews, 1988). In clinical practice with adults with concomitant language disabilities and mood disorders, I have observed the positive influences of neurotransmitter therapy. For example, relatively small dosages of neurotransmitter modifiers, such as imipramine or Prozac (fluoxetine), have ameliorated the manifestations of word-finding problems and short-term and working memory deficits in several adult clients over the long term. These observations parallel reports that memory functions (e.g., word recall) in adults following traumatic brain injury improve as the mood improves (Hertel, 1994).

SUMMARY

This chapter has portrayed the heterogeneity of language and communication disorders in adults with learning disabilities through personal quotes and perspectives, management scenarios to follow up on the personal perspectives, review of the literature of adolescent and adult language disabilities, and discussions of multidimensional assessments and holistic intervention options. The chapter also suggests future directions for the use of computer technologies, for example, for the assessment of adults, for research into the persistence and manifestations of language disabilities in adulthood, and for collaborative medical and psychoeducational management.

No single chapter can capture everything about the language and communication difficulties of adults and how to manage them. Therefore, I have attempted to catch the reader's attention and imagination by presenting real cases from my past and using these as a backdrop for the more theoretical discussions. I felt that it was important to emphasize the need for multidimensional assessments and targeted, holistic interventions for adults. The generic model introduced for the assessment and intervention planning process (Figure 11.1) will, it is hoped, bring cohesion to an otherwise cluttered landscape of management opportunities.

REFERENCES

American Psychiatric Association. (1994). *Diagnostic and statistical manual of mental disorders* (4th ed.). Washington DC: Author.

Bashir, A. S., & Scavuzzo, A. (1992). Children with learning disabilities: Natural history and academic success. *Journal of Learning Disabilities, 25,* 53–65.

Bashir, A. S., Wiig, E. H., & Abrams, J. C. (1987). Language disorders in childhood and adolescence: Implications for learning and socialization. *Pediatric Annals, 16,* 145–158.

Biederman, J., Newcorn, J., & Sprich, S. (1991). Comorbidity of attention deficit hyperactivity disorder with conduct, depressive, anxiety, and other disorders. *American Journal of Psychiatry, 148,* 564–577.

Blakeslee, S. (1994, August 16). New clue to cause of dyslexia seen in mishearing of fast sounds. *The New York Times,* pp. B7, B10.

Bloom, B. S., Engelhart, M. D., Furst, E.J., Hill, W. H., & Kratwohl, D. R. (1956). *Taxonomy of educational objectives: The classification of educational goals. Handbook I: Cognitive domain.* New York: David McKay.

Campbell, T. H., & Dollaghan, C. A. (1992). A method for obtaining listener judgments of spontaneously produced language: Social validation through direct magnitude estimation. *Topics in Language Disorders, 12*(2), 42–55.

Capute, A. J., Accardo, P. J., & Shapiro, B. K. (1993). *Learning disabilities spectrum: ADD, ADHD, and LD.* Baltimore: York Press.

Dalke, C. (1988). Woodcock–Johnson Psychoeducational Test Battery profiles: A comparative study of college freshmen with and without learning disabilities. *Journal of Learning Disabilities, 21,* 567–570.

Damico, J. (1992). Descriptive/nonstandardized assessment in the schools. *Best Practices in School Speech–Language Pathology, 2,* 1–143.

Damico, J. (1993). Language assessment in adolescents: Addressing critical issues. *Language, Speech, and Hearing Services in Schools, 24,* 29–35.

Damico, J., & Simon, C. (1993). Assessing language abilities in school-age children. In A. Gerber (Ed.), *Language-related learning disabilities: Their nature and treatment* . Baltimore: Paul H. Brookes.

Ditton, P., Green, R. J., & Singer, M. T. (1987). Communication deviances: A comparison between parents of learning-disabled and normally achieving students. *Family Process, 26,* 75–87.

Dollaghan, C. A. (Ed.). (1992). Analyzing spontaneous language: New methods, measures, and meanings. *Topics in Language Disorders, 12*(2), 1–82.

Dollaghan, C. A., & Campbell, T. F. (1992). A procedure for classifying disruptions in spontaneous language samples. *Topics in Language Disorders, 12*(2), 56–68.

Dreyfus, H., & Dreyfus, S. E. (1986). *Mind over machine.* New York: Macmillan.

Ellis, H. C., & Hertel, P. T. (1993). Cognition, emotion, and memory: Some applications and issues. In C. Izawa (Ed.), *Cognitive psychology applied* (pp. 199–215). Hillsdale, NJ: Erlbaum.

Ellis Weismer, S. (1985). Constructive comprehension abilities exhibited by language–disordered children. *Journal of Speech and Hearing Research, 28,* 175–184.

Ellis Weismer, S. (1992). Hypothesis-testing abilities of language-impaired children. *Journal of Speech and Hearing Research, 34,* 1329–1338.

Farr, R., & Farr, B. (1990). *Using portfolios in classrooms.* San Antonio, TX: Psychological Corporation.

Ferguson, M. L. (1993, September). Computer technology: Use in public schools. *American Speech–Language–Hearing Association,* 46–47.

Finch, F. L. (1991). *Educational performance assessment: The free response alternative.* Chicago, IL: Riverside.

Fitch, J. L. (Ed.). (1993, September). Computer technology. *American Speech–Language–Hearing Association, 35,* 35–51.

Gardner, H. (1991). *The unschooled mind.* New York: Basic Books.

Gerber, A. (1993). *Language-related learning disabilities: Their nature and treatment.* Baltimore: Paul H. Brookes.

Gerber, P. J., Ginsburg, R., & Reiff, H. B. (1992). Identifying alterable patterns in employment success for highly successful adults with learning disabilities. *Journal of Learning Disabilities, 25,* 475–487.

Gerber, P. J., Schneiders, C. A., Paradise, L. V., Reiff, H. B., Ginsberg, R. J., & Popp, P. A. (1990). Persisting problems of adults with learning disabilities: Self-reported comparisons from their school-age and adult years. *Journal of Learning Disabilities, 23,* 570–573.

Gilhooly, K. J. (1988). *Thinking: Directed, undirected and creative.* New York: Academic Press.

Gregg, N., Hoy, C., King, M., Moreland, C., & Jagota, M. (1992). The MMPI-2 profile of adults with learning disabilities in university and rehabilitation settings. *Journal of Learning Disabilities, 25,* 386–395.

Hertel, P. T. (1994). Depressive deficits in memory: Implications for memory improvement following traumatic brain injury. *Neurorehabilitation, 4,* 143–150.

Hoffmann, F. J., Sheldon, K. L., Minskoff, E. H., Sautter, S. W., Steidle, E. F., Baker, D. P., Bailey, M. B., & Echols, L. D. (1987). Needs of learning disabled adults. *Journal of Learning Disabilities, 20,* 43–52.

Joshi, P. T. (1993). Diagnosis and treatment of depressive disorders in children with learning disabilities. In A. J. Capute, P. J. Accarodo, & B. K. Shapiro (Eds.), *Learning disabilities spectrum: ADD, ADHD, and LD* (pp. 177–194). Baltimore: York Press.

Kamhi, A., & Catts, H. (1988). *Reading disabilities: A developmental language perspective.* Austin, TX: Pro-Ed.

Kamhi, A., & Koenig, L. (1985). Metalinguistic awareness in normal and language-disordered children. *Language, Speech, and Hearing Services in Schools, 16,* 199–210.

Kratwohl, D. R., Bloom, B. S., & Masia, B. B. (1964). *Taxonomy of educational objectives: The classification of educational goals. Handbook II: Affective domain.* New York: David McKay.

Lahey, M. (1988). *Language disorders and language development.* New York: Macmillan.

Lakoff, G. (1987). *Women, fire, and dangerous things: What categories reveal about the mind.* Chicago: University of Chicago Press.

Lapadat, J. (1991). Pragmatic language skills of students with language and/ or learning disabilities: A quantitative synthesis. *Journal of Learning Disabilities, 24,* 147–158.

Larson, V. L., & McKinley, N. (Eds.). (1987). *Communication assessment and intervention strategies for adolescents.* Eau Claire, WI: Thinking Publications.

Lavoie, R. (1990). *The F. A. T. City learning disability workshop* [Video]. Alexandria, VA: PBS VIDEO.

Lehrer, A., & Kittay, E. F. (1992). *Frames, fields, and contrasts: New essays in semantic and lexical organization.* Hillsdale, NJ: Erlbaum.

Levine, M. D. (1987). *Developmental variation and learning disorders.* Cambridge, MA: Educators Publishing.

Lewis, B., & Freebairn, L. (1992). Residual effects of preschool phonology disorders in grade school, adolescence, and adulthood. *Journal of Speech and Hearing Research, 35,* 819–831.

Long, S. (1991). Integrating computer applications into speech and language assessments. *Topics in Language Disorders, 11,* 1–17.

Long, S., & Masterson, J. J. (1993, September). Computer technology: Use in language analysis. *American Speech–Language–Hearing Association, 35,* 40–47.

Luria, A. R. (1980). *Higher cortical functions in man.* New York: Basic Books.

McKeown, M. G., & Curtis, M. E. (1987). *The nature of vocabulary acquisition.* Hillsdale, NJ: Erlbaum.

Malcolm, C. B., Polatajko, H. J., & Simons, J. (1990). A descriptive study of adults with suspected learning disabilities. *Journal of Learning Disabilities, 23,* 518–520.

Meltzer, L. (1992). *Strategy assessment and training for students with learning disabilities: From theory to practice.* Austin, TX: Pro-Ed.

Miller, J. F., Freiberg, C., Rolland, M., & Reeves, M. A. (1992). Implementing computerized language sample analysis in the public school. *Topics in Language Disorders, 12*(2), 69–82.

Miller, L. (Ed.). (1990). Language, learning, and literacy. *Topics in Language Disorders, 10*(2), 1–86.

Moreno, F. H. (1946). *Psychodrama: Vol. I.* Beacon, NY: Beacon House.

Nippold, M. (1993). Developmental markers in adolescent language: Syntax, semantics, and pragmatics. *Language, Speech, and Hearing Services in Schools, 24,* 21–28.

Reif, L. (1990). Finding the value in evaluation: Self assessment in a middle school classroom. *Educational Leadership, 47,* 2.

Rieber, R. W., & Carton, A. S. (1987). *The collected works of S. Vygotsky* (Vol. 1). New York: Plenum Press.

Roffman, A. J., Herzog, J. E., & Wershba-Gershon, P. M. (1994). Helping young adults understand their learning disabilities. *Journal of Learning Disabilities, 27,* 413–419.

Rourke, B. P. (1989). *Nonverbal learning disabilities: The syndrome and the model.* New York: Guilford Press.

Schank, R. C. (1982). *Reading and understanding: Teaching from the perspective of artificial intelligence.* Hillsdale, NJ: Erlbaum.

Secord, W. A., Damico, J., & Wiig, E. H. (1994). *Classroom communication and language assessment.* Chicago: Riverside.

Secord, W. A., & Wiig, E. H. (1992). *Developing a collaborative language intervention program.* Chicago: Riverside.

Semel, E. M., Wiig, E. H., & Secord, W. A. (1989). *CELF-R screening.* San Antonio, TX: Psychological Corporation.

Semel, E., Wiig, E. H., & Secord, W. A. (1990). *CELF-R scoring assistant.* San Antonio, TX: Psychological Corporation.

Semrud-Clikeman, M., & Hynd, G. W., (1990). Right hemispheric dysfunction in nonverbal learning disabilities. *Psychological Bulletin, 107,* 196–209.

Shames, G. H., Wiig, E. H., & Secord, W. A. (1993). *Human communication disorders* (4th ed.). Columbus, OH: Macmillan.

Silbert, J., Carnine, D., & Stein, M. (1981). *Direct instruction mathematics.* Columbus, OH: Merrill.

Smith, J., McNamara, R. K., Wiig, E. H., & Diller, H. (1995). Manuscript in preparation. *Learning disabilities and injury to a child.*

Starlin, C., & Starlin, A. (1973). *Guides for continuous decision making.* Bemidgi, MN: Unique Curriculum Unlimited.

Stone, C. A., & Forman, E. A. (1988). Differential patterns of approach to a complex problem-solving task among learning disabled adolescents. *Journal of Special Education, 22,* 167–185.

Swanson, H. L. (1989). Strategy instruction: Overview of principles and procedures for effective use. *Learning Disability Quarterly, 12,* 3–15.

Thomas, M., Sechrest, T., & Estes, N. (Eds.). (1994, March). *Deciding our future: Technological imperatives for education* (Vol. 2, pp. 695–1383) Proceedings of the Eleventh International Conference on Technology in Education, London.

Thomas, S. O. (1993). Rethinking assessment: Teacher and students helping each other through the "sharp curves of life." *Learning Disability Quarterly, 16,* 257–279.

Vygotsky, L. S. (1962). *Thought and language.* Cambridge, MA: MIT Press.

Wallach, G., & Butler, K. G. (1984). *Language learning disabilities in school-age children.* Baltimore: Williams & Wilkins.

Wansart, W. L. (1990). Learning to solve a problem: A microanalysis of the solution strategies of children with learning disabilities. *Journal of Learning Disabilities, 23,* 164–170.

Warden, R., & Hutchinson, T. (1992). *The writing process test.* Chicago: Riverside.

Westby, C. (1984). Development of narrative abilities. In G. P. Wallach & K. G. Butler (Eds.), *Language learning disabilities in school-age children* (pp. 103–127). Baltimore: Williams & Wilkins.

Westby, C. (1985). Learning to talk—talking to learn: Oral–literate language differences. In C. E. Simon (Ed.), *Communication skills and classroom success* (pp. 181–213). San Diego, CA: College-Hill Press.

Westby, C., & Erickson, J. (Eds.). (1992). Changing paradigms in language-learning disabilities: The role of ethnography. *Topics in Language Disorders, 12*(3).

Westman, J. C. (1990). *Handbook of learning disabilities: A multisystem approach.* Boston: Allyn & Bacon.

Wiggins, G. (1989, April). Teaching to the (authentic) test. *Educational Leadership, 46,* 41–47.

Wiig, E. H. (1989). *Steps to language competence: Developing metalinguistic strategies.* San Antonio, TX: Psychological Corporation.

Wiig, E. H. (1990). *Wiig Criterion Referenced Inventory of Language.* San Antonio, TX: Psychological Corporation.

Wiig, E. H. (1992). *Language intervention for school-age children: Models and procedures that work.* Chicago: Riverside.

Wiig, E. H. (1994). *A multi-dimensional assessment model.* Working paper, The Wiig Group, Arlington, TX.

Wiig, E. H., & Freedman, E. (1993). *The WORD book.* Austin, TX: Pro-Ed.

Wiig, E. H., Freedman, E., & Secord, W. A. (1992). Developing words and concepts in the classroom: A holistic–thematic approach. *Intervention in School and Clinic, 27,* 278–285.

Wiig, E. H., Jones, S. S., & Wiig, E. D. (in press). Computer-based assessment of word knowledge in teens with LD. *Language, Speech and Hearing Services in Schools.*

Wiig, E. H., & McCracken, J. (1992). *Daily dilemmas: Coping, compensation and communication strategies through social drama.* Chicago: Riverside.

Wiig, E. H., McCracken, J., & McPeek, D. (1995). Manuscript in preparation. *Experiential intervention for adolescents and adults with language-learning disabilities.* Arlington, TX: The Wiig Group.

Wiig, E. H., & Secord, W. A. (1989). *Test of Language Competence—Expanded.* San Antonio, TX: Psychological Corporation.

Wiig, E. H., & Secord, W. A. (1991). *Measurement and assessment: A marriage worth saving.* Chicago: Riverside.

Wiig, E. H., & Secord, W. A. (1992). *Test of Word Knowledge.* San Antonio, TX: Psychological Corporation.

Wiig, E. H., & Story, T. B. (1995). *Multidimensional adult language assessments: Experimental edition.* Chicago: Paradigm Press.

Wiig, E. H., & Wiig, E. D. (1993). *Test of word knowledge computer-based: Experimental.* Arlington, TX: Schema Press.

Wiig, K. M. (1993). *Knowledge management foundations: Thinking about thinking.* Arlington, TX: Schema Press.

Williams, J. M. G., Watts, F. N., MacLeod, C., & Matthews, A. (1988). *Cognitive psychology and emotional disorders.* New York: Wiley.

Wilson, R. (1980). *Test service notebook 37: Criterion-referenced testing.* San Antonio, TX: Psychological Corporation.

Wolf, D. P. (1989). Portfolio assessment: Sampling student work. *Educational Leadership, 46*(7), 4–10.

Wynn, M. K., Seaton, W. H., & Allen, R. L. (1993). Computer technology: Integration into office management. *American Speech–Language–Hearing Association, 1,* 50–51.

Ylvisaker, M., & Feeney, T. J. (1995). Traumatic brain injury in adolescence: Assessment and reintegration. *Seminars in Speech and Language, 16,* 32–44.

12

Literacy Needs for Adults Who Have Learning Disabilities

NEIL A. STUROMSKI

The issue of adult literacy has received considerable attention in the United States in the past few years. Whereas 50 to 60 years ago an individual was considered literate if he or she completed eighth grade (Beder, 1991), literacy is no longer just the ability to read and write. It also encompasses various other skills needed in daily life. To be regarded as literate today, an individual needs to understand more technical directions; understand and complete math computations; read and interpret records, charts, and graphs; fill out forms; and write notes and memos.

In the United States, the literacy problem is such that the skills of large numbers of adults are not adequate for them to meet the functional tests of everyday life. Moreover, as these tests become more difficult and complex, adult literacy seems to present an ever-growing challenge. The goals of adult students seeking to achieve a functional literacy level have changed over the past 50 to 60 years. Likewise, the field of adult literacy has expanded to include not only its original responsibilities—teaching basic reading and writing—but also a higher technical level encompassing such life skill functions as working on a computer, using an automated teller machine, balancing a budget, or having workplace know-how. Literacy today involves verbal communication, problem solving, and the ability to function on the job and in society and achieve goals. It involves developing knowledge and reaching potential.

The foundation of these literacy skills, in a broad sense, is a combination of traditional literacy and numeracy and the ability to pull together information from reading, to follow directions, and to use new technology. This requires organization, information processing, reasoning, and critical thinking capabilities, together with reading, writing, and math skills. This change in how literacy is viewed has occurred because of the rapid advances in technology and the ever-growing need for continuous job retraining in order to compete in today's job market.

In addition, in the past 10 years, the field of adult literacy has evolved from volunteers providing tutoring services and teachers offering night classes (often in connection with obtaining a General Educational Development [GED] certificate) to a variety of workplace, community, family, and English as a Second Language literacy programs. These programs are found in numerous agencies and organizations such as libraries, community colleges, secondary schools, prisons, municipal government departments, businesses and industries, nonprofit organizations, and volunteer literacy organizations (e.g., Laubach Literacy Action and Literacy Volunteers of America). Furthermore, there has been a growing awareness by adult education, job-training, and literacy professionals that a large number of adults in their programs may have learning disabilities. These professionals recognize that learning disabilities are real and they may affect many of the adults served in their programs.

Nevertheless, the adult literacy and the learning disabilities communities have been and are still operating in isolation from each other. They do not always share the same language or philosophy for how to best meet the needs of adults who have learning disabilities. However, they do share a common goal—to help adults who have learning disabilities acquire literacy skills. Therefore, there has been an increase in the demand by literacy and adult basic educators for information for and about adults with learning disabilities. In fact, most national and state conferences on adult education and literacy are now offering a larger number of sessions on adult learning disabilities.

Although the demand for information about adults who have learning disabilities has increased significantly, because of the limited amount of research and the lack of information about the problems and needs of adults with learning disabilities, it is difficult to determine appropriate intervention techniques and staff development and training needs. Although each of us has variations in our learning style, for most of us the things we are not good at do not present major barriers. For many adults who have learning disabilities, however, difficulties in learning lead to difficulties in employment, education, and daily life. Understanding the needs of those adults has become a more pressing issue due to the maturation of individuals who attended school when services for those students with learning disabilities were not widely available. As children, these individuals did not receive services, were not identified because learning disabilities were not understood, or were identified too late in their school careers for effective intervention.

As a result, larger numbers of adults who have learning disabilities are entering literacy, GED, job-training, and adult basic education (ABE) programs. Although these programs are intended to reduce students' frustration and failure, not all adults can profit from traditional adult education, job-training, and literacy programs; these programs are often not equipped to deal with adults who have specific learning disabilities. When programs cannot meet the needs of students with learning disabilities, frustration and failure continue, often with little hope for meaningful change.

DEFINITIONS:
LITERACY AND LEARNING DISABILITIES

Literacy is defined in various ways according to the manner in which individuals must function. The National Literacy Act (1991) defines literacy as "an individual's ability to read, write, and speak in English, and compute and solve problems at levels of proficiency necessary to function on the job and in society and achieve one's goals, and develop one's knowledge and potential." This definition includes the essential skills needed to be literate in today's world, understanding that the definition will change as the demands of work, family, and society change (Brizius & Foster, 1994).

"Learning disabilities" is an umbrella term that encompasses a wide variety of disorders, including disorders in one or more of the basic psychological processes involved in understanding or using spoken or written language. These may be displayed in a faulty ability to listen, think, speak, read, write, spell, or do mathematical calculations. It has become widely recognized that learning disabilities emanate from a neuropsychological base. A learning disability may be intrinsic to the individual through inherited or pre- and postnatal factors that produce a neurological delay or dysfunction (Chalfant & Scheffelin, 1969; Interagency Committee on Learning Disabilities, 1987; Smith, 1981, 1991; World Health Organization, 1980).

In 1988, the National Joint Committee on Learning Disabilities (NJCLD), a group of learning disabilities experts who represent the major national professional organizations in the field, included the phrase "may occur across the lifespan" in its definition of learning disabilities. These professionals, although previously perceiving this condition as a problem of childhood, now recognize that learning disabilities do not disappear when children leave school (Gottesman, 1992). However, from a survey of current practices on learning disabilities in ABE, it is clear that ABE directors feel that the lack of clarity in the definition of learning disabilities as it applies to adults presents a barrier in dealing with a number of fundamental issues in adult education and literacy programs: prevalence, identification, and training (Ryan & Price, 1993).

PREVALENCE

Approximately 30 million Americans are functionally illiterate (Payne, 1992; National Literacy Act, 1991). This constitutes one in every five U.S. adults. An additional 34% are considered marginally illiterate (Learning Disabilities Association of America [LDA], 1992). When examined by socioeconomic and cultural groupings, even larger differences are noted. For example, recent studies found 42% of urban, African American youth to be illiterate (Mullins & Jenkins, 1990), as well as 60% of prison inmates and 85% of juvenile offenders (LDA, 1992). Furthermore, the situation is not improving: of the United Nations' 156 member countries, the United States currently ranks forty-ninth in its rate of literacy, 18 positions lower than its 1950 ranking (LDA, 1992).

The Adult Education Amendments of 1988 required that the U.S. Department of Education submit a report to Congress on the definition of literacy and the nature and extent of literacy among adults in the United States. To accomplish this task, the Department of Education commissioned the National Adult Literacy Survey (NALS) to provide policymakers, educators, researchers, leaders in business and labor, and the general public with fundamental information on literacy in the United States. Although the survey provides no firm answers to the question of the adequacy of literacy skills of U.S. adults, one of the more noticeable findings was that 21% to 23% of the 191 million adults in this country demonstrated skills in the lowest levels of literacy. An additional 25% to 28% of the survey respondents exhibited skills in the next higher level of literacy (Kirsch, Jungeblut, Jenkins, & Kolstad, 1993). Furthermore, adults in the lowest two levels of literacy were less likely than their literate peers to be employed fulltime, earn high wages, and vote. Of the 3% of survey participants who self-reported a learning disability, 80% scored at the two lowest levels of literacy in the NALS (Reder, in press). This suggests that adults with learning disabilities are at a greater risk to be near or below the poverty level and most likely have not achieved satisfactory levels of employment that would, in turn, provide them with economic security.

However, when reviewing studies such as the NALS and examining *Assessing Literacy: The Framework for the National Adult Literacy Survey* (Campbell, Kirsch, & Kolstad, 1992), it becomes clear that research related to literacy and adults with learning disabilities is sketchy at best. Research questions on learning disabilities typically form tangential pieces of larger surveys. For example, the NALS survey respondents were asked to identify whether they had a type of physical, mental, or other health condition, of which learning disabilities was listed as one of the 10 possible category choices. In addition, these category choices were not mutually exclusive. Consequently, the results are unreliable as they use fluid variables such as self-reporting, self-knowledge, honesty, and perhaps even self-diagnosis. Another recent national survey commissioned by the Department of Labor and conducted by the Educational Testing Service to assess the literacy skills of job seekers in the United States reported results by variables such as age, sex, ethnicity, and educational and employment attainment but failed to look at disability-related variables (Kirsch, Jungeblut, & Campbell, 1992).

The range of estimates of the number of adult Americans with learning disabilities varies from 5% to 15% of the total population (Craig, 1990). The Learning Disabilities Association of America (1991) estimates that there are significantly more than 2 million adults with learning disabilities. Notwithstanding, estimates of the number of adults who have learning disabilities in literacy and ABE programs range from 50% to 80%, 15% to 30% of all Job Training Partnership Act (JTPA) participants, and 25% to 40% of all adults on Aid to Families with Dependent Children (AFDC) or in the Job Opportunities and Basic Skills (JOBS) program (Nightengale, 1991). However, unlike physical disabilities, learning disabilities have often been referred to as the hidden handicap because they are not visible. In addition, the lack of clarity in defining and diagnosing adults who may have a learning disability, as well as the tremendous diversity in the adult population, makes it all the more difficult to determine the exact number of adults with learning disabilities in literacy, ABE, JTPA, AFDC, and JOBS programs. With or without a diagnosis, adults with learning disabilities clearly make up the largest subgroup of individuals who seek to improve literacy skills in adult education and literacy programs (Anderson, 1994).

IDENTIFICATION

Adults who have learning disabilities may have many problems that have a significant impact on their lives, including: memory, left–right confusion, visual–spatial, motor, symbol-learning, language, cognition, organization, attention, and social behavior (Smith, 1991). Other factors contributing to the adjustment of adults who have learning disabilities include the severity of the learning problem, characteristics of the difficulty (e.g., visual, auditory, and spatial difficulties), intellectual level of the adult, gender, age, practical needs, the amount of social and environmental support, the presence of other disabilities (e.g., attention deficit with or without hyperactivity), and the social and financial condition of the individual (Osher & Webb, 1994).

Although the literacy and learning disabilities communities share a common goal—to help adults with learning disabilities acquire literacy skills—there is disagreement between adult literacy and learning disabilities professionals on the value of diagnosing learning disabilities. Professionals in the field of learning disabilities feel that in order to determine appropriate intervention strategies a clear diagnosis of a learning disability is essential (Alderson-Gill & Associates, 1989). Only by obtaining an educational history, cognitive ability assessment, and a thorough diagnosis of reading, written expression, spelling, and math can the appropriate instructional methods or combination of methods and techniques be determined for an individual with learning disabilities (Anderson, 1994). Furthermore, those individuals diagnosed as having a learning disability are assured basic opportunities through legislation such as the Rehabilitation Act (1973) and the Americans with Disabilities Act (1990). Only with a professional assessment and a diagnosis of a learning disabilities can these opportunities be realized. Psychologists, learning disabilities specialists, counselors, and social workers help to diagnose a learning disability; they make life-determining decisions for adults who come to them for help. Even for these professionals, diagnosing a learning disability in an adult is a difficult task; when the adult student has had poor teaching or is living in poverty, determining the cause of his or her problems becomes increasingly more complex (Osher & Webb, 1994).

Professionals in the literacy field suggest that it may do more harm than good to label a person as "having a learning disability." These professionals feel that there is negativity associated with the term "disability," and that it would be better to focus on the specific learning problems as they arise. Literacy professionals feel that a well-trained literacy tutor will be sensitive enough to recognize a learning problem and develop an approach to address that problem (Alderson-Gill & Associates, 1989). But most literacy practitioners agree that some basic screening is critical if only to eliminate the suspicion of learning disabilities.

Typically, the first stage of an evaluation is a screening. A screening is an informal way to interview or test in order to help identify those individuals who may or may not be "at risk" for a learning disability. A screening may include an interview, a record review, a brief test, and written answers to questions (HEATH Resource Center and National Adult Literacy and Learning Disabilities Center, 1994); the major risk in screening for learning disabilities is that the screen will be interpreted as a "diagnosis" of a learning disability. However, such a tool can provide clues to the appropriate intervention techniques in adult education or literacy settings. It may help tutors or teachers who have not been extensively trained in learning disabilities identify effective instructional strategies and techniques for students who may or may not have specific learning disabilities (Ross-Gordon, 1989). But a screening tool does not and cannot "diagnose" a learning disability. A literacy provider or adult basic educator who suspects that an adult has a learning disability should be able to provide a variety of options to that adult—including a complete assessment by a qualified professional that provides evaluation, diagnosis, and recommendations (HEATH Resource Center and National Adult Literacy and Learning Disabilities Center, 1994).

TRAINING

Literature on literacy and ABE reflects increasing evidence that adults who have learning disabilities represent a significant portion of the students in adult literacy and basic education programs (Bowren, 1981; Gold, 1981; Thistlewaite, 1983). Consequently, it becomes imperative that adult basic educators and literacy providers receive training in the specific area of learning disabilities. Klein (1989) indicates that teachers working in these programs are bewildered and frustrated by students who, although often bright and articulate, do not seem to acquire needed skills despite the use of varied teaching methods. Unfortunately, many tutors in literacy programs, teachers in ABE classrooms, and instructors in job-training programs have not received adequate training in adult learning disabilities. Furthermore, these educators have not received training in successful methods of screening adults who may have a learning disability or in the interventions that hold the greatest promise of success (Herbert, 1988).

Although a majority of ABE directors recognize the need for in-service training in learning disabilities, because of the lack of information and research on adult learning disabilities, ABE and literacy programs find it difficult to determine appropriate staff development activities (Ross & Smith, 1990). The growing number of sessions at national and state conferences on adults with learning disabilities indicates an increasing interest in this population. Practitioners who once overlooked the effect of a learning disability on an adult who attended a literacy or adult education program now search for techniques and interventions to address the needs of these adults (Osher & Webb, 1994).

But there is little that is certain about educating adults with learning disabilities. Padak, Davidson, and Padak (1990) state that ABE teachers face a major challenge in helping adult learners become competent readers. They explain that adult learners must be actively involved in instructional programs, must be able to effectively master and use reading strategies, and must be able to independently use and apply these strategies throughout their lives. It seems clear that adult learners cannot be taught in exactly the same way that children are taught (Knowles, 1989). Adults need to be intimately involved in their education and the process of learning. They need to help set objectives and goals. They also need to have the opportunity to review and change these goals and objectives. If given these opportunities, education becomes more meaningful for the adult learner; adult educators become helpers, guides, encouragers, consultants, and resources for adult learners.

Adult literacy programs that involve the adult with learning disabilities in the learning process find that adults can often provide invaluable information on what their needs are and how they learn best. Successful programs also recognize the importance of flexibility and creativity in their teaching approaches and learning-style assessments. They are starting to focus literacy lessons on more practical, functional material, matching instruction to the specific needs of the student. Instructors should be adept at modifying the pace of instruction, presenting varying approaches, locating and creating appropriate material, and becoming familiar with an adult student's interests, strengths, weaknesses, and immediate needs (Gottesman, 1992). The aim should be to develop approaches based on learner strengths, focusing on the individual, and enhancing the resources and abilities of the learner (Osher, Webb, & Koehler, 1993). Collaborative efforts are also occurring with more frequency at the local level between adult literacy and learning disabilities programs (PLUS Outreach, 1992).

But if literacy is no longer just the capacity to perform simple reading skills, we must provide literacy practitioners, adult basic educators, and job-training instructors with effective strategies and techniques that can teach adults not only reading but also writing, math, problem solving, organization, time management, and verbal communication. Programs are most effective when they are targeted to the specific needs of the adult learner. They must provide individuals with all the skills they need to function in daily life. And through appropriate training, adult educators who work with individuals who have learning disabilities can have an improved understanding of the adult learning process, reducing the risk that an individual might otherwise fall through the cracks of the adult education world.

ISSUES

Our inability to successfully address the needs of individuals who have learning disabilities appears to have a significant cost. Many adults with learning disabilities fail to achieve the skills necessary to obtain satisfactory levels of employment, economic security, and self-esteem (Smith, 1991). Smith also reports that all too often, adults who have learning disabilities are underemployed or on public assistance. She further suggests that a productive part of our work force will be lost if we do not properly educate adults who have learning disabilities. The need for appropriate education becomes more critical as technology advances and job retraining accelerates: Adults who have learning disabilities will be left even farther behind unless education and training address their needs. Proper education should include curricula designed to promote independent, lifelong learning and should aid the proficiency of individuals to deal with major life situations.

Goal Six of Goals 2000: Educate America Act (signed into law March 31, 1994) states that by the year 2000, every adult American will be literate, competitive in a global market, and representative of good citizenship. It is unlikely that the national adult education goal will be met unless effective teaching methods and strategies are developed to provide adults who have learning disabilities the knowledge and skills necessary to become literate.

However, adults with learning disabilities are not just children with learning disabilities grown up. The nature of the problem may continue, but life's demands have changed. Like other adults, they face the pressures of time, money, housing, health care, and employment needs and the need for acceptance and social relationships (Osher & Webb, 1994). In addition, one of the more important issues in dealing with adults with learning disabilities who attend literacy programs is low self-esteem. The panelists at the National Center for Learning Disabilities Summit (Ellis & Cramer, 1994) overwhelmingly stated that dealing with and elevating the self-esteem of adults who have learning disabilities were critical to increasing skills, improving self-worth, and making these adults productive members of society. Even when adults with learning disabilities, who have often felt "stupid" and "dumb" all their lives, succeed, they are not always comfortable with themselves. Their sense of a lack of competence is cemented by continuous defeat and failure. Because they are consumed by their defeat and failure, they often have minimal energy to devise strategies that will help them learn (Smith, 1994).

However, adults with learning disabilities need to acquire the skills to become independent learners. The desired outcome is to make the transition from instructor-directed activities, which teach individuals how to learn new information (as well as to learn from one's mistakes), to independent self-directed learning. Individuals must be able to apply the techniques and strategies learned through instruction to everyday situations. Instruction must provide the material on which learners can build and actively develop skills which they can generalize and use throughout their lives. Clearly, educators involved with ABE, literacy, and job-training programs need appropriate instructional strategies and effective teaching techniques to teach adults who have learning disabilities.

In a 1989 article, Malcolm Knowles explained that education is not perceived by the majority of people as a lifelong process. It appears that one of the most important aspects in helping people understand the educational process is to help them understand the concept of lifelong learning. Knowles discusses 15 dimensions of maturity that describe directions and growth from childhood and youth to adulthood. Individuals eventually reach a point at which they understand lifelong learning; therefore, they are able to continue to learn throughout life. Knowles states that one of the missions of the adult educator is to guide people through this maturing process. Therefore, one thrust of adult education should involve teaching adults "how" to learn for themselves, as opposed to trying to teach them everything the educator thinks an adult needs to "know." Knowles adds that society's demands are becoming so great that we need citizens who are willing and able to change with these new demands. He further states that for many, the ability to handle the changing world is falling behind the speed with which the world is changing. Without the "know-how" to adapt to their ever-changing environments, adults with learning disabilities will be left behind. Education and training programs designed to promote lifelong learning should aid individuals with learning disabilities to deal with our changing world.

There is a serious need for research to define and understand the adult learning disabilities population. In a survey of adult literacy and learning disabilities experts conducted by the Learning Disabilities Association of Canada (Alderson-Gill & Associates, 1989), a number of issues related to teaching literacy skills to adults with learning disabilities emerged that deserve mention because they continue to be true today. The study found that little research has been conducted related to teaching literacy skills to adults with learning disabilities; adult literacy practitioners have very little practical experience teaching literacy skills to adults with learning disabilities; and adult literacy and learning disabilities professionals have very different perspectives on teaching literacy skills to adults with learning disabilities. In addition, without increased research in best practices for screening, diagnosis, intervention, and training of adults with learning disabilities, we will continue to only make "best guesses" of effective techniques and interventions and our impact on the education of adults with learning disabilities who attend adult education, literacy, and job-training programs.

With insufficient research on this population, we must frequently turn to anecdotal accounts. Some adult literacy practitioners tell us that there are a significant number of adult learners who are much less responsive to literacy instruction than others, and the reality of the situation is that these learners can neither afford nor gain access to comprehensive learning disabilities assessments and specialized instruction. Other literacy practitioners suggest that (1) labeling a person with learning disabilities is potentially damaging; (2) well-trained literacy tutors can recognize learning difficulties and will alter their teaching style to accommodate most students' needs and, when a problem is too difficult, do seek out the appropriate assistance; (3) accurate assessment of learning disabilities may not be possible due to culturally and class-biased testing; and (4) standardized testing for adults with learning disabilities is often frustrating due to their history of failure in testing situations (Alderson-Gill & Associates, 1989).

Experts in learning disabilities further complicate the picture. Some emphasize the need for (1) quality training in learning disabilities for literacy tutors that is structured and standardized, (2) specialized literacy programs that address the unique needs of adults with learning disabilities, and (3) scientific assessment and standardized testing for the identification of learning disabilities (Alderson-Gill & Associates, 1989). Experts in the field of reading disabilities suggest that there may be few compelling reasons for diagnosing cases of specific reading disability (dyslexia) in adult practice. Their research suggests that the characteristics of reading that present the greatest problems (i.e., types of errors made, processes impaired, and effectiveness of various approaches to remediation) are seldom different for poor readers, regardless of the presence or absence of reading disability. Their work implies that a diagnosis may be unnecessary for successful remediation (Fowler & Scarborough, 1993).

CONCLUSION

The National Institute for Literacy (NIFL) was established under the National Literacy Act (1991, Public Law 102-73). An interagency group consisting of the Secretary of Education, the Secretary of Labor, and the Secretary of Health and Human Services provides the NIFL with policy guidance and administrative support, thus creating a unified force devoted to improving and expanding the nation's literacy service delivery system. The NIFL's primary mission is to provide leadership in achieving Goal Six of Goals 2000 (1994). To fulfill its mission, the NIFL is authorized to assist federal agencies to improve literacy services; conduct basic and applied research; assist federal, state, and local agencies to improve their literacy policies; provide training and technical assistance to literacy programs throughout the nation; collect and disseminate information; review and make recommendations with regard to reporting requirements and performance measures; and provide a toll-free telephone line for providers and volunteers (Irwin, 1992).

In October 1992, the NIFL's first Research Awards Program was launched, funding 36 basic and applied research and demonstration projects, totaling $3.2 million. These one-year awards were made to individuals, public and private nonprofit institutions, agencies, and organizations representing a cross-section of programs, including libraries, state and local literacy programs, school districts, universities, and research institutions, among others. Although the 36 awards reflected 11 broad categories associated with adult literacy, one funded project, located at the University of the Ozarks, focused specifically on the needs of adult learners with learning disabilities (NIFL, 1992).

In October 1993, as part of the NIFL's mandate to disseminate information on a national level, the National Adult Literacy and Learning Disabilities Center (the Center) was created to serve those adults who are illiterate and learning disabled.

The Center's focus is on enhancing awareness among literacy practitioners, policymakers, researchers, and adult learners about the nature of learning disabilities and its impact on the provision of literacy services. Clearly we need to bridge the gap between the fields of literacy and learning disabilities.

Building a bridge involves teamwork. It involves working together toward the same common goal. It involves building a solid foundation and structure. It involves connecting territory. It involves time, money, and commitment.

On one shore is the fullest possible participation in U.S. social and economic life: the ability to have a good job, to progress, and to gain new skills; the ability to figure sale prices in a store; the ability to read street signs; the ability to order a meal in a restaurant. Literacy is no longer just the capacity to perform simple reading and writing skills. It involves the ability to function on the job and in society and to achieve goals—to develop our knowledge and potential.

On the other shore are the estimated 30 million Americans who are functionally illiterate and the 34% who are considered marginally illiterate. A large number of those individuals are believed to have a learning disability.

There are many who are trying to build this bridge right now. Literacy, job-training, and adult education programs are intended to help adults find their way to the other shore. One of the main foundations of the bridge we are building is adequate training in learning disabilities for instructors in adult literacy, job-training, and ABE programs. Regular in-service training in learning disabilities is imperative.

Another important part of bridge building is that we work together—if we do not coordinate our efforts and work toward the same common goal, the bridge will not meet. In addition, if we become too protective of our territory, our time will be wasted and our bridge will not get built. Only by creating linkages among programs and agencies dealing with adult literacy and learning disabilities, and by providing training and technical assistance to adult literacy providers, can we strengthen the capacity of literacy practitioners to help adults with learning disabilities. It has been stated loudly and clearly by both the literacy and learning disability communities that literacy, job-training, and ABE program professionals need ongoing training in learning disabilities and that these professionals need to work together with the professionals in the learning disabilities community. Training needs include screening and intervention techniques that can provide the most effective and efficient instruction.

Training, screening, and intervention techniques are supported by another important building component: research. Not only do we have to build bridges between the adult literacy and learning disabilities communities, we need more research on the intervention techniques that can be used by ABE teachers, literacy providers, and job-training instructors when working with adults with learning disabilities. We need to bridge the gap between research and practice: Research cannot stop at the door of the university—practical applications of successful research interventions need to be delivered to the educators and the adults with learning disabilities.

Ultimately, what are bridges for? To move from one place to another—to get from one point in life to the next. From the estimated statistics, there are many adults who have low literacy skills and are in a less than desirable place in their lives. They are at a point at which their job skills are few, their self-esteem is low, and their frustration is high. In addition, it is estimated that a large number of these individuals are adults with learning disabilities. Many of these individuals have tried to cross the bridge but have been unsuccessful. They have tried to achieve literacy skills but have failed.

As we continue to develop techniques, methods, and strategies for working with adults with learning disabilities in literacy and adult education programs, we need solid foundations in training and research and must include in our structure adequate screening devices and a variety of intervention techniques. Again, this will take time, money, and commitment. Most important, the adult literacy and learning disabilities communities must coordinate their efforts to work as both partners and collaborators to construct a firm, solid, unshakable bridge for adults with learning disabilities who seek support from adult education and literacy providers.

REFERENCES

Alderson-Gill & Associates. (1989). *Study of literature and learning disabilities*. Ottawa, Ontario: Learning Disabilities Association of Canada.

Americans with Disabilities Act of 1990, 42 U.S.C.A. §§ 12101 et seq. (West 1993).

Anderson, C. W. (1994). Adult literacy and learning disabilities. In P. J. Gerber & H. B. Reiff (Eds.), *Learning disabilities in adulthood: Persisting problems and evolving issues* (pp. 121–129). Stoneham, MA: Butterworth-Heinemann.

Beder, H. (1991). *Adult literacy: Issues for policy and practice*. Malabar, FL: Krieger.

Bowren, F. F. (1981). Teaching the learning disabled to read. *Adult Literacy and Basic Education, 5*, 179–183.

Brizius, J. A., & Foster, S. A. (1994). *A governor's guide to literacy: A primer for state literacy policymakers*. Washington, DC: National Governors' Association.

Campbell, A., Kirsch, E. S., & Kolstad, A. (1992). *Assessing literacy: The framework for the national adult literacy survey*. Washington, DC: U.S. Government Printing Office.

Chalfant, J. C., & Scheffelin, M. (1969). *Central processing dysfunction on children* (NINDS Monograph No. 9). Bethesda, MD: U.S. Department of Health, Education, and Welfare.

Craig, J. L. (1990, November). The hidden handicap: Learning disabilities. *Menninger Clinic Perspective*, pp. 5–9.

Ellis, W., & Cramer, S. C. (1994). *Learning disabilities: A National Responsibility*. Report of the Summit on Learning Disabilities, National Center for Learning Disabilities, Washington, D.C.

Fowler, A. E., & Scarborough, H. S. (1993). *Should reading disabled adults be distinguished from other adults seeking literacy instruction? A review of theory and research*. Philadelphia: National Center on Adult Literacy.

Goals 2000: Educate America Act of 1994. Public Law 103-227.

Gold, P. C. (1981). The DL-LEA: A remedial approach for nonreaders with a language deficiency handicap. *Adult Literacy and Basic Education, 5*, 185–193.

Gottesman, R. L. (1992). Literacy and adults with severe learning difficulties. *Journal of the National Association for Adults with Special Learning Needs, 2*(1), 48–53.

HEATH Resource Center and National Adult Literacy and Learning Disabilities Center. (1994). *National resources for adults with learning disabilities*. Washington, DC: Author.

Herbert, J. P. (1988). *Working with adults who have learning disabilities* (Report No. CE 053 001). Topeka: Kansas State Department of Education, Manhattan Adult Learning and Resource Center. (ERIC Document Reproduction Service No. ED 310 237).

Interagency Committee on Learning Disabilities. (1987). *Learning disabilities: A report to the U.S. Congress*. Bethesda, MD: National Institutes of Health. (ERIC Document Reproduction Service No. ED 294 358).

Irwin, P. M. (1992). *CRS report for Congress. National Literacy Act of 1991: Major provisions of Public Law 102–73*. Washington, DC: Congressional Research Services.

Kirsch, I. S., Jungeblut, A., & Campbell, A. (1992). *Beyond the school doors: The literacy needs of job seekers served by the U.S. Department of Labor*. Washington, DC: U.S. Department of Labor.

Kirsch, I. S., Jungeblut, A., Jenkins, L., & Kolstad, A. (1993). *Adult literacy in America: A first look at the results of the national adult literacy survey*. Washington, DC: U.S. Government Printing Office.

Klein, C. (1989). Specific learning difficulties. *Adult Literacy and Basic Skills Unit, 32*, 2–5.

Knowles, M. S. (1989, August). Everything you wanted to know from Malcolm Knowles (and weren't afraid to ask). *Training*, 45–50.

Learning Disabilities Association of America. (1991). *Action alert*. Pittsburgh, PA: Author.

Learning Disabilities Association of America. (1992). *Illiteracy in America*. Pittsburgh, PA: Author.

Mullins, I. V. S., & Jenkins, L. B. (1990). *The reading report card, 1971–1988: Trends from the Nation's Report Card.* Washington, DC: U.S. Department of Education.

National Institute for Literacy. (1992). *Literacy News, 1*(6). Washington, DC: Author.

National Joint Committee on Learning Disabilities. (1988). Learning disabilities: Issues on definition. (Reprinted in *Journal of Learning Disabilities, 20,* 107–108).

National Literacy Act of 1991, Public Law 102-73, 105 Stat. 333 (1991).

Nightengale, D. (1991). *The learning disabled in employment and training programs: Research and evaluation report series 91-E.* Washington, DC: Urban Institute.

Osher, D., & Webb, L. (1994). *Adult literacy, learning disabilities and social context: Conceptual foundations for a learner centered approach.* Washington, DC: Pelavin Associates.

Osher, D., Webb, L., & Koehler, S. (1993). *Study of ABE/ESL instructor training approaches: Learning disabilities: Learner-centered approaches.* Washington, DC: Pelavin Associates.

Padak, N. D., Davidson, J. L., & Padak, G. M. (1990). Exploring reading with adult beginning readers. *Journal of Reading, 34*(1), 26–29.

Payne, M. (1992). Teaching tips: Meeting the needs of adults with learning disabilities. *GED Items.* Washington, DC: General Educational Development Testing Services.

PLUS Outreach. (1992). *Literacy/learning disabilities collaboration project.* Pittsburgh, PA: Author.

Reder, S. (in press). *Literacy education and learning disabilities.* Philadelphia: National Center on Adult Literacy.

Rehabilitation Act of 1973, Public Law 93-112, 87 Stat. 355 (1973).

Ross, J. M., & Smith, J. O. (1990). Adult basic educators' perceptions of learning disabilities. *Journal of Reading, 33*(5), 340–347.

Ross-Gordon, J. M. (1989). *Adults with learning disabilities: An overview for the adult educator* (Information Series No. 337). Columbus, OH: ERIC Clearinghouse on Adult, Career, and Vocational Education.

Ryan, A., & Price, L. (1993). Learning disabilities in adult education: A survey of current practices. *Journal of Postsecondary Education and Disability, 10*(3), 31–40.

Smith, S. L. (1981). *No easy answers.* New York: Bantam Books.

Smith, S. L. (1991). *Succeeding against the odds: Strategies and insights from the learning disabled.* Los Angeles: Jeremy P. Tarcher.

Smith, S. L. (1994). How not to feel stupid when you know you're not: Self-esteem and learning disabilities. In *Linkages* (pp. 1–2). Washington, DC: National Adult Literacy and Learning Disabilities Center.

Thistlewaite, L. (1983). Teaching reading to the ABE student who cannot read. *Lifelong Learning: The Adult Years, 7*(1), 5–7.

World Health Organization. (1980). *International classification of impairments, disabilities, and handicaps.* Geneva, Switzerland: Author.

13

Improving Employment Outcomes for Persons with Learning Disabilities

ESTHER H. MINSKOFF

Recent changes in federal legislation reflect a new view of intervention approaches for individuals with learning disabilities. Instead of focusing narrowly on school-based educational treatment, the current view of intervention is outcome-based and stresses postsecondary employment as one of the major goals of all programs for children, youth, and adults with learning disabilities. Preparing all students, not just those with disabilities, for employment is a nationwide trend that is reflected in the recently enacted school-to-work federal legislation (School-to-Work Opportunities Act, 1994). This emerging approach to intervention reflects a life-span view of services for individuals with learning disabilities rather than one limited to school-age individuals.

The shift from a school to a life-span orientation is a result of two areas of research: follow-up studies evaluating adult outcomes in individuals with disabilities after they exit school and studies of adults with disabilities. There are a large number of follow-up studies and studies of adults with all types of disabilities, but this chapter only examines research conducted with persons with learning disabilities. The National Longitudinal Transition Study (Wagner, Newman, & Blackorby, 1993) is the most comprehensive study of outcomes with individuals having disabilities who received special education. The follow-up 3 to 5 years after leaving high school yielded the following results for students with learning disabilities: 36% dropout rate, 16% postsecondary attendance, and 71% employment rate. Although the employment rate for these individuals with learning disabilities is comparable to that of individuals without disabilities, their employment rate is probably much lower because a larger percentage of them were not involved in postsecondary education (Michaels, 1994). The findings from the National Longitudinal Transition Study consistently have been supported by other follow-up studies assessing adult outcomes for individuals with learning disabilities (Wehman, 1992).

One of the first studies of adults with learning disabilities was conducted by the Research and Demonstration Project for Improving Vocational Rehabilitation for Learning Disabled Adults (Hoffmann et al., 1987; Minskoff, Hawks, Steidle, & Hoffmann, 1989). Surveys of 381 adults with learning disabilities who were found eligible for vocational rehabilitation services, 948 service providers who worked with persons with learning disabilities (e.g., psychologists, teachers, and vocational counselors), and 212 consumers and advocates indicated that adults with learning disabilities were perceived as having major academic, social, personal, and vocational problems. In a comparison of these 381 adults and 114 high school seniors with learning disabilities, the adults reported significantly more problems in all areas than did the high schoolers (Minskoff, Sautter, Sheldon, Steidle, & Baker, 1988). These problems were attributed to lack of self-perception and understanding of the reality of their situation by the high schoolers because of insulation from failure by special education. Other studies of adults with learning disabilities have consistently reported significant problems in academic, social, personal, and vocational areas (Wehman, 1992).

As a result of the research findings from the follow-up studies and the studies of adults with learning disabilities indicating less than satisfactory adult outcomes, transition programs have been legally mandated at the federal and state levels as a means of increasing the likelihood of successful adult outcomes, especially involving employment. However, there is limited research supporting the effectiveness of transition programs in improving adult outcomes for individuals with learning disabilities. Many of the studies that have been conducted have used simplistic research designs. If transition programs are to be accurately evaluated, they must be investigated using a multidimensional approach. Simplistic research designs that group persons with learning disabilities with other types of disabilities, or group all persons with learning disabilities as homogeneous, yield data of limited use. In addition, such research must examine the dimension of interventions received by students over their school careers, with special emphasis on specific transition practices. The influence of economic and geographic factors on employment also must be considered so the status of workers with learning disabilities can be contrasted with the status of all workers. Rusch, Enchelmaier, and Kohler (1994) propose a similar model for evaluating transition programs that involves a systems-level conceptual framework consisting of four levels: student and family, programs responsible for implementing educational interventions, organizational structure of the agencies that must be coordinated, and the community.

In order to explore the many issues underlying the relationships between employability and transition for persons with learning disabilities, this chapter concentrates on three areas. First, I review the research that relates specific components of transition programs to adult employability outcomes. Although the adult outcomes of employment, social and interpersonal relations, and independent living are interrelated (Michaels, 1994), this chapter only examines employability. Second, I present model transition programs based on the research findings on transition practices that seem to have contributed to the achievement of successful employment outcomes and the descriptive literature on transition programs. Third, I describe the studies designed to answer the multidimensional question, "*What components of transition programs are related to successful employment outcomes for what types of individuals with learning disabilities under what circumstances?*" These studies are being conducted by the Center for Learning Potential in association with the University of Georgia Learning Disabilities Research and Training Center.

REVIEW OF THE LITERATURE
Legal Mandates for Transition

In 1990, amendments to the Education for All Handicapped Children Act (1975, Public Law 94-142) were signed into law and renamed Individuals with Disabilities Education Act (IDEA, Public Law 101-476). Included in the IDEA are components that define and mandate transition planning and services for youth with disabilities. Transition services are defined in Section 602(a)(19) as follows:

> A coordinated set of activities for a student, designed within an outcome-oriented process, which promotes movement from school to postschool activities, including postsecondary education, vocational training, integrated employment (including supported em-

ployment), continuing and adult education, adult services, independent living, and community participation.

The IDEA also adds the following requirement of individualized education plans (IEPs):

> A statement of the needed transition services for students beginning no later than age 16 and annually thereafter (and, when determined appropriate for the individuals, beginning at age 14 or younger), including when appropriate, a statement of the interagency responsibilities or linkages (or both) before the student leaves the school setting. (IDEA, 1990, §602(a)(20))

In 1992, the Rehabilitation Act Amendments, reauthorizing the Rehabilitation Act (1973), were passed. One of the purposes of these Amendments is "to empower individuals with disabilities to maximize employment, economic self-sufficiency, independence, and inclusion and integration into society, through comprehensive and coordinated state-of-the-art programs of vocational rehabilitation." This legislation is designed to reduce service gaps between education and rehabilitation services when needed for students exiting school and to strengthen the coordination between vocational rehabilitation and the schools including exchange of information and data, provision of services, and access to rehabilitation service.

Another federal law, the Americans with Disabilities Act (ADA; 1990), prohibits discrimination against people with disabilities in employment, public accommodation, transportation, state and local government services, and telecommunications. The ADA opens the doors to employment for persons with learning disabilities, whereas the IDEA and the Rehabilitation Act provide possible means for achieving successful employment. With such job opportunities becoming available, it is imperative that factors related to maximizing the chances of fulfilling such job opportunities be identified. If persons with learning disabilities are not successful in meeting job challenges, job opportunities will wither and the promise of the ADA will be unfulfilled.

Studies of Best Practices in Transition

Kohler (1993) reviewed the literature on best practices in transition (i.e., those transition practices that have been substantiated or implied as having a positive impact on student outcomes). The subjects in the studies she reviewed ranged from individuals with learning disabilities to persons with severe disabilities, so generalization to learning disabilities may be limited. Another limitation stems from the lack of empirically supported evidence because much of the literature involved pseudo- and quasi-experimental studies and theory-based or opinion articles. Based on Kohler's review of 46 studies, three best practices in transition were cited in more than 50% of the documents reviewed: vocational training, parental involvement, and interagency collaboration and service delivery. Three other transition practices—social skills training, paid work experience, and individual transition plans—were cited in about one third of the documents reviewed. Based on her review of the literature, Kohler concluded that there is a lack of substantiated support for transition practices that have emerged as effective. However, there is implied support for some transition best practices. She cautioned that we cannot wait for empirical evidence of effectiveness before beginning transition programs. We must conduct research to substantiate best practices in transition, at the same time providing transition practices that have been implied as contributing to successful outcomes.

One aspect of the National Longitudinal Transition Study examined experiences while students were in high school (Wagner et al., 1993). High school vocational education experiences, work-study jobs, and paid work experiences were related to successful employment and should be considered best practices for a transition program. Students who were given tutorial assistance and other support services were more likely to graduate, thereby increasing their likelihood of successful adult outcomes. A school advocate, usually a special educator, seemed to be another component of a successful transition program.

In a survey of 168 project directors of federally funded model transition programs for students with all types of disabilities, 22 outcomes and 65 related activities were associated with employment (Rusch et al., 1994). Three outcomes that were identified as most important were IEPs, educating students alongside their peers who have no disabilities, and documenting progress in employment-related skills. In a review of nine exemplary transition programs for students with learning disabilities, the following components emerged: individualized planning and coordination; vocational preparation; academic remediation and support; academic, vocational, and social–personal counseling; support systems and services; job seeking and placement; and follow-up or follow-along (Rojewski, 1992).

Another approach for identifying best practices in transition involves follow-up studies at the local level so that the specific idiosyncrasies of local communities can be taken into account. In such a follow-up of students with learning disabilities in three local school districts in the Houston area, Fourqurean (1994) found which areas of vocational training in high school were correlated with employment in such jobs, thereby providing support for recommending such vocational areas to students in transition programs. He also found that most former students reported that not getting along with coworkers and supervisors was a common problem, supporting the necessity of infusing social skills training into secondary special education programs. Only 6% of the former students received any assistance from vocational rehabilitation, indicating the need for stronger linkages between the school and vocational rehabilitation.

Based on the literature on transition, the following best practices seem to be necessary for transition programs for students with learning disabilities: individual transition plans, vocational education and training, work experience, social skills training, parent involvement, interagency coordination, integration with nondisabled persons in vocational and work settings, academic support, vocational counseling, job seeking and job placement services, personal counseling, supportive services from an advocate, and program evaluation involving follow-up and follow-along.

PROPOSED IDEAS FOR CHANGE
Model Transition Programs

Using the limited research on transition and the growing body of literature describing transition programs throughout the nation, it is possible to tentatively identify best practices that should be included in transition programs for persons with learning disabilities and that should be the focus of empirical examination. A comprehensive transition program must involve three stages: planning for transition, the transition component of the IEP, and implementation of the IEP.

Transition Planning

Transition should not begin at the secondary level but, rather, must begin as soon as students are identified as having learning disabilities. If transition is to be effective, there must be life-span considerations starting in the preschool and early school years (Szymanski, 1994). Transition services need to be provided on an ongoing basis rather than being time-limited. Students with learning disabilities must develop skills in the following areas over their entire school careers: academic skills, life skills, self-awareness, social skills, work behaviors, and career knowledge.

Higher levels of academic achievement are necessary for the increasingly complex workplace (Carnevale, Gainer, & Maltzer, 1990); therefore, it is imperative that the academic skills of students with learning disabilities be developed to the highest level possible. In addition, the new school-to-work federal legislation seeks to provide a rigorous program of study designed to meet the same academic content standards as a particular state has established and to meet the requirements necessary to earn skill certificates in occupational clusters. If students with learning disabilities are to gain access to such programs, they must have high levels of academic skills. Poor academic achievement condemns many persons with learning disabilities to entry-level jobs, contributing to the underemployment that seems to be a problem for many individuals with learning disabilities. Because of the movement away from pullout special education programs to total inclusion for students with learning disabilities, many are not receiving remedial programs to improve their academic skills while they are in elementary and middle school. They are being integrated into classrooms where they cannot meet the academic requirements, and they are being carried along by such drastic classroom modifications as having all written materials read to them. Such wholesale mainstreaming neglects the need for intensive remediation of academic deficits and eventually limits students' abilities to meet the academic challenges of jobs above the entry level. Ironically, such students often seek academic remediation as adults, and many enter adult basic education and adult literacy programs taught by professionals untrained in special education methods or by volunteers with little expertise in teaching. Remediation of academic deficits by school personnel with specialized training has a greater chance of success than do postsecondary attempts at remediation and can minimize the damaged self-esteem that results from low academic performance in school.

Life skills such as those taught at the Life-Centered Career Education Program (Brolin, 1989) may be necessary for students with more severe learning disabilities. These functional skills (e.g., managing personal finances and getting around in the community) are vital for independent living, and students cannot just be trained at the secondary and postsecondary levels but must develop these skills over their entire educational career.

Many students with learning disabilities lack self-awareness. They may not have been told that they have learning disabilities, leaving them to flounder with their own self-diagnoses, which often involve fears of being mentally retarded or emotionally disturbed. Or, they may not have been helped to understand the nature of their strengths as well as their weaknesses. Self-awareness requires an ever-changing understanding of oneself and how one meets the challenges at each stage in life. With all good intentions, many parents and professionals protect students with learning disabilities from failure and create an unrealistic environment with little or no failure. Thus students fail to understand their disabilities while in school and receive a jolt when they get out of school, which Minskoff et al. (1988) found in their comparison of adults and high schoolers with learning disabilities. The classroom modifications that abound in a student's learning environment may not prepare the student for the workplace. Michaels (1994) cited three common modifications made in school so that students with learning disabilities can meet academic demands: doing less work, doing easier work, or having extra time for doing work. These modifications enable many students to receive adequate grades in their classes but may lead to unrealistic views of their abilities to meet demands in the integrated workplace setting where such modifications would not be made. They need to be given a balance of success and failure so that they develop a realistic perception of themselves and the challenges they must meet for success in school and the workplace.

The development of social skills has been identified as a best transition practice by Kohler (1993) and Fourqurean (1994). In a survey of 145 employers to identify the workplace social skills that are critical for job success, Minskoff and DeMoss (1994) found that compliance was most frequently rated as essential for job success, followed by cooperation, problem solving, civility, and verbal communication. Minskoff (1994b) designed the Trade Related Academic Competencies (TRAC) Workplace Social Skills Program to develop such social skills in students at the middle and high school levels and in postsecondary settings. Obviously, compliance and cooperation are social skills that need to be developed as soon as a student enters school so that these skills can first be applied to the school setting and eventually generalized to the work setting.

Work behaviors need to be developed starting at the preschool level. Szymanski (1994) cites the work personality (i.e., self-concept as a worker and work motivation) as developing during the preschool years and work competencies (i.e., work habits, physical and mental skills applicable to jobs, and work-related interpersonal skills) as developing during the school years.

Career knowledge needs to be developed through a comprehensive career education program that starts at school entry and changes as the student grows. Such education programs should include career awareness, career orientation, career exploration, career preparation, and career placement and follow-up. Career awareness should be introduced at the elementary level to develop knowledge of occupational clusters. Career orientation starts at the middle school level and seeks to match self-knowledge with an investigation of occupational clusters. Starting at the middle school and continuing through high school, career exploration leads to narrowing occupational alternatives. The School-to-Work Opportunities Act recommends that career awareness and exploration begin at the earliest possible age, but no later than seventh grade. At the high school level, career preparation, where students acquire entry-level skills in occupational clusters, should be provided. Finally, career placement and follow-up ensure that students bridge the gap between school and work.

Individual Transition Plans

Transition plans are to be included in a student's IEP at age 16 or, if necessary, earlier. The IEP committee should be made up of the student with learning disabilities, the parents, school personnel (i.e., special education teachers, regular education teachers, vocational educators, psychologists, and counselors), community agencies (e.g., vocational rehabilitation counselors), and any other people who will be involved in the implementation of the transition plans. It is critically important that students become active participants in their IEPs. Simply sitting and listening to others make decisions about them is not involvement. As students with learning disabilities become more knowledgeable about themselves and their goals, they should be trained to chair their own IEP meetings. Training in self-awareness, self-determination, and self-advocacy should be provided in conjunction with student involvement in the IEP process. Self-awareness (understanding one's strengths and weaknesses) must be the basis for self-determination (the ability to make appropriate choices involving all life decisions at home, school, work, and leisure). Self-advocacy should then be built on a foundation of self-awareness and self-determination. Self-advocacy training must lead to understanding one's legal rights under federal and state legislation. Once students reach the age of 18, legally they can make all decisions for themselves. We must make sure that they are ready to take on this role.

Parental involvement has been identified as a best practice in transition (Kohler, 1994). Parents need to be involved in all educational and transition decisions throughout their child's enrollment in school. Parents must be educated about their child's legal rights and the services that are due to them. Professionals have to balance the interests of students with learning disabilities with the interests of the school, but parents have only one interest—their children.

Although student and parent involvement is necessary for successful transition, support from an advocate is also essential. The School-to-Work Opportunities Act includes a school site mentor—a professional employed at the school who is designated as the advocate for a particular student and who works in consultation with classroom teachers, counselors, related services personnel, and the employer of the student to design and monitor the progress of the student's school-to-work program. If such a mentor is important for students without disabilities, such a professional is absolutely essential for students with disabilities. Special educators should be given expanded roles so that they can assume these different responsibilities and serve as school site mentors.

A common complaint from regular and vocational educators is that they are not invited to attend IEP meetings for students with learning disabilities who are mainstreamed in their classrooms. In some cases they are not allowed to see their students' IEPs. They cannot implement educational plans if they do not know what they are and why they are made. If the best practice of integration with the nondisabled is to be achieved, regular and vocational teachers must be partners in all decision making and, therefore, must be involved in the IEP process.

Community agency personnel, especially vocational rehabilitation counselors, should attend students' IEP meetings. Like Fourqurean (1994), I have found that many students with learning disabilities are not linked to vocational rehabilitation while in high school. This complicates the problem of implementation of IEP recommendations. Representatives from other community agencies such as the community service board, social services, or business should also attend IEP meetings if they are to be involved in implementation of transition plans.

The IEP must delineate the student's present level of performance in all areas necessary for decisions involving educational programming and transition. A student's present level of performance is determined from a comprehensive psychoeducational evaluation and vocational assessment. Hawks et al. (1990) have identified a model diagnostic battery for assessing adolescents and adults with learning disabilities. The purpose of vocational assessment is to gather employability-related information on a student's learning styles, work habits and attitudes, functional academic skills, specific vocational skills, interests, dexterity and endurance, and interpersonal skills.

The transition plan should include statements of desired postsecondary outcomes in employment, education, and adult living. For each of these three areas of postsecondary outcomes, specific goals and objectives should be generated. The IEP must include the services necessary to achieve the goals and objectives projected. One of the most important services involves vocational education and training. Some schools have successfully integrated students with learning disabilities into various vocational education programs in which the students have interests and aptitudes. Student interests and aptitudes should be identified in the vocational assessment. Students need to receive vocational counseling on an ongoing basis so that they can continue to identify their interests and aptitudes as they learn about new occupations and have experiences with different types of jobs. Also, they need instruction in job-seeking and job-keeping skills.

To ensure the success of such students, special educators should serve as consultants or resource teachers to vocational educators. Special educators must provide support to students with learning disabilities as well as to their mainstream instructors. Special educators can then provide assistance when students have academic problems with the vocational curriculum. The TRAC Program has been designed to assist special educators in training students with learning disabilities to meet the academic demands of 26 different vocational education areas in which these students frequently enroll (Minskoff & DeMoss, 1993). In addition, the special educator can advise and model for the teacher how to modify instruction based on a student's characteristics (e.g., giving written instructions as well as oral directions to a student with an auditory memory problem). It is important that the students learn to work with the nondisabled students in all vocational and regular classes because this will provide the basis for working with nondisabled persons in the workplace. Vocational preparation should be directed toward developing appropriate work behaviors for any job. There should be preparation for an occupational cluster, not for a specific job.

Because work experience while in high school has been correlated with increased employability in adulthood, it is important that the IEP include a goal relative to this. The parents and the school should work together to ensure that an after-school or summer job is obtained and any problems that arise in the workplace are solved with the assistance of the parents, school personnel, or both.

Implementing Transition Plans

Implementation has to be monitored at two levels: school and postschool. Implementation is easier to monitor at the school level because special education is accountable for providing all services in the IEP. However, barriers to implementation may result from limited access to mainstream services for students with learning disabilities. Access to vocational education programs for a student may be barred because of negative attitudes toward persons with disabilities by the vocational educators or because of unwritten quotas on the number of special education students allowed in certain vocational education programs. Vocational training has been identified as one of the most important best practices in transition; therefore, special educators, parents, and students with learning disabilities must advocate for such training. Students who do not receive vocational training, postsecondary education, or such other postsecondary services as vocational rehabilitation leave high school with *no* job skills and are doomed to permanent entry-level employment or chronic unemployment.

Implementation of transition plans is difficult at the postschool level because the school no longer has legal responsibility. If an individual is receiving vocational rehabilitation services after school, the vocational rehabilitation agency is responsible for implementation. If a student is enrolled in postsecondary education or training (i.e., vocational school, college, or university) and is eligible for special services under Section 504 of the Rehabilitation Act, limited services are available; however, such services are rarely as comprehensive as secondary school transition services.

If an individual does not receive vocational rehabilitation or postsecondary services, there is no agency legally responsible for implementation of plans needed to achieve adult outcomes. Most students with learning disabilities are not linked to vocational rehabilitation prior to or upon completion of high school, and most are not enrolled in postsecondary education of any sort. Follow-up studies have shown that most students with learning disabilities get jobs through family and friends (Fourqurean, 1994) and not through community agencies. For individuals without such connections, getting a job may be very difficult. The absence of legal responsibility for transition plans after a student leaves high school is one of the most significant barriers to the achievement of successful outcomes for individuals with learning disabilities, especially for those students who do not have parents who are advocates on their behalf or who have not been trained to advocate for themselves.

To ensure that transition services are available after students exit high school, the schools need to establish linkages with such agencies as vocational rehabilitation, social services, the community services board, mental health agencies, community colleges, colleges and universities, the state employment commission, private industry councils, and local employers in business and industry.

Ongoing transition services may be necessary throughout an individual's lifetime. Vocational retraining may be necessary because of job elimination, firing, personal crisis, social problems, independent living problems, or a change in personal goals. Some individuals with learning disabilities require ongoing services from birth to death. We have no mechanism in place to provide such services.

Research on Transition and Employability

One of the research strands of the University of Georgia Learning Disabilities Research and Training Center, which is being conducted by the Center for Learning Potential (CLP), focuses on the relationship between transition practices and employability of adults with learning disabilities. Three specific research studies are currently being conducted to answer the basic research question, "What components of transition programs are related to successful employment outcomes for what types of individuals with learning disabilities under what circumstances?" The CLP is examining this question with model transition programs using best practices that have been researched since 1983. These best practices are based on academic, psychosocial, and vocational interventions developed by the federally funded Research and Demonstration Project on Improving Vocational Rehabilitation for Adults with Learning Disabilities at Woodrow Wilson Rehabilitation Center from 1983 to 1987. From 1986 to 1989, interventions that were demonstrated to be effective with adults with learning disabilities were implemented with high school students with learning disabilities under another federally funded grant. These interventions are included in the model transition programs provided by the CLP to many Virginia school districts and funded by the Virginia Department of Rehabilitative Services. Nine CLP school districts are being used as sites for this research project.

Multidimensional Model

A multidimensional approach to this basic research question was undertaken to analyze five dimensions: (1) individual characteristics of persons with learning disabilities, (2) familial/cultural factors, (3) interventions, (4) economic and geographic factors, and (5) job factors. This multidimensional approach is similar to the conceptual framework for comprehensive transition outcome assessment proposed by DeStefano and Wagner (1993), which focuses on analysis of school content, school services, and individual, family, and community characteristics in relationship to student and young adult outcomes.

The CLP recognizes the heterogeneity of the population of individuals with learning disabilities and is investigating 10 variables involving individual characteristics in relationship to employability of adults with learning disabilities. Each of these 10 variables is being correlated with all the other variables on all the dimensions so that interactive effects can be identified. In this way it should be possible to identify best transition practices for subgroups of persons with learning disabilities having certain characteristics.

The following individual characteristics are being examined in relationship to employability outcomes.

1. *Gender.* Females with learning disabilities have consistently been found to have less successful employment outcomes in adulthood than males (Wagner et al., 1993; Fourqurean, 1994).

2. *High school graduation.* Dropouts have consistently been found to have poorer employment outcomes in adulthood than high school graduates (deBettencourt, Zigmond, & Thornton, 1989; Wagner et al., 1993).

3. *IQ.* Higher Verbal IQ and Comprehension and Information subtest scores on the Wechsler Adult Intelligence Scale—Revised have been related to more successful employment outcomes (Faas & D'Alonzo, 1990) and IQ has been identified as the best predictor of academic and vocational success (Hohenshil, Levinson, & Heer, 1985).

4. *Psychological processing deficits.* Deficits in psychological processing areas such as attention, memory, reasoning, and perception have a significant impact on job performance (Minskoff, 1994a).

5. *Academic achievement.* Because higher literacy levels are needed for the jobs of the future (Carnevale et al., 1990), adults with significant academic problems will find the challenges of increased literacy levels of future jobs daunting.

6. *Severity of disability.* Minskoff (1994a) contends that for some persons, learning disabilities may be more severe in adulthood than in childhood. Decisions regarding severity of disability based on seven variables have been suggested by Minskoff et al. (1989).

7. *Social participation.* Involvement in various social and com-

munity groups has been related to successful employment outcomes (Wagner et al., 1993).

8. *Social skills.* Workplace social skills have been identified as being crucial for successful employment outcomes (Minskoff & DeMoss, 1993).

9. *Psychological adjustment.* Hoffmann et al. (1987) found that 16% of the adults with learning disabilities surveyed reported having personal problems that made it difficult to get or keep a job.

10. *High school job experience.* Having part-time work experience has been related to successful employment outcomes (Wagner et al., 1993).

Both family and culture have a significant impact on employability for all persons as well as persons with learning disabilities. Four factors on this dimension are being investigated. The first factor is family socioeconomic status, which has been linked to successful employment outcomes for individuals with learning disabilities (Wehman, 1992). Persons with middle-class status value education as a means for their children to attain middle-class status for themselves, and thus they actively advocate for their children's needs. Persons who live in poverty may be more concerned about such critical issues as obtaining food and shelter than about their child's education and job success.

The second factor, public assistance (e.g., social security insurance, food stamps, and Aid to Families with Dependent Children), may be related to employability because public assistance may establish a reliance on dependence rather than employment. Third, racial, ethnic, or cultural group membership may be related to employability because different cultural groups place a different value on work. The fourth factor of family cohesion may be correlated with employability. Persons who come from supportive, loving homes where the parents believed in their children's abilities in spite of disbelief by others, especially school personnel, are more likely to achieve adult success. Supportive parents advocate for their offsprings, thereby obtaining the best possible services. For children who experience failure at school, a loving home provides a haven of safety and support for the development of a good self-concept. Related to family cohesion and social class may be living in a single-parent home.

The following school and postschool interventions that, singly or in combination with other interventions and variables on other dimensions, have been identified as being related to increased employability are being investigated: (1) vocational training and education during or after high school, (2) academic support by special educators, (3) specific transition practices as outlined in the IEP, (4) specific vocational rehabilitation practices, (5) special education services, amount of time in special education, type of secondary school curriculum, dropout prevention, and alternative education programs, (6) postsecondary education and training interventions (e.g., college and apprenticeship), and (7) social and psychological development (e.g., social skills, self advocacy training, counseling, and psychotherapy).

The dimension of economic and geographic factors considers the two variables of urban and rural settings and the impact of the local unemployment rate. This rate is related to the urban and rural factor because more jobs are found in urban settings. It is imperative that the state of the individual's local economy at a particular time be determined so that employment problems of individuals with learning disabilities are not attributed to internal factors when they may be due to the state of the local economy.

The dimension of job factors is being examined to discover how individuals with learning disabilities obtain and maintain employment because this was identified as a major problem by many adults with learning disabilities (Hoffmann et al., 1987). The relationship of the match between the characteristics and interests of an individual with the demands of the person's job is also being considered.

With the ADA opening the doors to many jobs for individuals with learning disabilities, it is important that job supervisors be educated about the special employment needs of this population. Minskoff, Sautter, Hoffmann, and Hawks (1987) found that only half of the 326 employers surveyed stated that they would hire persons with learning disabilities for the jobs that they supervised. They also found that 5% of these employers said they would fire an employee if they found out that they had unknowingly hired a person with learning disabilities. I know of some individuals who were fired after disclosing their learning disabilities to their employers. This creates a dilemma for adults with learning disabilities because if they self-disclose they may not be hired for a job or they may be fired. If they do not self-disclose, they cannot be guaranteed the assurances of the ADA. If individuals with learning disabilities are to be successful on the job, their job supervisors must be educated and given information and support. The relationship between employer knowledge of learning disabilities and attitudes toward persons with disabilities and job maintenance is also being investigated.

Research Studies

Three specific research studies are being conducted by the CLP to investigate the basic research question. The goal of Research Study 1 is to identify the effects of individual characteristics, familial and cultural factors, interventions, and economic and geographic factors on employment outcomes using a follow-up of individuals with learning disabilities who received model transition services in high school. The sample of 100 adults comes from nine Virginia school districts that use the CLP best practices transition model.

Research Study 2 is directed at assessing the effectiveness of transition and vocational rehabilitation services for increasing successful employment outcomes for individuals with learning disabilities by comparing individuals exposed to these services with persons not exposed to these services. Such a comparative study has not been done previously. A sample of 30 adults who did not receive transition services is being compared to 30 adults chosen at random from the population of 100 adults for Research Study 1. The adults who did not receive transition services come from a population of persons who graduated in the years prior to the introduction of transition services from one of nine school districts; therefore, the two groups differ only on the variable of transition services.

Research Study 3 focuses on identifying the effects of individual characteristics, familial and cultural factors, interventions, economic and geographic factors, and job factors on changes in employment outcomes for individuals with learning disabilities over the period of 1 year using a follow-along design. The random sample of 100 adults used for Research Study 1 is being followed for 12 months. The adults in the sample are being interviewed every 4 months to update their employment outcome measures and job factor measures. In addition, three of these clients are being examined in depth using a qualitative research design. Permission to interview their employers has been requested to obtain important data about their performance in the workplace and necessary job accommodation. The first two research studies use a follow-up format whereas the third study uses a follow-along format, which is important for getting qualitative information.

All data possible have been obtained from record reviews. Face-to-face interviews to obtain other information are being conducted by rehabilitation counselors and psychologists.

The following information is being obtained as measures of employment outcomes: (1) whether the individual is employed at the contact time, (2) the number of jobs the individual held in the target period, (3) successful and unsuccessful methods of finding jobs, (4) type(s) of jobs held, (5) hours worked weekly, (6) hourly wages earned, (7) benefits received, (8) if fired, the reason, (9) if quit, the reason, (10) job satisfaction, (11) job accommodations, and (12) performance review results.

FUTURE DIRECTIONS

Transition programs have been legally mandated as a means of improving employment outcomes for adults with learning disabilities. There is limited empirical support for the effectiveness of various components of transition programs; however, best practices have been tentatively identified and have been incorporated in a number of programs nationwide. Such best practices include individual transition plans, vocational education and training, work experience, social skills training, parent involvement, interagency coordination, integration with nondisabled persons in vocational and work settings, academic support, job seeking and job placement services, personal counseling, support services from an advocate, and program evaluation involving follow-up and follow-along.

Although there has been some research on transition and employability, most of it has used a simplistic research design. The CLP is conducting three specific studies using a multidimensional design to examine the basic research question. Research Study 1 is to identify the effects of individual characteristics, familial and cultural factors, interventions, and economic and geographic factors on employment outcomes using follow-up of individuals with learning disabilities who have received model transition services. Research Study 2 is to assess the effectiveness of transition and vocational rehabilitation services for increasing successful employment outcomes comparing individuals exposed to these services with persons not exposed to these services. Research Study 3 is to identify the effects of individual characteristics, familial and cultural factors, interventions, economic and geographic factors, and job factors on changes in employment outcomes over a 1-year period using a follow-along design. When these studies are completed, it should be possible to provide empirical support for transition practices that meet the needs of persons with different types of learning disabilities in different circumstances.

Although transition programs are being mandated, such programs are more likely to be promoted for students with more severe disabilities than for students with learning disabilities. Students with learning disabilities are encouraged to enroll in academic curricula with the understanding that they will enter postsecondary education and, therefore, do not require comprehensive secondary transition services. However, research has indicated that only a small number have access to postsecondary education. Even if they are involved in postsecondary education or training, they may not receive comprehensive services. Implementation of transition services at the secondary and postsecondary levels is and will continue to be a significant barrier for many persons with learning disabilities.

I would like to end this chapter on a personal note. I started in the field of special education in 1960 as a special education teacher in a high school program for students who were then labeled "mildly mentally retarded" but today would be labeled "learning disabled," "behavior-disordered," "attention-deficit-disordered," and "emotionally disturbed" as well as mildly mentally retarded. This secondary program provided intensive transition services starting with career education at the sophomore level, supervised work experience in the school at the junior level, and supervised work experience in the community at the senior level. The students were given a functional curriculum throughout all 4 years. *All* students were employed when they graduated from high school. This program unequivocally demonstrated to me that transition can be successful. But this program and others like it were eliminated as other educational fads were introduced. I sincerely hope that the transition programs that are starting nationwide will not be trampled by a new bandwagon.

REFERENCES

Americans with Disabilities Act of 1990, 42 U.S.C.A. §§ 12101 et seq. (West 1993).

Brolin, D. E. (1989). *Life-centered career education*. Reston, VA: Council for Exceptional Children.

Carnevale, A., Gainer, L., & Maltzer, A. (1990). *Workplace basics*. San Francisco: Jossey-Bass.

deBettencourt, L., Zigmond, N., & Thornton, H. (1989). Follow-up of postsecondary-age rural learning disabled graduates and dropouts. *Exceptional Children, 56*(1), 40–49.

Education for All Handicapped Children Act of 1975, Public Law 94-142, 89 Stat. 773 (1975).

Faas, L. A., & D'Alonzo, B. J. (1990). WAIS-R scores as predictors of employment success and failures among adults with learning disabilities. *Journal of Learning Disabilities, 23*, 311–316.

Fourqurean, J. M. (1994). The use of follow-up studies for improving transition planning for young adults with learning disabilities. *Journal of Vocational Rehabilitation, 4*(2), 96–104.

Hawks, R., Minskoff, E. H., Sautter, S., Sheldon, K. L., Steidle, E. F., & Hoffmann, F. J. (1990). A model diagnostic battery for adults with learning disabilities. *Learning Disabilities: A Multidisciplinary Journal, 1*, 94–101.

Hoffmann, F. J., Sheldon, K. L., Minskoff, E. H., Sautter, S. W., Steidle, E. F., Baker, D. P., Bailey, M. B., & Echols, L. D. (1987). Needs of learning disabled adults. *Journal of Learning Disabilities, 20*, 43–52.

Hohenshil, T. H., Levinson, E. M., & Heer, K. B. (1985). Best practices in vocational assessment for handicapped students. In A. Thomas & J. Grimes (Eds.), *Best practices in school psychology* (pp. 215–228). Kent, OH: National Association of School Psychologists.

Individuals with Disabilities Education Act of 1990. Public Law 101-476, 104 Stat. 1142 (1990).

Kohler, P. D. (1993). Best practices in transition: Substantiated or implied? *Career Development for Exceptional Individuals, 16*(2), 107–122.

Michaels, C.A. (1994). Transition, adolescence, and learning disabilities. In C. Michaels (Ed.), *Transition strategies for persons with learning disabilities* (pp. 1–22). San Diego, CA: Singular Publishing.

Minskoff, E. H. (1994a). Post-secondary education and vocational training: Keys to success for adults with learning disabilities. In P. J. Gerber & H. B. Reiff (Eds.), *Learning disabilities in adulthood: Persisting problems and evolving issues* (pp. 111–120). Boston: Andover Medical.

Minskoff, E. H. (1994b). TRAC *Workplace Social Skills Program*. Fishersville, VA: Woodrow Wilson Rehabilitation Center.

Minskoff, E. H., & De Moss, S. (1993). Facilitating successful transition: Using the TRAC model to assess and develop academic skills needed for vocational competencies. *Learning Disability Quarterly, 16*, 161–170.

Minskoff, E. H., & De Moss, S. (1994). Workplace social skills and individuals with learning disabilities. *Journal of Vocational Rehabilitation, 4*(2), 113–121.

Minskoff, E. H., Hawks, R., Steidle, E. R., & Hoffmann, F. J. (1989). A homogeneous group of persons with learning disabilities: Adults with severe learning disabilities in vocational rehabilitation. *Journal of Learning Disabilities, 22*, 521–528.

Minskoff, E. H., Sautter, S. W., Hoffmann, F. J., & Hawks, R. (1987). Employer attitudes toward hiring the learning disabled. *Journal of Learning Disabilities, 20*, 53–57.

Minskoff, E. H., Sautter, S., Sheldon, K. L., Steidle, E. F., & Baker, D. P. (1988). A comparison of learning disabled adults and high school students. *Learning Disabilities Research, 3*, 115–123.

Rehabilitation Act Amendments of 1992, Public Law 102-569, 106 Stat. 4344 (1992).

Rojewski, J. W. (1992). Key components in model transition services for students with learning disabilities. *Learning Disability Quarterly, 15*, 135–150.

Rusch, F., Enchelmaier, J., & Kohler, P. (1994). Employment outcomes and activities for youths in transition. *Career Development for Exceptional Individuals, 7*(1), 1–16.

School-to-Work Opportunities Act of 1994. Public Law 103-239, 108 Stat. 568 (1994).

Szymanski, E. M. (1994). Transition: Life-span and life-space considerations for empowerment. *Exceptional Children, 60*(5), 402–410.

Wagner, M., Newman, L., Blackorby, J. (1993, February). *Youth in transition: Secondary school and beyond.* Paper presented at the meeting of the Learning Disabilities Association of America, San Francisco.

Wehman, P. H. (1992). *Life beyond the classroom: Transition strategies for young people with disabilities.* Baltimore: Paul H. Brookes.

14

Service Delivery Models Effective with Adults with Learning Disabilities

ANNA H. GAJAR
JUDITH OSGOOD SMITH

NEED

The delivery of services to adults with learning disabilities has been identified as a priority by disabilities professionals who have noticed poor employment and life adjustment outcomes for this population. Adults with learning disabilities tend to be underemployed or unemployed and dependent on family members (Cobb & Crump, 1984; Fafard & Haubrich, 1981; Zigmond & Thornton, 1989). They exhibit problems in making vocational choices, acquiring and maintaining jobs, and receiving promotions (Humes, 1986) and often are put into job-training programs that only prepare them for low-level positions (Cummings & Maddox, 1987; Sitlington, 1981). Edgar and Levine (1988) found that 6 months after high school graduation, 35% of the adults with learning disabilities were unemployed. In addition, they were not involved in postsecondary training or other vocational activities. Finally, according to the U.S. Commission on Civil Rights (1983), unemployment among persons with disabilities was estimated to be between 50% and 75%, compared to 7% among nondisabled individuals. Based on these findings, a number of legislative mandates have been passed, transition programs have been proposed, and advocacy and position papers have been written, calling for a national commitment to providing services for adults with learning disabilities (Americans with Disabilities Act, 1990; National Joint Committee on Learning Disabilities, 1987; Will, 1984).

Legislation

Mandates passed since the 1970s have laid the framework for providing services to adults with learning disabilities. The Rehabilitation Act (1973, Public Law 93-112) emphasized services for individuals with severe disabilities. However, this law also contained landmark provisions for adults with learning disabilities. Section 504 of this Act included significant changes in training and hiring practices by prohibiting recipients of federal funds from discriminating against qualified individuals on the basis of their disability. The Vocational Education Act (1976, Public Law 94-482), the Education of the Handicapped Act (1983, Public Law 98-149), the Individuals with Disabilities Education Act (1990, Public Law 101-476), and the Carl D. Perkins Vocational and Applied Technology Education Act (1984, Public Law 98-524) include training, employment, community, and independent living as primary areas of focus for adults with learning disabilities. The Americans with Disabilities Act (1990, Public Law 101-336) prohibits discrimination in employment, public services, public accommodations, and transportation and provides for telecommunications relay services for adults with disabilities. In short, recent legislation establishes the mandate for providing services to adults with learning disabilities.

Transition Programs

Madeleine Will, former assistant secretary of the Office of Special Education and Rehabilitation Services (OSERS), stated that legislation established a new priority "to strengthen and coordinate education, training, and support services for handicapped youth in order to foster effective transition from school to the adult world of work and independent living" (Will, 1984, p. 12). Over the past decade a number of transition models have been proposed.

Advocacy and Position Papers

A number of research, opinion, program, and service articles have been published in leading journals, dealing with the need for service delivery for adults with learning disabilities (Vogel, 1990). A position paper by the National Joint Committee on Learning Disabilities (1987) presented a concise overview of the following concerns reported in the literature:

1. Learning disabilities are both persistent and pervasive throughout an individual's life.
2. At present there is a paucity of appropriate diagnostic procedures for assessing and determining the status and needs of adults with learning disabilities.
3. Older adolescents and adults with learning disabilities frequently are denied access to appropriate academic instruction, prevocational preparation, and career counseling necessary for the development of adult abilities and skills.
4. Few professionals have been prepared adequately to work with adults who demonstrate learning disabilities.
5. Employers frequently do not have the awareness, knowledge of, nor sensitivity to the needs of adults with learning disabilities.
6. Adults with learning disabilities may experience personal, social, and emotional difficulties that may affect their adaptation to life tasks.
7. Advocacy efforts on behalf of adults with learning disabilities currently are inadequate.
8. Federal, state, and private funding agencies concerned with learning disabilities have not supported program development initiatives for adults with learning disabilities. (p. 172)

Recommendations

1. Programs must be initiated to increase public and professional awareness and understanding of the manifestations and needs of adults with learning disabilities.
2. Selection of appropriate education and vocational training programs and employment for adults with learning disabilities is predicated on a clear understanding of how their condition influences their learning and performance.
3. Throughout the school years, individuals with learning disabilities must have access to a range of program and service options that will prepare them to make the transition from secondary to postsecondary or vocational training settings.
4. Alternative programs and services must be provided for adults with learning disabilities who have failed to obtain a high school diploma.
5. Adults with learning disabilities must have an active role in determining the course of their postsecondary or vocational efforts.
6. Consistent with the Rehabilitation Act of 1973 and regulations

implementing Section 504 of that act, appropriate federal, state, and local agencies as well as postsecondary and vocational training programs should continue the development and implementation of effective programs that will allow adults with learning disabilities the opportunity to attain career goals.

7. The development of systematic programs of research that will address the status and needs of adults with learning disabilities is essential for the provision of appropriate services.

8. Curricula must be developed and incorporated in preparation programs for professionals in such disciplines as education, vocational and rehabilitative counseling, social work, psychology, medicine, and law to inform these professionals about the problems and needs of adults with learning disabilities.

9. Mental health professionals must be aware of the unique personal, social, and emotional difficulties that individuals with learning disabilities may experience throughout their lives. (pp. 172–175)

Similarly, the Learning Disabilities Association of America (1994) posited that the needs of adults with learning disabilities "have not been addressed by program and policy makers; and . . . there is no consistent and ongoing recognition of and services to adult with learning disabilities among federal agencies" (p. 4). It recommended the following:

1. The U.S. Department of Education establish a national policy for life-long learning and education of adults with learning disabilities;

2. The U.S. Department of Education establish funding to provide for the education of adults with learning disabilities;

3. The U.S. Department of Education fund research and disseminate information about programs which have effectively served adults with learning disabilities; and

4. The U.S. Department of Education establish an interagency task force to provide effective program linkages among federal agencies which serve or employ adults with learning disabilities. (p. 4)

Based on the previously stated mandates, the call for transition programs, and written statements of concerns and recommendations for adults with learning disabilities, the following section of this chapter presents a review of service delivery systems cited in the literature for this population. An area framework section, including definitions, demonstration projects, conceptual models, service delivery components, and theoretical framework, is followed by descriptions of model programs for each of the following service domains (these domains are not exclusive and services often overlap) (1) transition (including secondary special education and vocational education programs), (2) vocational rehabilitation, (3) adult basic education (including literacy, General Education Development program, correctional and related services), and (4) postsecondary and higher education services.

REVIEW OF THE LITERATURE

Transition Service Framework

The reader is alerted to the fact that transition services are often exclusively directed toward young adults, ages 14–21. Gajar (1992a) proposed an arbitrary division between young adults with learning disabilities (14–21) and older adults ages 22 and over. Transition and associated mandates are largely directed toward service delivery for young adults. The services associated with this period, however, overlap with such service delivery areas as Mental Health and Vocational Rehabilitation, which are necessary at different transition periods, and which can be accessed by individuals throughout their lifetime. For the sake of organization, and from a service delivery perspective, this transition portion of the narrative will concentrate on the young adult population (ages 14–21).

Definitions

The Individuals with Disabilities Education Act (IDEA, 1990) defines transition services as follows:

> A coordinated set of activities for a student, designed within an outcome-oriented process which promotes movement from school to postschool activities, including postsecondary education, vocational training, integrated employment (including supported employment), continuing education, adult services, independent living, or community participation. (§§602[a], 20 U.S.C.)

An important element of transition services is the individualized transition plan (ITP). The contents of the ITP, however, are not clearly outlined or defined by legislation. Often a transition component is appended to the individualized education plan (IEP) mandated by IDEA. This component includes the following:

A statement of the needed transition services for students beginning no later than age 16 and annually thereafter (and when determined appropriate for the individual, beginning at age 14 or younger), including when appropriate a statement of the interagency responsibilities or linkages (or both) before the student leaves the school setting. (IDEA, 1990, §§ 602[a], §§ 1401[a], 20 U.S.C.

Demonstration Projects

Since 1984, the transition initiative sponsored by OSERS has resulted in more than 266 model demonstration projects utilizing a wide range of services facilitating the transition of young adults with disabilities from secondary schools to postsecondary and employment settings (Rusch, Chadsey-Rusch, & Szymanski, 1992). According to Rusch et al. (1992), "Of the more than 25,000 persons with disabilities receiving direct services, 85% were persons with learning disabilities" (p. 12).

A major thrust of transition is the development of interagency cooperative agreements for the purpose of facilitating service delivery. According to Rusch et al. (1992), interagency cooperative agreements within current model projects include local agencies (schools and residential rehabilitation facilities), state agencies, parent organizations, universities, private not-for-profit agencies, community colleges, Job Training Partnership Act programs, and others. Services provided by these partnerships are varied and based on a variety of conceptual foundations.

Conceptual Service Delivery Models

The OSERS transition model uses a bridge concept from high school to employment (Will, 1983). The bridges contain three clusters of transitional services: (1) transition without special services, (2) transition with time-limited services, and (3) transition with ongoing services. The first bridge (no special services) involves the services that are available to anyone in the community. Usually special accommodations for individuals with disabilities are incorporated within these generic services, such as those available at university and college settings. The second bridge (time-limited services) includes "temporary services that lead to employment . . . services such as vocational rehabilitation, postsecondary vocational education, and other job training programs to gain entry into the labor market" (Will, 1983, p. 6). The third bridge (ongoing special services) includes what has recently been labeled "supported employment."

As stated earlier, the major thrust of the OSERS model is employment. Other models, however, challenge the assumption that the ultimate goal of transition is employment. According to Halpern (1985), the ultimate goal of transition should be community adjustment. Based on this goal, Halpern added two additional dimensions to the employment dimension: (1) the residential environment and (2) the social and interpersonal networks of person with disabilities. In short, employment, residential environment, and social and interpersonal networks support the goal of community adjustment.

Wehman, Kregel, Barcus, and Schalock (1986) proposed a three-stage model including school instruction, planning for transition, and job placement. Their model emphasizes career and vocational training throughout the school career of the individual with a disability. Assumptions underlying this model are that (1) members of multiple disciplines and service delivery systems must participate, (2) parental involvement is essential, (3) vocational transition planning must occur well before 21 years of age, (4) the process must be planned and systematic, and (5) vocational service provided must be of a quality nature.

Two additional models warrant attention, the Brown and Kayser model (Brown & Kayser, 1982) and the Project Interface model proposed by D'Alonzo, Owen, and Hartwell (1985). The Brown and Kayser model stresses the match between the student with a disability and the environment and lists a number of strategies on how the environment can be modified to meet individual needs. These include (1) correction (correcting the constraints imposed by the environment), (2) compensation (increasing individual strengths and assets so that the match between student and environment is compatible), and (3) circumvention (altering the student–environment interaction so that it occurs at beneficial (levels).

The Project Interface model concentrates on providing access to community training programs to students who are not ready for competitive employment. The model involves four major activities: (1) identification of secondary students with disabilities, (2) intervention, including intake, vocational evaluation, employment training, and job placement, (3) employment, including following client progress and crisis intervention, and (4) follow-up, including continuous monitoring of employment and adjustment.

These models of service delivery during transition are based on the goal of what has been labeled "normalization," or what is usually conceptualized as a normal adult life.

Transition Service Delivery

Gajar, Goodman, and McAfee (1993), in a presentation of a schemata for transition, addressed components, and subcomponents of transition including special education, vocational education, career education, and vocational rehabilitation. The following sections of this narrative address programs within the first three transition-related components. A discussion of vocational rehabilitation, which often deals with older adults, will follow these three areas.

Special Education

Lists of secondary special education models of service delivery (often referred to as approaches) are readily found in the literature. Gajar et al. (1993) address the focus, features, strengths, and weaknesses of six instructional models for secondary-level students with disabilities as follows: (1) basic skills, (2) functional, (3) learning strategies, (4) tutorial, (5) vocational, and (6) compensatory.

The approaches or models described are limited in nature and concentrate on what might be considered a bandage approach to instruction. The instructional approaches do not prepare the young adult with learning disabilities for adult functioning. In contrast to these instructional models, Zigmond (1990) proposed a comprehensive high school program for students with learning disabilities, including four essential elements: (1) intensive instruction in reading and mathematics, (2) explicit instruction in "survival" skills, (3) successful completion of courses required for graduation, and (4) explicit planning for life after high school. Within these elements, the instructional features of the six instructional models can be incorporated.

Based on the elements for successful high school programs, Zigmond (1990) proposed two model programs for service delivery:

(A) Model One: Less But Very Special Special Education: This model is based on special education services being delivered in the special education resource room and contains the following five features:
    (i) Students are assigned to mainstream classes for math, content subjects required for graduation, and elective courses.
    (ii) One special education teacher is assigned as a support or consulting teacher to work with mainstream teachers in whose classes students with learning disabilities are placed.
    (iii) Additional special education teachers are responsible for yearly English and reading courses, one survival skills class,

and a supervised study hall in which students are scheduled to take each year of high school.

(iv) From the start of ninth grade, students interact regularly with a counselor for transition planning.

(v) Courses required for graduation are spaced evenly throughout the four years to reduce academic pressures, particularly in ninth grade. (pp. 21–22)

(B) Model Two: More Special Education: This model is based on special educators assuming the responsibility for the education of young adults with learning disabilities and contains the following features:

(i) All basic skills are taught by a special educator and instruction in basic skills is linked to transition planning.

(ii) Required 'content' subjects are taught by special educators.

(iii) Vocational education is provided in the mainstream and coordinated with transition planning within special education.

(iv) All ninth-grade students with learning disabilities will take a required course on survival skills taught by a special educator.

(v) Students' schedules would reflect a light academic load in ninth grade to ensure successful completion of the first year of high school. (pp. 23–24)

Delivery of services to young adults with learning disabilities in the secondary school environment is laden with difficulties; approaches to the delivery of instruction are presented, as are model programs. Each of these approaches and models, however, presents difficulties.

Vocational Education

Wermuth and Phelps (1990) identified 20 elements of exemplary vocational education programs. These are subsumed under five major domains: (1) program administration, (2) curriculum and instruction, (3) comprehensive support services, (4) formalized articulation and communication, and (5) occupational experience, placement, and follow-up.

Cobb and Neubert (1992) presented a number of observations in reference to these domains. For program administration, they noted that exemplary programs are characterized by strong administrative leadership, adequate financial support, the opportunity for staff development, and ongoing formative and summative evaluation. Exemplary elements of curriculum and instruction include "the capacity for individualized curriculum modifications, integration of academic and vocational curricula, appropriate (heterogeneous) classroom compositions, and opportunities to use one or more of the cooperative learning technologies" (p. 98). Comprehensive support services, consistently identified in the literature as essential, include "(a) assessment of students' vocational interests and abilities, (b) instructional support services (aides, tutors, and other forms of resource support), and (c) ongoing career guidance and counseling" (p. 99). Five formalized articulation and communication elements include "(a) family or parent involvement, (b) notification of students and parents of vocational education opportunities, (c) involvement by vocational educators in individualized planning, (d) formalized transition planning, and (e) intra and interagency collaboration" (p. 100). Finally, work experience opportunities, job-placement services, and follow-up of participants complete the list of elements associated with exemplary vocational special education programs.

Gajar et al. (1993) identified another set of characteristics for vocational training that appear to be most critical to success. These include (1) early exposure, (2) systematic instruction (a behavioral approach offers the most systematic means for providing efficient and effective instruction; however, vocational educators must guard against using this approach to promote dependence or immaturity), (3) community instruction, (4) comprehensive instruction (not just instruction in special work skills but training in skills necessary to find, obtain, and maintain employment), and (5) opportunity development (developing the capacity of employers to hire adults with learning disabilities).

The characteristics listed above and identified as components of exemplary vocational special education programs have been widely addressed in the literature. Phelps, Wermuth, Crain, and Kane (1989), however, noted that few empirical data supporting and or refuting these vocational special education elements are available. The following narrative considers two programs for which evaluative data are available.

Stodden and Browder (1986) developed and evaluated a community-based employment program, which included a number of adults with learning disabilities. The program involved five major activities:

1. *Assessment.* Participant behaviors were assessed in a variety of work situations to determine what skills individuals possessed and what skills needed to be taught.
2. *Preemployment training.* Training was aimed at work adjustment skills.
3. *Work experience.* Participants were provided with experiences in community jobs.

4. *On-site competitive work training.* Participants were place with local employers in entry-level jobs.
5. *Supported employment.* For a period of 1 year, assistance in the form of job coaching was provided.

Stodden and Browder (1986) concluded that the greatest needs of the participants were increased speed, greater consistency, ability to handle pressure, and better judgment.

Neubert, Tilson, and Ianacone (1989) described a federally funded transition program which included young adults with learning disabilities. The program included seven activities: (1) intake, (2) an 8-week employability course including vocational assessment, community-based career exploration, and job-seeking skills, (3) job tryouts at community employment sites, (4) job search support, (5) competitive placement and follow-up, (6) a job club, and (7) job change and advancement support. Extensive evaluative data were reported, including average hourly wage ($4.40), problems experienced (such as lower than acceptable productivity or work adjustment problems), and employment data after 6 months and 1 year (76% and 64%, respectively).

Career Education

Gajar et al. (1993) observed that career education "is not so much a specific way or content of training as it is a way of formulating the entire set of experiences that an individual needs to become an effective adult" (p. 325).

Brolin (1982) identified five stages of career development: (1) awareness (which begins in the elementary school and continues through secondary education), (2) exploration (which begins in junior high and entails hands-on experiences in elements of occupations and leisure activities), (3) preparation (which is experiential and involves use of community resources), (4) placement and follow-up, and (5) continuing education. According to Brolin, placement and follow-up, as well as continuing education, are in most instances neglected by educators. In addition, research on the effectiveness of career education programs is limited (Humes & Hohenshil, 1985).

Models associated with career education for the adult with learning disabilities include the Lifelong Career Development Model (LCDM), Transition Service Activity Center model, and Experience-Based Career Education (EBCE) model.

The LCDM includes transition centers located in community college settings. The rationale for the centers (Brolin, 1984) is that many individuals with learning disabilities either do not qualify for vocational rehabilitation services or do not want to be identified. In addition, the centers provide services throughout the life span. These services include (1) career assessment, (2) instruction on vocational skills, (3) assistance with independent living and personal adjustment, (4) professional training to improve services, (5) information and referral to other community resources, (6) career development planning, (7) collection of resources for the service needs of individuals with disabilities, and (8) advocacy. As an approach to transition, the centers provide services in three areas: (1) skills and competencies needed for successful community living, (2) identification and location of school, community, and home resources, and (3) assistance in various levels of career development.

The Transition Service Activity Center, proposed by Browder (1987), is similar to the LCDM in that the centers are located in the community. The model differs in that primary activities are conducted within a social–recreational context rather than from a curriculum base.

The EBCE model has been used for students at the secondary level. Larson (personal communication, 1982) identifies five aspects: (1) program is community based, (2) scheduling is individualized, (3) employer participation is voluntary, (4) experiences are exploratory, and (5) academics are developed in conjunction with the site. This model depends heavily on the cooperation of the school, family, and community.

The success of the delivery of services during the young adult years depends heavily on the cooperation and interaction among special education, vocational education, career education, and vocational rehabilitation service providers. In addition, many services need to be provided in environments outside the school setting and must be integrated between the disciplines. This has not always been the case (Gajar et al., 1993). Vocational rehabilitation, currently becoming an important service delivery avenue for transition, has historically been associated with older or out-of-school adults. The following section discusses the components and vocational rehabilitation service models dealing with adults with learning disabilities.

Vocational Rehabilitation Framework

The field of vocational rehabilitation includes three elements: rehabilitation, vocational education, and vocational guidance.

Definition

Brutting (1987) defines rehabilitation as "any process, procedure or program that enables a disabled individual to function at a more independent and personally satisfying level. This functioning should include all aspects—physical, mental, emotional, social, educational, and vocational—of the individual's life" (p. 1329).

Vocational guidance historically has been an important part of vocational rehabilitation. As early as the 1930s, guidance was emphasized:

> One of the most important services given by a rehabilitation agent is that of counsel and advisement. It is a continuous service designed to assist the disabled person in choosing, preparing for, entering upon and making progress in an occupation. (U.S. Department of the Interior, 1934, p. 49)

Conceptual Delivery of Services

The federal–state vocational rehabilitation program is administered on the federal level by the Rehabilitation Services Administration (RSA), a branch of OSERS. The RSA provides funds via state plans to respective state vocational rehabilitation agencies. Services are basically delivered by rehabilitation counselors (Szymanski, Hanley-Maxwell, & Asselin, 1992).

To be eligible for vocational rehabilitation, an individual must (1) have a disability that is a hindrance to employment and (2) be expected to be employable after receiving services. Eligibility, however, does not guarantee the availability of services. Services are determined by available funding. If sufficient funds are not available, the delivery of services is determined by the level of severity. Adults with moderate or mild disabilities, although eligible for vocational rehabilitation services, might not be able to participate (Szymanski et al., 1992).

Section 103 of the Rehabilitation Act as amended (1986) lists essential vocational rehabilitation services to be provided. These services are determined on a one-to-one basis and are designed to facilitate employment. Szymanski et al. (1992) presented a summary of these services which include primary services involving "evaluation of rehabilitation potential, counseling, job placement, physical and mental restoration services, and vocational and other training services including supported employment" (p. 158). Support services are often provided, and include such supports as interpreters, note takers, and reader services, "rehabilitation teaching, orientation and mobility services, and rehabilitation engineering" (p. 158). Services are provided via an Individualized Written Rehabilitation Program (IWRP), including sections similar to those found on IEPs, and ITPs. Finally, services are provided in many different settings and environments including the home, school, and places of employment. Integration of the individual into the community is anticipated; however, unlike the mandates for the school age population, supports in the mainstream or in the least restrictive environment are not required (Szymanski et al., 1992).

Vocational Rehabilitation Service Delivery

Adults with learning disabilities became eligible for vocational rehabilitation in 1981 when the RSA accepted specific learning disabilities as a medically recognizable disability (Gerber, 1981). However, the dilemma concerning assessment of a learning disability and the necessity of meeting eligibility requirements in order to receive services has resulted in a reluctance to serve adults with learning disabilities (Johnson, Bruininks, & Thurlow, 1987; Miller, Mulkey, & Kopp, 1984; Sanchez, 1984).

Miller et al. (1984) found that a number of vocational rehabilitation (VR) agencies serving adults with learning disabilities limit their services to the severely disabled. The practice of serving only severe cases has resulted in not only a small number of participants but also a large number of outcome failures. In other words, these individuals are considered unemployable. Fewer than 20% of VR clients with learning disabilities were referred to rehabilitation centers for work adjustment training, fewer than 5% were provided on-the-job training, and fewer than 1% received specific employer assistance. In support of these findings, Minskoff, Hawks, Steidle, and Hoffmann (1989) found that adults with learning disabilities in VR programs exhibited severe deficits including low-average general intelligence, low academic achievements, severe language deficits, and low self-esteem.

Smith (1992), in a study of postschool VR needs of a national sample of adults with learning disabilities, found that respondents were ineligible for rehabilitation services, dissatisfied with the services, or unaware of their rights in the eligibility process. In short, the delivery of VR services to adults with learning disabilities leaves much to be desired.

In summary, adults with learning disabilities have experienced difficulties in accessing and receiving appropriate vocational rehabilitation services. Effective VR service programs for this population are not cited in the literature. Szymanski, Dunn, and Parker (1989), however, presented an ecological framework for rehabilitation counselors who work with this population. The ecological framework for assessment and rehabilitation planning is based on seven tenets operationalized through the following dimensions: (1) individual attributes, (2) environmental attributes, (3) nature, quality, and sequence of interactions, and (4) perceptions of involved individuals. Basically, the VR client with learning disabilities brings certain attributes to the VR counseling and training sessions. These attributes interact with the testing or service situation and are based on previous interactions with home, school, community, and employment environments. Future environments, such as employment, in which the client will participate involve a number of environmental demands that must be considered in program planning (e.g., employer demands). Adults with learning disabilities have preconceived perceptions of how employment and life goals can be accomplished. Consequently, the nature, quality, and sequence of interactions between the client and future environments are based on how individual prospective and environmental demands are interpreted and integrated into a plan by the VR counselor.

As in the area of vocational rehabilitation, adult literacy and adult basic education agencies have experienced problems in the delivery of services for adults with learning disabilities.

Adult Education Services Framework

Literacy and adult education are national priorities. Agencies involved with literacy and adult basic education (ABE) have experienced problems with servicing individuals who have been identified or who exhibit the characteristics associated with adults with learning disabilities (Gold, 1981; Ross, 1987; Ross & Smith, 1990; Thistlewaite, 1983). A Canadian study of literacy and learning disabilities concludes that "it would be a mistake to assume that there exists a well established discipline of literacy instruction for adults with learning disabilities" (Literacy and Learning Disabilities, 1990, p. 1).

According to Ryan and Price (1993), ABE includes such services as adult secondary education and English as a Second Language. The services are provided in two general categories: (1) high school equivalency training to prepare for the General Education Development (GED) test and (2) tests and literacy skill building. These services have been directed by such mandates as the Adult Education Act (Public Law No. 100-297) and the National Literacy Act (Public Law No. 102-73).

A review of the literature shows that ABE is primarily involved with the delivery of services to individuals who have dropped out of high school or who are in need of a high school equivalency (GED) certification. Adults with learning disabilities compose a large part of this population. Westberry (1994) cited the following statistics: (1) the incidence of adults with learning disabilities without a diploma enrolled in ABE programs is as high as 80% and (2) 15–23% of Job Training Partnership Act participants and 25–40% of other federal employment training participants may have a learning disability (p. 202). Cobb and Crump (1984) found that of 100 adults with learning disabilities, half did not graduate from high school, 90% were unemployed, and only a handful completed the GED program.

Newman (1994) provided an overview of adult literacy programs, which include Laubach Literacy, Literacy Volunteers of America, business-sponsored literacy programs, and intergenerational and family literacy programs. A program or a system of service delivery specifically designed for adults with learning disabilities, however, does not exist. ABE providers have primarily concentrated on providing tutorial or remedial GED assistance for adults who have not graduated from high school. Evidence of systematic instruction in the remediation of basic skills, or provision of compensatory strategies for adults with learning disabilities has not been reported (Westberry, 1994).

A number of articles address the need for identification and diagnosis of learning disabilities and staff development in providing services for adults with learning disabilities by adult education service providers (Ross-Gordon, 1989; Ross & Smith, 1990; Ryan & Price, 1993; Westberry, 1994).

Adult Basic Education Service Delivery

Westberry (1994, p. 206) summarized a number of models used with secondary and postsecondary students with learning disabilities which would be applicable to ABE settings.

1. The tutorial model using pre-GED and GED materials. This model provides tutoring instruction of "text and vocabulary in a content area."
2. The Parallel Alternative Curriculum, a compensatory model that uses a nonreading format, "with taped books, videotaped materials, movies, slides, lectures, and various forms of discussion."
3. The reciprocal teaching models used to improve reading comprehension via "four strategies: summarizing, forming of potential test questions, clarifying ambiguities and predicting."
4. The strategies intervention model, which includes "strategies

for writing, reading, paraphrasing, work attack, and test taking, as well as for enhancing social and motivational skills."

Westberry concluded that the results of her review of learning strategies for adults with learning disabilities preparing for the GED exam revealed that specific learning strategies do not exist for this population. She suggested, however, that the most expedient model for ABE programs is a tutorial model incorporating peer tutoring combined with compensatory testing conditions. In addition, such compensatory intervention as taped texts and special-needs test accommodations was recommended. Finally, she urged the necessity for model development.

Postsecondary Services Framework

Adults with learning disabilities are the fastest growing group of individuals in need of services at the postsecondary level of education, including college, university, and technical school participants. Studies show that more than half of the 50,000 high school graduates who have been identified as learning disabled will go on to a postsecondary education environment (Mithaug, Horiuchi, & Fanning, 1985; Shaw & Shaw, 1989; White et al., 1982). The increase of adults with learning disabilities in postsecondary environments during the decade of the 1980s will continue into the decade of the 1990s and into the 21st century (Shaw & Shaw, 1989).

Legislation

The accommodation of adults with learning disabilities in postsecondary settings is mandated by the Rehabilitation Act (1973, Public Law 93-112), Section 504, which states:

> No otherwise qualified handicapped individual in the United States
> . . . shall, solely by reason of his handicap, be excluded from the
> participation in, be denied the benefits of, or be subjected to discrimination under any activity receiving federal financial assistance.

Based on this mandate, postsecondary institutions are obligated to adhere to a number of conditions, including:

1. An admission limitation on the number of qualified students with a disability cannot be imposed.
2. Preadmission inquiries as to a person's disability cannot be conducted.

3. Students cannot be excluded from taking a course solely on the basis of their disability.
4. Discriminating requirements must be modified to accommodate students who are disabled.
5. Accommodating devices such as tape recorders must be allowed in the classroom.
6. Devices that ensure full participation of a student in the classroom cannot be prohibited.
7. Alternative testing, when necessary, must be provided.
8. Faculty must, when required, use adaptive devices.
9. Students with a disability should not be counseled toward restrictive careers unless justified by certification requirements.
10. Students with a disability have a to right to due process if they encounter discriminatory behavior.

Hughes and Smith (1990), in a review of the literature on postsecondary students with learning disabilities, found a lack of empirical articles dealing with the effectiveness of treatment approaches. Bursuck, Rose, Cowen, and Yahaya (1989) reported that services for this population vary from campus to campus, and that postsecondary guides to services are either inaccurate or incomplete. Mangrum and Strichart (1984) found college programs lacking in meeting the needs of students with learning disabilities. Parks, Antonoff, Drake, Skiba, and Soberman (1987) reported that services provided by graduate and professional schools in the United States are at the minimum for compliance with legal mandates. Blosser (1984) reported a limited number of directors of college disabilities programs who have been trained in special education. In summary, as in the area of vocational rehabilitation and ABE, service programs founded on a strong research base for adults with learning disabilities in the postsecondary setting are not available. A review of the literature does, however, cite a number of university, college, and community college programs designed specifically for young adults with learning disabilities. Model components are diversified and include concerns about admission requirements, identification and diagnosis, service delivery, evaluation, financing, and research. The wide range of models and services offered appears to have evolved spontaneously (Gajar, 1992b). The following section on delivery summarizes the major services usually available in university and college settings or community college or vocational–technical institutions.

University–College Service Delivery Models

Referral

In a review of eligibility activities in postsecondary model programs, Gajar, Rusch, and DeStefano (1989) found a strong emphasis on referral and intake. Referrals were usually initiated by parents or by the individuals themselves. Reasons for referral included the following:

1. Students had been identified with learning disabilities prior to admission.
2. Students were experiencing severe difficulty in a number of areas: memory, taking tests, studying, reading (or spelling) writing, math, foreign language, time management, social skills.

Following referral, three types of admission policies are common in postsecondary programs (Mangrum & Strichart, 1984): open, regular, and special admissions.

Identification

A consensus on how to identify university students with learning disabilities has not been reached (Blackburn & Iovacchini, 1982; Cordoni, 1982; Gray, 1981; Hoy & Gregg, 1986). Nelson and Lignugaris-Kraft (1989) stated that "in some colleges services are available on request or following student and parent interviews . . . whereas other programs require lengthy psycho-educational testing to determine if there is a significant discrepancy between aptitude and achievement" (p. 247).

Services

Large universities usually provide instructional accommodations and assistance with study skills as well as self- and time management. Other services available to all students include mental health, tutoring, and career counseling. Smaller colleges often provide individualized remedial and tutoring services. For example, Barat College and the College of the Ozarks provide intensive individual instruction. Curry College provides tutoring in groups of two or three (Vogel & Adelman, 1981). Nelson and Lignugaris-Kraft (1989) reported that counseling services are often cited as necessary components of model programs. These services include personal or social counseling, academic or program counseling, and career or vocational counseling.

Personal Counseling. Counseling is often related to self-management and advocacy. Adelphi University, for example, provides individual and group counseling delivered by social workers (Barbaro, 1982). Emphasis is placed on time management, communication skills, and self-advocacy. Most universities, however, refer students to student mental health or psychological counseling services. The question arises whether institutions of higher education should, or are obligated to, provide specialized counseling for students with learning disabilities.

Academic Counseling. In a survey of postsecondary services for students with learning disabilities, Bursuck et al. (1989) found that most institutions provide some form of special services, including academic advisement, tutoring, counseling, advocacy, and progress monitoring. Some institutions provide IEPs and offer special classes. Accommodating course strategies as IEP objectives are also cited. A number of college programs emphasize remedial services incorporating basic skill training as the main objective.

Career Counseling. Types of career counseling include career awareness, career exploration, job maintenance, and vocational counseling (Hoy & Gregg, 1986; Salend, Salend, & Yanok, 1985; Siperstein, 1988; Strichart & Mangrum, 1985). Nelson and Lignugaris-Kraft (1989) reported that career counseling was reported as an important model component by only 3 out of 14 surveyed institutions. As with personal counseling, the need for specialized career counseling and the institution's obligation to provide this type of service are topics for debate. Most university settings, however, do provide career development and placement services for all students.

Community College–Technical Vocational Service Delivery

In a chapter on community college options for students with mild disabilities, Bursuck and Rose (1992) stated:

> In general, students with mild learning problems (particularly learning disabilities) tend to enroll in academic programs, whereas students with moderate to severe learning problems are more likely to take developmental courses or select vocational education programs. (p. 72)

They summarized Siperstein's (1988) three-stage transition model from high school to college and, finally, to employment. Each of the three stages requires specific types of services. For example, services needed for entry into a postsecondary setting include evaluation of the needs and potential of the individual student and the matching of these needs to the appropriate program. Entry into employment is made on realistic career choices and the acquisition of job-seeking and maintenance skills.

Bursuck and Rose (1992) described a number of community college-based programs leading to a vocational–technical education or an associate degree. In a vocational–technical education program developed at Northern Illinois University, a student, following assessment, may be directed toward a traditional program or a developmental program. The developmental program includes courses in occupational and work interests, occupational and work planning, and occupational work development and an internship. The program may also include developmental courses in English, math, and reading. Both the traditional and developmental programs include learning and social skill strategies, course accommodations, and tutoring.

In associate degree programs cited by Bursuck and Rose (1992), community college officials have "developed an increasing number of support services" (p. 80). These include faculty awareness sessions, "early availability of course syllabi, taped textbooks, permission to tape lectures, note takers, word processing programs, proofreaders, modified exam procedures, and modified course assignments" (p. 80). Another area of service includes "individualized education plans, specialized academic advisement, regular monitoring of academic progress, advocacy, content tutoring, support groups, specialized counseling and special courses in career awareness or learning strategies" (p. 80). In addition, remedial services are provided for basic skill areas such as reading, written language, oral language, and mathematics.

At first glance, the array of services available in different postsecondary settings is impressive. The graduation rates from many programs, however, are still low and a number of schools at all levels of postsecondary education do not provide many of the critical services. In reference to community college settings, Bursuck and Rose (1992) stated that "although community-college level services for persons with mild disabilities are increasing overall, there are not data to justify classifying existing services as anything but a good start" (p. 84).

PROPOSED IDEAS FOR CHANGE

Based on the review of the literature, the following ideas for change are suggested.

Life-Span Development

Brolin's model (1982) of career development views career education as extending from early childhood through retirement. His stages of career development are also applicable to service delivery approaches for adults with learning disabilities. First, awareness of adult roles must begin for children with learning disabilities at an early age and continue through high school. Exploration of service delivery options, including special education, vocational and career education, vocational rehabilitation, postsecondary education, and adult education services, should begin no later than junior high school. At this stage, vocational evaluation should take place and the planning process should include in-depth examination of the various community resources.

At the preparation stage for adult service delivery, students would focus on acquiring the competencies needed to negotiate the various postsecondary options. Following Brolin's (1982) suggestion, this stage would be heavily experiential, with the student working to develop the skills needed to work directly with future agencies and services providers. For example, following the suggestion of Shaw, Brinckerhoff, Kistler, and McGuire (1991), students could receive counseling and instruction to help themselves become self-sufficient so that they are able to self-advocate. They could also learn eligibility and admission procedures and receive instruction or assistance in negotiating the inevitable procedures required by service providers.

According to Brolin (1983), placement, follow-up, and continuing education are neglected components of service delivery. Service providers need to work closely with the individual and the family to ensure that the student has acquired the competencies in daily living and social skills. Follow-up may be necessary after the student has completed a program to ensure that further education or training is not necessary.

Family Involvement

Involvement in transition planning is mandated by law for both the individual with a learning disability and the family; however, care must be taken to ensure that they are full participants in the process. Families should be included in the process of planning for adulthood from the time a child is first diagnosed as having a learning disability.

Families need to be made aware of services, eligibility and admission procedures, and their rights and responsibilities. They may not be aware that many adult services are based on eligibility rather than entitlement by law. On the other hand, the Americans with Disabilities Act and Section 504 prohibit discrimination on the basis of disability. Clearly, information must be provided to help individuals with learning disabilities and their families gain access to appropriate services.

Training of Service Providers

An inadequate understanding of learning disabilities by service providers has been cited as a problem in the areas of adult education and vocational rehabilitation. Ross and Smith (1990) suggested staff development programs to include characteristics of individuals with learning disabilities, assessment techniques, and instructional strategies. Similarly, there is an urgent need to inform and train vocational rehabilitation counselors. A training program at the University of Pittsburgh School of Medicine is designed to assist counselors to develop skills in (1) identification of learning disabilities, (2) eligibility determination, (3) planning services, (4) identifying interventions and accommodations, (5) placement, and (6) development of community-based service delivery (McCue, 1988). Programs such as these are needed to eliminate knowledge gaps among service providers and improve services for adults with learning disabilities.

Interagency Agreements

Although federal and state laws mandate interagency agreements, lack of interagency collaboration has been identified as a barrier to receiving services (Gajar et al., 1993). Stodden and Boone (1987) identified conflicting classification procedures, language systems, and philosophies as barriers to interagency cooperation. School administrators and agency representatives need to concentrate, while the student is still in school, on improved communication between educators and human service providers.

Facilitator

Interagency collaboration will be more likely to occur if there is a designated facilitator for each adult receiving services. Under Part H (Grants for Preschool Children) of the IDEA, a case manager is responsible for the implementation of the child's educational plan, as well as coordination with all other agencies and persons working with the child. Given the fragmentation of services among service providers, a similar facilitator is needed for students who are making the transition to adult services. Similarly, adults who are receiving services should have a case manager who evaluates the individual's progress and coordinates ongoing services.

Dissemination of Findings of Model Programs

The current database concerning best practices in service delivery for adults with learning disabilities is very limited. Model programs are also frequently described in the literature; however, these descriptions are rarely accompanied by findings about program effectiveness.

Directors of federally funded programs are required to provide annual evaluations to their funding agencies. The federal government should be encouraged to disseminate these, as well as studies reporting effectiveness of practices and interventions, to other service providers.

SUMMARY OF AREA

This chapter has provided an overview of services for adults with learning disabilities in the areas of transition, vocational rehabilitation, adult education, and postsecondary education. Widespread recognition of the need for such services is evidenced in position papers by professional advocacy organizations as well as legal mandates. The extent of available services varies from discipline to discipline.

In the transition area, the federal government has historically focused on transition to employment. However, a more recent trend is to plan for the total community adjustment of the individual. Model programs exist in the areas of special education, vocational education, and career education. However, few empirical data are available to document the appropriateness or effectiveness of these models.

Adults with learning disabilities have experienced difficulty gaining access to and receiving appropriate vocational rehabilitation services. There is a paucity of vocational rehabilitation service delivery models for individuals labeled "learning disabled," and no effectiveness data are cited in the literature.

A high proportion of adult education students have learning disabilities. Nevertheless, there is no well-established discipline of instruction for this population within the adult education field. Programs focus on basic tutorial assistance or remediation for high school dropouts pursuing a GED. No specific learning or instructional strategies have been identified or documented for the population of adult education students with learning disabilities. In-service training is needed for adult educators.

Postsecondary education students comprise the fastest growing group of consumers of adult learning disabilities services. A wide array of services is available, from counseling to instructional accommodations and assistance with study skills. However, as in the other areas of service delivery, there is limited research documenting effective approaches or programs.

Finally, the literature points to some service delivery gaps in all these disciplines. To meet the needs of this population, we must consider the development of the individual over the life span and increase family involvement from childhood to adulthood. Training is needed for service providers with regard to both the nature of learning disabilities and appropriate intervention techniques. Interagency collaboration and coordination, through a facilitator or case manager, are essential. Finally, a recurring theme for each discipline reviewed is the urgent need for research. Based on this need, research seems to be the primary focus for the future.

FUTURE DIRECTIONS

The fact that there is little empirical information regarding successful programs or interventions for adults with learning disabilities may be, in part, because publication is not a requirement for the promotion or tenure of service providers except in the field of higher education (the one area in which research is beginning to appear). Research is traditionally the province of higher education faculty, who should be encouraged to collaborate with professionals from the various disciplines dealing with adults with learning disabilities to assist in conducting research and disseminating findings to appropriate audiences. This is not likely to occur without both federal funding and a collaborative norm among agencies (thus underscoring the need for interagency collaboration).

Gajar (1992a) reviewed the research dealing with adults with learning disabilities and found the existing database to be composed primarily of survey, descriptive, and group research. Based on this, she posited a need for (1) studies that identify specific samples within adult populations, (2) studies identifying successful intervention techniques, (3) research in a "variety of settings and encompassing critical periods of an individuals' life span" (p. 513), and (4) studies employing alternative methodologies to group designs. Qualitative and single-subject research designs are essential for the development of effective remedial and compensatory techniques for adults with learning disabilities in a variety of community and postsecondary settings.

Given legal mandates, services for adults with learning disabilities will undoubtedly increase. Program development must be based on research that examines the characteristics and demands of the settings with which adults with learning disabilities will interact, skills required in each setting, and successful intervention techniques. Finally, research is needed on the service delivery system itself to increase the possibility that it will successfully serve the needs of the adults who have learning disabilities.

REFERENCES

Adult Education Act of 1988, Public Law 100-297, 102 Stat. 302 (1988).

Americans with Disabilities Act of 1990, 42 U.S.C.A. §§§§ 12101 et seq. (West 1993).

Barbaro, F. (1982). The learning disabled college student: Some considerations in setting objectives. *Journal of Learning Disabilities, 15*(10), 599–603.

Blackburn, J. C., & Iovacchini, E. V. (1982). Student service responsibilities of institutions to learning disabled students. *College and University, 52*, 208–217.

Blosser, R. E. (1984). The roles and functions and the preparation of disabled student service directors in higher education. *Dissertation Abstracts International, 45*, 2395A. (University Microfilms No. 8425117)

Brolin, D. E. (1982). *Vocational preparation of persons with handicaps* (2nd ed.). New York: Merrill/Macmillan.

Brolin, D. E. (1983). Life-centered career education for exceptional children. In E. L. Meyen, G. A. Vergason, & R. J. Whelan (Eds.), *Promising practices for exceptional children: Curriculum implications* (pp. 379–402). Denver: Love.

Brolin, D. E. (1984). *Preparing handicapped students to be productive adults.* Paper presented at the Western Regional Resource Center Topical Conference, Servicing Secondary Mildly Handicapped Students, Seattle, WA.

Browder, P. M. (1987). Transition services for early adult age individuals with mild mental retardation. In R. N. Ianacone & R. A. Stodden (Eds.), *Transition issues and directions* (pp. 77–90). Reston, VA: Council for Exceptional Children.

Brown, J. M., & Kayser, T. F. (1982). *The transition of special needs learners into post-secondary vocational education.* Minneapolis: University of Minnesota, Department of Vocational and Technical Education.

Brutting, L. K. (1987). Rehabilitation. In C. R. Reynolds & L. Mann (Eds.), *Encyclopedia of special education* (Vol. 3, p. 1329). New York: Wiley.

Bursuck, W. D., & Rose, E. (1992). Community college options for students with mild disabilities. In F. R. Rusch, L. DeStefano, L. Chadsey-Rusch, L. A. Phelps, & E. Szymanski (Eds.), *Transition from school to adult life: Models, linkages, and policy* (pp. 71–91). Sycamore, IL: Sycamore.

Bursuck, W. D., Rose, E., Cowen, S., & Yahaya, M. A. (1989). Nationwide survey of postsecondary education services for students with learning disabilities. *Exceptional Children, 56*(3), 236–245.

Carl D. Perkins Vocational and Applied Technology Education Act of 1984, Public Law 98-524, 98 Stat. 2435 (1984).

Cobb, R. B., & Neubert, D. A. (1992). Vocational education models. In F. R. Rusch, L. DeStefano, L. Chadsey-Rusch, L. A. Phelps, & E. Szymanski (Eds.), *Transition from school to adult life: Models, linkages, and policy* (pp. 93–113). Sycamore, IL: Sycamore.

Cobb, R. M., & Crump, W. D. (1984). *Post-school status of young adults identified as learning disabled while enrolled in public schools: A comparison of those enrolled and not enrolled in learning disabilities programs* (Final report). Washington, DC: Office of Special Education and Rehabilitative Services. (ERIC Document Reproduction Service No. ED 253 029)

Cordoni, B. K. (1982). Postsecondary education: Where do we go from here? *Journal of Learning Disabilities, 15*, 265–266.

Cummings, R. W., & Maddox, C. D. (1987). *Career and vocational education for the mildly handicapped.* Springfield, IL: Charles C. Thomas.

D'Alonzo, B. J., Owen, S. D., & Hartwell, L. K. (1985). *School to work: Transition models for persons with disabilities.* Unpublished manuscript. (Available from the Illinois Transition Institute)

Edgar, E., & Levine, P. (1988). A longitudinal study of graduates of special education. *Interchange: The Secondary Transition Intervention Effectiveness Institute, 8*, 3–5.

Education of the Handicapped Act of 1983, Public Law 98-199, 97 Stat. 1357 (1983).

Fafard, M., & Haubrich, P. (1981). Vocational and social adjustment of learning disabled young adults: A follow-up study. *Learning Disability Quarterly, 4*, 122–130.

Gajar, A. H. (1992a). Adults with learning disabilities: Current and future research practices. *Journal of Learning Disabilities, 25*, 507–519.

Gajar, A. H. (1992b). University-based models for students with learning disabilities: The Pennsylvania State University Model. In F. R. Rusch, L. DeStefano, L. Chadsey-Rusch, L. A. Phelps, & E. Szymanski (Eds.), *Transition from school to adult life: Models, linkages, and policy* (pp. 51–70). Sycamore, IL: Sycamore.

Gajar, A. H., Goodman L., & McAfee, J. (1993). *Secondary schools and beyond: Transition of individuals with mild disabilities.* New York: Merrill.

Gajar, A. H., Rusch, F. R., & DeStefano, L. (1989). *A descriptive analysis of competition 84.078B postsecondary model programs.* Unpublished manuscript. (Available from the Illinois Transition Institute)

Gerber, P. J. (1981). Learning disabilities and eligibility for vocational rehabilitation services: A chronology of events. *Learning Disability Quarterly, 4*, 422–425.

Gold, P. C. (1981). The DL-LEA: A remedial approach for nonreaders with a language deficiency handicap. *Adult Literacy and Basic Education, 5,* 185–193.

Gray, R. A. (1981). Services for the LD adult: A working paper. *Learning Disability Quarterly, 4*(4), 426–434.

Halpern, A. S. (1985). Transition: A look at the foundations. *Exceptional Children, 51*(6), 479–486.

Hoy, C., & Gregg, N. (1986, Summer). Learning disabled students: An emerging population on college campuses. *Journal of College Admissions, 112,* 10–14.

Hughes, C. A., & Smith, J. O. (1990). Cognitive and academic performance of college students with learning disabilities: A synthesis of the literature. *Learning Disability Quarterly, 13*(1), 66–79.

Humes, C. W. (1986). From learner to earner. *Academic Therapy, 21,* 483–489.

Humes, C. W., & Hohenshil, T. A. (1985). Career development and career education for handicapped students: A reexamination. *Vocational Guidance Quarterly, 34*(10), 31–40.

Individuals with Disabilities Education Act of 1990, Public Law 101-476, 104 Stat. 1142 (1990).

Johnson, D., Bruininks, R., & Thurlow, M. (1987). Meeting the challenge of transition service planning through improved interagency cooperation. *Exceptional Children, 53*(6), 522–530.

Learning Disabilities Association of America. (1994). Resolution on adult education for persons with learning disabilities. *Journal of Learning Disabilities, 27,* 4.

Literacy and learning disabilities: A survey. (1990, November). *LDA Newsbriefs, 25*(6), 1, 16.

Mangrum, C. T., & Strichart, S. S. (1984). *College and the learning disabled student.* Orlando, FL: Grune & Stratton.

McCue, M. (1988). *Vocational rehabilitation of specific learning disabilities: Training for SLD resource counselors.* Pittsburgh: University of Pittsburgh, School of Medicine.

Miller, J. H., Mulkey, S. W., & Kopp, K. H. (1984). Public rehabilitation services for individuals with specific learning disabilities. *Journal of Rehabilitation, 50*(2), 19–29.

Minskoff, E. H., Hawks, R., Steidle, E. F., & Hoffmann, J. F. (1989). A homogeneous group of persons with learning disabilities: Adults with severe learning disabilities in vocational rehabilitation. *Journal of Learning, 8,* 521–528.

Mithaug, D. E., Horiuchi, C. N., & Fanning, P. N. (1985). A report on the Colorado statewide follow-up survey of special education students. *Exceptional Children, 51,* 397–404.

National Joint Committee on Learning Disabilities. (1987). Adults with learning disabilities: A call to action. A position paper of the National Joint Committee on Learning Disabilities, February 10, 1985. *Journal of Learning Disabilities, 20*(3), 172–174.

National Literacy Act of 1991. Public Law 102-73, 105 Stat. 333 (1991).

Nelson, R., & Lignugaris-Kraft, B. (1989). Postsecondary education for students with learning disabilities. *Exceptional Children, 56,* 246–265.

Neubert, D. A., Tilson, G. P., & Ianacone, R. N. (1989). Postsecondary transition needs and employment patterns of individuals with mild disabilities. *Exceptional Children, 55,* 494–500.

Newman, A. P. (1994). Adult literacy programs: An overview. *Learning Disabilities, 5*(1), 51–61.

Parks, A. W., Antonoff, S., Drake, C., Skiba, W. F., & Soberman, J. (1987). A survey of programs and services for students with learning disabilities in graduate and professional schools. *Journal of Learning Disabilities, 20*(3), 181–188.

Phelps, L. A., Wermuth, T. R., Crain, R. L., & Kane, P. (1989). *Vocational education for special populations: Options for improving federal policy.* Berkeley: National Center for Research in Vocational Education.

Rehabilitation Act of 1973, Public Law 93-112, 87 Stat. 335 (1973).

Ross, A. O. (1987). *Learning disabilities: The unrealized potential.* New York: McGraw-Hill.

Ross, J. M., & Smith, J. O. (1990). Adult basic educators' perceptions of learning disabilities. *Journal of Reading, 33,* 340–347.

Ross-Gordon, J. M. (1989). *Adults with learning disabilities: An overview for the adult educator.* Columbus, OH: ERIC Clearinghouse on Adult Career, and Vocational Education. (ERIC Document Reproduction Service No. ED 315 664)

Rusch, F. R., Chadsey-Rusch, J., & Szymanski, E. (1992). The emerging field of transition services. In F. R. Rusch, L. DeStefano, L. Chadsey-Rusch, L. A. Phelps, & E. Szymanski (Eds.), *Transition from school to adult life: Models, linkages, and policy* (pp. 5–15). Sycamore, IL: Sycamore.

Ryan, A., & Price, L. (1993). Learning disabilities in ABE: A survey of current practices. *Journal of Postsecondary Education and Disability, 10*(3), 31–40.

Salend, S. J., Salend, S. M., & Yanok, J. (1985). Learning disabled students in higher education. *Teacher Education and Special Education, 8,* 49–54.

Sanchez, S. (1984). Where do we go from here: A look to the future in rehabilitation of learning disabled persons. *Journal of Rehabilitation, 50*(2), 82–88.

Shaw, S. F., & Shaw, S. R. (1989). Learning disability college programming: A bibliography. *Journal of Postsecondary Education and Disability, 6*(1), 77–85.

Shaw, S. F., Brinckerhoff, L. C., Kistler, J. K., & McGuire, J. M. (1991). Preparing students with learning disabilities for postsecondary education: Issues and future needs. *Learning Disabilities, 2*(1), 21–26.

Siperstein, G. N. (1988). Students with learning disabilities in college: The need for a programmatic approach to critical transitions. *Journal of Learning Disabilities, 21,* 431–436.

Sitlington, P. L. (1981). Vocational and special education in career programming for the mildly handicapped adolescent. *Exceptional Children, 47,* 592–598.

Smith, J. O. (1992). Falling through the cracks: Rehabilitation services for adults with learning disabilities. *Exceptional Children, 58,* 451–460.

Stodden, R. A., & Boone, R. (1987). Assessing transition services for handicapped youth: A cooperative interagency approach. *Exceptional Children, 53*(6), 537–545.

Stodden, R. A., & Browder, P. M. (1986). Community based competitive employment preparation of developmentally disabled persons: A program description and evaluation. *Education and Training of the Mentally Retarded, 21,* 43–53.

Strichart, S. S., & Mangrum, C. T. (1985). Selecting a college for the LD student. *Academic Therapy, 20,* 475–479.

Szymanski, E. M., Dunn, C., & Parker, R. M. (1989). Rehabilitation counseling with persons with learning disabilities: An ecological framework. Special issue on learning disabilities. *Rehabilitation Counseling Bulletin, 33*(1), 38–53.

Szymanski, E. M., Hanley-Maxwell, C., & Asselin, S. (1992). The vocational rehabilitation, special education, vocational education interface. In F. R. Rusch, L. DeStefano, J. Chadsey-Rusch, L. A. Phelps, & E. M. Szymanski (Eds.), *Transition from school to adult life: Models, linkages, and policy* (pp. 153–171). Sycamore, IL: Sycamore.

Thistlewaite, L. (1983). Teaching reading to the student who cannot read. *Lifelong Learning: The Adult Years, 7*(1), 5–7, 28.

U.S. Commission on Civil Rights. (1983). *Accommodating the spectrum of disabilities.* Washington, DC: Author.

U.S. Department of the Interior. (1934). *Manual for case-workers* (Bulletin No. 175, Vocational Rehabilitation Series No. 23). Washington, DC: U.S. Government Printing Office.

Vocational Education Act of 1976 Public Law 94-482, 90 Stat. 2081 (1976).

Vogel, S. A. (1990). An overview of special topical issues on adults with learning disabilities. *Learning Disabilities Focus, 5,* 67–68.

Vogel, S. A., & Adelman, P. (1981). Personnel development: College and university programs designed for learning disabled adults. *CEC Quarterly, 1,* 12–18.

Wehman, P. H., Kregel, J., Barcus, M. J., & Schalock, R. L. (1986). Vocational transition for students with developmental disabilities. In W. E. Kiernan & J. A. Stark (Eds.), *Pathways to employment for adults with developmental disabilities* (pp. 113–127). Baltimore: Paul H. Brookes.

Wermuth, T. R., & Phelps, L. A. (1990). *Identifying components of effective vocational special needs programs: A preliminary framework.* Berkeley: National Center for Research in Vocational Education.

Westberry, S. J. (1994). A review of learning strategies for adults with learning disabilities: Preparing for the GED exam. *Journal of Learning Disabilities, 27*(4), 202–208.

White, W. J., Alley, G. R., Deshler, D. D., Schumaker, J. A. B., Warner, M. M., & Clark, F. L. (1982). Are there learning disabilities after high school? *Exceptional Children, 49*, 273–274.

Will, M. (1983). *OSERS Programming for the transition of youth with disabilities: Bridges from school to working life.* Washington, DC: Office of Special Education and Rehabilitative Services.

Will, M. (1984). *Bridges from school to working life: Programs for the handicapped.* Washington, DC: Office of Information and Resources for the Handicapped.

Zigmond, N. (1990). Rethinking secondary school programs for students with learning disabilities. *Focus on Exceptional Children, 23*(1), 1–21.

Zigmond, N., & Thornton, H. (1989). Follow-up of postsecondary age learning disabled graduates and dropouts. *Learning Disabilities Research, 1*(1), 50–55.

15

Learning Disabilities Policy and Legal Issues: A Consumer and Practitioner User-Friendly Guide

NOEL GREGG
YVONNE JOHNSON
CAROLYN McKINLEY

Consumers and practitioners often complain that they do not understand the policy and laws that protect adults with learning disabilities. Although legislation and regulations are catalysts for empowering adults with learning disabilities, they also create controversy and ambiguity pertaining to the interpretation of statutory regulations. It is easy to become confused by legal terminology and misinterpret the meaning of regulations meant to provide access, not deny, services for adults with learning disabilities. Such legislation as the 1992 reauthorization of the Rehabilitation Act of 1973 (Rehabilitation Act Amendments, 1992) and the Americans with Disabilities Act (1990) clearly state that individuals with learning disabilities are covered by these laws. Those laws also make employers and postsecondary institutions responsible for providing reasonable access and accommodation to all educational and vocational opportunities for the population with learning disabilities. The purpose of this chapter is to provide in a question-and-answer format a user-friendly guide to legislation, regulations, and policy relevant to the adult population with learning disabilities. Issues pertaining to the entire range of severity of adults with learning disabilities are discussed, including questions related to rehabilitation, special education, postsecondary colleges and university, corrections, and technical schools.

To understand legal protection, it is important to have a clear understanding of the terminology used to refer to sources of law. This chapter is meant to be a reference for consumers and professionals, not an inclusive critique or historical document of legislation and statutes pertaining to the rights of adults with learning disabilities. Therefore, a summary of the most frequently used legal terminology found throughout the literature exploring the rights of adults with learning disabilities is summarized in Table 15.1. This terminology is used throughout this chapter.

Such recent legislation as the Americans with Disabilities Act (1990, Public Law 101-336), the Technology-Related Assistance for Individuals with Disabilities Act Amendments (1994, Public Law 103-218), and the reauthorization of the Rehabilitation Act (Rehabilita-

TABLE 15.1. Legal Terminology

Term	Description
Law	Four types: constitutional law, state laws, local laws, and case law.
Policy	Rules and regulations developed to implement laws.
U.S. Constitution	The "supreme law of the land."
Case law	Law that emerges from court decisions.
State law	Statutory law enacted at the state level.
Litigation	Court cases (state or federal).
Rational basis test	Test the courts. Utilize to determine whether a state or state agency has discriminated.
Legislation	Laws enacted by the U.S. Congress and by state and local governments.
Statutes	Laws enacted by the U.S. Congress and by state and local governments.
Regulations	Rules developed to carry out legislation by an executive agency charged to do so.
Judicial interpretation	Commentary following judicial opinions referred to as dicta.

tion Act Amendments, 1992, Public Law 102-569) all reflect a paradigm shift in transforming and redefining disability in America (Kochlor, 1990). Gregg and Ferri (Chapter 2, this volume) discuss several theories currently influencing a paradigm shift in the field of learning disorders. The philosophy of several current theories and paradigms focuses on individual rights rather than deficits. According to Kochlor (1990), "The way to promote productivity and independence of people with disabilities is to remove the barriers that our society has created and restore the rights of citizens with disabilities to partake of the opportunities available to Americans" (p. 3). Attention is directed toward overcoming disabilities through education, rehabilitation, and technology. Systematic and attitudinal barriers can better be reframed when individuals have knowledge of the laws that protect their rights. Therefore, the following section reviews some of the major legislation that safeguards the rights of adults with learning disabilities.

WHAT STATUTES ARE OF PRIMARY SIGNIFICANCE TO ADULTS WITH LEARNING DISABILITIES?

This section identifies several statutes related to issues that affect adults with learning disabilities. The first two, the 1992 reauthorization of the Rehabilitation Act and the Americans with Disabilities Act, provide broad coverage against discrimination on the basis of disability by recipients of federal financial assistance (i.e., colleges and technical schools), providers of public services, and employers.

Americans with Disabilities Act

The American with Disabilities Act (ADA, 1990) provides protection for individuals with disabilities across programs and employers not covered by the Rehabilitation Act (1973). As of July 26, 1994, the ADA applied to all services, programs and employers with 15 or more employees. Although the passage of the ADA is often compared to the passage of other civil rights bills, Shapiro (1993) describes a striking difference:

> What made disability rights controversial—and trickier than granting rights to blacks, women, and other minorities—was that it could cost businesses money. The 1964 Civil Rights Act had simply required businesses to change their practices. But the ADA would require businesses to spend money, if necessary to avoid being discriminatory. (p. 115)

It is clear in the ADA legislation that the law applies to persons with learning disabilities and other "hidden disabilities," as well as to those individuals with visible disabilities (Grossman, 1994). Interestingly, Rothstein (1993) states that because colleges were already subject to the Rehabilitation Act, the ADA will not have as much of an impact on them regarding the population with learning disabilities. This statement by Rothstein (1993) ignores the fact that colleges and universities are "employers" of staff and faculty who might also demonstrate a learning disability and misleads us by ignoring the fact that students with learning disabilities who attend such facilities will be employees and employers in their near future. All employers and educational and service agencies will feel the impact of cases interpreted by either the ADA or the Rehabilitation Act. Accordingly, under Section 506 of the reauthorization of the Rehabilitation Act (1992), Congress amended Section 504 to comply with Title I of the ADA. Therefore, any institution subject to Section 504 will be measured by the "standards" of Title I of the ADA (Rehabilitation Act Amendments, §§ 506, 1992, Public Law 102-569). According to Grossman (1994), Title I and subpart A of Title II of the ADA together cover "virtually every state and local government employer" (p. 21). The ADA, as clearly stated by Ragsdale (personal communication, 1994), "levels the playing field for all the players involved in the game."

Rehabilitation Act and the Rehabilitation Act Amendments

The Rehabilitation Act (1973), Title V, prior to the ADA, has been the most significant piece of legislation protecting the rights of individuals with disabilities, particularly related to prohibiting employment discrimination on the basis of disability. Title V (specifically §§ 503), covers the federal government, every entity that receives financial assistance from the federal government, and anyone who does business with the federal government. The majority of colleges and universities in this country are recipients of federal financial assistance to some degree. A 1987 amendment to the Rehabilitation Act (Civil Rights Restoration Act, 1987, Public Law 100-259) clearly stated that if any part of a program or activity receives federal financial assistance, all the operations of the program are subject to Section 504.

Under Section 506 of the Rehabilitation Act Amendments, Congress amended Section 504 to achieve greater uniformity with Title I of the ADA. Therefore, any institution subject to Section 504 will have its conduct measured by the "standards" of Title I of the ADA.

Individuals with Disabilities Education Act

The Education for All Handicapped Children Act (1975, Public Law 94-142) was amended in 1990 and the new legislation was titled the Individuals with Disabilities Education Act (IDEA; 1990, Public Law 104-476). The term "handicapped" was eliminated from the law and replaced with the term "disabled." In addition, the definition of children with disabilities was extended to include those with autism and traumatic brain injury. The IDEA also mandated that transitional service be required and written into the annual individualized program for every child age 16 and over (age 14 when appropriate). Public Law 94-142 and its amended version, Public Law 101-476, provide protection for school-age children against discrimination due to a disability.

Education of the Handicapped Act

Section 626 of the Education of the Handicapped Act (1983, Public Law 98-199) is often called the Transition Amendment. Accordingly, its intent is to "stimulate and improve the development of secondary special education programs to increase the potential for competitive employment . . . " (Senate Report on the Transition Amendment of 1983, p. 20). The discretionary sections (C through H) of the Education of the Handicapped Act (1983, Public Law 99-427), which include Section 626, are currently being reauthorized through 1994.

Section 626 advocates implementation of statewide systems to help students with special needs make the transition into employment, postsecondary education, or other appropriate settings. In addition, the legislation focuses on starting the transition process early and establishing interagency links for cooperative services.

Technology-Related Assistance for Individuals with Disabilities Act Amendments

The Technology-Related Assistance for Individuals with Disabilities Act Amendments (1994; the "Tech Act") amended the Technology-Related Assistance for Individuals with Disabilities Act (1988, Public Law 100-407). The Tech Act has three main purposes:

> (a) to provide discretionary grants to states to assist them in developing and implementing (a) consumer-responsive, comprehensive, statewide program of technology-related assistance for individuals with disabilities of all ages; (b) to fund programs of national sig-

nificance related to assistive technology; and (c) to establish and expand alternative financing mechanisms to allow individuals with disabilities to purchase assistive technology devices and services.

The state grants program under the Tech Act is intended to be a catalyst for statewide systems change for the purpose of increasing access to appropriate assistive technology devices and services. These funds are to be used to support systems change and advocacy activities that will increase the availability of, funding for, and access to assistive devices and services.

Carl D. Perkins Vocational and Applied Technology Education Act

The Carl D. Perkins Vocational and Applied Technology Education Act Amendments (1990, Public Law 101-392) update the Carl D. Perkins Vocational Technical Education Act (1984, Public Law 98-524), which was designed to "assure that individuals who are inadequately served under vocational education programs are assured access to quality vocational education programs." The amended law eliminated set-aside monies from vocational education funds that were once earmarked only for individuals with disabilities in order to encourage local educational agencies (LEAs) to try to use set-aside monies with "assurances" to "enhance participation" of persons with disabilities. This change has a negative impact on individuals with disabilities because it allows LEAs to have the power in deciding the distribution of money among the many different special populations. In addition, the amendment applies a formula based on poverty level, for distribution of basic grant funds to meet greatest needs.

A primary mandate of the new act is that both secondary and postsecondary programs are responsible for ensuring ready accessibility to their programs. Postsecondary programs are responsible for providing transitional services and will be held responsible for assisting individuals with special needs with applications to their programs of study. During the Fall of 1995, this legislation will be reviewed by Congress and significant changes may impact on the adult population with learning disabilities.

WHAT DEFINITIONS APPLY TO THE ADULT POPULATION WITH LEARNING DISABILITIES?

Definitions of learning disabilities proposed by committees such as the National Joint Committee on Learning Disabilities (1989), the

Association for Children with Learning Disabilities (ACLD; 1986), and the Interagency Committee on Learning Disabilities (1987) have led to a better understanding of learning disabilities across the life span (Gregg, 1994). Yet the impact of these definitions on state and federal agencies has not been significant. Current efforts are being made across professional and federal agencies to adopt a more general definition of learning disabilities.

Statutory Definitions

Issues of definition and eligibility are easily confused, particularly as individuals begin to use more than one federal agency (e.g., special education, vocational rehabilitation, and Aid to Families with Dependent Children). First, it is important to understand what Section 504 of the Rehabilitation Act and the ADA set as criteria for who demonstrates a disability. Both of these laws apply to any individual in the United States who has a physical or mental impairment that substantially limits one or more major life activities, has a record of such an impairment, and is regarded as having such an impairment (the ADA, 1990). The term "specific learning disabilities" is included in the definition of mental impairments (Grossman, 1994), although no specific type of learning disabilities is noted in the ADA or its employment regulations. Grossman (1994) informs us that dyslexia is the only type of learning disability mentioned in the appendix and he encourages individuals with dysgraphia or dyscalculia to "analogize to dyslexia to establish they have an impairment" (p. 12).

"Major life activity" is another confusing term under the ADA and the Rehabilitation Act. Although an individual might establish that he or she has a disability, the individual must also document that this disability "substantially limits major life activity" (*Jasany v. United States Postal Service*, 1985). Major life functions include seeing, hearing, speaking, learning, and working. According to Grossman (1994), "processing visual or auditory information" should be considered a major life function. He cites support for this inclusion in the technical assistance manuals explaining the ADA (Equal Employment Opportunities Commission, 1992; Department of Justice 1992).

The ADA and the Rehabilitation Act also require that the individual disability identified must "substantially limit" one or more major life activities. The issue of "substantially limiting" is extremely sensitive and often ambiguous wording for the population of individuals with learning disabilities. Whereas Title I of the ADA and Title V of the Rehabilitation Act clearly state that individuals with learning disabilities are covered by the laws, the degree of severity for service eligibility has not been clearly defined and is awaiting further court decisions. Grossman (1994) completed a comprehensive search and "found at least seven cases in which the courts accepted the fact that a plaintiff with a learning disability was a disabled person within the meaning of employment discrimination law" (p. 23).

State and Federal Agency Definitions

For years, the definitions of learning disabilities that were applied to the adult population were those used by the public schools (Martin, Smith, & Zwerlein, 1985). The majority of state agencies adopted definitions using the model of Public Law 94-142 and its revision (the IDEA). Mercer, Hughs, and Mercer (1985) found that 44% of the states use the federally recommended Public Law 94-142 definition without modification, 28% have adopted it with modifications, and 25% have adopted different definitions. These definitions were child-oriented, not applicable to the adult population.

The Rehabilitation Services Administration (RSA) has struggled with a definition for learning disabilities. Prior to 1980, adults with learning disabilities were not eligible for vocational rehabilitation services unless a physical or mental disability was identified as defined by the *Federal Register* (November 29, 1979, Gerber, 1981; Martin, 1987). The RSA traditionally viewed learning disabilities as an educational problem rather than a medical condition. After many complaints by consumers and professionals, the RSA, in 1980, recognized learning disabilities as a discrete medical disability, thereby allowing adults with learning disabilities to become eligible for vocational rehabilitation services (RSA, 1981). The decision to recognize learning disabilities as a vocational rehabilitation disability category was certainly prodded by the inclusion of disorders related to learning disabilities in the third edition of the *Diagnostic and Statistical Manual of Mental Disorders* (DSM-III; American Psychiatric Association, 1980). The category of learning disabilities was converted to a neuropsychological classification code in 1985 by the RSA and the requirement for a physician's examination to document the case was deleted (RSA PPD-85-3). Since 1981, defining and serving individuals with learning disabilities have been enigmas to the RSA (Sanchez, 1984).

The RSA has modified the definition for learning disabilities several times. The current RSA definition is used by state vocational rehabilitation agencies that have no written learning disabilities policy. Table 15.2 includes the current learning disabilities definition used by the RSA, which stresses a neurological derivation. For comparison,

Table 15.2 includes the current United States Office of Education (USOE) definition of learning disabilities (IDEA, 1990), which uses the words "psychological processes" rather than "central nervous system processes." Clearly, this illustrates education's preference for using a *psychometrically* based diagnosis rather than a *medical one.* Also interesting is the RSA's reference to social competence and emotional maturity as identifying characteristics, which the USOE does not do. The proposal of the Interagency Committee on Learning Disabilities (1987) has also included the issue of social competence (see Table 15.2). This has caused quite a bit of controversy in the fields of special education and school psychology. Interestingly, the RSA and the Interagency definition recognize that learning disabilities can interfere with the ability to interact socially (Johnson & Blalock, 1987). According to Biller and White (1989), in the public schools, many individuals who demonstrate poor social skills are immediately classified and served under the category of emotional disturbance or behavior disorder, whereas in "adulthood such immaturity may not necessarily translate into an emotional disorder" (p. 7). Comparing the definitions used by 50 state departments of education and vocational rehabilitation, Biller and White (1989) found considerable agreement within fields rather than between fields related to the definition chosen for learning disabilities.

Diagnostic and Statistical Manual of Mental Disorders

The *Diagnostic and Statistical Manual of Mental Disorders,* fourth edition (American Psychiatric Association, 1994), often referred to as DSM-IV, is the classification system used by psychologists in classifying disorders for children or adults. The first version of the DSM was published in 1952, but it was not until the DSM-III in 1980 that a truly comprehensive classification of developmental disorders appeared (Hooper, 1992). Learning disabilities, although not a separate category, are classified under the following learning disorders categories: reading disorders, mathematics disorders, disorders of written expression, and not otherwise specified. In the same chapter, but not included in the index under a reference to learning disabilities, are the categories of phonological disorder, expressive language disorder, mixed receptive or expressive language disorder, and motor disorders. Clearly, the new DSM-IV identifies learning disabilities mainly with academic underachievement and other types of processing disorders (e.g., motor and attention) and separates language from what it call learning disorders. The new DSM-IV follows similar criteria as the DSM-III-R for the classification of learning disabilities. Emphasis again

TABLE 15.2. Federal, State, and Agency Definitions

Individuals with Disabilities Education Act (Public Law 99-147)	Specific learning disability means a disorder in one or more of the basic psychological processes involved in understanding or in using language, spoken or written, that may manifest itself in an imperfect ability to listen, think, speak, read, write, spell, or do mathematical calculations. The term includes such conditions as perceptual handicaps, brain injury, minimal brain dysfunction, dyslexia, and developmental aphasia. The term does not include children who have learning problems that are primarily the result of visual, hearing, or motor handicaps; of mental retardation; of emotional disturbance; or of environmental, cultural, or economic disadvantage.
Interagency Committee on Learning Disabilities (1987)	"Learning disabilities" is a generic term that refers to a heterogeneous group of disorders manifested by significant difficulties in the acquisition and use of listening, speaking, reading, writing, reasoning, or mathematical abilities or of social skills. These disorders are intrinsic to the individual and though a learning disability may occur concomitantly with other handicapping conditions (e.g., sensory impairment, mental retardation, and social and emotional disturbance), with social environmental influences (e.g., cultural differences, insufficient or inappropriate instruction, and psychogenetic factors), and especially with attention-deficit disorder, all of which may cause learning problems, a learning disability is not the direct result of those conditions or influences.
Rehabilitation Services Administration (1981)	Individuals who have a disorder due to central nervous system dysfunction involving perceiving, understanding, and/or using concepts through verbal (spoken or written language) or nonverbal means. This disorder manifests itself with difficulties in one or more of the following areas: attention, reasoning, memory, communicating, reading, writing, spelling, calculation, coordination, social competence, and emotional maturity. These disorders may constitute, in an adult, an employment handicap. The condition has an impact on employment.
National Joint Committee on Learning Disabilities (1981, 1987)	"Learning disabilities" is a generic term that refers to a heterogeneous group of disorders manifested by significant difficulties in the acquisition and use of listening, speaking, reading, writing, reasoning, or mathematical abilities. These disorders are intrinsic to the individual and presumed to be due to central nervous system dysfunction. Even though a learning

(continued)

TABLE 15.2. *(continued)*

	disability may occur concomitantly with other handicapping conditions (e.g., sensory impairment, mental retardation, and social and emotional disturbance) or environmental influences (e.g., cultural differences, insufficient or inappropriate instruction, and psychological factors), it is not the direct result of those conditions or influences.
Learning Disabilities Association (1985)	"Specific learning disabilities" is a chronic condition of presumed neurological origin which selectively interferes with the development, integration, and/or demonstration of verbal and/or nonverbal abilities. "Specific learning disabilities" exists as a distinct handicapping condition in the presence of average to superior intelligence, adequate sensory motor systems, and adequate learning opportunities. The condition varies in its manifestations and in degree of severity. Throughout life the condition can affect self-esteem, education, vocation, socialization, and/or daily living activities.

remains on academic underachievement, using a discrepancy-based model.

Some investigators have questioned the rationale for including developmental disorders in a psychiatric nosology (e.g., Garfield, 1986). According to Hooper (1992), there does appear to be a firm commitment to include learning disabilities in a system on mental disorders, "but the rationale for their inclusion must become stronger if they are to remain within such a classification framework" (p. 284). It is most disheartening, with the past DSMs, and even more so with the latest version, that there have been few attempts, if any, on the part of the American Psychological Association to take advantage of the literature related to children and adults with learning disabilities.

Such agencies as vocational rehabilitation, corrections, and institutes of higher education often contract with psychologists to evaluate learning disabilities for their clients and encourage individuals to pursue evaluations from private psychologists to document their need for accommodation and modifications. Professionals and consumers must be wary of the many psychologists who strictly interpret the DSM-IV when making their decision relative to an individual's demonstration of a learning disability. The result can lead to overidentification or misidentification of individuals with learning disabilities. Many professionals have voiced concern over the appropriateness of such classifications (Gregg, 1992; Reschly, 1992; Stanovich, 1992).

A critical issue for the adult population with learning disabilities centers on diagnostic evaluation (Glen Young, personal communication, 1994). Access to accommodation and modifications requires psychological documentation. Many literacy teachers, adult educators, corrections personnel, and employers express concern that the individuals with whom they work often do not have the financial means to pay for such an evaluation. Psychological evaluations on the open market can range anywhere from $300 to $1,500. Currently many insurance companies refuse to cover the cost of psychological evaluations, particularly related to documentation of learning disabilities and attention-deficit disorder. The problem is not just the insurance companies; many consumers do not have the means to carry insurance or work for companies that do not provide benefits. National advocacy groups are beginning to put pressure on government officials to explore the use of Medicaid to cover psychological evaluations. The LD/JOBS Project in the state of Washington is one of the initial examples of Medicaid paying for full-scale diagnostic testing at market rates (Glen Young, personal communication, 1994). More creative collaborative ventures like the Washington LD/JOBS Project will help stimulate the government and business interest in the issue of psychological evaluations and the adult population with learning disabilities.

WHAT IS THE DIFFERENCE BETWEEN ENTITLEMENT AND ELIGIBILITY?

Consumers under Public Law 94-142, now the IDEA, are provided accommodation, modifications, and services under this entitlement law. The ADA and the Rehabilitation Act are civil rights statutes with broader intervention and social objectives (Grossman, 1992). Although the IDEA is forced by fiscal demands to follow strict definitions as to who meets the criteria for learning disabilities, according to Grossman (1994) the ADA and the Rehabilitation Act are "intended to expand the number of workplaces available to persons with disabilities and to make industry assume the cost of employing persons who, with reasonable accommodation, can perform their jobs competently. These objectives are not well served by making it difficult to come under the overage of the statute" (p. 11).

Consumers and professionals dealing with academic or other educational-type agencies cannot always assume that court interpretations of the ADA and the Rehabilitation Act related to employment cases will follow suit in the academic world. The Supreme Court is usually more reluctant than employees to second-guess the decisions of educators (Grossman, 1994). Many issues pertaining to the rights of adults with learning disabilities and postsecondary training will be interpreted more from the academic than from the employment perspective.

Establishing pertinent identification criteria for learning disabilities services, entitlement, or eligibility statutes is not new to professionals working with children and adolescents at the elementary or secondary levels of schooling (Hammill, 1990; Kavale, 1987; Keogh, 1983; Reynolds, 1984–1985; Torgesen, 1987). Currently, there are no national standards for diagnostic and eligibility criteria for the child, adolescent, or adult population. Keogh (1986) relates differences in the identification procedures: (1) disciplinary or professional perspectives, (2) the specific formula used for determining a discrepancy between aptitude and achievement, (3) diagnostic methods and techniques, and (4) institutional constraints.

What Is Meant by Eligibility for Services?

The problem facing adults with learning disabilities and professionals rests not so much with definition as with the eligibility criteria used to operationalize the definition. Whatever definition an agency or individual evaluator follows, selecting the criteria by which to operationalize the definitions fairly remains difficult. Eligibility defines access to modifications and accommodation; therefore, it is the gatekeeper of services (Gregg, 1994). Eligibility criteria are the reliability component important in validating definitions. Many adults with learning disabilities quickly discover that there is no consistency across agencies and professionals related to the type of criteria selected. Therefore, an individual may be eligible for services at one agency but not at another. In addition, consumers must become aware of the strengths and weaknesses of the types of eligibility models used by a state agency. Different models appear to influence who is selected and who is denied services. Brackett and McPherson (Chapter 4, this volume) provide an extensive review of the literature related to identification and eligibility practices applied to the adult population with learning disabilities.

The type of model used by a state agency in determining eligibility affects the number and types of individuals identified (Chalfant, 1989; Gregg, 1994). The three most commonly used eligibility models by professionals in diagnosing learning disabilities include (1) looking at cutoff scores, (2) applying a discrepancy equation (regression model), or (3) using a differential diagnostic model or clinical model (Gregg, 1994).

Approximately 54% of state rehabilitation agencies and 84% of state special education departments use a discrepancy eligibility model (Biller & White, 1989). Researchers have documented that discrepancy models are biased against individuals who score lower on intelligence measures, such as adults with significant language learning disabilities or adults who do not fit the norm-referenced population of the assessment tools (Gregg, 1994). Many standardized intelligence measures have been seen as unreliable indicators of ability by experts concerned about race and cultural differences (Rogoff, 1989). Learning disabilities by definition encompass a heterogeneous group of individuals. Heterogeneity, however, should not preclude clear operational criteria for defining service eligibility and specific modifications or accommodation. The diagnostic category "learning disabilities" is not of a single dimension, rather it is a multivariate construct. As Biller and White (1989) state:

> In addition, delays in providing services may occur when individuals identified as having specific learning disabilities by the schools are referred to rehabilitation counselors, and the information needed by the counselors to determine eligibility is not available and must be obtained elsewhere, due to a difference in eligibility criteria between special education and rehabilitation. This situation is more than just a bureaucratic problem. Ultimately, the individuals with specific learning disabilities will pay the price through denied and delayed services. (p. 15)

Statutory Eligibility

Section 504 of the Rehabilitation Act and the ADA determine that individuals are eligible for protection against discrimination if they "have a physical or mental impairment which substantially limits one or more major life activities," have a "record of such an impairment," and are "regarded as having such an impairment" (the ADA, 1990). This broad coverage of who demonstrates a disability requires federal and state agencies to operationalize just who will receive services.

What Are the Eligibility Criteria Used for Rehabilitation?

Individuals with learning disabilities appear to have more difficulty accessing services from vocational rehabilitation than do individuals who demonstrate other disabilities (Chetkovick, Toms-Barker, & Schlichman, 1989; Dowdy & Smith, 1994). Consumers with learning disabilities often lack the ability to access services from vocational rehabilitation because professionals (special education, rehabilitation counselors, school psychologists, counseling psychologists, neuropsychologists) lack knowledge related to the adult population with learning disabilities, particularly in relation to assessment. In addition, there is a need for empirical research on reliable eligibility criteria and subgroups. Gregg (1993) reports that in a recent focus group with both rehabilitation and special education professionals, concern was expressed as to the effectiveness of many psychological and vocational assessments. These professionals receive reports from evaluators representing a variety of training and philosophical backgrounds related to assessment (e.g., behavioral, neuropsychological, psychodynamic, psychoeducational, and vocational or career) and, more often than not, they find that a professional bias or background philosophy determines eligibility rather than a consistent set of criteria. In addition, service providers suggest that many recommended assessment approaches address only one end of the severity continuum.

Professionals who provide vocational rehabilitation agency assessment use a variety of criteria to determine eligibility for services (discrepancy, intercognitive, interachievement, clinical). Depending on the eligibility model used, a consumer may or may not receive services. In a recent study (Hoy et al., Chapter 3, this volume) eligibility models were compared across a population of adults receiving state vocational rehabilitation services. There was little agreement across cutoff, discrepancy, and differential diagnostic eligibility models as to who was identified as demonstrating a learning disability.

Issue of Severity

An evaluator may identify an adult as demonstrating a learning disability, but the severity of the learning disability may not be severe enough by vocational rehabilitation services standards to be eligible for services. However, the issue of severity of disability has been inconsistently interpreted across states (Chetkovich, Toms-Barker, & Schlichman, 1989; Dowdy, 1992; Dowdy & Smith, 1994). Interestingly, Dowdy and Smith (1994), reporting RSA data, indicate that whereas 68% of all persons in the Vocational rehabilitation program are classified as individuals with severe disabilities, only 52% of individuals with learning disabilities meet this criteria.

The RSA in 1990 disseminated guidelines to address the issue of severity. The policy comes under the title of "order of selection" which means that a vocational rehabilitation agency may determine that it cannot serve all eligible individuals because of resource constraints. According to directives from the RSA, to determine whether an individual's learning disabilities are "severe" enough for program purposes, the following statutory and regulatory definition of "individual with severe handicaps" must be followed:

> An "individual with severe handicaps" means an individual with handicaps
>
>   1. Who has a severe physical or mental disability that seriously limits one or more functional capacities (mobility, communication, self-care, self-direction, interpersonal skills, work tolerance or work-skills) in terms of employability;
>   2. Whose vocational rehabilitation can be expected to require multiple vocational rehabilitation services over an extended period of time; and
>   3. Who has one or more physical or mental disabilities resulting from . . . specific learning disabilities . . . or another disability or combination of disabilities determined on the basis of an evaluation of rehabilitation potential to cause comparable substantial functional limitation. (RSA, 1981)

Once an individual is classified as having a severe disability, the state division of rehabilitation personnel will place the adult with learning disabilities in one of a number of categories that are called an order of selection. For instance, the first order of clients to be served by a vocational rehabilitation agency could be those who demonstrate two disabilities rather than just one. Therefore, an individual with learning disabilities could be eligible for vocational rehabilitation services but not receive the services if the state rehabilitation agency invokes an order-of-selection mandate for which the individual does not qualify.

Adults with learning disabilities may demonstrate additional disabilities, which has led to an increase in the number of dually diagnosed individuals with learning disabilities. A significant number of these individuals demonstrate learning disabilities and attention-deficit disorders. Professionals will require adequate training in assessment to identify disabilities that are often comorbid with learning disabilities. In addition, technical assistance focusing on appropriate interventions sensitive to dually diagnosed individuals is critical among professionals from many disciplines.

What Are the Eligibility Criteria Used for Colleges and Universities?

Eligibility criteria for college and universities have only recently received attention from professionals. Again, as with the RSA, little empirical research has focused on the issue of eligibility criteria for the adult population served by institutions of higher education. The majority of colleges and universities are simply requiring that students provide documentation to determine the existence of a learning disability. Therefore, a variety of models are used by professionals providing the assessments (Gregg, 1994). Vogel (1993) reports that at some colleges a minimum IQ cutoff score, in addition to documentation of a learning disability, determines access to specialized programs serving students with learning disabilities. Unfortunately, in this same chapter Vogel (1993) misrepresents the University of Georgia eligibility criteria and wrongly states that the California Assessment System for Adults with Learning Disabilities (CCC) is the only system that has a clinical eligibility model in place. Both the University of Georgia Learning Disabilities Center (LDC), in operation since 1982, and the CCC have similar eligibility models. Vogel (1993) describes the CCC model in depth. The University of Georgia LDC eligibility criteria for learning disabilities services are included in Table 15.3. These criteria have been adapted by the Georgia Board of Regents to be used at the other statewide assessment sites. In addition, Table 15.4 represents the eligibility criteria for attention deficit developed by the University of Georgia LDC.

Institutions of higher education, whether open or closed admission facilities, must be sure that they have clear eligibility criteria in the future so that the appropriate individuals will benefit from learning disabilities services. Clear eligibility guidelines will lead to consumers being able to receive appropriate services, not necessarily always learning disabilities' services. According to legal scholars (e.g., Rothstein, 1993), it is not unreasonable for an institute of higher education to "specify the documentation be done by a professional, be relatively recent, and include specific tests" (p. 34). The law will become a problem for institutions of higher education when they have no consistent policy related to eligibility or are inconsistent in the manner in which they operationalize these criteria. Eligibility criteria shown in Tables 15.3 and 15.4 also become teaching tools for professionals lacking experience in assessing adults concerned about demonstrating learning disabilities, attention-deficit disorder, or both.

TABLE 15.3. University of Georgia (UGA) Learning Disabilities Center (LDS)—Eligibility Criteria: Guidelines

1. Documentation must be within three years of the student's anticipated starting date at UGA.

2. A specific learning disability must be stated within the documentation submitted. If another diagnosis is applicable, please state it as well.

3. One of the following individually administered intelligence tests must have been utilized:
   WAIS-R (Wechsler Adult Intelligence Scale—Revised)
   WISC-III (Wechsler Intelligence Scale for Children)
   KAIT (Kaufman Adolescent and Adult Intelligence Test)
   Stanford–Binet
   Please list subscale scores.

4. Cognitive processing strengths, weaknesses, and deficits should be discussed. Clear documentation of deficit areas is necessary in order for the LDC to provide appropriate modifications. Please discuss the following processing areas:
   a. Visual–spatial abilities
   b. Memory (auditory and visual and short and long term)
   c. Fine motor dexterity
   d. Executive functions (verbal and nonverbal reasoning) (it is also helpful to know about the student's cognitive flexibility and automaticity with cognitive tasks)
   e. Attention (auditory and visual)

5. Oral language skills should be assessed and discussed. Formal instruments or an informal analysis of a language sample are appropriate. The LDC is primarily interested in whether or not a student's learning disability is affecting oral language and/or if a separate speech disorder is also present.

6. Social–emotional status should be assessed and discussed. Formal assessment instruments and/or clinical interviews are appropriate. The LDC is concerned with differential diagnosis of psychological disorders that affect academics from learning disabilities. The LDC is also aware that psychological disorders can be secondary to learning disabilities. College is typically quite stressful for students who have learning disabilities. In our attempt to best serve our students, it is helpful to know whatever we can about their personality characteristics, psychological welfare, self-esteem, and stress level.

7. Achievement assessment in the following areas is required:
   a. Written language (spelling and written expression). If a written language sample is available for the LDC to review, this is most helpful.
   b. Reading (decoding and comprehension). Please indicate the student's ability to comprehend longer passages, more typical of college texts than some assessment instruments provide.

(continued)

TABLE 15.3. (*continued*)

---

c. Mathematics (applied word problems and calculations). Please indicate whether or not the student was successful with algebra problems. Scores rarely provide this. For example, students can score within the low-average range on the WRAT-R (Wide Range Achievement Test—Revised) without attempting any of the algebra problems.

8. Utilize assessment instruments with age-appropriate norms for high school seniors/college freshman or older students. These can certainly be supplemented by informal assessment.

Note. With minor modifications, these criteria were adapted from an eligibility Noel Gregg developed for the University of Georgia Learning Disabilities Center and used from 1987 to 1993. Currently this adapted version is used by the Georgia Regents Systems.

What Documentation Is Necessary for Eligibility?

Controversy surrounds documentation of learning disabilities related to receiving services at the university and college level. The controversy surfaced when the ADA (1990) initially stated that for individuals to receive services related to their disability, a record of such an impairment must be available. Some advocates (Jarrow, 1992) interpreted this to mean that documentation, regardless of currency or content, would suffice for individuals to use as proof of their disability. Using such logic, a college student evaluated in first grade who was identified as demonstrating a learning disability could use this old, outdated evaluation as documentation in college for receiving services for learning disabilities. Rothstein (1993), a legal scholar, interprets the ADA (1990) quite differently when she states:

> While each college and testing service may have its own specific requirements, it would not be unreasonable for such a requirement to specify that the documentation be done by a professional, be relatively recent, and include specific tests. It is also permissible to expect that the student with LDs pay for the cost of such documentation. Although some students may have documentation from their public school years, and this may be acceptable for undergraduate education, it may well be viewed as unacceptable in a graduate or professional program. This is the case because the mental processes and effects can change significantly from childhood to adulthood. For that reason, it should be considered reasonable to require recent documentation (within the past three years, for example). (p. 27)

TABLE 15.4. UGA Attention-Deficit Disorder Guidelines

Criterion One:	Reported history of symptoms of Attention-deficit/hyperactivity disorder (ADHD) by age 6
Data source:	Clinical interview, past psychologicals, parent/spouse report.
Criterion Two:	Self-report of three major behaviors from the DSM-IV items.
Data source:	DSM-IV items
Criterion Three:	Observations from clinicians (two if possible) across the following setting: a. working independently b. working under direction c. working under time constraints Identification of the same three major behaviors across both observers.
Data source:	ADHD observational form.
Criterion Four:	Mandatory corroboration of behaviors by another adult (parent, spouse, relative, friend, with integrity of knowledge of client).
Data source:	Signed permissions to talk with other adult. Phone or in-person identification of at least three behaviors from the DSM-IV items.
Criterion Five:	Documentation on two rating scales of ADHD behaviors.
Data source:	Client Rating Form SCL-90; Brief Symptom Inventory Self-Rating; Symptom Checklist; others
Criterion Six:	Schizophrenia, borderline personality disorder, autism, and mental retardation is not the primary disability.

Note. Developed by Noel Gregg, Cindy Darden, and Carol Ronka. All clients must be given an anxiety and depression measure in addition to criteria one through six.

If one uses the American Psychological Association (APA) rules of ethics, Rothstein's (1993) interpretation is well supported by fact. Many evaluators not connected to a university or college to which students go for evaluation, as mentioned earlier, often follow the DSM-IV criteria. Therefore, the use of the APA Ethical Principles of Psychologists and Code of Conduct guideline appears appropriate. According to APA (1992),

2.07 Obsolete Tests and Outdated Test Results

> 1. Psychologists do not base their assessment or intervention decision or recommendations on data or test results that are outdated for the current purpose.
> 2. Similarly, psychologists do not base such decision or recommendations on tests and measures that are obsolete and not useful for the current purpose. (p. 7)

Therefore, in their eligibility criteria, it would be wise for universities and colleges to specify the assessment areas (cognitive, social or emotional, academic, language, etc.), types of scores reported (standard scores, percentile, or grade), and date of evaluation that need to be addressed in any evaluation utilized for learning disabilities documentation purposes.

Documentation for More than Eligibility

Consumers, as well as professionals involved in the provision of services to adults with learning disabilities, have voiced concern regarding the effectiveness of assessment for the purpose of academic, career, and vocational training (Brown, Gerber, & Dowdy, 1990; Gregg & Hoy, 1987; Hawks et al., 1990). Based on the results of a recent focus group, Gregg (1993) reports that approximately 40% of the responses from vocational rehabilitation and special education professionals pertain to the poor correlation between assessment scores and direct intervention or accommodation and modifications. Unfortunately, many professionals working with individuals with learning disabilities on employment skills often focus on program or curricula activities and ignore the role of evaluation in developing career goals (Hursch, 1989). Quite often secondary students with learning disabilities receive inadequate assessment to aid transition teachers in planning curriculum objectives or guiding the students in decision making. The heterogeneity of the population and the function of the assessment preclude the idea of designing a single test battery for adults with learning disabilities. Assessing the needs of consumers with learning disabilities at a university or college setting, as compared to the consumer with learning disabilities at a community-based supportive employment program, requires similar and different methods and techniques. (See Hawks, Chapter 7, this volume for an indepth discussion of this issue.) It is a critical for service providers to receive more training opportunities in matching client profiles, based on empirical research (i.e., cognitive, social, academic, and vocational), to the appropriate accommodation and modifications for individual independence.

What about Admissions to Universities and Colleges?

Universities, colleges, or other types of postsecondary training programs are not required to accept an individual who does not meet the standards or requirements of that program of study. Therefore, such institutions can require standardized tests (Scholastic Aptitude Test [SAT], Graduate Records Examination, etc.) to be part of the admissions process as long as the tests were administered with appropriate accommodation. Accommodation for a testing situation might include the use of tape recorders, note takers, taped test format, computers, specialized software, talking calculators, or spelling masters. For some individuals, taking the test in a quiet room is an appropriate accommodation. Currently, the Civil Rights Division of the U.S. Department of Justice is investigating the legality under the ADA of the Educational Testing Service (ETS) being able to print that a student took the SAT with special accommodation (Wodatch, 1994).

Because state licensing boards act as state agencies, they must provide testing accommodation options for persons with learning disabilities who might be sitting for licensure or certification examinations. Even if the test is being administered by a private agency (e.g., the ETS), Title III of the ADA prohibits discrimination on the basis of a disability. When a test is being administered by a private entity and the test score is being received by a state, local, or private agency, both the administration and receiving parties have responsibilities under the ADA.

WHAT IS THE PURPOSE OF AN IEP, ITP, ICP, OR IWRP?

The rehabilitation counselor and the special education teacher are required by federal law to develop individualized instructional plans for any person receiving services from either special education or vocational rehabilitation. The individualized education program (IEP), a key component of Public Law 94-142, and now Public Law 99-147 (known as the IDEA), provides the means by which this mandate can be operationalized.

For consumers and professionals involved with secondary and postsecondary schooling, the individualized transition plan (ITP) is the most relevant individualized program. It grew out of a concern for providing transitional services to students with special needs as they move from the public school to community agencies or in the world of work. Section 626 (Secondary Education and Transitional Services for Handicapped Youth Act) was added to the Education of the Handicapped Act (1983), authorizing funds for research, training, and demonstration programs in the area of transition. The Education of the Handicapped Amendments of 1986 further renewed the emphasis on transitional services. The ITP may be part of the IEP, but if so, must be addressed differently.

The transition process, according to the law, should begin by the ninth grade and include "joint involvement of school personnel who have the responsibility for training and job procurement, as well as human service providers who could offer support and follow-up during the student's adulthood" (Wehman, Moon, Everson, Wood, & Barcus, 1988). The student is considered a vital member of the ITP team.

Siperstein (1988) advocates the development of individualized college plans (ICP) for students in secondary programs who are planning to attend a postsecondary academic program. Because the needs of a student planning for college will be somewhat different from those of students considering more employment goals, the ICP is more specific to postsecondary academic goals.

The individual written rehabilitation plan (IWRP) is the formal tool used by the rehabilitation counselor and the client to develop a written plan of action. As with the ITP and ICP, the IWRP stresses the needs of a single individual—the consumer. Statements are to be consistently provided in all of these plans.

Empirical research investigating the efficacy of the ITP, ICP, and the IWRP for consumers with learning disabilities is a critical need in the fields of special education and vocational rehabilitation. Recommendations from the literature advocate the need for more and better in-service (Nadler & Shore, 1980) and preservice training (Schenck, 1981) and greater coordinated compliance enforcement (Dodaro & Savenmini, 1985). In addition, Dowdy (1994) stresses that "policies, processes, and procedures of a state VR [vocational rehabilitation] agency must be flexible enough to accommodate and respond to the unique dimensions of each client's rehabilitation needs" (p. 176). The National Longitudinal Transitional Study data (Wagner, 1992) for adolescents with learning disabilities indicates that outcomes for such individuals are not being effectively addressed particularly related to issues of diversity, in either ITPs or IWRPs.

ACCOMMODATION AND MODIFICATIONS

An institution or place of employment is required to make reasonable accommodation to any individual meeting the legal criteria for learning disabilities. By law, the term "accommodation" is a deliberately flexible standard to incorporate the different types of learning disabilities that individuals may demonstrate. A reasonable accommodation for one individual will not be the same as for another because of such factors as severity and type of learning disability. The appropriateness of accommodation for an individual must be evaluated on its own facts and merits (ADA, 1990).

What Is Meant by Reasonable Accommodation?

The Rehabilitation Act (1973) clearly set the stage for our current definitions and interpretations of reasonable accommodation. It mandated that employers that receive federal funds provide appropriate accommodation and modifications to qualified individuals. Future litigation related to the ADA will help to clearly define some of the gray areas related to determining appropriate accommodation and modifications. Under the ADA, accommodation and modifications are often referred to as methods of providing program access. Two definitions of reasonable accommodation that may help consumers and professionals are listed in Table 15.5.

The definition and discussion of reasonable accommodation in the ADA focuses on three positions in the employment process. The three positions include the following:

1. accommodations that are required to ensure equal opportunity in the application process;
2. accommodations that enable the employer's employees with disabilities to perform the essential functions of the position held or desired; and
3. accommodations that enable the employer's employees with disabilities to enjoy equal benefits and privileges of employment as are enjoyed by employees without disabilities. (Fed. Reg. 1991, p. 35,744)

According to some professionals, it might be more helpful to conceptualize reasonable accommodation as a type rather than a position in the employment process (Michaels, 1989; Young & Michaels, 1986). Using this model, Michaels (1989) identified three

TABLE 15.5. Definitions of Reasonable Accommodation

" . . . is a modification or adjustment made to the job application process, the work environment, the operational practices, and/or the conditions affecting the employee's ability to enjoy the benefits and privileges of employment" (Weyman, 1993, p. xxvii).

" . . . modification or adjustments to the work environment, or to the manner or circumstances under which the position held or desired is customarily performed, that enable a qualified individual with a disability to perform the essential functions of that position" (*Federal Register*, July 26, 1991, p. 35,735).

---

types of reasonable accommodation: "(1) environmental modifications—removal of architectural barriers; (2) equipment modifications—provision of assistive devices and special tools; and (3) procedural modifications—restructuring tasks, altering work methods and changing work schedules" (p. 71). For many adults with learning disabilities, Michaels's items (2) and (3) are the major types of reasonable accommodation most necessary to adjust academic or work situations.

The government, however, when writing the ADA was concerned that professionals focus on the process of identifying types of reasonable accommodation. Negotiating appropriate and reasonable accommodation will be a process, specific to each individual, that requires the input of consumers, advocacy groups, rehabilitation counselors, special education professionals, and the business community. The Equal Employment Opportunity Commission (EEOC) in this process has been one of problem solver and negotiator (Wehman, 1993). Congress suggested the following steps to facilitate the implementation of accommodation:

1. Identify barrier(s) to equal opportunity;
2. Identify possible accommodations;
3. Assess the reasonableness of accommodations in terms of effectiveness and equal opportunity;
4. Implement the most appropriate accommodation that does not impose undue hardship on the employer, or permit the employee to provide his or her own accommodations. (S. Rep. 116, 1989)

Do Employers Have to Provide an Accommodation for an Individual with Learning Disabilities?

Under the ADA, employers do not have to provide a particular accommodation if it would impose an undue hardship on the operation of the business. Undue hardship refers to any action that requires significant difficulty or expense in relation to the size of the employer, the resources available, and the nature of the operation. Several of the factors that would be considered when making a decision whether an accommodation would cause an employer undue hardships would be (1) the nature and net cost of the accommodation, (2) the financial resources of the facility making the accommodation, (3) the type of operation of the facility, and (4) the impact on facility operations if an accommodation would be provided to a consumer.

The ADA made it clear, however, that an employer may not claim undue hardship simply because the cost of accommodation is high in relation to an employee's salary. In addition, an employer may not claim undue hardship solely because it has a negative impact on the morale of other employees or because of disruption due to employees' fears about, or prejudices toward, a person's disability. An employer can, however, consider the impact of an accommodation on the ability of other employees to do their jobs.

What Are Examples of Reasonable Accommodations?

Consumers and professionals must always keep in mind that accommodation is determined on a case-by-case basis. Employers, as well as consumers, have rights provided by the ADA. It is up to the employer to determine the essential functions of a given job and to insist that only qualified persons be hired for a specific job. A person is considered qualified for a job if (1) he or she meets the necessary prerequisites for the job (e.g., education work experience, training, skills, and licenses or certificates) and (2) he or she can perform the essential functions of the job with or without reasonable accommodation. The burden is on the employer to show that a job duty is an essential function if it screens out an applicant with a disability. In addition, there is nothing in the ADA that prohibits employers from choosing the least expensive or most convenient accommodation. Some examples of types of reasonable accommodations are:

1. Reallocating or redistributing marginal job functions.
2. Altering when or how essential functions are performed.
3. Using part-time or modified work schedules.

4. Providing qualified readers or note takers.
5. Permitting use of accrued paid or unpaid leave.
6. Modifying modes of communication.
7. Modifying how training information is acquired.
8. Allowing individuals to provide their own accommodations.

Future litigation will be needed to determine the limits of the right to make use of self-accommodation (Grossman, 1994). Two important guides to help consumers and professionals interpret accommodation under ADA are the *Technical Assistance Manual for the Americans with Disabilities Act* (EEOC, 1992) and the *Technical Assistance Manuals Title II and III* (Department of Justice, 1992).

Are There Other Sources to Develop Accommodation and Modifications for Academic or Employment Settings?

The Job Accommodations Network (JAN) is an excellent resource for both consumers and professionals to get information related to types of accommodation and modifications appropriate for different individuals. Established in 1983 as a service of the President's Committee on Employment of People with Disabilities, JAN is an information network and consulting resource for qualified workers with disabilities. Businesses, rehabilitation professionals, and persons with disabilities can discuss their concerns and information needs with JAN's consultants and receive immediate suggestions on solutions to accommodation problems. JAN offers comprehensive information on methods and equipment that have proven effective for a wide range of accommodation.

Means (1994) reported that of the calls JAN has received during 1994 regarding learning disabilities and college, approximately 57% were about accommodation for the college program—whether schools have specific programs for learning disabilities, how the current college program could be modified, and the kinds of assistive devices that may benefit the college student with learning disabilities. Twenty-nine percent of the questions were about rights as college students under the ADA, and 18% concerned specific testing accommodations.

What Are the Limits of a Consumer to Make Use of Self-Accommodation?

For many successful adults with learning disabilities self-accommodation has constituted a mark of growth. Legal experts are seeking an interpretation of just what the limits are of the right to make use of self-accommodation. Future litigation will help consumers and professionals better understand this issue.

EMPLOYMENT AND POSTSECONDARY LITIGATION RELATED TO ADULTS WITH LEARNING DISABILITIES

Litigation surrounding adults with learning disabilities focuses on two specific arenas: academic programs and employment. Several excellent sources (i.e., Rothstein, 1993; Grossman, 1994) provide in-depth legal critiques of the recent cases and the decisions rendered by the courts related to adults with learning disabilities. Table 15.6 summarizes the results of some of the most recent cases affecting legal decisions related to the adult population with learning disabilities. The higher education cases appear to address issues of reasonable accommodation for an academic program of study, undue hardship on an institution providing reasonable accommodation, testing accommodation, and whether the institution bears responsibility for an instructor who refuses to allow an accommodation. In the area of employment, the cases focus on job functions and the impact of the disability, entry examinations and appropriate testing accommodation, communications, and appropriate job accommodation. It appears that, in the future, more legal cases will focus on issues of appropriate and reasonable tests, academic programs, and job accommodation for adults with learning disabilities. Grossman (1994) encourages consumers and professionals to "press the case that its members are included within the definition of disabled even for individual who are high functioning in some skill areas" (p. 34). Certainly, future research and professional training are needed to better understand and serve higher-functioning adults with learning disabilities.

FUTURE DIRECTIONS

The direction of economic forces are moving from what Reich (1991) calls a high-volume focus to a high-value focus. "In the high-value enterprise, profits derive not from scale and volume but from continuous discovery of new linkages between solutions and needs" (Reich, 1991, p. 85). Those of us interested in ensuring that adults with learning disabilities are prepared to meet the demands of the future world must be careful not to overrely on past directives, thus

TABLE 15.6. Select Historical Litigation Relevant to the Adult Population with Learning Disabilities

Case	Legal issue	Interpretation
Southeastern Community College v. Davis (1979)	*Higher education* • Admissions/ reasonable accommodation	*Question:* • Must an individual be qualified to perform essential requirements of a program despite disability? *Decision:* • School does not need to provide fundamental alterations to program.
United States v. Board of Trustees (1990)	*Higher education* • Undue hardship	*Question:* • Must a college ensure such auxiliary aids as taped text? *Decision:* • College may not use financial need of student as determiner for service.
Doe. v. New York University (1981)	*Higher education* • Safety	*Question:* • Concern related to safety of clients served if accommodation made for plaintiff. *Decision:* • College supported in concern over safety. • Plaintiff lost.
Salvador v. Bell (1986)	*Higher education* • Identification	*Question:* • Is college responsible if student has not identified self as LD? *Decision:* • University does not violate Section 504 when it does not know an individual is LD.

(*continued*)

TABLE 15.6. (*continued*)

Case	Legal issue	Interpretation
Wynne v. Tufts University (1991)	*Higher education* • Testing and accommodation	*Question*: • Is university compelled to utilize a specific test format? *Decision*: • Court did not compel Tufts Medical School to use a particular test format.
Dinsmore v. University of California (1990)	*Higher education* • Accountability of institution	*Question*: • Is college responsible for an instructor who refuses to allow an accommodation? *Decision*: • No reported opinion.
Di Pompo v. West Point (1991)	*Employment* • Job function • Safety	*Question*: • Impact of disability on essential functions of job role. *Decision*: • Reading was essential to the job requirements of specific case. • Plaintiff lost.
Fitzgerald v. Green Valley Area Educational Agency (1984)	*Employment* • Job function	*Question*: • Impact of disability on essential job role. *Decision*: • Driving not an essential function of specific case. • Plaintiff won.
Pandazides v. Virginia Board of Education (1992)	*Employment* • Testing accommodation • Test bias	*Question*: • Whether National Teachers Examination (NTE) discriminated against a person with LD.

(*continued*)

TABLE 15.6. (*continued*)

Case	Legal issue	Interpretation
		Decision: • In this case NTE did not discriminate. • Plaintiff lost.
Stutts v. Freeman (1993)	*Employment* • Testing accommodation on entrance examinations	*Question*: • Whether General Aptitude Battery (GAB) used for entry into a job discriminated against individual with dyslexia. *Decision*: • Required accommodation/modifications on test be provided. • Plaintiff won.
Sedor v. Postmaster General (1991)	*Employment* • Reasonable accommodation	*Question*: • Modification of due process dismissal procedures as a necessary reasonable accommodation. *Decision*: • Employer knowing employee has communication difficulties must take steps to address communication deficiency before holding employee responsible for communication.
American Fed. Gov't. Employees, Local 51 v. Baker, (1987/1992)	*Employment* • Accommodation	*Question*: • Whether organization of work affected job performance and required specific accommodation.

(*continued*)

TABLE 15.6. (*continued*)

Case	Legal issue	Interpretation
		Decision: • Employer cannot fire an employee until it hired an expert "with training and experience or job analysis, job restructuring and making accommodations to employees regarding accommodations." • Plaintiff won.
Nelson v. Thornburgh (1983/1984/1985)	*Employment* • Accommodation • Methodology for determining undue burden.	*Question*: • Are readers an accommodation? *Decision*: • Readers are a reasonable accommodation. • Plaintiff won.

diverting us from new linkages and solutions (Gregg, 1994). The passport to the future will require consumers and professionals from various disciplines to work cooperatively to provide access for all adults with learning disabilities to the tools and information available to them. Interagency and interdisciplinary collaboration are no longer a choice but, rather, the mandate for the future. Future policy directives need to better address three specific areas: (1) consumer empowerment, (2) underserved populations, and (3) funding and eligibility issues.

Changes in federal and state policy over the last few decades have led to greater participation of consumers in all phases of research and services. The Constituency-Oriented Research and Dissemination (CORD) policy, put into practice by the National Institute on Disability and Rehabilitation Research, has been a way to integrate the expertise of consumers, researchers, and practitioners. The focus of all future policy, research, and training activities related to the adult population with learning disabilities should be CORD-driven, utilizing methodology that ensures validity in answers and solutions (Gregg, in press). CORD-driven practices ensures valid solutions arrived at through applied research and the creation of alternative services to current practices and policy. All research and training projects funded by state and federal agencies should mandate the use of a CORD-like policy, including the National Institutes of Health, the Department of Labor, and the Department of Education.

Future policy must better address issues of gender, race, and culture. Multicultural issues (see Ross-Gordon, Chapter 5, this volume) have received little attention from professionals and consumer advocacy groups. Gregg (1994) discusses the gender inequities for females with learning disabilities in both academic and employment settings. In particular, women from minority backgrounds are the least served by current programs for adults with learning disabilities. Female students with learning disabilities are significantly more likely to be from minority and ethnic backgrounds (62%) than are male students (31%) (Wagner, 1992). The greater severity of disabilities and the minority status of females students with learning disabilities relative to males suggest that females might be more at risk for poor transition outcomes than are males (Wagner, 1992). Another group of underserved females with learning disabilities is the population of adults receiving welfare. A 1988 study for the Assistant Secretary for Planning and Evaluation (ASPE) on functional impairments of clients receiving services from Aid to Families with Dependent Children (AFDC) determined that nearly one in four women on AFDC under the age of 45 report themselves as functionally impaired in contrast to one in 11 non-AFDC women. A study completed in 1992 for the ASPE by Child Trends, Inc., evaluated AFDC mothers as potential employees (Functional Impairments, 1992). This study concludes that most of these women have a limited education, score below average on verbal and math skills tests, have had little work experience, are long-term welfare recipients, and report histories of learning disabilities and substance abuse.

Another underserved group for which future policy and research are critical is the adjudicated adolescent and adult population. Research findings document that a large percentage of these individuals demonstrate learning disabilities (Brier, 1994; Broder, Dunivant, Smith, & Sutton, 1981; Young, Pappenfort, & Malow, 1983). According to Brier (1989), approximately 30% to 50% of the adjudicated adolescent and adult population demonstrate learning disabilities. Future research funds should be channeled toward exploring the factors, social or cognitive, that contribute to individuals with learning disabilities being at risk for delinquent behavior (Gregg, 1994). Policy is required to guide professionals in the provision of appropriate assessment and services for such individuals.

The third area requiring greater leadership on the part of consumers and professional is related to definitions, appropriate accommodation and modifications, and eligibility criteria. Research should be funded that will explore how states are complying with the Carl D. Perkins Vocational and Applied Technology Education Act of 1990, Job Training Partnership Act, the Rehabilitation Act, Individuals with Disabilities Educational Act, and the American with Disabilities Act in relation to the population of individuals with learning disabilities. State and federal agencies should clarify contradictory or confusing polices and mandates (Gregg, 1994). In particular, there is a need for close examination of the financial investment of state governments with respect to providing services to adults with learning disabilities.

Future research and policy agendas for the adult population with learning disabilities require a life-span and life-space perspective (Szymanski, 1994). A life-span approach to issues facing the adult population with learning disabilities identifies the need for a longitudinal perspective in solving problems. Life space acknowledges the many life roles in which an adult participates (student, citizen, worker, partner, etc.) and encourages an ecological approach to habilitation and rehabilitation (Szymanski, Dunn, & Parker, 1989). Finally, the policy and research directives of the future must provide better solutions to the issues of inclusion, diversity, and leadership for the adult population with learning disabilities.

The changes to legislation and those agencies responsible for carrying out the directives of the policies generated by such legislation, has and will continue to be significant in the future. With philosophical changes in the way that services are provided in the future, policy will need to be revised to remain consistent with state and federal mandates. More power is being directed to state control through block grants. Such a change from federal to state governmental control will certainly have an impact on the quality and quantity of services to the adult population with learning disabilities. Professionals and consumers will need to remain informed of the various changes underway. In addition, it will be imperative that professionals and consumers become politically active in their state to insure that the rights of adults with learning disabilities remain protected.

REFERENCES

American Fed. Gov't Employees, Local 51 v. Baker, 677 F. Supp. 636 (N.D. Cal. 1987), *remanded*, 1992 WESTLAW 191099 (N.D. Cal. Jan. 28, 1992).

American Psychiatric Association. (1994). *Diagnostic and statistical manual of mental disorders* (4th ed.). Washington, DC: Author.

American Psychological Association (1992). *Ethical principles of psychologists and code of conduct.* Washington, DC: Author.

American Psychiatric Association. (1980). *Diagnostic and statistical manual of mental disorders* (3rd ed.). Washington, DC: Author.

Americans with Disabilities Act of 1990, 42 U.S.C.A. §§§§ 12101 et seq. (West, 1993).

Association for Children with Learning Disabilities. (1986, September-October). ACLD description: Specific learning disabilities. ACLD *Newsbriefs*, pp. 15–16.

Biller, E. F., & White, W. J. (1989). Comparing special education and vocational rehabilitation in persons with specific learning disabilities. *Rehabilitation Counseling Bulletin, 33*, 4–17.

Brier, N. (1989). The relationship between learning disabilities and delinquency: A review and reappraisal. *Journal of Learning Disabilities, 22*, 546–553.

Brier, N. (1994). Targeted treatment for adjudicated youth with learning disabilities: Effects on recidivism. *Journal of Learning Disabilities, 4*, 215–222.

Broder, P. K., Dunivant, N., Smith, E. C., & Sutton, L. P. (1981). Further observations on the link between learning disabilities and juvenile delinquency. *Journal of Educational Psychology, 73*, 838–850.

Brown, D. S., Gerber, P. J., & Dowdy, C. (1990). *Pathways to employment for people with learning disabilities: A plan for action.* Paper presented at the President's Committee on Employment of People with Disabilities, Washington, DC.

Carl D. Perkins Vocational and Applied Technology Education Act Amendments of 1990, Public Law 101-392, 104 Stat. 753 (1990).

Carl D. Perkins Vocational and Applied Technology Education Act of 1984, Public Law 98-524, 98 Stat 2435 (1984).

Chalfant, J. C. (1989). Diagnostic criteria for entry and exit from service: A national problem. In L. B. Silver (Ed.), *The assessment of learning disabilities* (pp. 1–25). Boston: Little, Brown.

Chetkovick, Toms-Barker, & Schlichman. (1989). *Evaluation of services provided for individuals with specific learning disabilities* (Final report). Washington, DC: U.S. Department of Education (Contract No. 300-87-00112).

Civil Rights Restoration Act of 1987, Public Law 100-259, 102 Stat. 28 (1988).

Department of Justice. (1992). *Americans with Disabilities Act of 1990, U.S.*

Department of Justice Technical Assistance Manuals Titles II and III. Washington, DC: Commerce Clearing House.

Dinsmore v. University of California, Berkeley (N.D. Cal. Sept. 23, 1990).

Di Pompo v. West Point Military Academy, 708 F. Supp. 540 (S.D.N.Y. 1989), 770 F. Supp. 887 (S.D.N.Y. 1991).

Dodaro, G. L., & Savenmini, A. N. (1985). *Implementation of P.L. 94-142 as it relates to handicapped delinquents in the District of Columbia.* Washington, DC: U.S. General Accounting Office.

Doe v. New York University, 666 F.2d 761 (2d Cir. 1981).

Dowdy, C. (1992). Identification of characteristics of specific learning disabilities as a critical component in the vocational rehabilitation process. *Journal of Rehabilitation, 58,* 51–54.

Dowdy, C., & Smith, T. E. C. (1994). Serving individuals with specific learning disabilities in the vocational rehabilitation system. In P. J. Gerber & H. B. Reiff (Eds.), *Learning disabilities in adulthood: Persisting problems and evolving issues* (pp. 171–178). Boston: Andover Medical.

Education for All Handicapped Children Act of 1975, Public Law 94-142, 89 Stat. *773* (1975.

Education of the Handicapped Act of 1983, §§ 626, Public Law 98-199, 97 Stat. *1357* (1983).

Equal Employment Opportunity Commission. (1992). *Technical assistance manual for the Americans with Disabilities Act.*

Federal Register, Vol. 46, No. 12, January 19, 1991, p. 5552.

Fitzgerald v. Green Valley Area Educational Agency, 589 F. Supp. 1130 (S.D. Iowa 1984).

Functional impairments of AFDC clients. (1992, March). *Report to the Department of Health and Human Services.* Washington, DC: Office of Inspector General.

Garfield, S. L. (1986). Problems in diagnostic classification. In T. Millon & G. L. Klerman (Eds.), *Contemporary directions in psychopathology: Toward the DSM-IV* (pp. 99–114). New York: Guilford Press.

Gerber, P. J. (1981). Learning disabilities and eligibility for vocational rehabilitation services: A chronology of events. *Learning Disability Quarterly, 4,* 442–425.

Gregg, N. (1992). Written expression disorders. In S. R. Hooper, G. W. Hynd, & R. E. Mattison (Eds.), *Developmental disorders: Diagnostic criteria and clinical assessment* (pp. 127–172). Hillsdale, NJ: Erlbaum.

Gregg, N. (1993, May 10). *Learning disabilities research and training center grant application* (C.F.R. §§ 352.32). Washington, DC: National Institute on Disability and Rehabilitation Research.

Gregg, N. (1994). Eligibility for learning disabilities rehabilitation services: Operationalizing the definition. *Journal of Vocational Rehabilitation, 4,* 86–95.

Gregg, N. (1994). *Adults with learning disabilities: Research directions leading toward inclusion, diversity and leadership in the new global economy.* Paper presented at the National Summit on Learning Disabilities, Washington, DC.

Gregg, N., & Hoy, C. (1987). Vocational rehabilitation needs of the nonverbal learning disabled adult. *Journal of Rehabilitation, 53*, 54–57.

Grossman, P. D. (1994). Developing issues for the learning disabled community under employment discrimination laws. In P. J. Gerber & H. B. Reiff (Eds.), *Learning disabilities in adulthood: Persisting problems and evolving issues* (pp. 20–45). Boston: Andover Medical.

Hammill, D. (1990). On defining learning disabilities: An emerging consensus. *Journal of Learning Disabilities, 23*, 74–84.

Hawks, R., Minskoff, E. H., Sautter, S., Sheldon, K. L., Steidle, E. F., & Hoffman, F. J. (1990). A model diagnostic battery for adults with learning disabilities. *Learning Disabilities: A Multidisciplinary Journal, 1*, 94–101.

Hooper, S. R. (1992). Epilogue: Developmental disorders. In S. R. Hooper, G. W. Hynd, & R. E. Mattison (Eds.), *Developmental disorders: Diagnostic criteria and clinical assessment* (pp. 283–289). Hillsdale, NJ: Erlbaum.

Hursch, N. C. (1989). Vocational evaluation with learning disabled students: Utilization guidelines for teachers. *Academic Therapy, 25*, 201–215.

Individuals with Disabilities Educational Act of 1990, Public Law 101-476, 104 Stat. 1142 (1990).

Interagency Committee on Learning Disabilities. (1987). Learning disabilities: A report to the U.S. Congress. Bethesda, MD: National Institutes of Health. (ERIC Document Reproduction Service No. ED 294 358)

Jarrow, J. (1992). *The ADA's impact on postsecondary education.* Washington, DC: Association on Higher Education and Disability.

Jasany v. U.S. Postal Serv., 755 F.2d 1244 (6th Cir. 1985).

Johnson, D. J., & Blalock, J. W. (1987). Summary of problems and needs. In D. J. Johnson & J. W. Blalock (Eds.), *Adults with learning disabilities: Clinical studies* (pp. 227–296). Orlando, FL: Grune & Stratton.

Kavale, K. A. (1987). Theoretical issues surrounding severe discrepancy. *Learning Disabilities Research, 3*, 12–20.

Keogh, B. K. (1983). Classification, compliance, and confusion. *Journal of Learning Disabilities, 16*, 455–460.

Keogh, B. K. (1986). Future of the LD field: Research and practice. *Journal of Learning Disabilities, 16*, 28–29.

Kochlor, C. (1990). Message from the project director: Policy crossroads for the 1990s. *Policy Network Newsletter,* pp. 1, 4, 19.

Martin, E. (1987). Developing public policy concerning "regular" or "special" education for children with learning disabilities. *Learning Disabilities Focus, 3*, 11–16.

Martin, E. W., Smith, M. A., & Zwerlein, R. A. (1985). Vocational rehabilitation and learning disabilities: The camel's nose is getting under the edge of the tent. In D. D. Duane & C. K. Leong (Eds.), *Understanding learning disabilities, International and multidisciplinary views* (pp. 167–178). New York: Plenum Press.

Means, C. (1994, October 21). *Job Accommodation Network, accommodation and modifications teleconference.* University of Georgia, Learning Disabilities Research and Training Center, Athens, GA.

Mercer, C. D., Hughs, C., & Mercer, A. R. (1985). Learning disabilities definitions used by state education departments. *Learning Disability Quarterly, 8,* 45–55.

Michaels, C. A. (1989). Employment: The final frontier—Issues and practices for persons with disabilities. *Rehabilitation Counseling Bulletin, 33,* 67–73.

Nadler, B., & Shore, K. (1980). Individualized education programs: A look at realities. *Education Unlimited, 2,* 30–34.

National Joint Committee on Learning Disabilities. (1987). Adults with learning disabilities: A call to action. *Journal of Learning Disabilities, 20,* 172–175.

Nelson v. Thornburgh, 567 F. Supp. 369 (E.D. Pa. 1983), *aff'd without opinion,* 732 F.2d 147 (3d Cir. 1984), *cert. denied,* 469 U.S. 1188 (3d Cir. 1985).

Pandazides v. Virginia Bd. of Educ., 946 F.2d 345 (4th Cir. 1991), 804 F. Supp. 794, (E.D. Va. 1992).

Rehabilitation Act of 1973, Public Law 93-112, 87 Stat. 355 (1973).

Rehabilitation Act Amendments of 1992, Public Law 102-569, §§ 106 506, Stat. 4344 (1992).

Rehabilitation Services Administration. (1981, July 27). *Memorandum from the task force on learning disabilities. Information memorandum RSA-IV-81-39.* Washington, DC: Author.

Reich, R. B. (1991). *The work of nations.* New York: Vintage Books.

Reschly, D. J. (1992). Mental retardation: Conceptual foundations, definitional criteria, and diagnostic operations. In S. Hooper, G. W. Hynd, & R. E. Mattison (Eds.), *Developmental disorders: Diagnostic criteria and clinical assessment* (pp. 127–172). Hillsdale, NJ: Erlbaum.

Reynolds, C. R. (1984–1985). Critical measurement issues in learning disabilities. *Journal of Special Education, 18,* 451–475.

Rogoff, B. (1989). *Apprenticeship in thinking: Cognitive development in social context.* New York: Oxford University Press.

Rothstein, L. F. (1993). Legal issues. In S. A. Vogel & P. B. Adelman (Eds.), *Success for college students with learning disabilities* (pp. 21–36). New York: Springer-Verlag.

Salvador v. Bell, 622 F. Supp. 438 (N.D. Ill. 1985), *aff'd,* 800 F. 2d 97 (7th Cir. 1986).

Sanchez, D. (1984). Where do we go from here: A look to the future in rehabilitation of learning disabled persons. *Journal of Rehabilitation, 51*(1), 80–88.

Schenck, S. U. J. (1981). The diagnostic/instructional link in individualized education programs. *Journal of Special Education, 14,* 337–345.

Secondary Education and Transitional Services for Handicapped Youth, Section 626 of the Education of the Handicapped Act Amendments of 1983, Pub. L. No. 98-199, 97 Stat. 1357 (1983).

Sedor v. Postmaster General, 756 F. Supp. 684 (D. Conn. 1991).

Senate Report on the Transition Amendment of 1983. (1989).

Shapiro, R. (1993). *No pity. People with disabilities forging a new civil rights movement.* New York: Times Books.

Siperstein, G. N. (1988). Students with learning disabilities in college: The need for a programmatic approach to critical transition. *Journal of Learning Disabilities, 21,* 431–436.

Southeastern Community College v. Davis, 442 U.S. 397 (1979).

Stanovich, K. E. (1992). Developmental reading disorder. In S. R. Hooper, G. W. Hynd, & R. E. Mattison (Eds.), *Developmental disorders: Diagnostic criteria and clinical assessment* (pp. 173–208). Hillsdale, NJ: Erlbaum.

Stutts v. Freeman, 694 F.2d 666 (11th Cir. 1983).

Szymanski, E. M. (1994). Transition: Life-span and life-space considerations for empowerment. *Exceptional Children, 60*(5), 402–410.

Szymanski, E. M., Dunn, C., & Parker, R. M. (1989). Rehabilitation of persons with learning disabilities: An ecological framework. *Rehabilitation Counseling Bulletin, 33,* 38–53.

Technology-Related Assistance for Individuals with Disabilities Act of 1988, Public Law 100-407, 102 Stat. 1044 (1988).

Technology-Related Assistance for Individuals with Disabilities Act Amendments of 1994, Public Law 103–218, 108 Stat. 50 (1994).

Torgesen, J. K. (1987). Thinking about the future by distinguishing between issues that have resolutions and those that do not. In S. Vaughn & C. Bos (Eds.), *Research in learning disabilities* (pp. 55–68). Boston: Little, Brown.

United States v. Board of Trustees of the University of Alabama, 908 F.2d 740 (11th Cir. 1990).

Vogel, S. (1993). The continuum of university responses to section 504 for students with learning disabilities. In S. A. Vogel & P. B. Adelman (Eds.), *Success for college students with learning disabilities* (pp. 83–113). New York: Springer-Verlag.

Wagner, M. (1992). Transition: Changes, challenges, cautions. In *What happens next? Trends in postschool outcomes of youth with disabilities* (pp. 4-1–4-6). Palo Alto, CA: SRI International.

Wehman, P. (1993). *The ADA mandate for social change.* Baltimore: Paul H. Brookes.

Wehman, P., Moon, M. S., Everson, J. M., Wood, W., & Barcus, J. M. (1988). *Transition from school to work: New challenges for youth with severe disabilities.* Baltimore: Paul H. Brookes.

Wodatch, J. (1994). Public policy and legislation. Paper presented at the National Summit on Learning Disabilities, Washington, DC.

Wynne v. Tufts University, School of Medicine, 932 F.2d 19 (1st Cir. 1991).

Young, J., & Michaels, C. A. (1986). *The hidden resource: Tapping the potential of workers with learning disabilities.* Albertson, NY: Human Resources Center.

Young, T. M., Pappenfort, D. M., & Malow, C. R. (1983). *Residential group care, 1966–1981: Facilities for children and youth with special problem needs* (Preliminary report of selected findings from the national survey of residential group care facilities). Chicago: University of Chicago, School of Social Service Administration.

16

Facilitating Alternative
Learning Techniques
for Adults
with Learning Disabilities
through the Use of Technology

ALICE F. GAY

If someone asked you, "Have you ever used assistive technology?" more than likely, without thinking, you would reply no. Well, just think about it.

We all use it—and have ever since the beginning, when men and women fashioned tools to mash, cut, scrape, and hammer. It has not always been called assistive technology, but it has always been around. Assistive technology can be described as using a combination of knowledge and implements to practice thought processing or manual skills while collecting materials or information. This is exactly what our ancestors did when they discovered the process of creating fire to prepare food or to keep warm—used assistive technology to enhance their ability to function in daily living.

Today we think of such technology as it is related to the computer age rather than to the stone age, but in juxtaposition to our levels of advancement in comparison to cave dwellers, the impact on our civilization is just as great. Just a few years ago, no one would have dreamed that personal computers would be commonplace in the home or that facsimile machines would change the routine course of a business day.

Watching young children sit down in front of a computer and begin searching the keyboard without hesitation shows us that technology can be easily conquered. Once we get used to the idea that using a computer or sending a fax is not intimidating, we are able to feel comfortable about further approaching technology.

We have all come to think of these changes as simple ways to make our methods of doing things easier, faster, and more efficient, but we do not think of it as assistive technology. Yet, each advancement toward using technological implements to assist us in accomplishing our tasks at hand is, in fact, just that.

Because we all use various means of assistive technology in many aspects of our lives, it is important for us to feel comfortable about the technology and its various delivery systems ourselves while promoting its use to others.

We hear about distance education, interactive television, electronic mail (e-mail), satellite downlinks, multimedia presentations, all of which sound intimidating. But they are here to stay—just like the first frightening fire power millions of years ago.

DEFINING ASSISTIVE TECHNOLOGY SERVICES AND DEVICES

The key issue discussed in this chapter is how to use assistive technology—and how to help others use it—not only in the academic setting but in the total environment. Its impact doesn't discriminate based on environments, age, gender, race, religion, or disability; using an assistive technology device produces independence, productivity, and integration in all of us. It is the enabler, the equalizer, the enhancer. It gives the user an option, and it becomes the tool.

To illustrate that fact, Congress, in the Technology-Related Assistance for Individuals with Disabilities Act (1988, Public Law 100-407), defined an assistive technology device as "any item, piece of equipment, or product system, whether acquired commercially off the shelf, modified, or customized, that is used to increase, maintain, or improve functional capabilities of individuals with disabilities."

One purpose of the Technology-Related Assistance for Individuals with Disabilities Act Amendments (1994, Public Law 103-218) was to provide discretionary grants to states to assist them to develop and implement consumer-responsive programs of technology-related assistance (Bailey, 1994).

According to the 1990 National Health Interview Survey on assistive devices conducted by the Census Bureau, more than 1.3 million people, about 5.3 percent of the population, were using assistive technology in the United States. While over half of these individuals purchased the devices themselves, or with the help of their families, more than 2.5 million Americans reported that they need assistive devices they did not have. (Tools for Life, personal communication, May 23, 1994)

But this issue was also addressed under assistive technology services, as defined:

Any service that directly assists an individual with a disability in the selection, acquisition, or use of an assistive technology service. Such term includes: (a) the evaluation of needs . . . including a functional evaluation . . . in the individual's customary environment; (b) purchasing, leasing or otherwise providing for the acquisition of assistive technology devices . . . (c) selecting, designing, fitting, customizing, adapting, applying, maintaining, repairing, or replacing of assistive technology devices; (d) coordinating with other therapies, interventions, or services with assistive technology devices, such as those associated with existing education and rehabilitation plans and programs; (e) training or technical assistance for an individual with disabilities, or, where appropriate, [his or her] family . . . and (f) training or technical assistance for professionals (including individuals providing education and rehabilitation services), employers, or other[s] who provide services to, employ, or are otherwise, substantially involved in the major life functions of individuals with disabilities. (Technology-Related Assistance for Individuals with Disabilities Act, 1988, Public Law 100-407)

Of course, to provide these services, funding is always necessary. Title II of the Technology-Related Assistance for Individuals with Disabilities Act (1988) addresses that issue in regard to national funding programs. Funding sources for individuals, may be public agencies, private foundations, civic organizations, or low-interest loan programs. Innovative resources may be using recycled or borrowed equipment or creating homemade devices.

THE BENEFITS OF ASSISTIVE TECHNOLOGY FOR ADULTS WITH LEARNING DISABILITIES

Traditionally, technology has always been viewed as some type of machinery or equipment, increasing productivity and cutting costs.

Used in education, technology, as explained by Amandam (1986), "makes distance and time irrelevant to teaching and learning," but more interestingly, she observes that "technology makes us smarter, better human beings" (p. 66).

Technology is not just equipment. Technology in education is an instrument for expression and communication. It incorporates all the materials and types of presentations we can access, from the text-book lecture with the chalkboard and overhead projector to the tele-conference with videotapes, computers, and laser disks. It is a teach-ing device and a learning tool.

"Adults whose motivation for learning is very different from that of the traditional student" (Duning, Van Kekerix, & Saborowski, 1993, p. 69) are often the primary audience for technology-based educa-tion. The advantages of assistive technology for adults with learning disabilities are autonomy, flexibility, and independence in a variety of environments (e.g., educational, recreational, and work settings). Assistive technology allows these individuals to retrieve, send, and receive information. Hawkridge, Vincent, and Hayes (1985) make the following observation:

> For many disabled people, communication problems are at the heart of their disablement and central to their personal struggle to learn to overcome their disabilities. This is the true whether they are young or old, whether they are male or female, whether they are disabled from birth or become disabled later in life. They are often left isolated, powerless, and dependent. They are deprived of im-portant ways of expressing their individuality. (p. 1)

Not being able to communicate effectively often leads to years of academic failure for adults with learning disabilities. Raskind and Scott (1993) outline two approaches for academic success for postsecondary students with learning disabilities—compensation and remediation—noting that compensation seems to be more effective for this group. Compensatory techniques should also prove to be more effective for adults with learning disabilities who are not in an academic setting. First, these adults have probably had many years of such training, with varying degrees of success or, more likely, failure. Second, all adults outside an academic setting will not have the resources avail-able to them for remedial training. Third, adults will probably not spend the time needed for remedial training; they may have immedi-ate needs such as obtaining skills for job placement, training, or ad-vancement.

Using technology can offset some deficiencies experienced by adults with learning disabilities. The particular deficiency will not be improved, but the method of counterbalancing the deficiency will be redressed. As technology advances, at an unbelievable pace, ways to offset learning difficulties will increase significantly. Voegel (1986) notes that we, as a society, are continually producing ways to compress, expand, and transform thoughts, ideas, and information from one medium to another in almost any kind of format. It is important for adults with learning disabilities to know, however, that technology, no matter how good it sounds, is not a cure-all. Simpson (1985) observes:

> Provided that we understand the limitations of each technology as well at its capabilities, and more importantly, provided that we understand the people we are trying to educate and the kind of education we are trying to give them, we can use technology in ways that will really help. (p. 91)

Manipulating technology is a coping strategy for adults with learning disabilities. Learning the technology, no matter how rewarding, can also be a challenge. Regardless, however, using technology should result in a noticeable improvement in handling knowledge (Voegel, 1986). For adults with learning disabilities, not only does technology enable them to use some of the same resources as everyone else, other assistive devices and systems "enable them to do what they could not without" (Hawkridge et al., 1985, p. 173).

Professionals need to realize that what works well for one student or client may not meet the needs of another. Adults with learning disabilities have individual needs; the technology introduced to the adult with learning disabilities should address a specific and immediate need, with an obvious connection between the function of the technology and the need of the adult (Raskind & Scott, 1993). Hawkridge et al. (1985) suggest asking two questions regarding the available technology: Can the technology improve communication and solve communication problems for the individual with the disability? Can the same devices and systems, or others specifically developed, meet the individual's needs? They outline three categories essential to consider in the needs assessment for adults with disabilities: the nature of the disability; the stage of the individual's intellectual, social, and physical development; and his or her educational level.

Voegel (1986) suggests that professionals utilize a systems approach by applying four components: (1) determining the adult's learning abilities, (2) developing instructional objectives in relation to curriculum, (3) utilizing instructional methods for appropriate student outcomes, and (4) monitoring a student's progress in relation to the previous three components.

ACCOMMODATION AND MODIFICATIONS
The Ins and Outs of Hardware

Lahm and Greszco (1988) divide hardware into two simple categories: input (information entering into the computer) and output (information coming out of the computer). Although the standard input method is through the computer's keyboard, alternative methods are what may be referred to as assistive technology devices (e.g., headpointers and voice recognition devices). Output devices may involve print, audio, telecommunications, or video.

Computers

Seeing the computer as a tool used to present a wide variety of media and learning material, Heinich, Molenda, and Russell (1989) list its advantages (1) instantaneous response to student input, (2) extensive capacity to store and manipulate information, and (3) ability to serve many individual students simultaneously. There is a need for educators and researchers not only to use computers but to understand their functions and instructional capabilities—to become computer literate. "Computer literacy involves knowledge, attitudes, and skills. Knowledge of hardware, software, and data-processing concepts is necessary as well as the applications of computers" (Heinich et al., 1989, p. 367).

Amandam (1986) sees computer technology as offering "educators the opportunity to shift their focus from teaching to learning" (p. 67) and lists among its advantages providing information in reduced time, being effective at raising the achievement of low-achieving students, and increasing motivation and attention span.

Recognizing the rapid change in how information (data, text, audio, visual) is disseminated, Cook (1988) sees the positive aspects of moving to a screen-based society:

> The value of the computer lies in its ability to manipulate many kinds of information under the control of the user, information that already exists as published software (from adventure games to physics simulations) and information that is entered directly by the user into a software tool (such as a word processor or a database manager). In an educational setting, it is the user's interaction

with the content of a computer program, in particular the degree of personal control of the information exchange, that sets the computer apart. Interaction requires involvement, which in turn can enhance the learning experience. (p. 220)

Adaptive Devices

Everyday, new and exciting adaptive devices are created in the technology world. They vary in complexity, cost, and availability. Using simple adaptive devices is often overlooked (e.g., using books on tape with a tape recorder, colored plastic overlays, and spell checkers for the allure of the new high-tech products). Often the best approach is to use a combination of both high- and low-tech tools. Vendors are becoming more willing to allow individuals to try out new devices before purchasing.

Currently some popular adaptive devices are widely recognized as effective for both adults with learning disabilities and those with dual diagnoses (e.g., having learning disabilities along with fine or gross motor skill difficulties or visual impairments) and are outlined by Green and Brightman (1990):

1. Key repeat eliminators shut off the repeat function of the keyboard, preventing rows of unwanted characters mistakenly entered by the individual with fine or gross motor skills.
2. Headpointers (on an adjustable headset) and mouthsticks can be used to press keys on the keyboard.
3. Keylatches (attached to the keyboard) allow more than one key at a time to be pressed when a program command requires it.
4. Keyguards (flat boards fitting over the keyboard) prevent the user from accidentally hitting more than one key at a time.
5. Keyboard mouse allows the user to control the mouse by using the numeric pad on the keyboard.
6. Head-controlled mouse (using a special headset) sends mouse signals to the computer, allowing the movement of one's head to control mouse functions.
7. Joysticks and trackballs are stationary alternatives to the traditional mouse and are easy to control.
8. Voice recognition system allows the user to control all functions of the computer by speaking into a microphone without any physical contact with the computer.
9. Large-size monitors may be a simple way to assist the user in seeing screen images more clearly, with the user keeping in mind that everything on the screen is enlarged, not just selected areas.

10. Hardware magnification lenses can be attached to most computer monitors to enlarge the screen image.
11. Large print processors allow the user to magnify selected graphic portions of the screen image on a second monitor,
12. Tactile output systems are of two types: one gives an exact tactile representation of letters and lines on the screen; the other uses a Braille display processor to convert the text on the screen into Braille.
13. Speech synthesizers produce sound by means of a phoneme generator, which converts written texts with artificial speech (Sammon, 1988).
14. Braille printers, connected to the computer utilizing special software, produce embossed text in Braille.

The Selection of Software

Although software may have a predetermined sequence of learning activities (Smith & Koep, 1988), attention to an individual's variables should be a consideration. Garrett and Dyke (1988) suggest that a good software program should have clear, documented objectives based on sound pedagogical principles, user-friendly operations for the individual's capabilities, and reasonable and immediate reactions for success during the learner's manipulation of the program.

Identifying key strengths and weaknesses of software, Anderson (1991) cites the following: (1) identification (type of program, target audience), (2) technical details (hardware required, printer, scanner), (3) ease of operation (screen readability, help functions), (4) enhancements (sound, speech, graphics, interactivity), (5) stated objectives (well-defined objectives), (6) content (accurate, appropriate, varied), (7) user orientation (alternative speeds or levels of operation), (8) interaction (stimulating, challenging), (9) cognitive level (knowledge, application, evaluation), (10) feedback (effective, appropriate), (11) evaluative teaching methods (pretest, posttest, recordkeeping, diagnostic testing), and (12) prerequisites (specific skills).

Software Programs

Software provides directions for operating and maneuvering the hardware, and as computers are more often being used in special education, both educators and researchers need to pose the following questions:

For which students, in what context, under what conditions, with what teacher interventions, and for what purpose is this piece of software appropriate? Choosing the right software for special education students demands as much care and attention as choosing any other course materials. Similarly, supporting good software with an appropriate teaching-learning environment is essential. (Russell, Corwin, Mokros, & Kapisovsky, 1989, p. 1)

Russell et al. (1989) advocate putting students in "control of learning activities, challenging them to be the ones to solve problems and have outlined characteristics of learner-centered software as follows (a) offers students choices in selecting the goal of an activity, the strategies to reach the goal, or both, (b) provides feedback that is informational rather than judgmental, (c) allows, emphasizes, or encourages prediction and successive approximation, and (d) encourages learning within a meaningful context for students, building on students' intrinsic motivation" (pp. 4–7).

Green and Brightman (1990) describe several categories of software available for individuals with specific impairments, keeping in mind that many individuals with learning disabilities are dually diagnosed; they may also have fine or gross motor skills difficulties or speech or visual impairments. Voice recognition software is available for those with motor skills difficulties; for speech impairments, software is available for talking, assessment, therapy, and alternative communication (e.g., speech reading, sign language, and finger spelling); for visual impairments, Braille, large print, and magnification software is available.

Although there is not specific software for individuals with learning disabilities, there is a variety of traditional educational software that can be used in such academic areas as reading, writing, math, and research. Word processing programs allow the user to compose and edit, with the assistance of a spell checker, grammar checker, and thesaurus. Writing software gives the user options with word prediction and allows for brainstorming; outlining programs help the individual to focus and organize thoughts. Spreadsheet programs provide a practical way to understand mathematical basics. Scheduling software assists individuals with learning disabilities in keeping track of tasks and appointments.

There are several programs (e.g., SuperCard, Allegiant Technologies; HyperStudio, Roger Wagner Publisher; Authorware Professional, Spinnaker Corporation; and ToolBook, Asymetrix Corporation) that not only offer ways to organize and display information but allow users to design and write their own applications without having to be computer programmers. HyperCard (Apple Computer), for example, presents information on the screen in the format of a card; a series of these cards is called a stack. Clicking buttons on the screen links one card with another; some of these buttons perform functions (e.g., playing sound and showing visuals). The user can modify existing stacks of cards or customize new ones by typing in data or adding illustrations. Markman (1988) describes HyperCard as a multimedia application that "simplifies the mechanics of creating presentations that students and teachers now can make this type of presentation a routine classroom activity" (p. 333).

Bissell (1990), working with both secondary and higher education institutions, found that multimedia technology appears to be effective because it does the following:

> (a) helps to make learning a genuinely active and interactive process; (b) offers simulated "real life" situations, which are interesting and meaningful to students; (c) facilitates immediate feedback to all students; (d) enhances cooperative learning, which is demonstrably valuable for students at all grade levels; (e) provides multiple representations of central curriculum content, increasing conceptual understanding and the likelihood that students with different prior experiences will be able to learn; (f) individualizes instruction, so that it addresses varying learning; (g) combines text, graphics, animation, still frames slides, moving video segments, and dual sound tracks in multiple languages so that learning need not be dependent on language alone; and (h) allows instruction to be designed around key concepts rather than being driven by textbooks at the expense of other resources. (p. 59)

Bowe (1984) observed that "in the past, the teaching of other subjects had to be delayed for several years while educators concentrated on the arduous task of instruction in reading" (p. 8). With the current integration of technology and knowledge skills, this is no longer the case. Individuals with learning disabilities can benefit from assistive technology in the development of memory, concentration, and organization, affecting all academic areas.

Resources

There are so many new resources available for the adult with learning disabilities that it can be a frustrating experience to search for special needs products. Adults with learning disabilities may find a software program that fits their needs and then realize that they do not have enough memory on their computer to operate the program. It takes an organized plan of action to sift through all the available product information. To alleviate this time-consuming and confusing task, there are several resource guides currently on the market to assist both the professional and the consumer in making choices regarding assistive technology.

Lazzaro (1993) has organized a checklist for individuals to determine the type of equipment and software that best fits their needs, along with technical requirements (e.g., brands, memory, and hardware). Providing a comprehensive list of hardware and software, he divides adaptive technologies into the following system categories: speech synthesis, magnification, Braille, optical character recognition, Baudot/ASCII modem, beep indicator software, computerized sign language training, adapted keyboard, keyboard modification software, alternative input systems; voice recognition, and alternative communications devices.

Brandenburg and Vanderheiden (1987) cross-reference adaptive technological devices and software (e.g., management, recreation, and personal tools) with product name and vendor. Along with a description and cost, each product listed tells the user what type of computer is needed and the manual format (print, audiotape).

Providing one of the most inclusive resource guides, McCormick (1994) not only looks at assistive technology products for those with learning disabilities and multiple disabilities but furnishes a comprehensive list of resources, including the full text of the Americans with Disabilities Act of 1990.

DISTANCE EDUCATION AND LEARNING THROUGH TELECOMMUNICATIONS

Teaching and Learning Processes

Distance learning only used to consist of correspondence courses in which the adult would register for a course, receive lessons, return completed assignments, and get instructor feedback, grades, and certification—all by mail. Today, distance education can be accomplished through the use of interactive television, satellites, computer network systems, and desktop videoteleconferencing. All these media employ assistive technology, including both hardware and software.

Verduin and Clark (1991) identify several educational systems that deliver distance education to adult learners: (1) postsecondary educational institutions offering college degrees to new students, (2) postsecondary educational institutions offering degrees to previous students, (3) conventional universities that offer independent study or continuing education credits, (4) consortia of education-related institutions providing common distance education courses, and (5) educational media developed by educational organizations and used by distance learners without the assistance of an educational organization or institution.

Adults with learning disabilities can employ one or a combination of these systems in the distance learning process; Frick (1991) states that "education occurs in an environment consisting of the surrounding community and its culture" (p. 16). He believes that education cannot occur without a teacher, "but a teacher can guide without instructing directly" (p. 14). Reinforcing that technology conveys the message while a teacher supplies the content, Frick restructures the educational system using six modules with flexible boundaries and schedules. In each module, with the use of both technology devices and worldwide access to information, the teacher becomes the manager of the student's learning experiences while the student controls his or her learning pace.

Tobin (1988) states that "those with learning disabilities have different cognitive processing problems and must be diagnosed and instructed based on individual needs" (p. 146). Hansen (1984) agrees, seeing individualized teaching as "one of the few unambiguous common features of special eduction" requiring the following effective individual educational material characteristics:

1. It should be able to motivate the pupil to start a given educational sequence and to maintain his motivation until the sequence is completed.
2. It should be adaptable to the *cognitive* level of the individual pupil, so that the optimum relationship is generated between the pupil's current achievement potential and the level demanded by the given learning situation.
3. It should place the pupil in a perceptual situation, where a maximum of sensory learning paths are activated, and it should ensure particularly that pupils with reduced or lost sensory functions have the possibility to learn by means of the functions that are still intact.
4. It should ensure that the pupil feels *emotionally* secure in the learning situation, balanced between relaxed confidence and dynamic learning, so that the learning element forms a harmonic part of the multifaceted development of personality.
5. Despite its individual starting point, it must be well-suited for integration into the overall educational planning of the group or class, so that it also has a positive influence on the pupils' social development.
6. To the extent appropriate, it should be able to challenge the pupil's *motor function* so that learning is followed and supported by ac-

> tion in the presentation and processing in response to a learning
> task. (p. 25)

Each of Hansen's criteria can be accomplished using assistive technology, and the advance of such distance learning delivery systems as
desktop videoteleconferencing and e-mail instruction can promote
individualized materials. The materials should be appropriately designed and presented for the learner's cognitive framework (Purdy,
1986).

Purdy (1986) sees the problem for distance learning in the challenge of individuals "to think and reason, to respond actively and
critically to the course" (p. 10). Purdy suggests that courses should
(1) have clear, concise, interesting and flexible components; (2)
achieve academic standards including accuracy, objectivity, and com-
pleteness; (3) include important, exciting, and relevant subjects; and
(4) be supported by appropriate student services by the educational
institutions.

Instructional Design and Development

To achieve Purdy's objective of producing "quality materials that utilize the qualities of the medium" (p. 11). One should look at instructional design and development. According to Ely, LeBlanc, and Yancy
(1989), both design and development involve (1) needs assessment,
(2) task analyses, (3) learner characteristics, (4) message design, (5)
product development, and (6) motivational strategies.

Ely et al. (1989) define instructional design as that which relates
to the product itself, focusing on "artificial intelligence, expert systems, interactive video, and problem solving" (p. 10). It is the device
that delivers the information. Holmberg (1989) stresses the importance of instructional design in the development of course materials
as "a system for bringing reasonable expectations, experiences, and
insights into useful order" (p. 20).

Knirk and Gustafson (1986) stress that the following data are
needed to provide effective individualized instruction for the learner:
(1) information-processing style (e.g., need for materials that involve
redundancy, positive reinforcement, self-pacing, and tactile activities), (2) use of senses for perception or reception of stimuli (e.g.,
preferences for motion, visual, auditory stimuli); (3) emotional needs
(e.g., expressive reinforcement, self-motivation, perseverance, and
sense of responsibility), (4) social needs (e.g., peer socialization and
peer approval), and (5) physical and emotional needs, real or felt
(e.g., noise levels, room temperature, and time of day).

Telecourses and Presentations

One of the most important aspects of instructional development involves distance education and course development (Ely et al., 1989). Garrison (1989) states, "The regularity, immediacy, and naturalness of communication by teleconferencing also makes possible a full range of instructional techniques" (p. 61).

According to a study by Aslanian and Brichell (cited in Duning et al., 1993), adults choose a telecourse because of (1) its nearby location, (2) type of program, (3) low cost, and (4) academic quality.

Holmberg (1989) finds that "many adults prefer distance study to other forms of learning because they feel it makes them more independent" (p. 25). Ironically, most educators who resist using electronic technologies while teaching do so because they lack know-how and feel a loss of control and privacy (Duning et al., 1993). However, as Azarmsa (1993) points out, "Teleconferencing is not intended to replace the classroom teacher, but rather, to extend the classroom beyond the immediate walls" (p. 156).

Communications, either one-way or two-way, can be offered in both direct and mediated deliveries. According to Garrison (1989), lectures (direct) and broadcast (moderated) are examples of one-way communications; and face-to-face dialogue (direct) and teleconferencing (mediated) are two-way communications. He further breaks down mediated communication into real and simulated:

> Real forms of mediated communications include telephone (immediate) and electronic mail (delayed). In both these examples, there is an individual reacting to a transmitted message. In a simulated conversation one does not really communicate with another person. Responses have been programmed which are contingent on the message received. (pp. 21–22)

In addition to using teleconferencing for teaching, it is advantageous for in-service training and development. Teleconferencing is also useful for updating timely information and providing inexpensive training for large groups. Azarmsa (1993) suggests such other uses for professionals as receiving credentials through special programming, interacting with several sites, watching different models of teaching at several schools, and visiting other facilities by means of an electronic field trip.

Program Delivery

Azarmsa (1993) identifies three elements in a telecommunications system: transmitter or source, medium, and destination or receiver.

She illustrates, "In a classroom, for example, the instructor can be a source, the students are the destinations, and the lecture is the medium" (p. 44). Including the basic components of hardware, software, data, procedures, and personnel, Azarmsa (1993) defines telecommunications as "a process of transmitting information over a distance by an electrical or electromagnetic system. This information may take the form of voice, data, image, or message" (p. 2). She adds, however, that there must be some involvement, understanding, and interpretation on the part of the receiver to complete the exchange of information and ensure communication.

Program Content

Holmberg (1989) sees the following as essential functions of course materials: (1) to arouse attention and to motivate, (2) to share expected student outcomes, (3) to integrate previous knowledge and interest, (4) to present the material to be learned, (5) to guide and structure, (6) to activate, (7) to provide feedback, (8) to promote transfer, and (9) to facilitate retention.

Preparing the lesson, graphics, and activities is important, but Portway and Lane (1992) point out that one of the most important features of the program should include planned interaction strategies when utilizing content materials.

Program Instruction

There often seems to be more of an interest in providing stimulating visual presentations in a telecourse than in the traditional classroom, as if the distance learner bores more easily than the regular classroom participant. Fortunately, for all learners, there is exciting educational technology that can be integrated into the delivery of instruction. This chapter lists only a few examples.

CD-ROM. CD-ROM (Compact Disc Read-Only Memory) not only has an enormously large storage capacity (the equivalent of almost 300,000 printed pages) but "the unique ability of integrating text, complex graphics, voice and images at relatively low costs . . . " (Sammon, 1988, p. 186). Storing its information in digital bits, compact discs are an economic way to store text, images, and sound. Although limited in its live motion capabilities, CDs are an excellent way to provide a vast amount of data in an interactive format.

Videotapes. Initially used only for broadcast, videotape was costly and cumbersome (Gano, 1988). Today, videocassette recorders (VCR) in the home are commonplace. Consumers frequently use VCRs to tape and watch movies and, with the introduction of simple operating compact video cameras, can make and edit their own movies. This widespread familiarity with video equipment has greatly enhanced educational activities, giving instructors and students interactive opportunities.

Videodiscs. A laser videodisc is similar in size to a long-playing record, storing up to 54,000 frames on each side. Sounds and images are presented in an analog or continuous form.

Unlike playing a videotape, one can quickly and precisely jump to various positions on the disc; labeling it "a random access" medium. Being practically indestructible, thus a prime archival source, Gano (1988) lauds the use of the videodisc, "Random access, coupled with stable still frame and variable-speed play, allows people to probe and peruse a videodisc as they might a book" (p. 256). He also sees it as the "potent technology" because videodiscs can play moving images as well as store high-density digital information (e.g., compact discs).

Combining the videodisc and the computer, Garrison (1989) observes that it "makes it possible to develop computer assisted learning materials that combine the logical control and flexibility of computer software with the audio–visual characteristics of the laser videodisc" (p. 87).

Netta and Staub (1988) give the following advantages of the laser videodisc:

1. It is easy to use.
2. The disc will not wear; it is robust and reliable
3. Each item of information is clearly identified via frame and section numbers.
4. It can be cross-referenced to written material via unambiguous addresses.
5. Each item of information can be accessed directly.
6. Search times are extremely short.
7. It allows high speed perusal (scanning).
8. Frames can be frozen at any time and for any length of time. (scene-freezing).
9. Reproduction is extremely flexible.
10. It allows mass storage of individual frames and mixtures with films.
11. Moving sequences can be presented in compressed form by series of frames.
12. It has two separate sound channels.
13. It can be linked to external computers.

14. It can be used interactively as an instructor's aid or for self-teaching work stations. (pp. 179–180)

There are some definite disadvantages, however, in using videodiscs. It is an expensive medium and requires a computer, a monitor, and a laser disc player, and there are not a plethora of videodiscs available to the general public. Although Paine and McAra (1993) acknowledge that the videodisc remains supremely effective in delivering full-frame, full-color moving video, it is an "ageing rather than an advancing technology" (p. 51).

Virtual Reality. Virtual reality (VR) is a three-dimensional audio–visual interaction in which the user encounters a simulated, computer-generated experience. Paine and McAra (1993) identify two types: immersive and desktop. The immersive VR requires the individual to utilize a headset, which offers the user three-dimensional images and sounds generated and controlled by computers. Immersive VR provides the illusion of alternative environments. This type of VR is mostly used for entertainment.

With desktop VR, the user can participate in a real-time interactive experience by viewing a three-dimensional environment on a computer monitor. The desktop VR offers educational and vocational applications, by conveying "the correct visualization of objects and relationships within three-dimensional environments" (Paine & McAra, 1993, p. 53). Future applications using VR should be investigated for specific disabilities, especially in the areas of job training in the work place.

Program Method

Heinich et al. (1989) observe, "After years of slow growth, teleconferencing has become one of the fastest-growing segments of the telecommunications industry as more and more corporate and educational institutions embrace the teleconference as an efficient means of informing and educating their constituents" (p. 264).

Current technology offers several teleconferencing formats.

One-Way Video with Two-Way Audio. One-way video with two-way audio has been the most common form of teleconferencing. This format is used in the transmission and reception of satellite signals. A satellite dish transmitting the signal is an uplink. It is sending signals from earth up to the satellite. The satellite dish receiving a satellite signal is a downlink; it is receiving those signals from the satellite back to earth.

Now widely prevalent in industry, schools, and homes, satellite reception is becoming simpler and cheaper. A presentation in full-motion video, along with audio, is broadcast. Audio may be received back from other receptions sites via the telephone. The transmission of this type of teleconference is the most sophisticated and costly, requiring a studio setup with TV cameras, microphones, telephone, and speaker system for incoming telephone calls.

Two-Way Video with Two-Way Audio. Two-way video with two-way audio may be accomplished using the full-motion advantage of satellite if the selected locations serve as satellite uplink and down-link sites. Each is sending a signal up to the satellite and each, in turn, is receiving a downlink. Simply, to send messages, one has to uplink; to receive messages, one has to downlink.

Another method is using compressed video, converting analog signals to digital bits via the telephone. Some refer to this method as interactive television.

Interactive television is becoming a more popular form of tele-conferencing. Its advantages best fit the definition offered by Garrison (1989), "Of all the means used to support distance education, teleconferencing most closely simulates the transaction between teachers and students in a contiguous or conventional form of education" (p. 66). He further adds, "The exchange is conversation in nature, it may be spontaneous, and it is immediate."

Instructors can use a variety of options to present classroom materials, including videotapes, slides, overheads, computer-generated materials, and even an electronic writing board.

As systems within states are recognizing the advantages of inter-active television, coordinated efforts will be emphasized for comprehensive planning to maximize networking potential educational activities and outreach opportunities.

Two-Way Audio. Two-way audio, most effective when visuals are not needed, is information sent via the telephone line. The audioconference involves the transmission of voices over telephone lines, with speaker phones at each site. Usually a main speaker makes a presentation and listeners respond with comments or questions. When speaker phones are used to amplify the sound, the number in the listening audience is unlimited. This is the most common and the most cost-efficient method of teleconferences and, relying only on the sense of hearing, the hardest to keep the attention of listeners. To retain and focus the attention of participants, interesting print materials should be on hand, along with any other appropriate supplemental activity to keep the listener involved.

Computer Conferencing. Posing the question of how on-line environments may improve learning, Harasim (1990) looks at the collaborative learning theory in computer conferencing. Noting the shared attributes with distance learning and face-to-face interaction, she characterizes traits of conferencing systems: many-to-many communication, place independence, time independence, text-based, and computer-mediated interaction.

With the many-to-many communication aspect of on-line conferencing, the learner is able to formulate ideas into words through the responses of others. All users read the same messages and share the same files. In addition to alleviating possible problems of traditional place-based education (e.g., disabilities, geographic isolation, and family responsibilities), Harasim points out the definite advantages of the characteristic of place independence: accessibility to experts, collaboration with peers, union with a diverse participant population, availability of global resources, and commonality of shared interests.

Time independence is identified by Harasim as the third attribute of on-line education. Instruction can be presented so that learners may participate at a time convenient to each individual, facilitating self-pacing.

New systems, such as desktop videoconferencing, are real-time communications in which learners have immediate feedback through video, audio, interactive software sharing, and electronic writing boards.

Using the text-based characteristic of on-line education, the user may respond immediately or take time to consider responses. Harasim (1990) sees an advantage, "The need to verbalize all aspects of interaction within the text-based environment can enhance such metacognitive skills as self-reflection and revision in learning" (p. 49).

Since Harasim noted that on-line communication was limited to a text-based format, such network applications as Mosaic and Netscape have been widely introduced. They allow the user to access World Wide Webs. With these applications, the user can retrieve visuals and audio in addition to text from all over the world.

Computer-mediated interaction is described by Harasim as the ability to present, receive, process, and manage information, with the advantages of being revisable, archivable, and retrievable. A conference, using this characteristic, would be recorded with an entire transcript stored in the system database which can be read, scanned, or reviewed at a later date.

1. *Desktop videoconferencing.* According to Portway and Lane (1993), the biggest significant trend in the area of conferencng has been the concept of desktop videoconferencing. When this type of technology becomes widespread, it will probably be

one of the major educational advancements for individuals with disabilities. With the proper hardware (including a small camera) and software, individuals, using a modem or a direct link to a file server or mainframe, can see one another, share data, and work together on projects simultaneously.

2. *Electronic mail.* In addition to the typical message transmission and reception feature, e-mail can assist educators in administering tests, monitoring a student's progress, and providing explanations, resources, and even lectures. Using a telephone line along with a computer, modem, communications software, and any needed adaptive technological devices, this is a particularly useful media for those who are unable to access others immediately due to their disabilities. It provides both professional and social contacts; it is interactive.

Network Systems. Being on the network can mean several things. It can mean that one is on a local area network in which individual computers share data, courseware, and printers. One computer serves as the file server, storing all the network files; individual computers, accessing the file server, can use these files and any available networked printers. This network may also have point-to-point capabilities which connect individual computers with data sharing functions.

Reynolds and Anderson (1992) point out that networks can provide individualized yet coordinated task performance; produce quick updating of course materials and records; render interaction among students with one another, as well as with the instructor; and provide the same versions of software to all users.

Being on the network can also refer to internet, commercial on-line services, and bulletin boards. These wide-area networks provide individuals with learning disabilities perhaps one of the most empowering capabilities technology has to offer—literally, a global outreach to quickly access vast amounts of information, data, and resources using the gamut of available adaptive technological devices.

1. *Internet.* The internet is a massive, worldwide connection of computers in corporations, universities, government agencies, and military and other public and private organizations. Individuals can exchange information, transfer files, even read and respond to specific subject-related newsgroups. There are a number of newsgroups that exchange information on disabilities.

2. *Commercial on-line services.* For a small monthly fee, indi-

viduals can access commercial on-line services with large databanks and fax and e-mail capabilities.

3. *Bulletin boards.* Bulletin boards are smaller versions of the commercial on-line services, with users sending and receiving information. There are quite a large number of bulletin boards that specifically relate to a variety of disabilities.

Accessing information through the use of technology is becoming popular. Using Houle's (1961) model of motivational orientations for continuing education, McCreary (1990) distinguishes participants using computer-mediated communication (CMC): goal-oriented, activity-oriented, and learning-oriented. Goal-oriented participants, typically sporadic users who respond to specific needs, are going to use CMC to fulfill a managerial or administrative task. Activity-oriented participants, engaging in continuing education for fellowship, escapism, or satisfaction, will usually be drawn to the social networking aspects of CMC. McCreary expands this set of participants into two subsets: exploration-oriented and social explorers. The exploration-oriented are fascinated with the technology aspect of CMC, searching services and networks, while the social explorers are interested in lure of social interaction with others in diverse geographic locations. Finally, the learning-oriented, traditionally driven by a desire to know, have been identified by McCreary as those professional educators and researchers who will use CMC for such activities as library and database searching and on-line testing.

Kinner and Coombs (1995) found that CMC works well with adult learners, facilitating the integration of "disabled learners into a mainstream class. Physical disabilities vanish from sight, and participants interact on the basis of their contributions" (p. 66).

Evaluation

Verduin and Clark (1991) enumerate F. S. Future's evaluation factors in distance education as (1) access (numbers, target groups, geographical coverage, media availability, awareness), (2) relevance to needs and expectations (societal, individual, employment-related, needs assessment-related, market research-related), (3) quality of programs offered (instruction, learning materials, education or training, total learning experience, diplomas or certificates, satisfaction or recognition), (4) learners' outcomes (output and input, time, failures, repetition, dropouts, entry and exit qualifications), (5) impact (overall success, students, graduates, employees, enrollment), (6) effectiveness and efficiency (needs, demands, cost), and (7) generation of knowledge (new practices, new ideas, new directions).

SUMMARY

Regardless of what aspects of technology one uses, there are structured ways to enhance the learning experience. In looking at how private industry approaches facilitating the learning process, Nevis, DiBella, and Gould (1995) outlined guidelines for developing and implementing strategies. These strategies, modified, can be used by any organization or educational institution:

1. Before attempting new things, study and evaluate what you have and what you are doing now.
2. Introduce changes slowly. People accept change when they experience success with modest, focused, and specific changes.
3. Consider pertinent factors (e.g., specific learning disabilities and cultural factors) in choosing and implementing any strategy.

As Holmberg (1989) summarizes, "Of course, it is what a medium can do and not what it is like technically that is important in selection situations. This means that we must pay attention to the relevant attributes of media rather than the media themselves" (p. 74).

As we look to the attributes of technology and what it does, we can look to ourselves and to each other—how we wish to learn, to perform, to contribute—and we want to do it all.

We may not learn like everyone else; we may not perform in the traditional way—sometimes all it takes is a little modification, a little accommodation—but we all endow our own individual traits and qualities in our contributions.

Facilitating the learning experience can benefit the learner and the educator alike. Using technology as a tool, simple or complex, adds to our ability to experience awareness, knowledge, and success. Tools are facilitators, used to build, construct, and mold unformed components into something new, something whole. Sometimes the process is a scary or frustrating process, but the results can be exciting and rewarding. Like those before us, just think what we can do with a little fire power.

REFERENCES

Amandam, K. (1986). Technology for education: Promises and problems. In G. H. Voegel (Ed.), *Advances in instructional technology: New directions for community colleges* (Vol. 55, pp. 65–72). San Francisco: Jossey-Bass.

Americans with Disabilities Act of 1990, 42 U.S.C.A. §§§§ 12101 et seq. (West 1993).

Anderson, J. (1991). *Technology and adult literacy*. London: Routledge.

Azarmsa, R. (1993). *Telecommunications: A handbook for educators*. New York: Garland.

Bailey, N. (1994, Summer). What you need to know about the Tech Act. The LD Link, p. 1.

Bissell, J. (1990). Fostering multimedia in K-12 and higher education: A case study. In J. Cash (Ed.), *The power of multimedia: A guide to interactive technology in education and business* (pp. 53–60). Washington, DC: Interactive Video Industry Association.

Bowe, F. G. (1984). *Personal computers and special needs*. Berkeley: Sybex.

Brandenburg, S. A., & Vanderheiden, G. C. (1987). *Communication, control, and computer access for disabled and elderly individuals. Resource book 3: Software and hardware*. Boston: College-Hill Press.

Cook, P. (1988). An encyclopedia publisher's perspective. In S. Ambron & K. Hopper (Eds.), *Interactive multimedia: Visions of multimedia for developers, educators, and information providers* (pp. 219–240). Redmond, WA: Microsoft Press.

Duning, B. S., Van Kekerix, M. J., & Saborowski, L. M. (1993). *Reaching learners through telecommunications: Management and leadership strategies for higher education*. San Francisco: Jossey-Bass.

Ely, D. P., LeBlanc, G., & Yancey, C. (1989). *Trends and issues in educational technology*. Syracuse, NY: Syracuse University Press.

Frick, T. W. (1991). *Restructuring education through technology*. Bloomington, IN: Phi Delta Kappa Educational Foundation.

Gano, S. (1988). Multimedia technology is for casual everyday use. In S. Ambron & K. Hopper (Eds.), *Interactive multimedia: Visions of multimedia for developers, educators, and information providers* (pp. 255–264). Redmond, WA: Microsoft Press.

Garrett, J., & Dyke, B. (1988). *Microelectronics and pupils with special educational needs: Support material for the in-service training of teachers*. Manchester, UK: Manchester University Press.

Garrison, D. R. (1989). *Understanding distance education: A framework for the future*. London: Routledge.

Green, P., & Brightman, A. J. (1990). *Independence day: Designing computer solutions for individuals with disability*. Allen, TX: DLM.

Hansen, J. (1984). *Teaching and training the handicapped through the new information technology: Computerized special education*. Luxembourg: Office for Official Publications of the European Communities.

Harasim, L. M. (1990). On-line education: an environment for collaboration and intellectual amplification. In L. M. Harasim (Ed.), *On-line education: Perspectives on a new environment* (pp. 39–59). New York: Praeger.

Hawkridge, D., Vincent, T., & Hayes, G. (1985). *New information technology in the education of disabled children and adults.* San Diego, CA: College-Hill Press.

Heinich, R., Molenda, M., & Russell, J.D. (1989). *Instructional media and the new technologies of instruction* (3rd. ed.). New York: Macmillan

Holmberg, B. (1989). *Theory and practice of distance education.* London: Routledge.

Houle, C. O. (1961). *The inquiring mind.* Madison: University of Wisconsin Press.

Kinner, J., & Coombs, N. (1995). Computer access for students with special needs. In Z. L. Berge & M. P. Collins (Eds.), *Computer mediated communication and the on-line classroom* (Vol. 1, pp. 53–68). Cresskill, NJ.: Hampton Press.

Knirk, F. G., & Gustafson, K. L. (1986). *Instructional technology: A systematic approach to education.* New York: Holt, Rinehart & Winston.

Lahm, E., & Greszco, K. (1988). Therapeutic applications and adaptive devices. In M. M. Berhmann (Ed.), *Integrating computers into the curriculum: A handbook for special educators* (pp. 29–58). Boston: College-Hill Press.

Lazzaro, J. J. (1993). *Adaptive technologies for learning and work environments.* Chicago: American Library Association.

Markman, M. J. (1988). Epilogue: HyperCard. In S. Ambron & K. Hopper (Eds.), *Interactive multimedia: Visions of multimedia for developers, educators, and information providers* (pp. 233–239). Redmond, WA: Microsoft Press.

Mathias, H., Rushby, N., & Budgett, R. (Eds.). (1988). *Aspects of educational technology: Designing new systems and technologies for learning* (Vol. 21). London: Kogan Page.

McCormick, J. A. (1994). *Computers and the Americans with Disabilities Act: A manager's guide.* Blue Ridge Summit, PA: Winderest.

McCreary, E. K. (1990). Three behavioral models for computer-mediated communication. In L. M. Harasim (Ed.), *Online education: Perspectives on a new environment* (pp. 117–129). New York: Praeger.

Netta, F. & Staub, U. (1988). The video disk as a teaching aid. In F. Lovis (Ed.), *Remote education and informatics: Teleteaching* (pp. 179–184). Amsterdam: Elsevier.

Nevis, E., DiBella, A., & Gould, J. (1995, Winter). Understanding organizations as learning systems. *Sloan Management Review*, pp. 78–85.

Paine, N., & McAra, P. (1993). Interactive multimedia technology: A summary of current developments. In C. Latchem, J. Williamson, & L. Henderson-Lancett (Eds.), *Interactive multimedia practice and promise* (pp. 39–56). London: Kogan Page.

Portway, P. S., & Lane, C. (1992). *Technical guide to teleconferencing and distance learning.* San Ramon, CA: Applied Business Telecommunications.

Purdy, L. N. (1986). Teleconferences: Using technology to serve distant learning. In G. H. Voegel (Ed.), *Advances in instructional technology: New directions for community colleges* (Vol. 55, pp. 3–12). San Francisco: Jossey-Bass.

Raskind, M., & Scott, N. (1993). Technology for postsecondary students with learning disabilities. In S. Vogel & P. Adelman (Eds.), *Success for college students with learning disabilities* (pp. 240–275). New York: Springer-Verlag.

Reynolds, A., & Anderson, R. H. (1992). *Selecting and developing media for instruction* (3rd ed.). New York: Van Nostrand Reinhold.

Russell, S. J., Corwin, R., Mokros, J. R., & Kapisovsky, P. M. (1989). *Beyond drill and practice: Expanding the computer mainstream.* Reston, VA: Council for Exceptional Children.

Sammon, P. (1988). CD-ROM as storage medium for computer aided instruction. In F. Lovis (Ed.), *Remote education and informatics: Teleteaching* (pp. 185–190). Amsterdam: Elsevier.

Simpson, B. (1985). Heading for the ha-ha. In D. Sloan (Ed.), *The computer in education: A critical perspective* (pp. 84–94). New York: Teachers College Press.

Smith, D., & Koep, R. (1988). Computer software as text: Developments in the evaluation of computer-based educational media and materials. In H. Mathias, N. Rushby, & R. Budgett (Ed.), *Designing new systems and technologies for learning. Aspects of educational technology* (Vol. 21, pp. 197–204). London: Kogan Page.

Technology-Related Assistance for Individuals with Disabilities Act of 1988, Public Law 100-407, 102 stat. 1044 (1988).

Technology-Related Assistance for Individuals with Disabilities Act Amendments of 1994, Public Law 103-218, 108 Stat. 50 (1994).

Tobin, D. (1988). Computer assisted instruction in special education. In M. M. Berhmann (Ed.), *Integrating computers into the curriculum: A handbook for special educators* (pp. 145–178). Boston: College-Hill Press.

Verduin, J. R., Jr., & Clark, T. A. (1991). *Distance education: The foundations of effective practice.* San Francisco: Jossey-Bass.

Voegel, G. H. (1986). Instructional technology mix: Some considerations. In G. H. Voegel (Ed.), *Advances in instructional technology: New directions for community colleges* (Vol. 55, pp. 73–82). San Francisco: Jossey-Bass.

Index

Ability–achievement discrepancy
model, 57–58, 59, 63, 74
vs. clinical model, 76–77
weaknesses of, 79
Academic skills. *See also* Education;
Reading
and subtyping of learning
disabilities, 191–192
and transition programs, 283
Accommodation and modifications
and assistive technology, 373–378
and legal issues, 352–356, 357–
360
Achievement. *See* Ability–achievement discrepancy model;
Achievement-only model;
Discrepancy model; Intra-
achievement discrepancy
model; Underachievement
model
Achievement-only model, 186–187
ACID profile, 189
Adaptive devices, 374–375
Adelman, H. S., 88–89
Adult basic education, 102–104,
312–314. *See also* Remedial
education
professional training for,
267–269
Adult Education Amendments, 264
Adulthood, definition of, 81–82
AFDC (Aid to Families with
Dependent Children), 361

African Americans. *See* Blacks
Age, and psychosocial adjustment,
210
Aid to Families with Dependent
Children (AFDC), 361
American Federal Government
Employees Local 51 v. Baker,
360
American Psychological Association, 348–349
Americans with Disabilities Act,
280, 299, 331–332, 335,
342
documentation required by, 347
and employment, 292, 340–341
and "reasonable accommodation," 352–353, 354–355
Asch, A., 23
Assessment. *See* Diagnosis
Assistive technology, 368–389.
See also Computer technology
and accommodation and modifications, 373–378
benefits of, 370–373
definition of, 369–370
and distance education and
learning, 378–389
Association of Children with
Learning Disabilities, 6–9. *See
also* Learning Disabilities
Association
Association of Learning Disabled
Adults, 7

393